www.wadsworth.com

wadsworth.com is the World Wide Web site for Wadsworth Publishing Company and is your direct source to dozens of online resources.

At *wadsworth.com* you can find out about supplements, demonstration software, and student resources. You can also send e-mail to many of our authors and preview new publications and exciting new technologies.

wadsworth.com
Changing the way the world learns®

The Natural Investigator

A Constructivist Approach to Teaching Elementary and Middle School Science

Michael Bentley, Ed.D
Virginia Polytechnic Institute

Christine Ebert, Ph.D.
University of South Carolina

Edward S. Ebert, II, Ph.D.
Coker College

Wadsworth
Thomson Learning™

Australia • Canada • Denmark • Japan • Mexico
New Zealand • Philippines • Puerto Rico • Singapore
Spain • United Kingdom • United States

Education Editor: *Dianne Lindsay*
Assistant Editor: *Tangelique Williams*
Editorial Assistant: *Keynia Johnson*
Marketing Manager: *Becky Tollerson*
Project Editor: *Trudy Brown*
Print Buyer: *April Reynolds*
Permissions Editor: *Joohee Lee*
Production Service: *Publishing Support Services*

Text Designer: *Andrew Ogus*
Copy Editor: *Darlene Bledsoe*
Illustrator: *Joan Carol*
Compositor: *G&S Typesetters*
Cover Designer: *Ellen Kwan*
Cover Image: *David Young-Wolff, PhotoEdit; Craig Tuttle, The Stock Market*
Cover and Text Printer/Binder: *Custom Printing*

Printed in the United States of America
1 2 3 4 5 6 03 02 01 00 99

For permission to use material from this text, contact us:
    Web: www.thomsonrights.com
    Fax: 1-800-730-2215
    Phone: 1-800-730-2214

Library of Congress Cataloging-in-Publication Data
Bentley, Michael Lee.
    The natural investigator : a constructivist approach to teaching elementary and middle school science / Michael Bentley, Christine Ebert, Edward S. Ebert II.
        p.   cm.
    Includes bibliographical references (p.) and index.
        ISBN 0-534-12912-9
        1. Science—Study and teaching (Elementary) I. Ebert, Christine, 1946– .   II. Ebert, Edward S., 1953– .   III. Title.
    LB1585.B36   2000
    372.3'5'044—dc21   99-41930

♲ This book is printed on acid-free recycled paper.

For more information, contact
Wadsworth / Thomson Learning
10 Davis Drive
Belmont, CA 94002-3098
USA
www.wadsworth.com

International Headquarters
Thomson Learning
290 Harbor Drive, 2nd Floor
Stamford, CT 06902-7477
USA

UK/Europe/Middle East
Thomson Learning
Berkshire House
168–173 High Holborn
London WC1V 7AA
United Kingdom

Asia
Thomson Learning
60 Albert Street #15-01
Albert Complex
Singapore 189969

Canada
Nelson/Thomson Learning
1120 Birchmount Road
Scarborough, Ontario M1K 5G4
Canada

Table of Contents

List of Figures

List of Activities

List of Photographs

Preface

Those who have meditated on the art of governing humankind have been convinced that the fate of empires depends on the thorough education of youth.

—Aristotle

This book is about the teaching of science in elementary and middle schools. It is written for those of you who are preparing to teach and also for those of you who want to become more skilled in teaching. It is written, in particular, for those who can understand that teaching involves much more than the repeating of information. Education is a profession that calls for thinkers who can communicate the beauty and value of well-developed human thought.

From the beginning you should be advised that a conscientious study of science teaching is complex and challenging enough to keep you busy learning even after years of classroom experience. For this reason, we have written this book to be useful as a guide and as a resource for many years to come.

Three of us worked together to write this book. Combined, we share more than three-quarters of a century of experience in teaching science and in helping individuals develop themselves as science teachers. We hope that what we have to share with you in these pages will help you define for yourself the challenges of the classroom, and help you to better understand the nature of science and science education. Obviously, teaching and learning science have been of interest to the three of us our entire adult lives. We hope that ultimately you will share our enthusiasm for the subject.

You will see that the book contains fourteen chapters clustered in five sections. The three chapters of Section I are provided to give you a perspective of science and its place in elementary and middle school curricula. Though science was likely always a part of your educational experience, it has not always held a strong position in the educational curriculum of our relatively young country. You may be surprised to learn of some of the trials and tribulations of science education through the years.

Section II is intended to provide you with insights about how children learn, and how to find out what they *really* think about a particular topic. Though many times you will believe that you have presented a lesson just as clearly as it could be done, the way it relates to what children already know can yield a completely different result from that which you intended.

Section III focuses squarely on the teaching of science with the philosophy of constructivism as its referent. You will not find pages here about preparing lectures. Nor will you find discrete activities to occupy your school year. Rather, everything that we present will be offered as a component of a dynamic, interactive, hands-on and minds-on approach to education that capitalizes on the inherent curiosity of children. Your ability to develop meaningful science lessons given any topic is the goal of this textbook. Taken together, these chapters are intended to help you make science easily the most exciting time of each class day.

In Section IV we will shift to a more detailed look at the bigger picture of science in the curriculum. Issues of science, technology, and society, as well as discussions of key science reform efforts will demonstrate the far-reaching implications of science in elementary and middle schools. Also included in this section will be our discussion of assessment. In a time of clarion calls for school accountability, it is more important than ever that the classroom teacher be able to accurately determine the gains made by children as a result of instruction.

Finally, Section V will provide you with a compendium of resources and a lengthy list of references. These portions of the book provide you with the means for extending your study by virtue of the many resources available to you as a classroom teacher, as well as offering direction for pursuing any aspect of this text in much greater detail. We encourage you to make frequent use of the information provided here.

In particular, this book offers you a very valuable resource for use during your science methods course. The subscription to Info-Trac College Edition that could have been packaged with this text allows you to get the most up-to-date information about any topic that is discussed. In the dynamic world of education, new information is always becoming available, debates about pedagogy continue, and educational technology progresses at a rapid pace. Fundamentals, however, endure. And that is what makes Info-Trac College Edition useful to you. We can provide you with sound, fundamental pedagogy in this text, and InfoTrac College Edition can keep you at the cutting edge of each topic.

Throughout the text are many activities based on InfoTrac College Edition. But don't feel bound by these activities. Use InfoTrac College Edition whenever it suits your needs. You may want another opinion about what has been expressed. Perhaps you find yourself particularly interested in a specific topic, and so will use InfoTrac College Edition to locate additional information. And in addition to providing you with access to a tremendous body of knowledge, your use of InfoTrac College Edition will provide valuable experience in using the Internet as a true investigative tool.

You will likely note very early in your work with this textbook that each chapter begins with a quotation that we considered to be pertinent to the material to follow. In all cases, wise and erudite individuals have been cited. In some cases, their wisdom was borne of many years considering this world; in others, it is the wisdom that can only come from those who have yet to reach their tenth birthday. We can learn from each.

A last word now, a more personal word, before you begin. In the years that the writing of this book have occupied, three children and two grandchildren have been born into the families of your authors. Even experienced educators are reminded of the degree to which children depend on the nurturing care of loving family members. What develops is a physical, emotional, and intellectual exchange that will continue throughout their lives. And when those children go off to school, it will be the nurturing guidance of teachers, such as you, to which they will turn. As a teacher, it has been said, your influence will last an eternity.

You can address this considerable responsibility by becoming a teacher who not only knows the topic, but who also knows *how* children learn and how to *value their thinking*. That bigger picture, which goes far beyond a series of neat little activities, is what this book tries to convey. As you work now to become a professional educator, or to hone your professional skills, you may find yourself challenged to change your own attitude about science. It is never too late to arouse your curiosity. It may be true that such an awakening may be more important to your ultimate success as a teacher of science than what you learn from this textbook or from your methods course. Indeed, the responsibility of being a teacher is awesome, but you are to be commended for choosing a career in which you truly can make a difference in the world.

ACKNOWLEDGMENTS

Though the names of three authors appear on the cover of *The Natural Investigator,* there are in fact many other people involved in bringing a book such as this to the reader. We offer our thanks to all of those individuals who did their job so well, and left us with a product that we are pleased to offer to you. To whatever degree possible, we'd like to take a moment to thank some of those people with whom we were so often in communication.

Regarding the photos in the book, we would like to acknowledge 5th grade teacher Teresa Auldridge and her class (South Salem Elementary School, Salem, Virginia), and 4th grade teacher Betsy Bursey and her class (Community School, Roanoke, Virginia). Then there were the children at Pontiac Elementary School (Elgin, South Carolina), whose teachers, Sally Huguley, Melissa Klosterman, Molly Phipps, Stella Wilkins, Jennifer Layton, Sharon Williams, Kristi Haltiwanger, and Tara Thompson, all allowed us enthusiastic access to science in their classrooms. And we wish to thank our friend and colleague, Chen Long, for his assistance in photographing the children.

Many people have reviewed the content of this book, either in the capacity of formal reviewers, colleagues offering guidance, or students in our own classes working with the materials as part of their teacher education experience. We would like to thank all of those students who have worked with us, provided valuable recommendations as the work progressed, and demonstrated the effectiveness of what we offer here to you.

A key aspect in our work has been the welcoming, professional, and collegial atmosphere offered by the administrators, teachers, and staff at Pontiac Elementary School. In particular we express our appreciation to Dr. Richard Inabinet, Principal, and Mrs. Beth Elliot, Assistant Principal. This spirit was also offered to us by 2nd grade teacher Judy Whiting (Boyce Elementary School, Boyce, Virginia), and middle school teachers Jane Turner (Addison Middle School, Roanoke, Virginia), and Mary Ann Reynolds (James Madison Middle School, Roanoke, Virginia). Our appreciation goes as well to Dr. Vito DiPinto and Dr. Fred Wilkins, National-Louis University, Evanston, Illinois.

The manuscript for *The Natural Investigator* was reviewed by many of the leading individuals in science education across the country. We gratefully acknowledge their work and are pleased to recognize them here: D. Daryl Adams, Minnesota State University, Mankato; Glenda Akins, Valdosta State University; Charles R. Barman, Indiana University; Joseph A. Baust, Murray State University; Sylven S. Beck, The George Washington University; Karen S. Brown, Indiana Wesleyan University; John R. Cannon, University of Nevada, Reno; Vito M. DiPinto, National-Louis University; James J. Gallagher, Michigan State University; Leonard J. Garigliano, (emeritus) Salisbury State University; Penny Hammrich, Temple University; Louis A. Iozzi, Rutgers University; Delmar Janke (retired), Texas A & M University; Vince Mahoney, Iowa Wesleyan College; Edmund A. Marek, University of Oklahoma; R. W. McClure, Saint Mary's University; Milton Payne, Stephen F. Austin State University; Ava F. Pugh, Northeast Louisiana University; Judy Reinhartz, The University of Texas, Arlington; Karen E. Reynolds, San José State University; Donald Schmidt, Fitchburg State College; David Stronck, California State University, Hayward; Marvin Tolman, Brigham Young University; and Robert Yager, University of Iowa.

And finally, particularly in the last year of developing this project, it has been our pleasure to work with two individuals who facilitated finalizing the manuscript and seeing it through production. We would like to thank our Production Editor, Vicki Moran of Publishing Support Services, for her ability to make this such a smooth process (at least from the perspective of the authors!). And we very much thank our editor at Wadsworth / Thomson Learning, Dianne Lindsay, for getting all of us through all of this! Thank you. We look forward to our continued collaboration.

Michael Bentley
Christine Ebert
Edward S. Ebert, II
1999

The Natural
Investigator

Section I   Considering the World of Science

CHAPTER 1   **Perspectives on the Nature of Science**

CHAPTER 2   **Scientific Knowledge for the Elementary/ Middle School Years**

CHAPTER 3   **Science Education: The New "Basic" in the Classroom**

Section I contains three chapters that share the common theme of describing science, though each chapter does so in a different context. These chapters are provided to form a *foundation* for the teaching of science. It is our belief that a solid foundation is necessary in order to understand the breadth of the academic discipline. The organization of the chapters is intended to move the reader from a consideration of science to a discussion of science as it is represented by educational curricula, and finally to an explanation of the teacher's role in the presentation of science as an academic subject.

Chapter 1, "Perspectives on the Nature of Science," considers the discipline in terms of its characteristics, relationship to our culture, and philosophy. The intent is to demonstrate that science is much more than just a collection of facts in a textbook. Our goal is that the reader will be able to appreciate the importance of understanding the *nature* of science before trying to *teach it* to other people.

Chapter 2, "Science Knowledge for the Elementary/Middle School Years," introduces those aspects of science in the curriculum that the classroom teacher typically does not control. Though it is our hope that the reader will one day become a participant in the process of curriculum design, it is most likely that a beginning teacher will be given a curriculum to be followed. This chapter explains educational efforts at the state and national levels to build frameworks that identify the most appropriate and important domains of science for children to experience in school. Contrasted with chapter 1, with its focus on scientific investigation as human endeavor, this second chapter is concerned with the social (and perhaps political) aspects of including science in the curriculum.

"Science Education: The New "Basic" in the Classroom," chapter 3, describes science education in the particular context of the classroom teacher. The history leading up to science becoming a part of the curriculum is discussed. In addition, a considerable portion of the chapter is devoted to a discussion of an additional element in the teaching of science: teaching for feeling and valuing. Chapter 3 is intended to provide the reader with a clearer idea of why teaching is referred to as both an art and a science.

1 | ⚜ | Perspectives on the Nature of Science

What Is Science?

Science and Culture

Science and Philosophy

Conclusion

Your Academic Roadmap

Study of this chapter should help you to understand the following concepts:

- The study of science is open to all.

- Science is a multidimensional endeavor with complex interrelations with society.

- Science is creative and inquiry-oriented.

- Science is dynamic and continues to be constructed in each new generation.

- A constructivist philosophy values children's inherent curiosity as teachers arrange experiences to allow the construction of knowledge.

Our century is a century of explorations: new forms of art, of music, of literature, and new forms of science.

—**Illya Prigogine,** *From Being to Becoming: Time and Complexity in the Physical Sciences*

WHAT IS SCIENCE?

Science, like "art" or "creativity," is a term that people typically assume they can define. Consequently, our topic question is one of those that people don't wrestle with unless specifically put on the spot to do so. Yet, isn't it an important term to understand? Without question, the scientist needs an understanding of the term in order to conceptualize the work he or she is to do, and to internalize the purpose of that work. Teachers of science certainly need to be able to define the term in order to understand what is to be taught to students and why. Likewise, students benefit from understanding what science is as a way of organizing the experiences that follow when "science" begins. In fact, we all should be able to verbalize our conceptual-

ization of what science is in order to understand and avail ourselves of the contributions science makes to our lives.

In this chapter we approach the question of just what science is by looking at scientists and what they do, the relationship of science to culture, and by examining the philosophies and logic that characterize endeavors in science. Though it is not our intent to provide you with a "canned" answer to the question, by chapter's end we hope you will be able to verbalize your own conceptualization of what is referred to as *science*.

What Distinguishes the Scientist?

When you think of a scientist, what image first comes to mind? This question has been presented to a lot of children in the Draw-A-Scientist Test (DAST). Try asking some children to draw the first picture that comes

FIGURE 1.1 Children's drawings of scientists. Used by permission.

to mind when they think of a scientist. Examples of responses from two children are illustrated in Figure 1.1. Many children respond to the DAST by drawing the familiar, stereotypical image of the scientist. The first drawing in Figure 1.1 illustrates many of the components found in just such an image: a Caucasian male dressed in a lab coat and surrounded by the "stuff" of his trade—such as test tubes, flasks, Bunsen burners, computers, electrical equipment, and, of course, the ubiquitous pocket liner. Typically, fewer children draw scientists who are women or minorities. Researchers who have studied children's images of scientists find that children perceive scientists more and more stereotypically as they progress through successive grade levels (Chambers, 1983). Why do you think this happens?

The stereotypical scientist is the caricature often seen in comic books, television shows, and movies. For example, Gary Larson's well-known "Far Side" cartoons often depict scientists this way. The average prime-time TV viewer can expect to see two scientists on the screen each week. Fortunately, "good" scientists appear five times more often than "bad" scientists. On the other hand, the scientists depicted are more likely than other occupational groups to be involved in some form of fatal activity. Studies of the media report that, overall, scientists are portrayed in a positive way, but they are often associated with a "sense of evil, trouble, and peril" (Gerbner, Gross, Morgan, & Signorielli, 1985, p. 12).

Scientists, of course, are not the only professionals that get stereotyped—think about doctors and lawyers, for example. Are these occupations any easier to define than the scientists? Stereotypes may contain some element of truth in that people recognize and pass them along, but at best stereotypes communicate only a part of the picture. How do scientists you know compare with the stereotype? Try Activity 1.1 with a friend or classmate.

ACTIVITY 1.1

The Stereotyped Scientist

Think about the following and discuss with a classmate.

1. Does the stereotype of the scientist fit the scientists you know?

2. In what ways do the following scientists fit, or not fit, the stereotype?

Carl Sagan	Jane Goodall
Annie Jump Cannon	Lynn Margolis
Percy Julian	Mary Leaky
Jocelyn Bell	Henrietta Leavitt
Eugenie Clark	Rachel Carson

3. Look up some recent Nobel Prize winners. How do they match up with the stereotype?

4. What criteria are used, or should be used, to identify quality work in science?

There are tens of thousands of people working in the United States today who consider themselves scientists. Though science is an enterprise with ancient roots, most of the scientists that ever lived are now alive. And most of these, as the stereotype suggests, are white males. Only 15 percent of working scientists, mathematicians, and engineers are women. African Americans and Hispanics each represent only 2 percent of scientific workers (Oakes, 1990).

Why do you suppose that women and minorities have a low rate of participation in the science and technology workforce? There certainly has been an historic pattern of cultural bias against women and nonwhite ethnicities in most of the professions, but those who have studied the matter say there is no single culprit that can be identified (Bullock, 1996). Children are influenced from very early in life by the society in which they are reared, and many societies in the multiethnic culture of the United States hold persistently to certain beliefs about the natures and potential of people of the female gender and non–Anglo ethnicities (Banks, 1994). For one reason or another, many children in our society construct stereotypes of scientists and their work, stereotypes that act as barriers to their access to science and their participation in it. We can infer from the results of many studies that these stereotypes are retained through typical experiences in the classroom science program (Larochelle & Desautels, 1991).

The good news is that the issues of access and equity now are recognized throughout the intellectual community, and affirmative action programs have been making an impact. While women and people of various ethnicities are still in the minority as scientists, the participation of these groups in science at all levels has been increasing. There are more women scientists and scientists of non–Anglo ethnicity working now than the total number of scientists working a century ago. As an elementary teacher, you can plan and implement a classroom science program supportive for all children. You can encourage all children to pursue their interests and develop their talents in science as well as any other area.

Stereotyping according to gender and ethnicity is just one of the misconceptions that children (and many adults) have about scientists. What do *you* think qualifies a person to be called a scientist? In Activity 1.1 you had the opportunity to consider and discuss your ideas regarding who gets counted as a scientist. For example, did you think anthropologists count as scientists? How about engineers? Did people working in economics or sociology make your list? And what of geographers?

The line of demarcation between science and other pursuits can be fuzzy: Not everyone agrees on which disciplines belong under the "science" umbrella. To complicate matters even further, there is the issue of science and technology. Are these two names for the same thing? Are you prepared to help children to distinguish between what is science from what is not? With all of the questions that have arisen in this chapter already, it is little wonder that defining science is more difficult than one would first have expected. So, having determined that neither gender nor ethnicity are the determining characteristics of scientists, let's try to look more closely at what science *is* and what scientists *do* in order to answer our initial question. As a beginning, complete Activity 1.2 on your own, and then discuss your ideas with one or more of your classmates.

ACTIVITY 1.2

What Is Science?

Think about the following and discuss your ideas with a classmate: What *is* science? What features or characteristics distinguish science from nonscience?

1. What do you think about this statement: Science is the search for truth.

Strongly Disagree 1 2 3 4 5 Strongly Agree

2. Compared to knowledge in other disciplines, scientific knowledge is more objective and unbiased.

Strongly Disagree 1 2 3 4 5 Strongly Agree

3. In research, scientists use the scientific method to solve problems and verify findings.

Strongly Disagree 1 2 3 4 5 Strongly Agree

4. In science, if a theory is proven true, it becomes a law.

Strongly Disagree 1 2 3 4 5 Strongly Agree

5. Biological knowledge would be different today if the historic proportion of men biologists versus women biologists had been reversed.

Strongly Disagree 1 2 3 4 5 Strongly Agree

6. Most of the new ideas in science are produced by brilliant individuals.

Strongly Disagree 1 2 3 4 5 Strongly Agree

7. If experimental results fail to support a theory, scientists reject the theory and seek other alternatives.

Strongly Disagree 1 2 3 4 5 Strongly Agree

8. Disagreements among scientists about a theory are normally solved when new data are generated related to the problem.

Strongly Disagree 1 2 3 4 5 Strongly Agree

An Operational Definition of Science

Somewhere in your life in school you probably have been asked to write a definition of science. More likely than not, your high school and college science textbooks started off with a consideration of the nature of science (or biology, or physics . . .). The topic may have been dropped as the course focus quickly shifted to the details of science content. Nevertheless, your own concept of the nature of science developed from your experiences in school and college classes, and, as we have already mentioned, from how you saw science depicted in the media and wider culture. Whatever it is, you will draw upon your concept of science in your teaching.

It should be clear to you by this point that science is a term that encompasses many disciplines, and so when we ask "What is science?" the question goes to the *nature of the endeavor* rather than simply the content of a particular discipline, such as chemistry or geology. This point is important because the teacher of science should help children develop their *knowledge of science* as well as *scientific knowledge*. According to the National Science Teachers Association, communicating the nature of science is one of the general goals of science education (National Science Teachers Association, 1982). The American Association for the Advancement of Science identifies the nature of science as one of four categories of knowledge, skills, and attitudes essential for all citizens (American Association for the Advancement of Science, 1989). In its Project 2061, three principle aspects of the nature of science are emphasized:

1. *The scientific worldview.* The world is understandable, scientific ideas can change, scientific knowledge is long-lasting, science cannot provide complete answers to all questions.

2. *Scientific methods of inquiry.* Science demands evidence, science blends logic and imagination, science explains and predicts, scientists try to identify and avoid bias, science is not authoritarian.

3. *The nature of the scientific enterprise.* Science is a complex social activity, science is organized into content disciplines and is conducted in various institutions, ethical principles govern the conduct of science, scientists participate in public affairs both as specialists and as citizens (AAAS, 1990).

ACTIVITY 1.3
INFOTRAC COLLEGE EDITION
INVESTIGATION:

Project 2061

What is Project 2061? And why was the number 2061 used in the title? Use Info-Trac College Edition to locate information about this effort. Try to answer the following questions in addition to the two above:

- What is the goal of Project 2061?
- For whom is it intended?
- How will the goal be reached?
- Is there any opposition to Project 2061?

Your own nature of science (NOS) concept becomes an important part of your content knowledge as a teacher and will come into play when you make decisions about what to teach and how to teach it. What you believe about the nature of science—how scientists come to know what they know—will influence how you might respond to children in the classroom as well as your own motivation to learn more science.

Science is a multidimensional and complex social activity involving practitioners at many levels of education and training. Now wait just a moment before you underline that sentence as if it will answer the "What is science?" question on your next examination. Rather than being an answer in and of itself, that sentence provides you with the parameters that must be considered in the conceptualization of an answer. What are those multiple dimensions? What are those complex social activities? And who are those practitioners? Are you among them?

The word science is based upon the Latin *scire* (skee-ray), meaning "to know." In this case, meaning to know about nature, the physical environment and phenomena. Just over a century ago the word science meant "systematic inquiry." It means the same in its Japanese, French, Tamil, and Turkish counterparts. The German word for science, *Naturwissenschaft,* means "inquiry into the external world" (McCloskey, 1995, p. 19).

The famous Danish physicist Niels Bohr has said that the aim of science is to extend our experience and reduce it to order. But many other aims of science are discussed in the literature, including the aims of simplicity of explanation, convergence on truth, instrumental control, problem solving, the free flow of ideas, and technological gain.

Science is naturalistic, which means its scope is limited to what can be tested empirically. Anything regarded as supernatural is outside the scope of science. This idea was accepted as the foundation for what science is and what it is not from a legal standpoint by Judge Overton of the Louisiana Supreme Court. In overturning a state law requiring the teaching of creationism whenever evolution was taught in science, Judge Overton (*Edwards v. Aguillard,* 1987) determined that these criteria be applied for determining what is science:

1. Science is guided by natural law.
2. Science has to be explanatory by reference to natural law.
3. Science is testable against the empirical world.
4. Science is tentative
5. Science is falsifiable.

From these criteria we see that science is intimately tied to the world around us, but there is clear acknowledgment that, at any point, our explanations of that world may be taken into question. Science, in fact, specifically asks those questions that force us to reconsider, or consider further, what we "know" of nature. Questions of such things as religion or belief, on the other hand, are less empirically determined, and more answered in faith. It is faith that holds any system of beliefs together even when events might call those beliefs into question. In either approach, science or religion, we seek explanations of our world, of our environment. Science, in particular, may be seen as a human endeavor that systematically seeks to understand the world around us, with full awareness that our understanding is a work in process and that further questions and revision are expected.

Science as Problem Solving

If science is considered to be the process of understanding the world around us, that is, finding answers to a myriad of questions from multiple perspectives, then that activity might properly be referred to as problem solving. Questions provide the impetus for scientific investigation. That in itself should be obvious enough. Yet we all face questions that require answers throughout each day of our lives. "How will I get to class if it rains today?" "What time should I leave for the grocery store?" "What would be good for dinner?" These are all problems to be solved. But are they scientific problems? As stated, they are questions that can be answered by applying information already known. Known procedures, time constraints, and dietary requirements can be applied in these situations to arrive at suitable solutions. The activity would be problem solving, but not the particular problem solving that characterizes science.

The questions—the problems—in scientific investigation differ from most other types of questions that people face. The key difference is that the answer to a problem in scientific investigation is information that is not already known. The answer produces new information. Even if the investigation verifies a previous experimental result, the additional result changes (strengthens) information about the earlier findings. For this reason, Ebert and Ebert, in their book *The Inventive Mind in Science* (1998), refer to problem solving in science as *creative* problem solving. It is creative because investigations in science must necessarily question the implied or established parameters of the problem in order to find new perspectives and responses. Without questioning the "rules" of the problem, nothing new is likely to emerge.

The creative dimension of science permeates both its nature and its processes. Asking questions for which there is no answer is

© Austin MacRae

PHOTO 1.1 Marine scientist

a bold endeavor. Yet it is what children do all the time. Children struggle to make sense of the world around them with limited information. They easily ask the questions, of themselves and others, that will require knowledge beyond their current level of understanding. And similarly, children rarely confine themselves to particular rules for finding answers to their questions. The imposition of rules is learned. Exploration with a willingness to change what one already knows, is science.

The Processes of Science

Despite what you may have heard, the processes of knowledge building in science cannot be reduced to a single method. You might remember reading about or being taught the "scientific method." Even today children are often told the scientific method consists of a series of steps beginning with observations or questions, proceeding to the formation of hypotheses and then tests, and ending in conclusions (e.g., in Moyer & Bishop, 1986, 28). Sociologists who have studied scientists' work report that the stepwise scientific

method is more a format used by scientists in writing up their work for peer review than it is a description of the steps they took in an investigation. The journal article is often a reconstruction of what actually went on in an investigation (Weininger, 1990).

In practice, scientists use many different methods, and some are particular to the disciplines. For example, chemists rely heavily on experiments, whereas archeologists and astronomers, because of the nature of their subject matter, rarely use experimental methods. As discussed earlier in this chapter, the stereotypical scientist wears a white coat and is surrounded by lab equipment. But some scientists spend most of their time in the field; others, such as theoretical physicists, work mostly with mathematical models, doing what Einstein did best, "gedanken" (thought) experiments. In the words of David Bohm,

> The essential activity of science consists of thought, which arises in creative perception and is expressed through play. This gives rise to a process in which thought unfolds into provisional knowl-

edge which then moves outward into action and returns as fresh perception and knowledge. This process leads to a continuous adaptation of knowledge which undergoes constant growth, transformation, and extension (Bohm & Peat, 1987, p. 56).

Bohm perceives science as a dialectic activity involving thought and action. Science is cumulative in that new ideas are built on previous work. In chapter 6, "Developing the Skills of the Natural Investigator," you will find a detailed discussion of the processes of thought, The Basic Science Process Skills, that characterize scientific inquiry. Chapter 7, "Investigations in Science," will explore the activities, the investigative techniques, that scientists use in their work, and that you can use with your students. Taken together, these processes of thought and action will enable your students to *do* science rather than simply read *about* science.

Quick Review

This discussion of what science is all about has involved a look at who scientists are, the nature of science, and the processes that it employs. We find that scientific investigation is not an activity that excludes people based on gender or ethnicity, though women and minorities in the United States have long been underrepresented among the ranks of scientists. We have found that science has a nature that goes deeper than any specific scientific discipline. It is, in fact, a multidimensional endeavor with complex interrelations with society. At its foundation, science is a creative and inquiry-oriented enterprise that seeks to solve problems and answer questions about the world around us. In the scientific community, understanding is built with a combination of thought and action. With all of this said, let's take some time to consider

the cultural and philosophical perspectives of scientific inquiry.

SCIENCE AND CULTURE

At the outset we want to acknowledge that the world has always been composed of cultural groups and each group developed its own ways of interpreting experience related to the environment. We can refer to peoples' different ways of investigating their environment and ordering their understandings as traditional ecological knowledge (TEK), or just traditional science (Snively, 1995). Science as a way of knowing has grown out of Western culture as one kind of social endeavor people pursue for work or pleasure.

One reason it is important for teachers to recognize and value TEK is that children of different cultural backgrounds frequently interpret scientific terms and ideas differently than children of the majority culture. There have been studies of the differences between Euro-American children and aboriginal children (for example, the Native American, the Maori in New Zealand, the African Caribbean, African American, and Inuit). Aboriginal children may have "very different beliefs about the concepts of time, life cycles, growth, death, taxonomy, food chains, energy, evolution, tidal cycles, weather, causation, and resource management" (Snively, 1995, p. 58). Science in the elementary curriculum should help children understand the world, but we need to be clear that we mean the world of the child, not the world of the dominant culture (Atwater & Riley, 1993). Science is often associated with the world of the dominant culture, but there can be constructive dialogue among the different worlds. Children in public schools are educated very often with the clear purpose to be citizens in the common society, and this means being able to understand science.

It is not difficult to grasp the notion that science influences culture, and that culture influences science. For instance, electric lights used for sporting events took what was an afternoon and weekend pastime and made them available in evenings throughout the week. What effects do you suppose this had on patterns of family interaction? Similarly, the many reform efforts in public education in the United States can be traced to the prevailing cultural priorities. As in ages past, science today provides rich material for writers and artists. Contemporary writers such as Michael Crichton and Stephen King often use science in their writing, but even Chaucer wrote about the astronomy and medicine of his day (Weininger, 1990). Michael Reiss, in his book *Science Education for a Pluralist Society* (1993), says that many children "have no idea of the extent and significance of the contributions made to science by non-Western cultures" (p. 13). He argues that every science is an *ethnoscience*: ". . . a scientist's *perceptions* of the natural world, as well as her interpretations, come through her senses, herself as a person, and her culture. There is no single, universal, acultural science" (p. 24). Similarly, Western scientific ideas, widely disseminated in our time, emanate from our own cultural context and permeate scientific development in other countries to the extent that they are culturally compatible.

Western scientists have gradually come to acknowledge the contributions of science traditions in other cultures. An extensive literature has been accumulated by ecologists, geologists, climatologists, biologists, and others that is identified as TEK: traditional ecological knowledge (Snively, 1995). The goal of multicultural science education is that children understand the consensus version of science, but not be required to give up their traditional cultural beliefs. We are just beginning to value the cultural knowledge of the "long-dwelling" peoples of the world.

The Impact of Language and Metaphor

Language is another aspect of science's human roots. Every language is a human cultural construction. Scientific knowledge is built on a framework of metaphor. Theories and models draw upon cultural metaphors, and metaphors play an important role in communicating scientific ideas. Western societies often relate to nature through mechanistic metaphors, for example, the "functioning" of the brain or the ecosystem. Traditional peoples, on the other hand, depend more on metaphors of kinship, as well as animal, vegetable, and landscape metaphors (Snively, 1995).

Gloria Snively (1995) reminds us that "language is a necessary medium for thinking and learning" (p. 59). Precision in language often is associated with science. Yet scientific terms frequently cover a whole range of meanings among scientists. Sometimes this is a problem, but plasticity of concepts also can be helpful in science. Somewhat open-ended scientific metaphors enable scientists to find further applications for concepts and theories, and also their limits (Weininger, 1990). Scientists also use common expressions to communicate special scientific meanings. The words "living" and "acceleration" can mean different things to scientists working in their fields than what they would mean when used in everyday conversation. "Equilibrium" was first used in science but now has diffused to the wider culture and has acquired everyday meanings.

ACTIVITY 1.4
INFOTRAC COLLEGE EDITION
INVESTIGATION:

Science Education around the World

As you might expect, science education in the United States may not be the same as science education in another country, particularly those countries with significantly different cultures. Use InfoTrac College Edition to help you answer the following questions:

- How does science education differ around the world? Select three countries other than the United States and find out what "science education" means in those countries.

- What trends can you identify in science education among the three countries you have researched and the United States?

- What are the implications of what you have found when considering the idea of the common goals of a global community?

Hypotheses, Models, Theories, and Laws

The scientific knowledge people construct takes many forms, such as models and stories, or theories. Scientists both tell stories and build models as forms of explanation. For example, Newtonian physics is mostly mathematical modeling, whereas Charles Darwin's biology is almost entirely story with no mathematical models (McCloskey, 1995). Scientific work involves both creating the stories and models and testing them. Models, theories, laws, and hypotheses— the products of science—are idealizations that represent the physical reality that is beyond our reach. And although the cultural effects of language use sometimes confuse the issue, each of these four terms represent very distinct products to the scientist.

Models and theories, both being kinds of explanations for the accumulated data, differ in that theories require the support of more evidence than models and in fact often encompass models. More specifically, models

seek to explain *how* parts interact, whereas theories go further by attempting to explain *why* parts interact as they do. For example, a model of the solar system would show how the planets are arranged relative to the sun, but would not explain why they are arranged in such a manner. On the other hand, the Big Bang theory attempts to explain why the universe is as it is.

Theories and laws are the most important products of science. Theories do not ever become laws, or vice versa. Rather, they are different categories of representations just as apples and oranges are different categories of fruit. Theories are *explanations* in which scientists place a great deal of confidence as a result of the greater support by evidence. Many scientific laws, however, were known long before any theories were developed to explain them. For example, do you recall Boyle's law from your chemistry classes? Robert Boyle performed a number of key experiments on gases in the seventeenth century. From those experiments came Boyle's law, which can be stated as: The volume of a confined gas whose temperature is held constant will vary in inverse proportion to the pressure on the gas. You'll notice that Boyle's law does not explain *why* gases behave in this way, but rather it describes the behavior of gases as repeatedly observed. And that is what laws are: *descriptions* of natural systems whose behavior has been repeatedly observed. Here's an example in everyday terms: The law may be that the maximum speed for driving on the interstate highway is 65 mph. That is, 65 mph is the maximum rate at which you may operate an automobile (description of behavior) without being cited for a violation. This law exists, and can exist quite well in the absence of your own theory (explanation) of why there is such a law.

The hypothesis is yet another category of statement in science. Cultural dilution of the meaning of the term has resulted in most people defining the hypothesis as "an educated guess." As quaint as this might be, there is considerably more strength behind a well-formed hypothesis. Hypotheses are tentative explanations or descriptions that guide investigations (Ryan & Aikenhead, 1992). The hypothesis states an anticipated relationship based on the information the scientist has available with regard to a model, theory, or law. Testing the hypothesis will yield information that strengthens or weakens the scientist's confidence in the model, theory, or law under consideration.

Models and theories, then, are *explanations* of observations. Laws are *descriptions* of natural systems that have been repeatedly observed. And hypotheses are tentative statements of an *anticipated relationship*.

Science and Technology

The distinction between science and technology is another issue that children increasingly have difficulty making. In fact, many adults do not distinguish much between science and technology. Ebert and Ebert (1998) discuss the mutually beneficial relationship between the two, as one discipline facilitates the work of the other and vice versa. They are, however, careful to elucidate the very distinct difference between the two: "Simply stated, science seeks to understand the world around us, and technology takes scientifically generated knowledge and gives it *practical value* by developing processes and machines that extend capabilities" (p. 56). Henry Nielson (1992), author of *The Endless Spiral,* suggests another perspective of technology: "Technology is changing materials, information, and energy from one form into another."

Science and technology can be contrasted in other ways. In science, theories are validated through observations of natural phenomena, whereas in technology, tools, materials, and processes are applied to develop human adaptive systems (Sanders, 1993). From a sociocultural view, Ryan and Aikenhead (1992) assert that the social purpose of science is to generate new knowledge, while the social purpose of technology is to respond to human and social needs.

For the scientist, as Ebert and Ebert (1998) suggest, technology is a tool as well as the toolmaker. Theoretical scientists, bench scientists, and engineers all need to be creative and logical—and all use tools in their work. Some of the tools used by scientists are intellectual tools, such as mathematics, while others are physical tools, such as instruments for measuring, observing, and analyzing. Data processing tools, like calculators and computers, are now ubiquitous in science and technology work. Unlike scientists, however, children rarely use tools in their attempts to construct understanding of the world. Children often believe that what they cannot see does not exist. Hence, there is a failure to appreciate the important distinction between science and technology.

Unwarranted conceptions such as these reveal that through their schooling and the wider culture, many children construct inflated and unrealistic ideas about what is possible through science. No doubt a contributing factor is the mystique of technology as something comprehensible only to a very few individuals. Taken together, these beliefs fall under the umbrella of what has been called *scientism.* Scientism is the notion that our only "true" knowledge is produced by science (Fetzer & Almeder, 1993). Scientism includes the idea that scientific knowledge can serve as the basis for social and ecological control. A related idea, *technologism,* is the notion that there is a technological solution to all of our problems (Goldsmith, 1992). Scientism and technologism lead people to false expectations of science and technology, that is, that by these means we will have the power to find out everything there is to know and to solve all of our problems.

PHOTO 1.2 Teachers working with science equipment

Quick Review

So far we have asked you to think about and examine your beliefs about the nature of science, what scientists do, the outcomes of scientific work, the relationship between science and technology and between science and society/culture/language. Without a doubt, this represents a substantive exercise in introspection. However, the scholarship in all these areas is quite active, and science continues to be constructed in each new generation—along all of these dimensions as well as in terms of content. We have only scratched the surface of this great conversation. As you practice your craft in the classroom, we hope you will take time to reflect again and again on these foundational issues relating to science. That pause to reflect, especially on the underlying questions, is *the* catalyst for professional development. Even more to the point, your willingness to engage in thought *about* science is indicative of your ability to consider the most fundamental questions, those related to the nature of science. The next section of this chapter considers two philosophical perspectives on scientific inquiry. One of them, construc-

tivism, characterizes all that has been done thus far in this book and is the foundation for all that follows.

SCIENCE AND PHILOSOPHY

Like everything else in people's minds, the concept of science is a construction negotiated with others. What people think about the nature of science has changed over time. Contemporary scholars have constructed a picture of science very different than what prevailed a few generations ago. The degree of change amounts to what philosopher of science Thomas Kuhn (1962) has called a paradigm shift—meaning that the "big picture" has changed. While scholars still differ on many issues, the consensus is that the earlier view of science, called *positivism,* is now discredited. Even when positivism was the consensus view, a minority were arguing for an alternative. Early thinkers who planted the seeds for what is now called *constructivism* were Immanuel Kant, Henry James, Charles Sanders Peirce, and John Dewey. Crafters of postpositivist philosophies of science include

Kuhn and other historians, philosophers, and sociologists of science. Despite decades of conversation about the nature of science, there is by no means uniformity of opinion. There are many unsettled issues about the nature of science and knowledge.

Our own view is that scientists' work is creative and takes many diverse forms. As we see it, the main goal of scientific work is to create models and theories of nature that are warranted by the evidence, help us make sense of our experience, and are useful. In Hestenes's (1992) words:

> The great game of science is modeling the real world, and each scientific theory lays down a system of rules for playing the game. The object of the game is to construct valid models of real objects and processes. Such models comprise the core of scientific knowledge. To understand science is to know how scientific models are constructed and validated. (p. 732)

What follows is more background on the evolution of the contemporary view of science and a comparison of positivism and constructivism. Finally, and most important, are some thoughts on how all of this applies to day-to-day life in the elementary classroom.

Positivism

The nineteenth-century philosopher, Auguste Comte, coined the term positivism, but its roots can be traced back to Francis Bacon, the "father of modern science" (Isaac Newton and René Descartes were founders of modern science, too). The positivist conception of science developed in the centuries that followed, and took its most extreme form in nineteenth-century European work. Lincoln and Guba (1985) have identified five basic assumptions that underlie and characterize positivism as a philosophy of science:

1. A single, tangible reality exists "out there" that can be broken apart into pieces, which can be studied independently (the whole is just the sum of the parts).

2. The observer can be separated from the observed (or the knower from the known).

3. Observations are separated in time and context, such that what is true at one time and place may be true at another time and place.

4. Causality is linear; there are no effects without causes and no causes without effects.

5. Objectivity is possible; methodology guarantees that the results of an inquiry can be free from the influence of any value system.

ACTIVITY 1.5

Your Beliefs About Scientific Knowledge

Consider the following, and then discuss your opinions with a classmate.

1. What do you believe about scientific knowledge? Refer back to your responses in Activity 1.2. Compare your own beliefs with the five major positivist assumptions.

2. Do you agree or disagree with the positivist assumptions? Where do you feel unsure? What do you still need to know?

Science, like any other form of knowing, has to be built upon assumptions, but most philosophers today no longer consider the assumptions of the positivists to be logically defensible. The problem for teachers is that many science textbooks and classroom programs may still reflect positivist views. Positivism is exemplified, for example, when children are told that scientists have "proven" something, or when science is depicted as nothing more than a mound of facts.

Why do these old ideas die hard? In later chapters you will have an opportunity to learn about research, such as that conducted by the Learning in Science Project in New Zealand. This work represents abundant evidence regarding the *tenacity of beliefs,* even after extensive instruction (Osborne & Freyberg, 1985). You might be surprised at what children really believe about things.

There is another reason that old ideas die hard. Sometimes it takes a long time for an idea to be discussed and negotiated among people. Cultural historians talk about a century as the order of magnitude in time for the diffusion of a major concept through culture!

Constructivism

From a constructivist view of science, instead of seeking proof, scientists work to convince their peers that what they propose reasonably fits the available data, aids understanding, and is useful in making predictions and decisions. In other words, scientists seek to show that their idea meets criteria of *warranted assertability* and *viability* (von Glasersfeld, 1989). Scientists can show that their models and explanations work, but they cannot prove a one-to-one correspondence to external reality. Constructivists perceive science as a complex of meanings *negotiated* in a community of practitioners. Constructivist assumptions include:

1. Curiosity is the fundamental driving force in science.
2. Science is a dynamic, ongoing activity.
3. Science aims at comprehensiveness and simplification.
4. Science utilizes many methods.

5. The methods of science are characterized by attributes that are more in the realm of values than techniques.
6. A basic characteristic of science is a faith in the susceptibility of the physical universe to human ordering and understanding.
7. Science has a unique attribute of openness.
8. Tentativeness and uncertainty mark all of science (Kimball, 1968).

Comparing Positivism with Constructivism

Within the positivist camp, *verificationism* is the idea that conclusions reached through experimental science represent proof. This is the view that scientific knowledge can be known with certainty. But is proof a reasonable expectation? Science is perceived by constructivists as one way of knowing that has its own particular scope and limits. Proof is beyond those limits. Inductive reasoning (reasoning from the particular to the general), the kind of logic used in science experiments, cannot lead to absolute certainty about any results because, for one thing, scientists can never account for all cases. Actually, experiments cannot prove anything (Garrison & Bentley, 1990). It is not even clear what can be disproven by inductivist scientific methods. The point is that an emphasis on proof is infinitely less important in a world that we scarcely understand than is an emphasis on understanding as being dynamic and ever changing. Our experiences lend support to our theories.

You probably had not expected that a book about how to teach science in the elementary school would be discussing such deep philosophical issues. And quite understandably, you may be asking yourself what all of this has to do with growing lima beans or building simple circuits. Keep in mind that it is these questions about the nature of science, the nature of inquiry, that have yielded the vast amounts of information and understanding that we do have at this time. Without this impetus, a systematic attempt for understanding would not have been able to develop. So resist the temptation to shy away from these excursions. They will, ultimately, provide you with a stronger foundation for the teaching of science than you had ever expected to possess.

A final issue between positivists and constructivists is the nature of the relationship between observation and theory. Positivists see the observer (or the knower) and the observed (what is to be known) as clearly separate. This separation is reflected in the positivist view that theories (explanations, beliefs) are sharply distinct from observations (data, facts). They hold that observations are facts and can be made objectively, without bias. They see little or no role for subjectivity in well-designed scientific experiments. This *objectivism* is a key positivist assumption, "that reality can be confirmed by matching our inner and outer worlds" (Segal, 1986, p. 19). Hence, observations, and especially the data from experiments, are highly valued by positivists. In positivism, theories are created to explain observations a posteriori, or after an open-minded gathering of data. Does this sound consistent with what you have been taught about science? Very likely it does.

On the other hand, constructivists argue that in order to see anything meaningful at all, the observer must have some notion of what to expect, that is, a theory. In other words, all of your experiences are necessarily bound up in some context based on all of your previous experiences. And it is not possible for you to completely separate that context from any new experience. Constructivists would say that observations, the data, are *theory-laden,* that is, they are influenced by a per-

son's expectations and beliefs. Ken Tobin and Deborah Tippins (1993) put it this way:

> From a constructivist perspective data are not collected, but are constructed from experience using personal theoretical frameworks that have greatest salience to the goals of the individual doing research. . . . Decisions to categorize data as relevant or nonrelevant can be made at the time data are created, analyzed, or interpreted. . . . The assumption is that the data that are created are representative of the objects, events, and phenomena that occurred in the unit of time. However, the fact remains that the data recorded as relevant conform to the researcher's personal theories of what is relevant in a particular context. (pp. 15–16)

For example, data regarding size is quantifiable. And here is where this impacts directly on your work in the classroom. It is you who will provide the opportunities for your students' engagements with this environment, and you who will attempt to guide your students as they develop personal frameworks of understanding. From this view, you cannot *give* your students a scientific conceptual scheme; all such schemes are constructed by each individual as he or she interacts with others in conversation, in books, and so forth. You can only facilitate the construction of that scheme by providing guidance with appropriate experiences.

A similar situation was long ago recognized by theologians. The medieval Christian saint and scholar, Anselm, wrote, "*Credo, ut intelligam*"—"I believe, that I might understand." In positing theories, scientists too make leaps of faith to understand the natural world. Of course, they try to make the leaps as short as possible. As constructivists, we believe that objectivity can be approached and should be attempted, but cannot be achieved. We agree with the philosophers

Christine Ebert

PHOTO 1.3 Even for children, scientific investigation requires access to the appropriate tools.

who argue that an element of subjectivity is involved in all knowledge, including science.

Constructivism and the Teaching of Science

Through their work with each other, conducting investigations and constructing knowledge, children can develop a richer and more realistic conception of the nature of science. In your own classroom, you can become aware of the initial conceptions among the children and challenge children to think more about these notions (just as we have been challenging you to think about them throughout this chapter). Also, you can purposefully weave more explicit instruction about the nature of science into your program, gearing the content to the children's readiness.

A number of implications for teaching practice can be derived from a constructivist view of science (Duschl, 1989; Duschl & Hamilton, 1992). One is that more attention should be paid to the theory side of scientific investigations (Gowin, 1987). This means helping children make their beliefs more ex-

plicit and helping them to see how expectations and beliefs affect observation and data selection. You help children make their ideas more explicit by asking them why they say such-and-such, and in encouraging them to elaborate in their explanations.

Another practical implication of a constructivist view of science is that classroom activities and investigations should be less like cookbook recipes and more like the open-ended investigations of real scientific work. Further, instructional activities and situations should engage students in more student-to-student discussion of scientific ideas and more cooperative group work (Lemke, 1990; Larochelle & Desautels, 1991).

Children can use tools as scientists do in their investigations and deliberations. Children can take measurements, organize, and analyze their data. Elementary children can use measuring tools such as:

- rulers, tape measures, trundle wheels (all for measuring length or distance)

- measuring cups or graduated beakers (for capacity)

- thermometers (for temperature)

- spring scales (for weight)
- equal-arm platform balances (for mass)
- stopwatches, sundials, hourglasses, and clocks (for time)

Of course, the computer is a tool scientists use in a variety of ways. Like scientists, children can use computers with sensors on probe attachments to directly measure phenomena such as temperature. Also like scientists, children can use computers for modeling and simulating physical systems. The scientific simulation creates a "microworld" in which children can observe contrived systems and make and test their hypotheses and predictions (di Sessa, 1982).

Still another implication of constructivism for science teaching is that more attention be given to the history of science and technology. Studying exemplars of the creation and negotiation of scientific knowledge can help students learn about the human face of science (Matthews, 1987).

Some teaching methods that particularly address the nature of science are shown in the concept map, Figure 1.2.

Quick Review

It is not necessary that you adopt a constructivist philosophy in order to teach science. A philosophy is a very personal choice, and that sentiment, by the way, is very much in keeping with a constructivist view. A constructivist perspective can, however, have a profound influence on your approach to the teaching of science. One of the significant characteristics of a constructivist view is that it recognizes the value of the inherent curiosity that children bring to your class. Constructivists see science as dynamic rather than static—that is, it is a continual process of increasing one's understanding of the natural world. Constructivists view the actual construction of knowledge as occurring within each individual through the interaction with other people and with phenomena. From a constructivist perspective, your task as a teacher is to arrange the engagements that will allow your students to construct knowledge, and to continually monitor the knowledge structures that emerge in order to see that your own instructional goals are being met.

CONCLUSION

This chapter has focused on developing your understanding of what science is, its underlying philosophy, and how it relates to culture. Though this is an important exercise for all people, it is particularly important for you as a teacher. Why? Because of the ideas that children bring to your classroom, those ideas that have developed over the years as a result of the many experiences of their lives. Indeed, it would be much easier for you as a teacher if all children came to you, to use Locke's simile, as a tabula rasa—a blank slate. That, however, is simply not the case.

One large research study involved nearly eleven thousand high school seniors from across Canada. Each was asked to respond to a statement and write a short paragraph explaining their views about science. One finding of the study was that most students had an all-inclusive "technoscience" concept, not distinguishing between science and technology. For example, most equated scientific research with medical research or agricultural research.

Many students in the Canadian study believed "the scientific method" entails rigidly following prescribed steps. They also expressed confidence in scientists and engineers in making decisions on science-related social issues. They put more faith in a technocratic rather than a democratic approach (Aikenhead, nd).

Another finding in that study was that most of the students viewed scientific knowl-

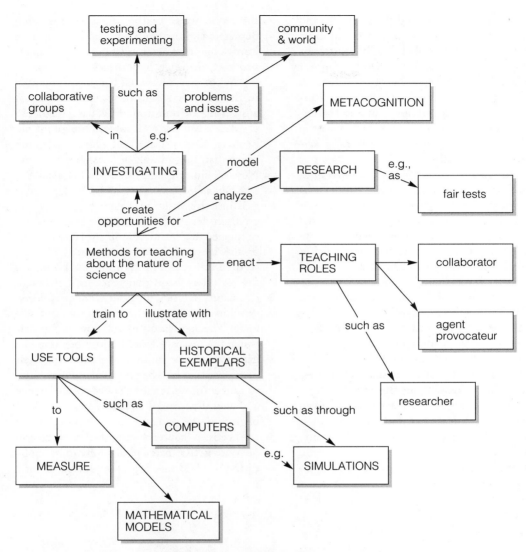

FIGURE 1.2 A web of teaching strategies that help children develop the concept of the nature of science.

edge as tentative—but for different and conflicting reasons. Some held that "old knowledge is reinterpreted in light of new ideas, old knowledge was in error, and old knowledge was 'added to,' thereby giving a different picture" (Aikenhead, nd). The researchers also found that students viewed science as closely interrelated with society. Stu-

dents felt scientists are and should be concerned with the effects of their work. Most of these students also expressed an awareness that social interactions affect the creation of scientific knowledge, and that politics affects science.

The study revealed that both male and female students equally favor more women becoming scientists and engineers, and equally believe that social conditions have affected the present imbalance. Interestingly, in this study few gender differences appear in student opinions, "except that females tended to believe more in creative, non-rigid thinking as an attribute of good scientists, while males tended to believe more in the objectivity and social isolation of science" (Aikenhead, nd).

The Canadian study gives us a portrait of typical ideas about science among older students. We might wonder what influences those ideas. That schooling and mass media are among those influences should indicate how important it is that the classroom teacher be prepared with a thoughtfully developed conceptualization of the nature of science and its relationship to culture and society. Think once again about your results in Activity 1.2. Discuss the answers with your classmates. How do your views compare with those of the Canadian seniors?

Many teachers are still unfamiliar with constructivist ideas about the nature of science. Consequently, the view of science still being communicated in most classrooms is that science is a body of knowledge compiled through the steps of the scientific method. This is not surprising since through the authority of textbooks, science is often depicted as thoroughly objective, value-free knowledge that accumulates as experiments prove or disprove hypotheses and theories.

As you consider what has been presented in this chapter it will become obvious that answering the question of "What is science?" is still left for you to resolve. Our intent has been to demonstrate that science is much more than just a book of facts about nature. New teaching guides, like the *National Science Education Standards* (NRC, 1996), propose that instruction be oriented toward helping children develop a conception of the nature of science that is different in a variety of ways to the view many of us learned when we studied science. Throughout this book, we discuss many ways that teachers can orient classroom practice in order to help children develop more sophisticated notions of science. The key recommendation in the National Standards is that children become engaged in active inquiry and through their own investigations be provided opportunities to reflect on what they believe about science and scientists. And it all begins here, and it all begins now, as you consider for yourself what science is. (Chapter 4 extends this discussion of constructivism as a philosophy to its application to children's cognitive development.)

2

Scientific Knowledge for the Elementary/ Middle School Years

Scope of Elementary/Middle School Science

National Science Education Standards

Obstacles to Implementing a
Depth-Oriented Science Program

Conclusion

Your Academic Roadmap

Study of this chapter should help you to understand
the following concepts:

- An effective science education program is one
  that seeks depth rather than breadth.

- A "framework" approach to the development of
  a science curriculum serves to show how topics
  relate to one another.

- An awareness and understanding of the National
  Science Education Standards underlies a sound
  pedagogy.

- There is a need to move away from the "textbook" approach to science education.

- Many resources can supplement a science
  textbook.

The present curricula in science and mathematics are overstuffed and undernourished.

—F. J. Rutherford and A. Ahlgren,
Science for All Americans

SCOPE OF ELEMENTARY/MIDDLE SCHOOL SCIENCE

The scope of science is enormous, and so is the scope of the elementary school science curriculum. It is unlikely that you will know all the science content, but every teacher eventually has to teach unfamiliar subject matter. The challenge is even greater for those who never seriously studied science and lack a meaningful conceptual framework with which to structure the subject matter. A lot of science may seem useless without the "big picture." As chapter 1 was intended to help you expand your perspective on the nature of science, chapter 2 focuses on the structure that underlies science in the school curriculum. With these two ele-

ments of the picture in place, chapter 3 addresses the varied dimensions of science as a subject that you will teach.

The kind of elementary school curriculum advocated by typical state curriculum guides and by the National Research Council's *National Science Education Standards* (1996) requires basic content in the physical, life, and earth-space sciences, as well as some background knowledge of the history and philosophy of science. As a teacher, you may have a science textbook to guide you, but no textbook could possibly provide all the background information you need to prepare your lessons. Consequently, the task of planning your classroom science program may seem overwhelming. Grasping the big picture, however, and having a basic framework will get you started. Having on hand some good resources will help you get the details together. As you teach science, you will gradually appropriate the content so that your knowledge and confidence should grow with each year you teach.

The science content discussed in this chapter is based on the framework developed by the National Committee on Science Education Standards and Assessment for the National Science Education Standards, released in 1996 (NRC, 1996). The standards represent a broad framework designed to help teachers plan a science program. The standards have already influenced what is taught in most public schools in the United States. So, regardless of where you teach, you need to understand the standards' content framework.

Less Is More

The notion of "less is more" can be traced back to the Greek poet Hesiod (ca. 700 B.C.E.). Mies van der Rohe, the architect of unadorned, functional buildings, adopted the phrase as a guiding principle for his work. The notion was applied to education by Theodore Sizer (1984) in his book *Horace's Compromise,* which focuses on improving U.S. secondary schools. In science education at all levels, the emphasis now is on "big ideas"—fewer concepts but in greater depth, with more emphasis on understanding and less emphasis on the recall of terminology. With "less is more" as a guiding principle in planning units and lessons, *depth* is preferred over *coverage.* This in itself should make sense to you, since "to cover" refers to concealing something rather than exposing it for consideration. When teachers try to cover too much content, their students tend to get stuck at the low level of thinking required for simply remembering information. The consensus in the profession now is that it is better for students to comprehend the richness and complexity of a few topics than to be superficially exposed to many topics.

Studying something in depth also leads to better retention and increases the chances that what has been learned will be applied in other situations. Instead of being overwhelmed by a multitude of facts and concepts, students engaged in in-depth studies experience the achievement of mastering the particular material. You will want your students to "go beyond simple declarative statements to differentiation, elaboration, qualification, and integration" (Newmann, 1988, p. 346). A wonderful intellectual experience is possible for those students who reach the point in their study where they can perceive the limits of knowledge on a topic and can generate new questions that lead them into creative inquiry. A recent metaphor used to describe the ideal curriculum balance is "postholing." Students should generally become familiar with the topography but aim to "posthole" selected spots on the terrain in greater depth.

Frameworks for Science Content

In order to bring an end to the constant addition of new material to the science curriculum, efforts have been made to establish frameworks that would delineate the categories of scientific inquiry and the general concepts that would be most appropriate for a school curriculum. The science program that results consists of the sum total of science-related experiences available for children in the school and the classroom. Since schooling is an intentional process ultimately directed by the larger society, people at many levels have a stake in what is taught. As a teacher, you will have ample opportunity for your own creative curriculum making, but you will also be constrained by society's dictates. These dictates range everywhere from local school board policies (for example, on the use of animals in the classroom) to state education department curriculum documents and the national standards.

In the past, many different frameworks have been used to organize the science

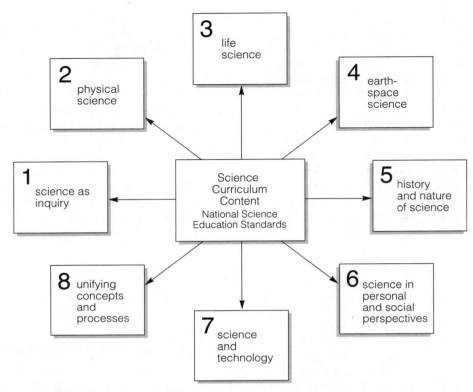

FIGURE 2.1 A framework for science program content devised by the *National Science Education Standards.*

content of the elementary curriculum. One framework involved dividing all of science into two broad categories: physical science and life science. Another approach has been to divide science three ways: physical science, life science, and earth–space science. In other schemes, the science processes (observing, measuring, etc.) have been emphasized as a content category. There are certainly many ways to organize science, and there are good arguments for each approach. This chapter uses the framework adopted by the *National Science Education Standards* (NRC, 1996). For grades K–8, the science content of the curriculum is divided into three content categories:

Physical science (physics and chemistry)

Life science (biology and ecology)

Earth and space science (astronomy, meteorology, oceanography, and geology)

The national standards then add these five additional content categories:

Science as inquiry

Science and technology

Science in personal and social perspectives

History and nature of science

Unifying concepts and processes

Figure 2.1 depicts this framework graphically. The categories of "science as inquiry" and "history and nature of science" are addressed in this book in this chapter and in chapters 6 and 7. The categories of "science and technology" and "science in per-

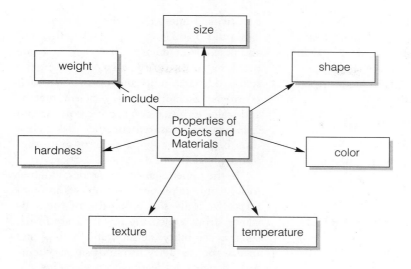

FIGURE 2.2 Concept map showing properties of objects and materials for a primary unit.

sonal and social perspectives" are addressed in chapter 10. "Unifying concepts and processes" are addressed in chapters 7 and 9. The next section of this chapter provides an overview of each of the first three content areas: physical science, life science, and earth-space science.

Quick Review

In the best of all possible worlds, every elementary teacher would be thoroughly familiar with every curriculum topic to be taught, but the actual practice of teaching usually fosters teachers' learning and leads many to feel comfortable with most topics. The approach we recommend is to be less concerned about covering a lot of content and to instead focus on creating instructional units in which your students will be able to explore some part of the content in depth. Start your unit planning by thinking about the major ideas involved in the topic. If you are developing a physical science unit for primary grades, one of the major ideas may be the properties of objects and materials. Create an outline or sketch out a concept map, such as the one in Figure 2.2. This will help you expand and connect ideas using a

"framework" approach to the development of relevant learning activities.

NATIONAL EDUCATION STANDARDS

In the *National Science Education Standards* (NRC, 1996), science content is considered in clusters of grades. On the basis of children's cognitive development and teacher experience, grades are grouped K–4 and 5–8. In each cluster, the standards address the major concepts in the physical, life, and earth-space sciences, and these are discussed in the next three sections of this chapter. You will find a listing of the standards in chapter 14, "A Compendium of Resources for Teaching Elementary Science."

Physical Science

The physical science content in the elementary curriculum is about forces and motions, and matter and energy. Forces include pushes and pulls, friction, and gravity. Motions vary in starting position, speed, and direction. Forces and motions are also related to machines. Matter is studied by investigating the properties of things. Energy includes the areas of mechanical energy, sound, light, heat, electricity, and magnetism. In the physical sciences, the National Science Education Standards call for all students in grades K–4 to develop an understanding of

- properties of objects and materials,
- position and motion of objects, and
- light, heat, electricity, and magnetism.

For grades 5–8 the standards call for students to develop an understanding of

- properties and changes of properties in matter,
- motions and forces, and
- transformations of energy.

Children explore the physical world in their day-to-day environment by observing and manipulating objects. They need many experiences with a variety of objects and contexts, so that they can compare, sort, and describe what they experience as their understanding develops. Children use qualitative terms to describe objects and materials and how they behave and change. As their knowledge develops, they will also use quantitative descriptions.

Primary children do not usually develop complex scientific ideas. For example, a young child who sees water boiling away sees the water as disappearing rather than as changing state. Young children do not distinguish heat and temperature, and they tend to think of electricity as moving away from its source to a target, rather than forming a circuit.

Investigations children carry out in their early years can provide a basis in experience for conceptual growth. Experiences with heat that focus on changes in temperature, for example, can later be drawn upon when children grapple with the difference between degrees and calories.

As they go through school, children find that they can extend their descriptions by

measuring things. First, they use nonstandard units (hand lengths, pencil lengths, etc.) and measuring devices that they've made (markings on a board, etc.), and later, the standard metric units and instruments such as rulers, measuring cups, thermometers, and scales and balances. From recording and graphing the measurements they make, children begin to recognize patterns and order in the physical world.

In the upper elementary grades, children move from the properties of objects and materials to study the properties of the substances from which the materials are made, such as solubility, density, and boiling and melting points. They also study simple chemical changes and learn about elements and compounds. Children learn that some substances, such as acids or metals, share characteristics and can be grouped. Figure 2.3 maps additional properties of materials as appropriate for upper elementary children to study. Compare this map with the map of the properties for primary children in Figure 2.2.

Another important physical science topic for elementary children is force and motion. Children can experience the motions of simple objects, such as marbles, balls, and toys, and can move from qualitative descriptions in primary grades to more quantitative descriptions. They can learn to represent motion on a graph, and they can describe the forces acting on objects. They can learn that friction is a force that slows down a ball rolling across the floor. Children are likely to believe, however, that as long as the ball keeps rolling, a force is acting on it to keep it moving. Yet, as Newton pointed out, it is inertia that explains why objects remain at rest and continue to move once set in motion. Children also have difficulty conceptualizing balanced forces in equilibrium. For instance, when a flower pot weighing 1 kilogram (2.2 pounds) rests on a table, the table "pushes up" with a force of 1 kilogram. If the flower pot were replaced with another flower pot, this one weighing 2 kilograms,

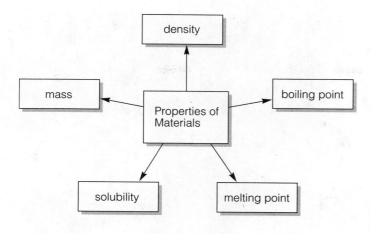

FIGURE 2.3 Concept map showing physical science unit for grades 5–8.

the table would now be "pushing up" with a force of 2 kilograms. If not for equilibrium, either the table would fall apart or the flower pot would be launched into the air.

Children's understanding of energy is developed through early experiences with sound, light, heat, electricity and magnetism, gravity, and the motion of objects. From such experiences, children develop the idea that energy comes in different forms and from many sources. They learn to identify the sun as a major source of energy for changes on the earth. In the upper elementary grades, children begin to understand more complex notions, such as that light consists of different wavelengths, and that energy can be transferred from one form to another. In studying energy, children should be provided with opportunities to experience many kinds of energy transformations, such as the chemical energy of fire being converted to light and/or heat, magnetism being converted to electricity, and electricity being converted to sound.

Life Science Content

The life science content in the elementary grades includes the study of different kinds of organisms, their behaviors and functioning, habitats and life cycles, interactions and relationships. Life science is also about the parts of an organism, including their structure and how they function in the organism. In the elementary grades, the emphasis is on plants and animals. In the life sciences, the National Science Education Standards call for all students in grades K–4 to develop an understanding of

- characteristics of organisms,
- life cycles of organisms, and
- organisms and environments.

For grades 5–8, the standards call for students to develop an understanding of

- structure and function in living systems,
- reproduction and heredity,
- regulation and behavior,
- populations and ecosystems, and
- the diversity and adaptations of organisms.

In the early grades, children should be able to experience and study many different kinds of living things and their habitats. From their observations, children can begin to demarcate living from nonliving and can categorize living things. Young children also begin to understand the needs of living things and how organisms behave to meet their needs. Organisms possess specific kinds

Chen Long

PHOTO 2.1 Classroom pets such as this guinea pig help children to understand the needs of living things.

of structures that function in particular ways to help them meet these needs. Early experience with living things is the basis for understanding biological diversity and the dependence of organisms on both the living and the nonliving environment for survival. Such experience also is the basis for realizing that all organisms, including humans, cause changes where they live, and that such changes may be either beneficial or harmful to themselves and other organisms.

Young children should also have experiences with organisms in the different stages of the life cycle. In the early grades, children may not understand the continuity of life through different stages, such as from egg to tadpole to adult. While young children realize that an organism resembles its parents, they are not likely to understand the inheritance of traits. They may think traits come from only one parent or are just a blending of both parents' characteristics. In addition, many features of an organism are changed or become developed through the organism's interactions with its environment.

In the upper elementary years, children move from a focus on individual organisms to studying both larger and smaller dimensions,

the context of ecosystems, and the units of organisms and cells. Their investigations can be increasingly quantitative, and they can use instruments such as the microscope. These children begin to develop concepts of nutrient and energy flows in an ecosystem, and relate heritability of characteristics across generations to adaptation and evolution. In learning about ecosystems, children can understand food webs, food pyramids, and trophic levels—producers, consumers, decomposers. They also can learn about ecosystem carrying capacity and the concept of niche.

In the upper elementary grades, children can recognize the complementarity of structures and functions at different levels of organization—cells, organs, systems, organisms, and ecosystems. Children can understand more about the nature of disease, how some diseases are the result of the failure of a bodily system while others are caused by infectious agents. They can understand the difference between asexual and sexual reproduction, the role of the specialized gametes—sperm and eggs—and how hereditary information is carried by genes on the chromosomes of every cell.

Children in the upper grades are particularly interested in their own bodies, which makes this a good time to help them relate life science concepts to the human organism and its environment. Preteens become involved in activities such as sports, music, and the arts. One way to help them realize the relevance of life science to their lives is to help them see how their performance in sports or on the stage is related to the functioning of their bodily organs and systems.

Earth and Space Science Content

The earth and space sciences include a wide range of topics from several scientific disciplines. These include physical and historical geology, astronomy and cosmology, meteorology and climatology, and oceanography.

The National Science Education Standards call for all students in grades K–4 to develop an understanding of

- properties of earth materials, and
- objects in the sky.

For grades 5–8, the standards call for students to develop an understanding of

- the structure of the earth system,
- Earth's history,
- Earth in the solar system.

In the early grades, science instruction in this area should be focused on the concrete everyday world that children experience. Young children should be encouraged to use their observational skills to become aware of interesting details and changes. They should develop their abilities to describe and explain what they observe in their environment. It is through talking about and drawing what they see and think about that children create the background for understanding more abstract concepts later.

Primary grade children can study the properties of earth materials (rocks, soils, water, and air). They can learn that the proper-

Christine Ebert

PHOTO 2.2 Studying rocks from the local area allows children to make systematic observations of the world around them.

ties of these materials make them useful, such as for making things and for supporting life. They also can learn that such materials may be made up of parts or composed of different kinds of materials. Children can observe different constituents in some rocks, for example. At this level, it isn't important that the constituents be identified as minerals, or that they learn what geologists call the rock, or even that they classify the rock by its source (sedimentary, igneous, or metamorphic). Such ideas, however, can be meaningful to middle grade students. Younger children can describe how different rocks, and their different constituents, look and feel. They also can start rock and fossil collections.

In children's study of both life and earth sciences, they should visit outdoor study sites regularly. By observing changes in a specific place on a regular basis, they come to realize that the earth is changing constantly, and that some of these changes occur in patterns. The idea of change can be extended so that children realize there are many time scales for change. Young children can appreciate that fossils are evidence of creatures that lived in the distant past.

Even as early as first grade, children can keep science or nature journals as a way of recording and processing their experiences (Gallas, 1995). Later, they can use instruments such as thermometers and metersticks to take and record measurements. They can organize their measurements in charts and simple graphs. For example, primary grade children can study the changes in the position of objects in the sky, such as the sun and the moon. They can draw the shape of the moon as it changes through a lunar cycle. These drawings can be arranged in sequence and displayed in the classroom as a reminder of this predictable cyclical change. Young children can understand that the phases relate to changes in the position of the moon relative to the sun and the earth. However, modeling how the celestial bodies are positioned in space is more appropriate for the later elementary grades.

By the middle school level, children are more able to understand the positions, distances, and dynamics between the earth, the sun, and the moon, and can work with a model of the system, such as the one in Figure 2.4.

Middle grade children are able to consider the earth as a system in which four components interact—geosphere, hydrosphere, atmosphere, and biosphere. Children at this level can also understand the unique physical and chemical properties of water; for example, that water is a solvent that dissolves minerals and gases and carries them to the oceans. They can understand plate tectonics, a unifying geological theory about the

earth's crust that explains how most earthquakes and volcanoes occur, and helps explain different patterns of climate in the past and even the distribution of plants and animals around the world. Children can study the earth's history and speculate on how predicted movements of the earth's plates might make the earth different in the future.

In addition, middle grade children can understand more about geophysical and geochemical cycles, such as the rock cycle and the water cycle, and constituent processes, such as weathering, erosion, evaporation, and condensation. They can understand how some geological events or processes, such as earthquakes and erosion, are destructive, while others, such as volcanic eruptions and sea-floor spreading, are constructive. Most children this age will have little trouble with the concept of evaporation, but conceptualizing condensation will be more challenging.

Concepts such as gravity and the causes of the seasons could be challenging to children at this level. Gravity can be explained in different ways. From the perspective of Newtonian physics, gravity is an attractive force that "holds" the planets in orbit about the sun. From the perspective of Einstein's theory of relativity, however, the planets orbit the sun because of the "shape" of space. Massive objects distort or warp space. The sun, being 99 percemt of the mass of the whole solar system, is at the "bottom" of the well. The earth stays in place due to its orbital velocity. Thus, in Einstein's view, gravity is not a force, but an aspect of inertia and the shape of space.

The seasons occur because the energy from the sun that hits the earth's surface varies during the year due to the tilt of the earth's rotational axis. There are long periods of daylight and more direct solar rays in summer, whereas the days are short and the rays more slanted in winters. At a given time, seasons are opposite in the Northern and Southern Hemispheres. Children in the

sun

moon

Earth

FIGURE 2.4 Position of sun, Earth, and moon at quadrature (quarter phase).

middle grades are able to understand the relationship between the sun and the many phenomena on the earth that are related to solar energy, including ocean currents, winds, and the growth of plants.

The Additional Content Areas

In addition to the traditional subject matter areas of physical, life, and earth–space science that are discussed in the previous section, the National Science Education Standards add five other categories of content:

> science as inquiry
>
> science and technology
>
> science in personal and social perspectives
>
> history and nature of science
>
> unifying concepts and processes

This chapter provides only an overview of each of these areas since they are dealt with in greater detail in other chapters of the book. Keep in mind that these five additional content areas can be integrated into the curriculum by being organized in relation to concepts and principles in the physical, life, and earth–space sciences.

Science as Inquiry In the standards, the content standard for scientific inquiry and the standard regarding the history and nature of science overlap considerably. As to the former, the standards state that as a result of activities, all students in kindergarten to grade 8 should develop both the skills necessary to do scientific inquiry and an understanding about scientific inquiry. According to the standards, scientific inquiry refers to the many ways scientists study nature and propose explanations for natural phenomena based on the evidence they derived in their work. In the classroom, inquiry refers to the activities in which children develop their understanding of scientific ideas and their understanding of how scientists conduct their work (NRC, 1996). Inquiry also is an approach to teaching in which children are enabled to conduct scientific inquiry themselves. You will find more about the topic of inquiry in science in chapters 6 and 7.

History and Nature of Science The standard for the history and nature of science states that as a result of activities, all students, K–8, should develop understanding of science as a human endeavor. For grades 5–8, students should also develop an understanding of the nature of science and the history of science. Science is a human endeavor in that people of different cultures have always sought to understand the world and to solve problems encountered in the environment. Over time, people have learned much from their experiences and have made a variety of contributions to our understanding of nature. In today's global society, many people choose to do science as a vocation. There are many types of employment in science, from which people can earn a good living as well as gain satisfaction in their work.

Yet another aspect of science as a human endeavor is that scientific work is accomplished through human abilities and skills, and depends on human values. Human values related to science include openness, skepticism, and honesty.

Teachers typically have not emphasized the improvement of students' conceptions of the history and nature of science (NRC, 1996). Children can gain much insight from the study of science in history. Through the use of short stories, teachers can integrate into instruction historical examples of people who have made contributions to science, including women and people from various ethnicities. We address the topics of feeling and valuing in science in chapter 3.

Science and Technology Regarding the standard for science and technology, the standards state that as a result of activities, all students in K–4 should develop

- abilities to distinguish between natural objects and human-made objects,
- abilities of technological design, and
- understanding about science and technology.

The latter two aspects of the standard are also repeated for grades 5–8. The science and technology standard extends the idea of inquiry in science to the parallel idea of design in technology. Young children often are able to carry out design activities with more understanding of the processes involved than is the case with inquiry activities. They are able to follow the four-step process:

1. State the problem.
2. Design and implement a solution.
3. Evaluate the solution.
4. Communicate the problem, design, and solution.

Older children can tackle more complex problems and can begin to distinguish between science and technology. More is said about science and technology in chapters 7 and 10. You also may wish to refer to Ebert and Ebert's *The Inventive Mind in Science* (1998) for a thorough treatment of how to incorporate creative thinking in science through inventing-based strategies.

Science in Personal and Social Perspectives The standard for science in personal and social perspectives states that as a result of activities, all students K–8 should develop their understanding of personal health. In addition, K–4 students should develop an understanding of

- characteristics and changes in populations,

- types of resources,
- changes in environments, and
- science and technology in local challenges.

Students in grades 5–8 also should develop an understanding of

- populations, resources, and environments,
- natural hazards,
- risks and benefits, and
- science and technology in society.

The content specified in this standard provides a foundation for the understandings and actions required of citizens. This standard also connects science in the curriculum with social studies and health education, which makes it a focus for curriculum integration. Younger and older children alike can learn about and act on problems and issues related to science and technology in their own communities. By becoming engaged with real-world problems and issues, children can develop their understanding of concepts such as population growth, carrying capacity, resource depletion, environmental degradation, and risk-benefit analysis. They can come to realize that science cannot answer all questions and that technology cannot solve all human problems or meet all human needs. Chapters 9 and 10 relate to this dimension.

Unifying Concepts and Processes The standard for the unifying concepts and processes lists the following major scientific themes, which are content for the curriculum from K–12:

Order and organization

Evidence, models, and explanation

Constancy, change, and measurement

Evolution and equilibrium

Form and function

These are some of the interdisciplinary "big ideas" that can be found as threads in the fabric of science. As such, they are discussed throughout this text. Other curriculum framework documents, such as *Science for All Americans* and *Benchmarks for Science Literacy* (AAAS, 1989, 1993), also have emphasized the value of such conceptual themes in organizing the science curriculum.

ACTIVITY 2.1

Standards around the United States

All fifty states have their own frameworks or standards for the science curriculum. These can be accessed on the Web at http://putwest.boces.org:80/standards.html

1. Access your state's science standards.
2. Compare your state's standards to the National Science Education Standards discussed in this chapter.
   - What are the content areas in your state's science program?
   - Select any grade level, and look to see in what ways the content for your state is like or different from the nationwide standards.

Quick Review

The five "new" content categories can and should be integrated into the three basic subject matter categories. Taken together they provide you with the themes and tone of science instruction. For instance, a life science unit about plants should incorporate some important historical studies, the scientist(s) who conducted relevant investigations, and the methods and technologies used in the particular research under study. Stephen Hale's fascinating experiment to determine where plants obtain the materials for their growth is a good example. He was the first to show that plants "draw through their leaves some part of their nourishment from the air" and also showed that a great proportion of the weight of the plant must come from the air and not from the soil (you might find that many of your students believe that new plant growth comes from soil nutrients) (in Richards, 1987, p. 35).

ACTIVITY 2.2
INFOTRAC COLLEGE EDITION
INVESTIGATION:

Are the Standards Worthwhile?
Who Decides?

With all that has been said about the establishment of these standards, the next question is whether they are really worthwhile. In fact, as mentioned earlier, different states have different standards.

Use InfoTrac College Edition to help you address the following questions:

- What seems to be the primary reason for adopting national and/or state standards?

- Is there a counterargument to the adoption of standards?

- Who writes the standards?

- Who decides whether to adopt the standards?

OBSTACLES TO IMPLEMENTING A DEPTH-ORIENTED SCIENCE PROGRAM

There are many obstacles to creating a depth- and inquiry-oriented science program. One is that few prospective elementary teachers have experienced this kind of science teaching as students. The cliché that "one teaches as one has been taught" points to the need for positive role models for teaching science. Your own experience may have been dominated by coverage-oriented science classes. Designing a depth-oriented inquiry classroom program, then, may be a challenge for you simply because it is a way that is new and unfamiliar.

In addition to the lack of models, another obstacle is that many teaching resources are not designed to support an inquiry approach. Teachers who must plan lessons dealing with unfamiliar subject matter are more likely to rely on textbooks, work sheets, and "cookbook" activities. Unfortunately, as discussed in chapter 1, many of the activities in the published materials do not appropriately represent the nature of science. They offer mainly closed-end activities that have a single right answer (Carlsen, 1991). Further, many textbooks try to cover a wide range of topics and consequently treat each topic superficially.

Another obstacle to designing and implementing an in-depth and inquiry approach is that many children who will be your students have been culturally conditioned to expect to be taught in the traditional way. Because so many teachers in the past have relied exclusively on textbooks as a guide for what to teach, many students have learned that they can succeed by relying on rote memory.

Related to this is the fact that many American children now bring a culturally conditioned attitude to their schoolwork that undermines sustained concentration on a single topic. Typically, these children have been rewarded in school mainly for completing discrete tasks and remembering bits of information. Many have spent far too many hours watching television. Children who watch a lot of television often want sound bites— quick, simple, unambiguous answers. They have little patience for in-depth studies (Newmann, 1988, p. 347).

Another obstacle is the misconception among many students and their parents that teachers should be "fonts of knowledge." It may have been possible as late as the 1700s for a single individual to be thoroughly familiar with most scientific knowledge (perhaps Thomas Jefferson was one such *pi dion*). But since then, the sciences have become quite specialized. Individual human beings just are not able to master all knowledge (Newmann, 1988, p. 346). As a teacher, you will undoubtedly encounter some student's expectation that you should "know it all."

It is also inevitable that a child in your class will ask you a science question that is beyond your scope of knowledge. Because your own experience as a student has perhaps taught you that teachers should be experts, you may feel inadequate. K. C. Cole (1982), a physicist, described an experience she had some years ago, just after she completed a book on light and optics. She was sailing on a sloop in the Virgin Islands and had noticed the brilliance of the shimmering deep blue and green colors of the sea. She asked her sailing companions about the cause of this effect. The colors, they quickly and unambiguously replied, depended on the angle of the sun, the shade of the sky, and the contour of the shore. Feeling ashamed and embarrassed at her own ignorance, Cole "crawled back into the cabin, vowing never to let my stupidity out in public again" (p. 18). But the story does not end here.

Later, back in the science museum where Cole worked, she asked three physicist friends why the waters of Tortola glimmered so in blue and green: "To my surprise and delight, they argued about the issue for days—and no one pretended to have a single right answer" (p. 18). This anecdote illustrates a very important point: In science, there are no stupid questions. Cole continues:

Many people shy away from science because they are afraid to ask stupid ques-

tions. Somewhere along the line they have been led to believe that all scientific questions have clear, unambiguous answers. They have been taught that science is all work and no play, all logic and no guesswork, all knowledge and no wonder. The truth is that the more complete the answer in science, the juicier the next question. . . . Mark Twain used to say that the best thing about science was the enormous amount of conjecture one earned for such a trifling investment of fact. (p. 18)

Of course, science isn't the only subject area where teachers are expected to be experts and are afraid of asking "stupid questions" or of giving wrong answers, but it is certainly one area where many teachers lack confidence in their knowledge. It is important to remember, however, that ignorance, not knowledge, is the real subject matter of science. The experience of many top scientists has been that the more they learn, the more they are aware of what they don't know. Lewis Thomas (1978) has said, "The greatest of all the accomplishments of 20th century science has been the discovery of human ignorance" (p. 15). As Cole (1982) concludes in her essay, "asking stupid questions is usually worth the price in humility or embarrassment; because asking stupid questions is often a very good way to get smart" (p. 18).

ACTIVITY 2.3
INFOTRAC COLLEGE EDITION
INVESTIGATION:

What Progress Has Been Made in Implementing the Standards?

Obviously, having standards written is not enough. Use InfoTrac College Edition to see where science education is right now in terms of implementing the standards. Try to find information that will answer the following questions:

- What obstacles make implementation of standards difficult?
- What sort of legislative support is required for implementation of the science standards?
- Which states have adopted and implemented (at the classroom level) new science education standards?

CONCLUSION

This chapter was intended to help you think about the overall picture of the science content of the elementary curriculum. We acknowledged the trend to teach fewer topics and details in exchange for gaining greater depth. Our focus to that end has been on the National Science Education Standards (NSES) content standards as a model framework for an elementary science program. We also suggested that many teachers find switching to an inquiry- and depth-oriented curriculum approach, as endorsed by the NSES, difficult. Not least among the difficulties is the process of overcoming a number of obstacles, including the textbook-dominated curriculum and the mistaken belief of many children that the teacher should know it all.

The NSES framework and a science textbook are by no means your only resources as you plan what science will be in your classroom. When you begin your work in a particular school, you also should check to see what *curriculum guides* are used in that school or school district. Don't be shy about asking for these; they are not secret documents. Rather, they exist to facilitate instruction. You should also have access to the *state and local curriculum guide for science,* as well as a *professional resource library.* Check these guides first to see what specific science content is designated for the grade or grades you will be teaching.

Find out what resources you will have to work with as you teach. Of course, you will also study the *science textbook,* if there is one (many schools use multiple resources for science instead of a single textbook), both for content and for organization. If a textbook is available, compare the content of the school district curriculum guide with the content of the textbook. It is very likely that the two will not match perfectly. Note which chapters of the textbook match the content designated for your grade in the curriculum guide. Note also if there are topics for your grade that are omitted in the textbook. Find out if topics in your textbook are designated to be taught in earlier or later grades. Finally, you may find it helpful to create an outline or concept map of the basic material you will be teaching.

The content that you have mapped out may seem overwhelming, but there should be no shortage of ideas on what to teach. There are many more resources for you to tap. Your school library should be stocked with science-related tradebooks. Your local public library also will have children's tradebooks as well as books on science at many levels. These materials will help supplement your own background and serve as unit- and lesson-planning resources (see chapter 14 for additional resource suggestions). Without question, science is not a subject that can just "happen" in your classroom without adequate preparation (accomplishing that preparation is what makes you a professional). But there is also no doubt that a well-prepared and well-presented program of science can be the most dynamic educational endeavor that your school has to offer. Using resources such as those described here, along with the frameworks discussed in this chapter, you can build an exemplary program for the learning of science.

3 | ❧ | Science Education: The New "Basic" in the Classroom

Science in the School Curriculum

Why Science Is Important in the Elementary and Middle School

Teaching for Feeling and Valuing

Implications for the Aspiring Teacher

Conclusion

Your Academic Roadmap

Study of this chapter should help you to understand the following concepts:

- Issues in science education are typically influenced by the prevailing social climate.

- One way to improve science education is to see that teachers experience quality science education.

- By engaging in science, doing science, children foster both creative and critical thinking in a problem-solving context.

- Teachers have the opportunity to encourage the development of positive self-concepts through their science (and other) teaching.

- Science, as a journey that results in the construction of knowledge, is as dynamic and equally important as the other basics of the curriculum.

The nation that dramatically and boldly led the world into the age of technology is failing to provide its own children with the intellectual tools needed for the 21st century. . . . We must return to the basics, but the "basics" of the 21st century are not only reading, writing, and arithmetic. They include communication and higher problem-solving skills, and scientific and technological literacy—the thinking tools that allow us to understand the technological world around us.

—National Science Board Commission on Precollege Education in Mathematics, Science, and Technology,
Educating Americans for the 21st Century

SCIENCE IN THE SCHOOL CURRICULUM

In the past, science has not been the most prominent subject in the elementary school curriculum. Rarely has science been considered as important as reading, math, or language arts. It has not been uncommon for science to be scheduled as the last subject to be taught in the school day, or even to be neglected altogether.

Yet despite the neglect of science education in the past, today science is increasingly recognized as a basic, core subject in the elementary grades. This chapter focuses on how the science program has come to be a part of the curriculum, and takes a look at the condition of science education in contemporary American school systems. We also offer some reasons why we believe that studying science is worthwhile for young people. After all, science can be useful in many ways for children as they grow into citizenship. Finally, we discuss the implications that all of this holds for teachers and teaching. You will find that, unlike chapter 1, the focus here is specifically on science as a subject taught in school. So pause for a moment and think about your own opinions regarding school science. Discuss your responses to the questions in Activity 3.1 with a classmate.

*Reflecting Back on Being
a Science Learner in School*

Think about the following and then discuss
your opinions with a classmate.

1. Think back on your own experience
    as a science learner in school. What
    was science like for you?
2. Can you recall any teachers whose sci-
    ence teaching was exceptionally good
    (or bad)? What made it so?
3. Can you recall any "critical incidents"
    when you were particularly attracted
    to (or discouraged from) the study of
    science? What happened?
4. Why do you think science should
    (or should not) be taught in grades
    1–8?

A Brief Overview of How Science Became a Part of Education

In the United States before 1850, science was
taught at the elementary school level chiefly
to support children's theological education.
The pedagogy of those days was generally
dominated by recitation methods. Children
had to memorize a lot of factual knowledge.
In the middle of the nineteenth century,
American science education was influenced
both by British educational literature and
by German Pestalozzian pedagogy; however,
only the wealthy social classes had access to
British-type schooling.

Science gained popularity with the
American public in the 1870s. It was during
this period that the first organized science
program officially became part of the elementary curriculum in a public school district (in St. Louis, Missouri). Interest spread,
and before the end of the century, science
was part of the curriculum in most public
schools across the country. Science curricula
and instruction then were however, not as
you have known it. Rather, the curriculum
of many schools included the study of nature,
but the focus was generally related to supporting theology, and memorization was a
main teaching method.

An early reform model for science teaching was the Oswego Method, introduced in
the 1850s and championed by the upstate
normal school that is today part of the State
University of New York. This method was
an adaptation of Pestalozzi's object teaching,
which emphasized observing and describing
objects. The goal was mainly to prepare children for secondary school science. Unfortunately, the Oswego Method neglected interpretation and understanding and produced a
fragmented, unorganized science program
(Carin & Sund, 1981).

In the late 1800s, industry was expanding in the United States and people were mi-
grating from rural areas to the cities. Two science program models competed during this
time. A nature study movement pushed for
more direct experiences for children, and
also for helping children understand and appreciate their environment. The impetus for
this model was to counteract the abandon-
ment of America's farms. The competing
model, the elementary science movement,
put its emphasis on basic physical science and
technology content. This movement was
more urban-oriented and promoted the
development of the emerging industrial-
technological society (Bybee, 1977).

After the first world war, science education was influenced by the rise of pragma-
tism and the progressive education movement, led by John Dewey. Dewey criticized
the prevailing emphasis on memorizing and
called for programs centered around reflective thinking, problem solving, and experimenting. Innovative teachers in this period

attempted to link science to children's lives and interests by relating science concepts to health, safety, and career possibilities (Carin & Sund, 1981).

Science was an important subject in the progressive schools. The progressive education curriculum sought to cultivate children's attitudes and appreciations as well as their understanding of scientific methods of investigation. As a reform movement, however, even at its peak, only a minority of U.S. schools followed a progressive education model.

The Great Depression hit at the end of the 1920s. The austerity of the times led to a return to "the basics," which meant memory work for schoolchildren. In the 1930s and 1940s, efforts to improve school science programs focused on articulating and sequencing the content from kindergarten through high school. A primary objective was to teach children the major scientific principles and their applications. For example, children learned physical science concepts in studying how the telegraph and other machines worked.

Science education, as a national priority, began to emerge with the reforms following World War II. The war had a major impact on all dimensions of American life. For one thing, it produced a shortage of personnel with scientific and technical knowledge and skills. For another, "The war revealed through the testing of recruits and officer candidates that more people than expected were deficient in basic literacy and quantitative reasoning skills" (DeBoer, 1991, p. 128). Armed conflict also made many people aware of the importance of science, mathematics, and technology in military matters.

Science education attracted even more public interest in 1957 when America's Cold War foe, the former Soviet Union, launched Sputnik, the first artificial satellite. Perhaps "public interest" is too mild a description.

Americans were horrified to find that the Soviet Union had moved so far ahead in this highly technological endeavor. As a result, in the 1960s and early 1970s federal funds were provided to improve science education in American schools (DeBoer, 1991). New nontextbook science curriculum materials were created, and teachers were provided with many opportunities for professional development through subsidized science workshops and courses. This reform movement has been referred to as the "new progressivism" because of the similarities between the educational values of the two periods. The reform of the late 1960s and the 1970s also reflected a public reaction to the unpopular Vietnam War and a tremendous growth in environmental awareness issues. Interestingly, the emphasis on science education in the second half of the twentieth century was ushered in as the social consequence of one war, and ushered out as a social consequence of another war. Nonetheless, the gains in science education perspective and curriculum development during this period were substantive. More is said about these innovative programs in chapter 11.

Interest in science waned during the late 1970s and the 1980s, however, as the public focused on the priorities of several conservative federal administrations. During that period, funding by the National Science Foundation for improving science education completely dried up. After years of neglect, science education is again the focus of political and academic discussions regarding educational reform. Beginning in the early 1980s, hundreds of state and national studies and reports cited science as a crucial part of the curriculum that needed attention.

In 1989, all of the state governors and the president, meeting for the first education summit, declared six national educational goals. As three of the six goals addressed mathematics and science education, science education clearly has been identified as a national educational priority (Raizen & Michelson, 1994).

The declaration of the national goals has encouraged several national initiatives to improve science education. Many new curriculum materials have been designed and are now on the market (these are also discussed in chapter 11). The Eisenhower mathematics and science education programs, administered through the U.S. Department of Education, provides funding for teacher education in these subjects. The Eisenhower National Clearinghouse for Mathematics and Science Education and ten regional consortia provide help to schools for curriculum development, assessment, and in-service professional development. The National Science Foundation (NSF) has funded "systemic initiatives" in a number of states and cities across the country. NSF's systematic approach to reforming science and math education has created a number of exemplary model programs.

The National Science Education Standards, released in 1996, are another outcome of the national education goals. The math standards were the first to come out (NCTM, 1989). The science standards were developed by the National Research Council of the National Academy of Sciences and followed in the footsteps of Project 2061 of the American Association for the Advancement of Sciences (AAAS, 1989, 1993) and the National Science Teachers Association's Scope, Sequence and Coordination Project (NSTA, 1992).

Senta Raizen and A. M. Michelson (1994) characterize this latest round of reform and the new curriculum materials in this way: "All these projects stress a vision of learning grounded in new conceptions of pedagogy that stress thinking and solving problems in real-world contexts and the creation of schools as collaborative learning environments" (p. 6). Clearly, we are seeing a shift from science as a collection of facts to science as a dynamic force in both understanding and problem solving.

The Contemporary Condition of Science in the Public Schools

Contrary to being something that "has been taught forever," you can see that science education in our country has a checkered past. It is not surprising that the lack of continuity has led to outcomes that we would not consider desirable. From what you already know of science education in the elementary/middle school system, how would you evaluate it? As an aspiring teacher, whose responsibility it will one day be to assign grades representing thoughtful evaluation, what grade would you give to science education in our country, in your hometown? As is the case with all aspects of education, science education has provided researchers with fertile ground for study. The information that follows may assist you in assigning that grade.

Headline-grabbing studies periodically report that American students remain "scientifically and technologically illiterate." A Gallup poll in the late 1980s reported that 55 percent of American teenagers believed that astrology works, while another study found 40 percent believed that particular numbers are lucky (Lauerman, 1988). Another study reported that most adults who own air conditioners do not use the thermostats as intended by the manufacturers because they do not understand how the device works (Van, 1988). In a large survey of more than a thousand adults, almost half did not identify the sun as a star. Subjects were asked, "Would you say that the sun is a planet, a star, or something else?" Fifty-five percent responded that it was a star; 25 percent said a planet; 15 percent said something else; and 5 percent either did not know or refused to answer (Lewenstein, 1988). In another survey, fewer than half the adults who were interviewed expressed the scientific concept that the earth revolves around the sun, and most thought antibiotics kill viruses (Culliton, 1989).

Do these above points make you want to change your grade on the schools? Of course, the subjects of these studies were high school students or adults, but younger school students also generally do not score well on standardized tests in science. One study of academic achievement in science, the National Assessment of Educational Progress (NAEP), reported that science proficiency across all the grades remains "distressingly low" (Mullis & Jenkins, 1988, p. 5). The researchers who analyzed the 1990 NAEP study of 25,000 students reported that students had a difficult time going beyond a general understanding of a written passage to discuss and explain what they had read. In another study, the International Science Assessment, researchers found U.S. students were among the lowest achievers of all participating countries (International Association for the Evaluation of Educational Achievement, 1988).

What might be behind the low test scores? The NAEP researchers reported that nearly half of fourth-graders and over 60 percent of eighth-graders read ten or fewer pages a day for school, yet over 60 percent of both the fourth-graders and the eighth-graders said they watch at least three hours of television each day. The researchers reported that outside school, nearly one-third of eighth-graders say they never read for fun.

Beginning in the 1980s, student performance on the various standardized tests has actually changed slightly upward, with the most notable gains among African Americans (Suter, 1993). Two disturbing trends are discernable: first, that most U.S. students are becoming proficient in only the most basic skills, comparatively few attaining higher levels of achievement; and second, that the gap between whites and minorities increases dramatically up the grades (Haury, 1994). The average proficiency of thirteen-year-old African American and Hispanic students remains at least four years behind similar Euro-American children (Mullis & Jenkins, 1988).

As for increasing the participation of girls and women in science, gender performance differences on standardized tests have also been noted. In the NAEP physical science test, the performance gap by gender was "extremely large" (Mullis & Jenkins, 1988). Further, Byrne (1993) documents the cumulative and progressive loss of female enrollments in science courses, the "cascading losses," as cohorts move upward through the grades. For the cause of this situation, Byrne points to "conditions and unexamined policies and practices" (p. 2).

Studies and reports like the ones cited above cast doubts on the effectiveness of science education in America's schools. Many standardized tests measure the child's recall of scientific knowledge, although some gage scientific, or logical, reasoning as well. The tests do not assess either an understanding of the nature of science or scientific habits of mind, such as attitudes and motivation. Nevertheless, such results disturb just about everyone—teachers, parents, scientists, business and industrial leaders, and public policy makers.

ACTIVITY 3.2

Designing a Science Literacy Test

It is one thing for researchers to make claims about science literacy and other such issues. And it is quite another to find out for yourself. Take this opportunity to do just that.

- Work in a group with several of your classmates to design a science literacy test. Each group should choose a different grade level of science textbook from your curriculum library. Grades 3, 5, and 8 might be good choices, but you are free to design this test as you like.

- Construct a test of no more than fifteen questions from chapters throughout the textbook. The questions need not be extremely detailed. Rather, look for general concepts. You can select your own question format—multiple-choice, fill-in-the-blank, open-response, etc.

- Administer your test to a predetermined population, for example, freshmen at your college or university, or perhaps high school seniors if you have access to a local school. (*Note:* Be sure that you have the principal's and the teacher's permission. Also, you will have to be certain to protect the anonymity of your respondents. Remember, you are not assessing individuals, but rather general scientific literacy.)

- Compile your results, look for trends, and make recommendations to your science methods class based on your data.

Trying to Explain What Has Been Found

Most experienced science educators lament the general state of science education in our schools. What can explain the poor state of science instruction? The situation is not solely the fault of teachers, who themselves could be the victims of inadequate or ineffective instruction. In fact, many elementary teachers admit that they are uncomfortable about teaching science; they report not liking science and/or feeling inadequate, or unqualified to teach it. Yet, teachers are ultimately the key to the success of science in the curriculum.

Those who have studied the matter say that reading and basic arithmetic skills still dominate the curriculum in the average American elementary classroom, and science remains a low priority (Raizen & Michelson, 1994). Teachers still devote very little time to science in comparison with other school subjects (Weiss, 1994; Harms, 1981). Many observers report that instruction is centered on the teacher and dominated by the use of whole class lectures with question-and-answer, chiefly based on information in the textbook. One researcher went so far as to say that "over 90 percent of all science teachers use a textbook 95 percent of the time; the textbook becomes the course outline, the framework for the students' experience, testing, and world view of science" (Cole & Griffin, 1987, p. 32).

Because of the dominance of textbook/workbook-oriented lessons, children have few opportunities to learn science through the experiences of objects and phenomena. Hands-on science is rare even today, and even rarer is instruction that occurs outside the classroom, such as on field trips. As a result of the way children are taught, they come to perceive scientific processes to be the verification activities found in the experiments they occasionally carry out. Worse, as a result of the way students are taught, they often perceive little value or use of science in their everyday lives (Yager & Brunkhorst, 1986).

There is little evidence that teachers are addressing goals related to children using science in everyday life, or understanding science for solving problems or making civic decisions. Instruction is rarely focused on improving thinking processes or developing children's attitudes and values. Rather, teaching is typically focused on specific content, which is often communicated as true and unchanging knowledge. This, as pointed out in chapter 1, is specifically what science is *not*.

Most science instruction is narrowly aimed at preparing children academically for the next grade or level (Cole & Griffin, 1987).

It should not be surprising, considering the above, that researchers report that children do not like science. In one study, children in all but the middle grades rated science as their "least favorite" subject. But don't be too encouraged by that news about the middle school students, as only social studies rated lower in their hearts. Many children come to believe they are incompetent to learn science and so avoid science learning opportunities. This attitude toward science later translates into the fact that few high school graduates chose to take three years of science, and only about 15 percent chose to take physics. Further, young women avoid science almost double the rate of young men (Tressel, 1987).

Quick Review

Issues in education are typically influenced by the prevailing social climate. The haphazard inclusion of science in the curriculum, along with its varying degrees of emphasis, is testament to that fact. The fluctuating condition of science instruction is not a surprising consequence. Yet the state of science in the elementary/middle school curriculum could be improved if teachers could experience quality science education themselves. Many teachers have only the minimum amount of science coursework required for their state's certification, sometimes as few as two courses. Counting both high school and college, elementary teachers sometimes have taken only biology courses. In an attempt to improve science education, most states have increased the number of science courses required both for high school and for elementary and middle school teacher certification. There have also been efforts, such as the Eisenhower grant program, to improve the science education of teachers already in the classroom.

In our opinion, a well-rounded science background for teaching science would include some coursework in physics, chemistry, biology (including content in botany, zoology, physiology, and genetics), and the earth-space and environmental sciences (including content in ecology, geology, astronomy, oceanography, and meteorology). For elementary teachers, the Standards for Science Teacher Certification of the National Science Teachers Association (NSTA) specify 12 semester hours of laboratory or field-oriented science, including coursework in the biological, physical, and earth sciences. The standards specify 24 hours for middle grade teachers and 45 hours for junior high teachers, as well as 9 hours of mathematics and computer science (access NSTA at http://www.nsta.org/about/teacher.html for a complete explanation of the standards). By accessing http://www.iuk.edu/faculty/ sgilbert/draftstand.htm on the World Wide Web, you can find additional information about the standards for the preparation of science teachers. Of course, we realize that simply taking more courses is not the answer if the coursework continues to have the same focus as has been typical of the past. And so you can see, the problem of science education is not just a matter of what goes on in your local elementary school; improvement over the status quo requires attention from kindergarten all the way through professional teacher certification.

WHY SCIENCE IS IMPORTANT IN ELEMENTARY AND MIDDLE SCHOOL

To this point, we have explained how science became a part of the curriculum. We have

Christine Ebert

PHOTO 3.1 A study of forces and motion could result from the interest in riding this scooter.

also discussed where the science part of the curriculum stands with regard to outcomes, and have entertained some of the reasons for that standing. As you ask questions of yourself and others about what to do about science in your own classroom, you would be wise to consider some of the *reasons* for children to study science. Since most people would agree that scientific pursuit is of value in one way or another, the focus here is to address why it is important for *children* to study science. There are two basic arguments in support of our claim: the utilitarian argument and the humanistic argument. Advocates of each view are typically at odds with each other. Fortunately, the study of science offers the best hope for a peaceful reconciliation.

Science Is Utilitarian

The utilitarian argument is that science is important in the curriculum because science is *useful* for students to know. Remember, primary children today will be adults in C.E. 2020. Science and technology are pervasive in today's world. In becoming global citi-

zens, children will benefit from understanding the basic ideas in the physical, life, and earth-space sciences and from understanding the role of science and technology in society and culture. This benefit will come from having multiple frameworks for real-world problem solving and decision making.

Science also will be useful to know for those children who have talents and interest in scientific or technical work. If current trends are a guide, scientific and technological fields will provide many kinds of jobs at many levels in the future. During the elementary grades, children form their attitudes and develop lifelong interests from which career decisions are made. The elementary school curriculum should include opportunities for all children to learn about and experience science, and to learn about science-related possibilities in the world of work.

Regarding the value of science for *all* children, an issue in science education at all levels is equity. A special effort will be required to increase the participation of women and minorities in science and engineering. As discussed in chapter 1, most scientists and engineers are men; in the United States, most are white men. Women comprise only 15 percent of American scientists and engineers. The situation for blacks and Hispanics is even worse, with each making up only 2 percent of the science-engineering workforce. Among both minority groups, the high school dropout rate is high and fewer numbers of youngsters continue schooling to complete college degrees (Holden, 1989). Appropriate elementary school science instruction can help dispel the myth that science is only for boys and Euro-Americans. Sensitive teachers can encourage all children to consider pursuing hobbies and careers in science and technology (Sprung et al., 1986).

It would be naive, of course, to argue that better instruction in science will cause all students to become enthralled with the subject. It will always be the case that some students will have a greater inclination toward math, some toward English, and so on. Individual preference is a valuable aspect of human nature. Because of that, we would like to make our goal as clear as possible. By improving the quality of science education for all children, science educators such as ourselves hope to bring the *wonder of science* to each child. We believe that the more appropriate presentation of science instruction will remove the barriers that have discouraged children from the study of science, and so let the nature of science speak for itself.

Encouraging children to embrace the wonder of science becomes particularly important because many problems in today's world relate in some way to science and technology. In the political world, nearly half of all legislative bills are related in some way to science and technology (Bybee, 1985). Though chapter 10 specifically addresses the movement in science education called Science/Technology/Society (STS) education, the point here is that science and technology education can help people learn how to solve a range of problems, from practical everyday problems to environmental ones. Science education can help children develop creative thinking ability that allows them to see problems from multiple perspectives. It can also facilitate the development of critical thinking ability and practice in using evidence in decision making (Sivertsen, 1993).

The advent of the nuclear age provides a clear example for problem-solving ability among the citizenship of a society. It is not always the case that decision makers dealing with science-oriented questions are scientists. And in such instances, the value of knowing basic science cannot be overstated. With regard to this particular issue, human beings now have access to a power capable of destroying the world as we know it. Nuclear weapon technology has spread to many countries around the globe. Scientists and engineers may or may not be responsible for the decisions that have contributed to the possibility of a truly devastating event. However, people in and out of the scientific community will have to address and resolve these questions.

Many people only began to realize the vulnerability of the earth's life support systems after seeing photographs of Earth from space. Earth was revealed as an island in space. Buckminster Fuller coined the phrase "spaceship earth," suggesting we are passengers on a giant self-contained starship (which, in a way, we are).

While photographs of the earth from space have raised human consciousness about our relationship to the ecosystem, other information relayed from earth orbit continually documents the effects of human activities on that life support system. Cameras and other sensors on satellites hundreds of kilometers above Earth now provide a stream of data on the physical and ecological condition of the planet. Satellite cameras can see objects only 10 meters (33 feet) across from a distance of over 800 kilometers (500 miles). Special sensors can focus on particular bands

©NASA

PHOTO 3.2 Spaceship Earth

of light to provide data about heat stress in plants, sediment in bodies of water, and hazardous waste buried underground. Scientists use satellite images to measure such things as the sea level change, ocean current movements and temperatures, ocean plant life populations, the rate of deforestation, and the effects of acid rain on forests (Ryan, 1989). The hole in the ozone shield over Antarctica was first discovered from such data.

As a result of these technologies, combined with studies conducted on the surface, we now understand more about the state of the planet than we ever dreamed of knowing before. There is widespread agreement among scientists from many life and earth science disciplines that serious environmental problems threaten the ecosystem's ability to provide for future generations the quality of life we now enjoy in the industrial societies (Brown et al., 1995, 1996). The distinguished journalist and news commentator, John Chancellor, once commented that we need to adopt the proper perspective on the problems that the planet faces. He noted that the planet got along just fine before we were around, and no doubt will do just fine after

we have finally brought about our own extinction. The question then, is not about saving the planet, but rather about saving ourselves. Very likely, he was quite correct. Better science education will be a key to solving the problems that "the planet" faces.

The photos of Earth from space helped catalyze the worldwide movement to protect environmental quality and conserve resources. The breadth of scientific investigation, however, extends in many directions. Another image of the era of science and technology is the image taken first by Swedish physiologists of a human embryo in its amniotic envelope. Contemplating these two images, the philosopher Gerald Holton (1992) remarks,

> The blue-green Earth system and the reddish brown embryonic system at first glance are quite unrelated—one is as large as our whole world beneath the stars, the other hidden and tiny. Yet, precisely during these decades, the health of these two systems has become profoundly related; each depends on the well-being of the other. (p. 110)

Holton goes on to declare,

> . . . if the child that grows from the embryo is not taught the lesson of stewardship over the external ecological system, that insensitivity will only accelerate the subversion of the health of the globe as a whole. In short, the globe of Earth and the globule of the foetus are now linked together far more tightly than before. (p. 110)

Developing problem-solving skills becomes very important because there is much evidence that the world of the twenty-first century will be even more complex and more precarious than the world of today (Brown et al., 1992). Of all the school subjects, science is the one that focuses on the future. We believe elementary children should have opportunities to think about the future and understand the concept of *contingency*. That concept was brought to science through Scholastic philosophers of the twelfth century who wrote that what happens in the world is contingent on our behavior now. Children can learn by the end of the elementary years that the choices they make now will influence what happens, what is known, and what exists later.

As a teacher in the twenty-first century, you will be responsible for preparing children to be not only citizens in a complex technological society but also members of a biospheric community whose ecological health is endangered on many fronts. Scientific knowledge can help people understand both the natural and designed worlds, and, we hope, help them find solutions to our environmental and social problems. In the words of *Science for All Americans* (AAAS, 1989),

> Education has no higher purpose than preparing people to lead personally fulfilling and responsible lives. For its part, science education . . . should help students to develop understandings and habits of mind they need to become compassionate human beings able to think for themselves and to face life head on. (p. 12)

Science Is Humanistic

A compelling argument for the study of science in grades 1–8 is its utility, but equally important, if not more so, is that science gives pleasure and enriches children's lives. This is the humanitarian argument for science in the curriculum. The physicist, James Trefil, said it this way,

> In the end, the purely instrumental utility of scientific knowledge may be less important than the wider value to be gained from being acquainted with science as one of the great expressions of the human spirit. Science has been and continues to be one of the noblest achievements of mankind. From a humanistic point of view, its attainments are on a par with great achievements in art, literature, and political institutions, and in this perspective, science should come to be known for the same reasons as these other subjects. (1983, p. 147)

Children, particularly younger children, will come to your classroom with an indefatigable curiosity. And you, with knowledge that you might otherwise take for granted, will be able to mystify and inspire them. Children want and need to make sense of what they see around them. It is, in fact, what they do. Though their methods are not necessarily systematic, and their conclusions not necessarily logical, their thinking is nonetheless directed toward finding reasons and explanations for their observations and experiences. And they *will* form conclusions. Science will become interesting to them when it satisfies their need to know about the environment. Many children enjoy and find science rewarding to learn because it satisfies a deep curiosity about the natural world. This natural curiosity can be your strongest ally in the classroom.

Quick Review

The nature of scientific inquiry is a natural point of departure for working with curious and wondering children. With this one course of study, the effective teacher has the means to provide children with answers to their questions, build foundations for future investigation, and establish a literacy in the discipline that will serve them throughout a lifetime. By engaging in science, *doing* science, children foster both creative and critical thinking in a problem-solving context. As John Dewey asserted, genuine thinking is fostered through the solving of real problems.

ACTIVITY 3.3

Science as Utilitarian versus Science as Humanistic

Consider the big picture of science for a moment by taking a look at science as it manifests itself all around you. For instance, do electric lights illuminate your classroom? Is the air quality in your building better or worse than in other areas of the building, campus, town, state? With this approach in mind, do the following with the help of several of your classmates. The challenge will be to see which group can develop the most extensive list.

- Prepare a "Science in Action" list that represents examples of how science, or a knowledge of science, impacts your daily life.

- Review your list one item at a time, and indicate whether the item represents science in its utilitarian nature or its humanistic nature.

- Compare the results from your group to those of the other groups.

- From all lists compiled, eliminate the duplicates, come to a consensus on the question of utilitarian versus humanistic, and compile one master list. How many items were you able to list?

TEACHING FOR FEELING AND VALUING

The notion that science is important because of its utilitarian and humanistic dimensions speaks to a domain of educational objectives outside of the more familiar cognitive domain. In the Taxonomy of Educational Objectives: Cognitive Domain (you may have heard this referred to as Bloom's Taxonomy) the emphasis is on the acquisition and manipulation of information. The affective domain is concerned with feeling and valuing. Though these two domains (there is also a third category: the psychomotor domain) can be distinguished for academic purposes, they each relate to who you are and to the context within which you go about constructing knowledge. As such, attention to the affective domain is just as much a part of teaching as is attention to the content of any particular discipline. Addressing your students' needs in terms of the affective domain is not something that should be "sprung" on you as an afterthought or during student teaching. So we include this discussion of it here with our introduction to the teaching of science.

The Affective Domain in Science Education

Feeling and valuing may strike you as being an unusual topic in a textbook about science teaching methods. Scientists, after all, seem to

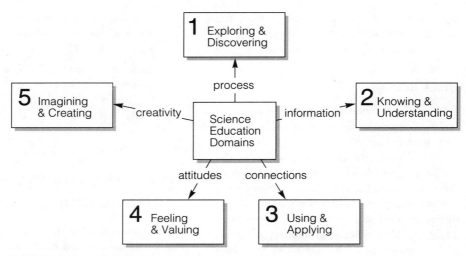

FIGURE 3.1 The five domains of science education.

be detached and unemotional in their work. Nevertheless, as discussed in chapter 1, scientists rarely fit this stereotype. Feeling and valuing actually drive the scientific enterprise. The great philosopher Charles Sanders Peirce noted, "For it is not knowing but the love of learning that characterizes the scientific man." Carl Sagan (1991) put it this way: "Science—pure science, science not for any practical application but for its own sake—is a deeply emotional matter for those who practice it . . ." (p. 10).

The domain of feeling and valuing is more academically known as the affective domain. Within science in particular, feeling and valuing comprise one of the five domains of science education (Yager, 1994; Yager & McCormack, 1989). These domains are illustrated in Figure 3.1. Later chapters in this book address teaching strategies related to the domains of knowing and understanding, exploring and discovering, imagining and creating, and using and applying.

Having discussed the specific content areas for a science program in chapter 2, we now address the link between knowledge and feeling and valuing. We believe that attention to the affective domain results in facili-

tating cognitive development. Children's attitudes and values influence the way in which they think about things and the degree to which they will engage in consideration of various topics. For this very reason, childrens' attitudes and values should be developed as part of their participation in the classroom science program.

Because people differ in the values they hold, the values promoted in the public school curriculum can be a politically hot issue in a community. Before going any further, think for a moment about your own beliefs related to teaching values. Activity 3.4 is an opportunity to reflect and to talk with a classmate about this issue.

ACTIVITY 3.4

Values Education in Public Schools

Think about the following and discuss your responses with a classmate.

1. Americans have all kinds of opinions about the role of the public schools in teaching values. What is your opinion? Where does the affective domain, the

domain of feeling and valuing, fit into the curriculum?

2. Is a value-neutral curriculum desirable, or even possible?

3. Can you identify any values that will be part of the curriculum in your classroom?

ACTIVITY 3.5
INFOTRAC COLLEGE EDITION INVESTIGATION:

Current Perspective on Values Education

In Activity 3.4 you were asked to reflect on your own opinions regarding values education, and to discuss them with your classmates. However, as you are likely aware, this is a question that has occupied the minds of educators, legislators, parents, and other citizens for a very long time.

Use InfoTrac College Edition to find out the state of the current debate over values education in the schools.

- According to the educational literature, where—if at all—does the affective domain fit into the curriculum?

- Is a value-neutral curriculum desirable, or even possible?

- In the United States, do the educational values of the nation differ from those that a state might support?

The Affective-Cognitive Link The first point is that the domain of feeling and valuing is of central importance in science teaching. One reason this is so is because an emotional valence may be attached to some or all of our perceptions. Emotion provides the energy to learn, and *learning,* the outcome of the effort, is found to be emotionally satisfying.

Feelings not only cue and reinforce learning, but form the underlying structure of thought itself. Creative individuals have described how ideas first came to them as vague and diffused bodily sensations, "feeling-tones" that gradually became defined into concepts. Einstein noted this experience in relation to his creative work.

William Gray, a Massachusetts psychiatrist, has portrayed a theory of learning in which emotion is the key to memory, recognition, and the origin of new ideas (Ferguson, 1982). Gray believes a person's cognitive ability corresponds to the range of emotions from which he or she can draw. In Gray's view, humans are smarter than animals because humans possess a greater repertoire of emotional nuance.

Regardless of the particular neural interconnections involved, psychologists recognize that emotion and cognition interact strongly in learning. According to Jerre Levy (1980), optimal brain functioning of an individual depends on the integration of the emotional and rational functions. Our best mental work is produced when our emotional and cognitive systems function in a concurrent or synchronous way, as when attention and interest are focused on the same objective. In other words, children are *likely to understand more when they are interested in what they are studying.* This is so because they are more likely to become emotionally engaged in the topic or task when they are interested to begin with. Success in making sense of something reinforces the child's effort and produces confidence in the child that he or she can learn more. As a teacher, your attention to the affective dimension in the classroom is ultimately the key to your students' success as science learners.

Csikszentmihalyi's Model of Development Many cultures have ideas of development embedded in their beliefs and traditions. In psychology there are many models of human growth and development. University of Chicago psychologist Mihalyi Csikszentmihalyi (1991, 1994) offers a model for development that illuminates the critical interaction between affect and learning. According to Csikszentmihalyi, the individual's first task in development is *individuation,* which involves self-identification and increasing independence. The urge to individuation becomes involved in a long-term struggle with the person's opposite need for affiliation, or belonging. These processes result in an increasing complexity of consciousness.

Csikszentmihalyi's model of development places a lot of emphasis on the role of *intrinsic* motivation in learning. For most creatures, motivation is not a problem because when a conflict comes up, the organism either acts in an appropriate manner, such as to run away, or it ends up as dead meat. Motivation becomes a problem for us, however, when our *choice* of what to do is in doubt. As we develop and our mental complexity increases, choosing may become ever more difficult. If we no longer have a clear focus for our attention, we experience confusion. Anxiety, a uniquely human characteristic, occurs when we experience *conflict* even though nothing in our immediate environment is causing conflict. Unlike other creatures, humans can recall and fret over situations or events that are distant in time and/ or space. When we have too many goals, the result also is a lack of mental harmony. The emotional and the cognitive dimensions lose the synchrony that leads to further development.

There is a desired state in all of this. The optimal condition is what Csikszentmihalyi refers to as *flow.* In this case there exists a mixture of positive feelings that fosters *autotelic* experience—the behavior is self-reinforcing and no external reward is required. The experience of flow can occur in any activity. Csikszentmihalyi characterizes the flow situation as one in which the challenge is well matched with the individual's skill. For example, you might experience flow in playing tennis. Your opponent is challenging enough to draw out your best effort and finest performance. A less skillful opponent isn't fully engaging, while one too skillful might prove frustrating or humiliating. In the experience of flow, one's goals are clear and feedback is immediate. There also is a sense of potential control, and a merging of action and awareness. A contemporary equivalent for this may be "being in the *zone.*" Do you think you could arrange experiences to put your students in a *science zone*? Can you imagine how exciting that could be?

Tapping the Learning Potential of the Child

When children are treated as capable persons, they will generally rise to the occasion. As Levin (1994) suggests, teachers can involve children in taking charge of their own learning. Fortunately for you as the teacher, human nature is on your side. The inclination to learn is in our Homo sapiens genes. Psychologists such as Carl Rogers and William Glasser talk about a child's predisposition toward growth. Everyone is intrinsically motivated to grow and to construct concepts about the world (Weiner, 1984). The child *wants* to understand: The process of theory building is characteristic of all children.

Toward Increasing Autonomy and Developing Self-Concept As children mature and individuate, they generally become more able to direct themselves. They become increasingly competent and independent. Accordingly, a goal in teaching can be to facilitate this development of autonomy. Chaillé and Britain (1991) note that "children's needs to develop both intellectual and moral autonomy should be taken into account when we develop curricula and determine how adults should and should not interact with young children" (pp. 8–9). Many teaching methods, however, work against autonomy. For example, autonomy is not promoted by science activities that children work through like following a recipe with predetermined results.

The characteristics of the child as a social being and as an increasingly autonomous being are related to the child's developing self-concept: "By giving children opportunities to be independent, to make choices where appropriate, and to rely on themselves rather than on adults for materials and direction, we can greatly influence their sense of self, their confidence and sense of mastery, and their awareness of themselves as active constructors of knowledge—all aspects of being autonomous" (Chaillé & Britain, 1991, p. 8).

Toward Meeting Basic Biological Needs

One of the classic insights in psychology is Abraham Maslow's notion that motivation is related to satisfying basic biological needs. Glasser (1990), following Maslow, has proposed that everyone is motivated to satisfy five basic biological needs: (1) survival, (2) love, (3) power, (4) fun, and (5) freedom (p. 43). Glasser believes these needs are built into our genetic structure.

According to Glasser, the desire to know and understand is based on satisfying one or more of the five basic needs. Academic knowledge does not necessarily satisfy any basic need, and so school learning may *not* be so natural. In Glasser's (1990) words, ". . . the fact that students choose not to do schoolwork does not mean they lack motivation. If, however, what we are asked to do also satisfies one or more of our basic needs, a great deal of work gets done" (p. 42). The key to motivation, for Glasser, is to identify a child's particular needs and help him or her meet them. If these needs are being met, the child is more likely to be a happy and productive learner.

Michael Bentley

PHOTO 3.3 A child in thought is one who is constructing new levels of understanding.

Values Formation

Some people believe that values should not be part of the curriculum in school, that they should be taught at home or in the church, synagogue, or mosque. But there really is no way to avoid teaching values in school. For one thing, teachers are second only to parents as role models for children. Children want to like and respect their teachers, and most usually do. In both obvious and subtle ways, children perceive what their teacher values. That is one reason why the teacher's attitude toward the subject matter is so important.

Values are part of the curriculum, whether people want them to be so or not. The mere selection of the subjects to be included in a curriculum is a value statement. Certainly, the survival of our democratic

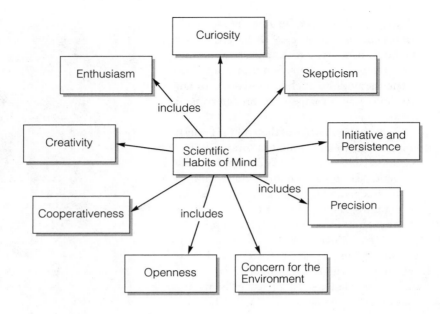

FIGURE 3.2 Scientific habits of mind relate to both the affective and the cognitive domains.

society depends on the prevalence of certain values among the citizenry. The only question is whether the values will be out in the open, or part of a hidden curriculum. Our opinion is that the values of the curriculum should be made explicit and therefore open to public scrutiny. As a teacher, you ought to be aware of the values content of the curriculum. School people, parents, and community members ought to reflect on and discuss the values that are promoted in the classroom.

What values should be promoted in school? As you might guess, people have different answers for this question. The values of justice and fairness, persistence, generosity, loyalty, and social cooperation have been recommended (Benniga, 1988). In science class, considering the present state of the world (see chapter 11), a good case can be made for promoting pro-environment values. The American Association for the Advancement of Science (AAAS), in *Science for All Americans* (1989), advocates teaching the "scientific habits of mind," which includes both values and attitudes. These habits of mind are mapped in Figure 3.2.

Motivating Children to Learn Science

The individual differences among children are astounding and a wonderful source of inquiry for teachers. For example, one child might get into a flow experience through involvement in a science project. Another child might be turned on by scientifically exploring a woodland or pond habitat. It is important to support the science learning of all children by providing a variety of kinds of opportunities for children to learn.

You can forgive yourself if you don't manage to turn on every one of the children to science (or to any intellectual pursuit). In the end, as we emphasize throughout the book, children have to do the learning themselves. But you can provide diverse learning opportunities in the situations you set up in the classroom. Not everything has to be a "unit project" or an activity with multiple levels of interactions. You can, for example, incorporate techniques such as "Science Talks," a method developed by Karen Gallas (1994, 1995), a first-grade teacher-researcher. This method can engage children at the affective and intellectual levels simultaneously. In conversations with others during Science Talk, children process their experiences based on what they know and what is co-constructed in the interactions with ideas of others. The outcome of that process, the learning, is a function of the child's interest and engagement, the energy put into listening to others, and reflecting. Gallas also recommends coupling journaling as a teaching strategy along with Science Talks.

ACTIVITY 3.6

Discussing Science

The Science Talks approach developed by Karen Gallas provides you with the opportunity to practice engaging people in discussions about science. Keep in mind that rather than trying to *teach* science, your focus here is to allow people to *consider* science. What you will gain from this activity (particularly if you seek out opportunities to continue practicing this) is a sense of how people think about and express their knowledge of science.

- Select a topic in science to use as your discussion topic. Generate a question that would initiate conversation about this topic.

- With a small group of students in your field service or practicum placement, conduct an informal discussion. As the facilitator, your job will be to help others join into the conversation.

- As soon as possible after the discussion, write out your reflections on what occurred (perhaps in your journal if you are keeping one for this course). What conclusion could you draw in terms of the science knowledge that the participants possessed? What can you say about the confidence that the participants had in their knowledge of science?

- What do you suppose would happen if you tried this with a group of your colleagues? Did you try it? What happened? Did you note any similarities or differences between the way your colleagues discussed the topic and the way children enagaged in the conversation?

Motivating the Unmotivated: Locus of Control Research Always remember that, as a teacher, nature is on your side: All children want to understand. That is the good news. The bad news is that an opposing natural tendency in every organism is the need to conserve energy—that is, there is a need to get by with the least effort. More bad news is that much of learning is effortful. And so, every classroom teacher has run into the problem of an "unmotivated" child. We place unmotivated in quotation marks because, as we have already discussed, people are always motivated. Unfortunately, that motivation is not always in the directions that we would like.

Psychologists who have studied children's beliefs about their own efficacy, or power to act in their own behalf, have developed a model called *attribution theory*. This model is about children's perceptions of the locus of control. For children who have grown up in Western culture, success or failure in anything is typically attributed to one or more of four causes:

- native ability,
- effort,
- task difficulty, or
- luck (Hunter & Barker, 1987).

To attribute one's success or failure to native ability is self-limiting because talent typically is regarded as a fixed characteristic given at birth (though it is not). On the other hand, effort is a factor under a person's control. We cannot control the talent or ability we have, but we can control how much we put into a project. Effort has been found to be greatest in children who attribute their performance to internal, or controllable, causes (Brophy, 1987). The child who attributes his or her success to a combination of ability and effort, and his or her failure to a lack of effort, has the greater potential for success. If the child applies this attribution pattern to schoolwork, he or she will be more likely to achieve academically. Such an attribution pattern is characteristic of a positive self–concept.

As a teacher, you can identify a child's attribution pattern and help the child recognize that a choice is involved in the matter. You can also encourage more effort in learning science by tapping into the child's interests. More effort will be exerted to learn about something the child values. The effort exerted by the child is a product of *expectancy* and *value* (Feather, 1982). Expectancy is the child's estimate that a given behavior will lead to certain outcomes, such as being able to perform a task successfully when he or she applies the effort. Value is the degree to which participation in the task itself is appreciated. Value can also be thought of in terms of the benefits or rewards anticipated upon completing the task.

In teaching, you can help children recognize how they might benefit from knowing the particular science involved. You can also be careful to assign tasks at the appropriate level: challenging—but capable of being accomplished, assuming a reasonable effort is applied. There are two things to be done: (1) to focus children's awareness on the value of the science to be learned—why it is important, useful, or worthwhile, and (2) to match the children's abilities to the level of difficulty of the assigned learning tasks. Both of these relate to our earlier reasons for teaching science: Science is useful and personally rewarding.

The level of difficulty of the academic tasks is important because children will get bored if the task is too easy and will get frustrated if it is too hard. You can surely recall an experience of your own where you struggled to understand something that seemed beyond your ability to know.

That the academic tasks assigned should be challenging yet within the range of your students' abilities is also implied in Csikszentmihalyi's model of development. The ideal situation to achieve is high expectations for children while not frustrating them. Children are motivated by knowing that you expect them to achieve. This tells children that you respect them. Respect, like empathy, is a powerful emotion that can elicit a strong response from children.

Your high expectations will also set some level of stress for your students. Stress is an emotion that can interfere with the mental work required in learning science. Research on stress has revealed that while some degree of tension or stress is desirable and motivating, too much stress can impair adaptability (Selye, 1956). It appears that anxiety, expressed in the biochemistry of the limbic area of the brain, actually shuts down the higher cognitive centers of the brain (Restak, 1995; Krech, 1969). A child's fear of failure or humiliation can be psychologically demobilizing. In a supportive environment, risk–taking is not penalized and mistakes are accepted as part of the learning process. In a supportive environment, with the appropriate level of expectations, students are able to think at higher levels (Clark, 1986, p. 22). Again, the idea is to set expectations that the child can reasonably meet.

All of this is easy to say, but not so easy to achieve in practice. For one thing, assigning tasks of appropriate difficulty takes real skill. This is complicated by the fact that children within every class have a range of abilities and interests. This is one reason why nongraded groupings of students may foster more of

Chen Long

PHOTO 3.4 Children of various ages enjoy science.

some kinds of learning. Another bit of good news: Most teachers gain a sense of what is appropriate with experience. You will develop this ability if you pay attention to the feedback you receive from your students and adjust your teaching behaviors accordingly.

ACTIVITY 3.7

Looking for Locus of Control

You can easily conduct a ministudy to compare locus of control as it appears in children and in students of your age range.

- The next time you take another exam, ask several of your classmates what they thought of it, and how they think they did. (Certainly, you don't want to ask about their grades, so be sure to do this after the test, but before the results come back.)

- Talk to several students in your field service or practicum placement after they have taken a test. Ask the same questions as mentioned above. (Keep in mind that the test need not have

been a science test. In this activity the emphasis is on locus of control, not on science knowledge.)

- What can you say about locus of control, based on the responses you have received?

- And of course, where do you tend to place locus of control for your own academic performance?

Teacher Behaviors That Motivate So far we have considered the relationship of emotion and cognition to children's engagement in the study of science. Children's attitudes toward themselves as learners, the influences of a supportive learning environment, and the level of difficulty of the academic work contribute to the overall picture of a student's academic motivation. The following are teacher behaviors that establish excellence in professional practice in the affective domain. Keeping these in mind will help you to create a supportive and motivating classroom environment for science learning. Teachers nurture learner growth when they

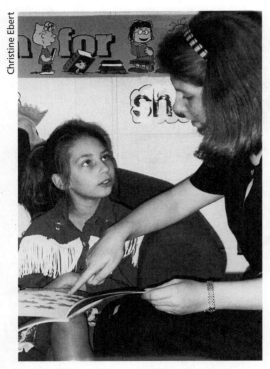

Christine Ebert

PHOTO 3.5 A caring attitude between teacher and student is important.

- exhibit a caring attitude,
- model enthusiasm and interest by example,
- provide choices and share control,
- explain the rationale for tasks and assignments, and
- use a variety of teaching strategies, including inquiry activities, hands-on opportunities, field study experiences, and cooperative group methods.

Exhibit a Caring Attitude Perhaps the most basic thing you can do is to exhibit a caring attitude toward each child. Children behave differently toward teachers whom they perceive as caring about them as individuals (Simpson, 1979). Showing empathy for children is a powerful way to build rapport. It means being able to convey that you understand how the child feels, that you have experienced the same emotions and similar situations yourself. Exhibiting a caring attitude also means knowing your students as persons, remembering their individual interests and designing science activities around those areas of interest. To John Dewey, the entire curriculum proceeds from the children's interests. But incorporating children's interests into the curriculum does not mean abandoning the content of the school's prescribed curriculum. Dewey's notion was not that we ask each child what games or activities he or she likes. Rather than think in terms of children's interests, think in terms of the *interests of children*. The utility of a scientific principle to an adult is likely quite different than the utility of that same principle to a child.

Model Enthusiasm and Interest by Example
Another way to motivate children to put effort into learning science is to present yourself as an example. For instance, you can model curiosity and enthusiasm for science topics and questions throughout your teaching. Children watch adults to find out how grown-ups act, and teachers are among the most significant grown-ups in children's lives. As a teacher, you can encourage children to be more curious by communicating your own inquisitiveness. Besides inquisitiveness, the following attitudes and values can be modeled to motivate children:

- Appreciation of the usefulness and value of knowledge
- Pride in work
- Carefulness in work, including careful observing, listening, and reading
- Positive self-concept as a science learner, moderated by a sense of fallibility
- Respect for other opinions (Nickerson, 1981, p. 24)

Providing Choices for Students Still another way you can motivate students is by providing opportunities for them to make choices. As Glasser (1969) has noted, children need to experience control over their own lives. If your students are to become responsible learners, you must provide opportunities for them to experience choice and shared control. There are two aspects to this. First, the children have to perceive that choice and control are available to them. Second, they have to believe they are competent (or can become competent) to make good choices and achieve their goals (Clark, 1986).

There are many kinds of choices that even young children can handle. Some examples would be choices among topics for study, choices of assignments or of activities in which to participate, choices as to arrangement of events in the daily schedule, and choices of teammates in cooperative learning groups.

An important area of student choice concerns the evaluation system. Most of us have never experienced schools without grades, but there is much evidence that grades often impede and inhibit learning. Grades are external rewards and sometimes are experienced by the child as a form of punishment. Grades certainly affect self-esteem. Students who consistently make grades of D or F come to believe that they cannot succeed academically.

As a teacher, you may not have a choice about whether to give grades. But you can communicate to your students that the only purpose of grades is to give feedback and show what they know according to some scale. A low grade does not mean failure, but simply that the child has not yet learned enough (Glasser, 1990, p. 53).

It is helpful to let each child have a voice in setting his or her learning goals and evaluation criteria. When designing the rubrics for assessing activities and projects you can invite children's suggestions and negotiate mutually acceptable criteria. Children are more apt to work toward meeting criteria they had a share in deciding. If grading is based on mutually determined standards, children are more likely to take responsibility for the learning tasks involved.

Providing Explanations Can you recall any experience of being told to do something solely on the basis of adult authority? "Do this because I say so!" Do you remember how you felt toward that adult, and toward the task? Explaining important teaching decisions to children demonstrates that you respect them. It is motivating to children to know why particular behaviors are being requested of them, or how completing the assigned tasks relates to helping them understand. An example of this kind of teaching is when, on the kindergarten playground a teacher explains the prohibition against throwing rocks or running around carrying sharp sticks. In science class, children might be given reasons why they are expected to follow particular safety rules, or why they are assigned a science project.

Of course, your explanations should make sense, and what you teach should be worth learning. As Jere Brophy (1987) has put it, "It is not reasonable to expect students to be motivated to learn if they are continually expected to practice skills already thoroughly mastered, memorize lists for no good reason, copy definitions of terms that are never used in readings or assignments, or read material that is not meaningful to them because it is too vague, abstract, or foreign to their experience" (p. 42).

Using Multiple Strategies Another way to motivate learning is to use a variety of instructional methods, including inquiry activities, hands-on experiences, and cooperative group methods. Children generally respond better to a variety of teaching strategies. By using many kinds of teaching strategies, you also reach children with different learning styles.

There is a place for text reading, lecturing, and recitation in science teaching, but *inquiry*—the exploration and experience of objects and phenomena—is at the heart of science and should be the core teaching strategy for science. Glasser (1990) says that "learning together as a member of a small learning team is much more need-satisfying, especially to the needs for power and belonging, than learning individually" (p. 48). Cooperative group methods and inquiry are a dynamic combination for the learning of science.

In a supportive and nurturing environment, as established by these teacher behaviors, children are accepted for being themselves and respected as individuals. In a nurturing environment, children are actively engaged in meaningful tasks. Their needs as learners are recognized and responded to. They know that it is safe to make mistakes. At the same time, they know that they are expected to learn.

Quick Review

In *Science for All Americans,* the AAAS (1989) proclaims, "In the science classroom, wondering should be as highly valued as knowing" (p. 191). The affective domain includes the values and habits of mind that are part of the science content of the curriculum. The affective domain is also about children's feelings toward science and toward themselves as science learners. We have presented a model for development that demonstrates the affective-cognitive connection and argued that feeling and valuing underlies cognitive development. As we have noted, there are many ways for the teacher to encourage children to develop positive concepts of themselves as

science learners and to motivate them to achieve to their abilities.

IMPLICATIONS FOR THE ASPIRING TEACHER

With all that has been discussed in this chapter, what does it mean for the prospective teacher? Clearly, science is not a matter of just opening a textbook and reading a chapter. The teaching of science is much more dynamic than that, and there is much to be learned. We hope that this book will get you started. As ever, a good place to begin is with your own imagination. Think for a moment about the *process* of education. What is it like? What images or metaphors come to mind?

Metaphors of Instruction

Our thoughts often take the form of images or metaphors. In education, there are at least three principal guiding metaphors in the conceptualization of what school is all about. In this century the most prominent of the three in American education has been the *industrial* metaphor. Perhaps this is due to the dominance of business and industry in the United States. In this view, the school is a factory and the students are the raw materials to be processed. The teachers are workers on an assembly line. Each year, students are passed along to the next station, or grade, where another teacher contributes to the processing and passes the student along. Some students get rejected by quality control and are retained to be reprocessed. The teacher's work is guided by production goals and objectives from upper levels of the corporate hierarchy. In this metaphor, teachers do things *to* students. Language such as "input," "output," "management-by-objectives," and the like are marks of this perspective. Does it sound at all familiar to you?

An alternative to the industrial metaphor is the *garden* metaphor. In this view, students are seeds and teachers are farmers. The job of the teacher is to prepare the soil (the classroom environment) so that it will promote growth. The teacher is concerned with the "climate" and with helping the students develop their potential. Like seeds, children have all of their potential inside, and the task is to let them unfold and bloom. Similarly, Socrates used to say that men were "pregnant with knowledge." That is, the information was within them, and it was Socrates' job to draw that knowledge out. In this view, teachers do things *for* students.

The final metaphor may be the most ancient and is the least in evidence today. It is the metaphor of the pilgrimage, or *journey*. In this view, you and your students are travelers on the road to faraway destinations. As teacher/guide, you have more experience as a traveler; you have been to faraway places before. However, the journey represents a new experience for you, too, because every journey is unique and somewhat unpredictable. Even if the journey is to a familiar place, you are a learner on the way as well. The teacher, as a guide, wants the journey to be a good experience for the pilgrims. The guide wants them to get the most out of their trip. The guide knows that different pilgrims will experience the various destinations on the journey in different ways. In this view, the teacher does things *with* the students. This metaphor, too, has left its linguistic fossils. The original meaning of the term, a "course," was a stretch of path to be run.

Which of these metaphors do you recognize from your own experience with schooling? Can you imagine how these three visions of the *process* of education would be translated into very different teacher behaviors? In particular, envisioning education as a journey is a way to give permission to yourself to learn alongside the children as the journey proceeds. There is really no better way: There is simply more to teaching science than you could possibly know as you are just beginning. We encourage you to think positively about the journey of learning that stretches out ahead of you through the courses you are now taking. And keep in mind that the journey will continue throughout your professional career as a teacher. Learning is truly one of life's greatest adventures and greatest pleasures.

ACTIVITY 3.8

Observing Teaching Styles

In your field-study experience or clinical placement, look for these various metaphors being expressed in teaching. Obviously, you will need to obtain permission to visit a number of different rooms. You should be able to ascertain very quickly which of the metaphors is in use.

Find classrooms where you can identify each of the metaphors in practice, and observe the classroom for a few minutes.

- What can you say about the interaction between student and teacher?

- How would you describe the educational "atmosphere" of the classroom?

- What conclusions do you draw from comparing these three styles?

What You Need to Know

The "knowledge base" for teaching science in the elementary school is multidimensional. Elementary and middle school teachers should have the following:

- Knowledge of students, how they learn science, what they already know when they arrive in the classroom

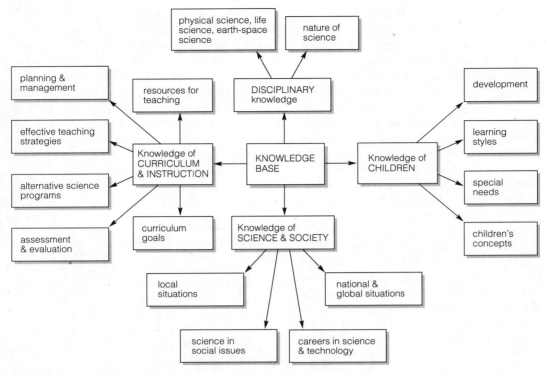

FIGURE 3.3 Knowledge base concept map.

- Knowledge of the world the students live in (and will live into) and its relation to science and technology
- Knowledge of science as a way of knowing, the methods and significant ideas of science
- Knowledge of the varieties of science programs in the elementary and middle school curriculum, how the science program can be organized and integrated with the other subjects in the curriculum
- Knowledge of teaching strategies, ways to communicate scientific knowledge and processes, and develop your students' scientific habits of mind

A concept map of this knowledge base appears in Figure 3.3. To look this over, you might feel as though you would have to spend all of your time teaching science. You will find, however, that such is not the case. There is much of science content that can be integrated, for example, into social studies, math, and language arts. This book will go a long way toward helping you prepare.

Quick Review

The instructional metaphors provide you with a way of conceptualizing your role as a teacher. Of the three described, that of the journey is most realistic in that it acknowledges that as you guide students to particular instructional experiences, you are also learning from a new experience yourself. Allowing your students to be aware of your learning will model for them the idea that learning does not take place only in school, and only in grades K−8. Similarly, we offer the "knowledge base" for science teaching as indicative of the fact that science content is only one piece of a much larger web. You can understand and relate one part of the web with another, and your science teaching—all of your teaching—will benefit from the much broader perspective that you will possess as a professional educator.

CONCLUSION

In reflecting on the value of science learning to the child, George DeBoer (1991) has written the following:

> Science education, as all education, should lead to independent self-activity. It should empower individuals to think and act. It should give individuals new ideas and investigative skills that contribute to self-regulation, personal satisfaction, and social responsibility. Knowledge that is richly interconnected, intellectual skill that allows individuals to work with what is known, and an awareness of the contexts within which that knowledge and those skills apply—all of this should be part of science education. (p. 240)

In this chapter, we have considered the historical development of science education, the rationale for science in the elementary and middle schools, the powerful dimension of feeling and values, and the implications of these issues for the aspiring teacher. Our view is that science is as important as the other "basics" because it is useful, because it is part of our cultural heritage, and because it helps satisfy basic needs, especially the need to know. We remind you again that children's curiosity about the world will always be your strongest ally as a teacher.

Also in this chapter, we have considered the present state of science instruction in the schools. The science program in the schools can and should be improved such that children can benefit from instruction in the ways envisioned by DeBoer. From what we have observed in many places across the United States, science programs limp along on too little support. For a variety of reasons, many teachers provide too little time in science instruction, and many are not prepared or eager to teach science. The most frequently used teaching strategies do not help children understand and do not create a positive affect about science. In many cases this is due, at the bottom, to the teacher's own lack of science understanding. And if science instruction is to become what it is capable of becoming, teachers will need to appreciate that for all its facts and information, science is dynamic because of how people feel about and value learning. That affective aspect of science will likely not be included in the textbooks that your students use, or in the teacher's edition on your desk. The affective, humanistic dimension of science that *you* bring to your classroom is what demonstrates why teachers cannot be replaced by computers and software.

In this chapter, we have also considered what all of this means to you as a prospective elementary or middle school teacher. When you read about the results of the studies cited here and the conclusions of the researchers, did you recall your own experience as a student? How many of your teachers overly relied on the textbook? On the other hand, did you ever experience teachers who made learning science exciting to learn? And now, as you begin your study of methods of teaching science, what do you imagine about yourself as a classroom practitioner?

Perhaps you think that you will be among the majority of teachers who feel uncomfortable or inadequate teaching science. If such is the case, now is the time to commit to changing your perspective. If elementary or middle school teaching is indeed to be your vocation, we hope you will invest time and effort into your professional development in this critical area as an educator. We believe this is a worthwhile pursuit, because science is truly important for your students.

Section II   Psychological Foundations for Teaching Science

CHAPTER 4   **Children's Cognitive Development and the Learning of Science**

CHAPTER 5   **Eliciting Children's Conceptions about Science**

This section contains two chapters that focus on the way children think and learn. Knowing *how* they think is the focus of chapter 4; knowing *what* they think is the focus of chapter 5.

Chapter 4, "Children's Cognitive Development and the Learning of Science," provides a discussion of how children's science is similar to, and different from, scientists' science. The point is made that simply providing information in a classroom is not necessarily sufficient to bring children to the level of understanding that you may have intended. The construction of knowledge utilizes all of the experiences that a child has had, the vast majority of which have occurred outside of a classroom. This chapter presents a stepwise model to help clarify the task of systematically moving children from one level of understanding to the next.

With an understanding of how children make sense of the world around them, chapter 5, "Eliciting Children's Conceptions about Science," provides a method for finding out just what makes sense to your students. You will find that what you think they believe and what they actually believe may be very different. The chapter details the technique of interviewing your students in order to elicit this information. The interview, however, is a distinctly noninstructional situation. The intent of interviewing students is purely to determine what they really know or believe about a topic prior to planning instruction. For this reason, we have placed it in this section on psychological foundations rather than with teaching methods or assessment.

4 | ❀ | Children's Cognitive Development and the Learning of Science

Children's Science and Constructivism

Facilitating Conceptual Development

Conclusion

Your Academic Roadmap

Study of this chapter should help you to understand the following concepts:

- The instructional outcomes intended by the teacher are not necessarily the same as the actual outcomes.

- Children and scientists construct knowledge from the materials available to them.

- Teachers provide opportunities for experiences that facilitate conceptual development.

- Changing a child's concept of a topic in science requires that the new explanation be as personally satisfying as the child's previously held explanation.

What is science?
You find out all the things about the earth. You find out about animals. . . . It's asking questions and finding out why. That would probably cover it.

—Stephanie, eight years old

CHILDREN'S SCIENCE AND CONSTRUCTIVISM

Children learn, even if they don't attend school. They are naturally curious and eager to make sense of the world around them. In that regard, they are very much like scientists. Both search for explanations about how things work and why things behave as they do. However, as our previous discussion of constructivism has indicated, these explanations are of a very personal nature. An individual's knowledge of the world must be based on that individual's experience with the world. The result is that what makes sense to one person may not make sense to someone else. For instance, the idea that the world was flat made sense to people based on their experiences with, and knowledge of, the world. Our knowledge and range of experience today make such a belief unacceptable. Yet we can only construct with the materials available.

By acknowledging the personal nature of "sense making," a constructivist approach to education provides the teacher with considerable insight about what students know as they enter the classroom, what occurs during instruction, and how to account for the eventual outcomes of instruction. By looking at the intended outcomes of instruction versus the actual outcomes, we will be better able to understand the difference between children's science and scientists' science. That distinction will emphasize the value of constructivism as a referent for instructional planning. Even so, misconceptions can, and will, arise. And so it will be important to draw another distinction: incomplete understanding and misconception. Taken together, each of these topics will lead to a discussion of a model for facilitating conceptual development.

Intended and Actual Outcomes of Instruction

While visiting the teachers' workroom in an elementary school one day, we listened as a couple of teachers were talking. The conversation focused on the changes noted by each teacher as they were in the process of implementing new strategies for teaching science as presented in a staff development program. The following is part of that conversation.

Why is it that when I teach science, several of the children miss the point of the lesson? I plan lessons which allow the students to be actively involved, doing lots of science process skills. The children have opportunities to explore the concepts by working with manipulatives and they seem to enjoy an investigative approach to learning. Yet when the lesson is over, there are still gaps in some students' explanations of the concept.

The question, asked by many teachers who have experienced this same situation, is an important one. It indicates the sensitivity of teachers to the effectiveness of instruction. Even as teachers are changing instructional strategies and improving student learning, actual student outcomes do not always match the teachers' intended outcomes.

However, by reflecting a little about the basic premise used in the approach to the teaching of science as described above by the concerned teacher, and by knowing what children's science is, you can expect a variety of learning outcomes and realize why teachers' expectations differ from what students learn. If the children are encouraged to *discover* the concepts and scientific principles— that is, if learning is dependent on using manipulatives to conduct personal investiga-

tions—then learning will vary from one discoverer to the next. Discovery, according to Ebert and Ebert (1993), is a creative endeavor that involves the search for patterns, perspectives, and relationships. Each student has a unique set of experiences from which personal knowledge is constructed. It is that personal knowledge and unique perspective that is engaged when the student pursues the creative endeavor of scientific investigation. The patterns and relationships discovered are bound to vary from one child to another.

The great amount of similarity in children's conceptual development, at least in part, is a result of similar learning opportunities for the children, due to the control that the teacher has with regard to formal instruction. Knowing that children have personal experiences resulting in unique sets of knowledge, and recognizing the differences in their use of language, it is understandable, and even predictable, that children will achieve different outcomes given the same science activity.

Eight-year-old Jeremy alludes to his own experiences with his explanation of rain and reveals his own version of the "water cycle."

What is rain?
It comes down.

Where does it come from?
When the cars and houses get washed.

Is there water in the sky?
Yes.

How does it get to the sky?
When we use our sink, it goes up in the sky so our houses and cars can get washed.

As children's experiences broaden, their ideas will inevitably change. The teacher, however, should not feel compelled to correct these explanations. With time and experience, these conceptualizations will change.

Classroom studies by Osborne and Freyberg (1985) and Wittrock (1974) suggest the following as major differences between the

Chen Long

PHOTO 4.1 The teacher needs to remain accepting of a child's responses and reasoning during the interview.

teacher's intentions and the actual learning taking place. Disparities exist between

- the *ideas* brought to the lesson by the children, and the assumptions made by the teacher about those ideas;
- the *scientific problem* as perceived by the teacher, and what the children perceived the problem to be;
- the *activity* the teacher proposed, and the activity undertaken by the children; and
- the *conclusions* as stated by the children, and the teacher's proposed conclusions.

It is necessary to recognize that a teacher's intentions cannot be directly transferred into student conceptualizations. Language is not a simple conduit carrying information from one mind to another. Students, through interactions with materials, teachers, and peers, will construct their own *purposes* for the lesson, develop their own *intentions* regarding the activities, and formulate their own *conclusions*. These constructs may or may not be similar to the teacher's intentions. Therefore, it is important that the teacher attempt to reduce the disparities by recognizing and

appreciating the perceptions that the children bring to the classroom.

For example, a sixth-grade teacher designed a lesson to help her students understand that all living things are composed of cells. She wanted them to learn that plant cells have rigid cell walls and that animal cells have membranes that are not rigid. The activity involved having children preparing and looking at microscope slides of onion cells and cheek cells.

The following statements from children in the class are in response to the question, "What did you learn today?"

Keysia: You have to be really careful with that stain. It can really make a mess and it stains your hands and stuff.

Matthew: Each of those little squares have little dots and stuff in them and there are lots of little square things.

Mikel: I learned that there are these things that are inside my mouth . . . these cells that grow there . . . and everybody has them.

Andrea: Onion cells look like blocks, purple blocks, and cells that live in

FIGURE 4.1 Examples of invented explanations.

What is thunder?

"Thunder is God bowling."

"Thunder is the clouds clapping."

"Thunder is God yelling at the angels like my mom does to me."

> my mouth are pale . . . they're white, kind of like circles.
>
> **Zack:** It is hard to see in that microscope. My partner and I had a hard time. We found some stuff but it was hard.

As you might expect, none of these responses matched the teacher's objectives. That does not mean that the lesson was a failure. It does mean that the outcomes are different from what was intended. The teacher was expecting a generalization related to plant and animal cells. The children, on the other hand, were involved in the details of the activity and the specific observations. And that is what they verbalized. It is probable that many experiences will be required before the children begin to see patterns emerging and therefore be able to make generalizable statements. The one experience, however, is a starting place, and can be built upon to facilitate growth and the emergence of the intended concept.

ACTIVITY 4.1

Actual Outcomes

This notion of intended outcomes versus actual outcomes is easy enough to investigate. Try the following in your field service or practicum placement:

- Arrange with your cooperating teacher for you to be there to observe an entire lesson, and to speak with several children after the lesson is concluded.
- Ask the teacher to tell you, before the lesson, what concepts the lesson will address.

- As the lesson proceeds, jot down what you consider to be the major concepts.
- Finally, talk with several students after the lesson, and ask what they learned that day.

Note: Keep in mind that the teacher might do an extra special job of trying to get concepts across because the two of you have arranged this little investigation. So, try to approach this in a manner that is just as normal as possible. The information you collect will be of value to you and to the teacher.

Children's Science versus Scientists' Science

The major difference between the scientist's approach to developing explanations or theories and the child's approach is the way observations are used. Children, as they attempt to make sense of the world around them, do so in terms of personal experiences, their current knowledge, and their own use of language. Young children's ideas are scientific in that they are based on available evidence. That evidence, however, tends to be limited to directly observable characteristics. Whereas the scientist seeks to derive explanations objectively from the observations, the child is inclined to invent explanations to account for observations such as the ones reported in Figure 4.1.

Despite what other people might think, the explanations in Figure 4.1 make sense to each child. The logic represents the child's own level of logical thinking. It is these ideas and explanations about how and why things behave as they do that Osborne and Freyberg call "children's science." From the child's point of view, these ideas are coherent and sensible, as illustrated in Figure 4.2.

Explanations such as these, which are personally adequate, are frequently inaccurate from the scientific viewpoint. Typically, the

FIGURE 4.2 One child's perspective on animals.

Damon: An insect is a little crawly thing and they bite.

Interviewer: Is an insect an animal?

Damon: Oh, no. Animals are like dogs and cats and horses and things. They have legs and make animal noises.

explanations will change as the child's experiences broaden.

Summarizing the information on the perspectives of children (Osborne and Freyberg, 1985), the following generalizations provide insight into children's science:

- Children tend to have self-centered or human-centered viewpoints.

- Their views are based on everyday experiences and common use of language.

- They are interested in specific explanations rather than coherent theories.

- They endow inanimate objects with characteristics of humans and other animals.

- Children consider nonobservables as nonexistent.

From the list above, we can begin to see how children's science differs from what we call scientists' science. As a way of knowing, children's science succeeds in finding explanations for naturally occurring phenomenon. After all, children, like scientists, support their ideas on evidence. Children, however, construct their versions of science by observing naturally occurring phenomena in everyday surroundings using only their unassisted sensory abilities. Adult scientific pursuits make use of technologically advanced equipment, such as electron microscopes, electronic probes, and computers; and scientists work in specially designed environments created for scientific research, such as laboratories and spaceships. And scientists' science approaches the task of understanding more *systematically* and with more *objectivity*.

Interestingly, it is not just the similarities between children's science and scientists' science, or just the differences, that are important. Rather, an awareness of both are what Osborne and Freyberg (1985) consider to be "of central importance in the teaching and learning of science." As a teacher, you are very methodically trying to arrange opportunities for experiences that will enable children to construct the concepts you want them to understand. Unlike scientific endeavors, you (usually) do know what you want your students to find. Very much like in scientific endeavors, your students do the finding. Figure 4.3 provides information describing and comparing the two types of science. As you look over the list, you will find that scientists' science is just a more sophisticated version of what most of us do as a

FIGURE 4.3 Children's science versus scientists' science.

Children's Science	Scientists' Science
Ideas based on evidence	Ideas based on evidence
Explanations sometimes derived from observations	Explanations derived from prior theory and observations
Explanations sometimes invented to account for observations	Observations used to test explanations
Unassisted senses used to make observations	Sophisticated equipment used to make observations
Nonobservables considered nonexistent	Nonobservables may be detected through instrumentation
Self-centered or human-centered	Objective perspective sought

natural attempt to make sense of the world around us.

An important similarity that is not listed in Figure 4.3 is that ideas once constructed and accepted as satisfactory, whether by children or scientists, are difficult to change. In the case of children, changing to a more scientific viewpoint typically comes with the broadening of one's experiences. The change, however, is not always easy to facilitate through the teaching of science. Researchers have found that the ideas held by children not only affect how students make sense of new information or data, but that the ideas can remain intact throughout new instructional settings and can persist even when faced with counterevidence and argument. Since children's ideas are often held strongly, even tenaciously, they may remain uninfluenced by instruction. Another possibility is that the ideas can be influenced in unanticipated ways. Thus, a problem important to the teaching of science is that scientific explanations are often too different from the viewpoint of children and, consequently, are unattractive alternatives to what the child already believes.

Posner, Strike, Hewson, and Gertzog (1982) suggest that children will change their ideas only if their present ones are unsatisfactory in some way. Dissatisfaction with an idea, however, is not necessarily a sufficient reason for discarding it. In fact, Posner et al. suggest four conditions that must be met in order for a child to accept a different conceptualization (see Figure 4.4).

Obviously, we can say that the same conditions are necessary for changing the mind of an adult. These conditions are particularly important for a teacher, however, because teachers are in fact *change agents*. At every turn, a teacher strives to encourage students to change their ideas by providing experiences that introduce concepts in ways that day-to-day life does not. The techniques for accomplishing this task—that is, allowing

FIGURE 4.4 Conditions for conceptual change (from Smith, 1991).

- The student must become *dissatisfied* with his or her current understanding.

- The student must have available an *intelligible alternative*.

- The alternative must seem *plausible* to the student.

- The alternative must seem *fruitful* to the student.

for conceptual development generated from experiences that broaden understanding and from consideration of plausible alternatives to naive conceptualizations—is what the constructivist approach to science teaching is all about.

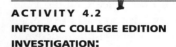

ACTIVITY 4.2
INFOTRAC COLLEGE EDITION
INVESTIGATION:

Holding On

People, children or otherwise, have a tendency to hold onto concepts that have become satisfying to them in some way. Pseudoscience is a term that refers to what might be called "nonscientific" scientific conceptualizations. Use InfoTrac College Edition and search headings such as pseudoscience, paranormal, or myth to find contrasting views on what we typically consider to be science.

Constructivism in Practice

In chapter 1, we discussed constructivism as a philosophy. Here, we want to make the philosophy pragmatic by considering it as a referent for educational theory and for the selection of instructional strategies. Piaget, in his early work, focused on the relationship between language and thinking. That and his work on animism (attributing animal characteristics to inanimate objects) and egocentrism (regarding everyone's perspective to be the same as one's own) are still relevant to the teaching and learning of science.

Piaget (1977) purported that as a learner strives to organize personal experiences in terms of preexisting mental schemes, knowledge is constructed. We do this by matching new situations to those we have already experienced. A situation that is similar to what we already know is *assimilated* into our understanding. When we assimilate, we make slight changes in a preexisting schema. For example, going to a new restaurant may be a different experience, though essentially similar to the overall experience of dining out. Sometimes, however, an experience is very new or different than anything done before. In that case, the experience requires *accommodation*. Accommodation may involve significantly changing a preexisting schema, or perhaps constructing a brand-new schema. While Piaget's schema theory is not accepted by all, constructivists agree that learners, in their search for understanding, look for patterns within their realms of experience, developing personal explanations for natural phenomena and constructing their own forms of reality. Knowledge, therefore, is constructed in the minds of the learners. Thus, the constructivist theory of knowledge is a logical outgrowth of Piaget's model of intellectual development.

Consider this example of how a child might construct a personal explanation for shadows: The child notices his or her shadow while playing outside on a sunny day. An adult identifies the shape as the child's shadow and also indicates the existence of the adult's shadow. Some playful manipulation of arms and legs helps the child recognize the ownership of the shadows. The child, over a period of time, continues to observe his or her own shadow and begins to associate its existence with sunny conditions. At this point, the child's understanding of the concept might be explained somewhat like the excerpt from the following interview with Jackie, a fourth-grader.

What can you tell me about shadows?
"They are black and if the sun is above you the shadow is right where your feet are. If the sun is in the west, your shadow is in the east. If the sun is in the east, your shadow is in the west."

Where does a shadow come from?
"It comes from you."

How does it come from you?
"The sun shines on you."

Jackie's explanations for shadows are based on her own experiences with shadows. Given opportunities to study and manipulate shadows using artificial sources of light and a variety of objects, she may construct a more complex level of understanding of the concept of shadows to include generalizations regarding sources of light. The following interview with Jason, another fourth-grader, is an example of a more complex construction.

What can you tell me about shadows?
"There are reflections on the ground from a light or the sun. If you stand in front of a light or the sun, the light can't go through you so it makes a black spot that appears on the ground."

Where does a shadow come from?
"Well, from the sun mostly. The sun or a light shines on you, and it can't shine through you so a shadow appears on the floor".

However, children frequently invent explanations to account for observations. This is obvious in six-year-old Marla's explanation regarding phases of the moon.

Is the moon always the same shape?
"No."

Why does the moon's shape change?
"Because I think the moon sometimes is shy and in the evening it just shows a little bit of it and at night it finally comes out."

Marla's explanation is an example of an anthropomorphic response, in that human-like characteristics are attributed to inanimate objects. This is not surprising considering that Marla's range of experiences likely includes many instances in which cartoon representations of the sun, the moon, trees, and so forth, were represented with faces and voices. What she perhaps knows about timidity in herself and other people is applied to this situation, inventing an explanation for the difference in the appearance of the moon that seems quite reasonable in terms of children's science.

That children learn by constantly constructing new knowledge seems easy enough to accept. What we need, however, is an effective means of instruction that facilitates the construction of concepts identified in the curriculum. In that regard, there are a number of things a teacher can do to put children into situations that will facilitate the construction of their understanding. The emphasis of such techniques is on having children actively involved in the *manipulation of materials* and the *consideration of their own ideas and those of others*. This requires some expertise on the part of the educator, in that it involves challenging student's preinstructional conceptualizations in a nonthreatening manner. Figure 4.5 lists techniques teachers can use to help children conceptually.

The degree to which student thinking and activity is integral to the educational plan is evident in the list of teaching techniques provided in Figure 4.5. What is not as evident is the considerable professional expertise required to establish a classroom science program based on a constructivist perspective. You will notice that throughout the

PHOTO 4.2 Children may have unexpected explanations for the nature of shadows.

list of techniques, there exists a *dynamic* nature to the conduct of the lesson. This is particularly reflective of Piaget's notion that knowledge is dynamic in that it is ever expanding, spiralling to encompass more and more experiences and meaning.

Children's Misconceptions

It is inevitable that if there are twenty students in the classroom, there will be twenty versions of what happened in school that day. And each version could be accurate. This brings us to the topic of misconceptions. As the constructivist philosophy empowers each individual with the responsibility for building his or her own knowledge, it also provides an explanation for how what you intended to be taught may have been

FIGURE 4.5 Teaching practices consistent with constructivism (adapted from Brooks, 1990).

1. Encourage and accept student autonomy, initiative, and leadership.

2. Whenever possible, use interactive and physical materials to allow students to collect their own data.

3. Use cognitive terminology such as *classify, analyze, predict,* and the like when framing tasks.

4. Allow student thinking to drive lessons, and shift instructional strategies or alter content based on student responses.

5. Ask students for their ideas about concepts before sharing your understanding of those concepts.

6. Encourage students to engage in conversation about the topic, both with the teacher and with one another.

7. Encourage students to elaborate on their initial responses.

8. Challenge students' initial hypotheses and then encourage a response. This process will require considerable diplomacy; an idea must be challenged without attacking an individual's whole perspective.

9. Foster student inquiry by asking thoughtful, open-ended questions and encouraging students to ask questions of others.

10. Allow *wait-time* after posing questions. Effective questioning requires allowing three to five seconds' pause for students to think before responding.

11. Provide opportunities for students to discover relationships and create metaphors.

12. Require students to reflect on experiences and actions and make predictions.

13. When designing lessons, organize information around conceptual clusters—of problems, questions, discrepant situations. (See "The Learning Cycle" in chapter 8.)

14. Align the curriculum with appropriate developmental needs of students.

15. Identify students' alternative conceptions, and design subsequent lessons to address any misconceptions.

influenced by what the child already knows. If, as we suggest in this book, you take the time to ascertain what each child actually believes about important educational topics, you will be able to identify misconceptions that they might hold. From that point, you will be able to design lessons to specifically challenge and address those ideas.

For the sake of completeness, we will first admit that some scholars argue that there is no such thing as a misconception. After all, a concept is a concept whether it corresponds to the scientific community's explanation or not. Practically speaking, in an environment in which students are tested and evaluated with regard to their science knowledge, it is important to help them move toward accepted scientific understandings. So, at this point, it is important to make some distinctions that will guide the remainder of this chapter.

The terms "incomplete understanding" of a concept and "misconception" are some-times used differently by those conducting research in this area. The variety of terms that are found in related research include "preconceptions," "misconceptions," "naive theories," "alternative conceptions," and "alternative frameworks." The use of "preconceptions" is often based on Ausubel's (1968) work, which uses the term when referring to expressed ideas that are not yet generalized understandings characteristic of conceptual knowledge. "Misconception" connotes a wrong idea or an inaccurate assimilation of a theory or model. Those authors who use the phrase "naive theories" see children's ideas as being not fully developed and often similar to the theories expressed by "scientists" centuries ago. The term "alternative frameworks" suggests that children have developed autonomous frameworks for conceptualizing their own experiences of natural phenomena.

As used in this context, a misconception is a belief expressed by a child that is incorrect from the perspective of the scientific community. An incomplete understanding of a concept is partially correct as opposed to being entirely correct. The explanation includes information that is supported by the scientific community but lacks additional information that is necessary to the complete understanding of the concept. For example, a child who believes that seasons are caused by the distance of the earth from the sun during its annual revolution is operating with a misconception. A child who believes that the seasons are caused by the earth's orientation on its axis relative to the sun, but is unable to explain how that changes the seasonal temperatures, is operating with an incomplete understanding. In the first case, the teacher is faced with changing the student's understanding. In the second case, the teacher has the task of broadening the student's understanding. Do you see how these are two very different instructional tasks? Activity 4.3 provides a list of students' scientific concepts. Read each of them and try to determine which represent misconceptions and which represent incomplete understanding.

ACTIVITY 4.3

Misconceptions and Incomplete Understanding

Consider each of the following statements. Indicate whether you think the statement is an example of a misconception or an incomplete understanding. Be sure to explain your reasoning.

- The sun rises in the east and sets in the west.
- Magnets attract metal objects.
- Plants get their food through roots.
- With a light source and an object you can make a shadow.

- Stars do not shine in the day because the sun is too bright.
- If the sun is shining while it is raining, you can see a rainbow.

Quick Review

The four topics discussed in this first half of the chapter have been presented in a way that demonstrates the circular nature of cognitive development and the learning of science. We began by discussing an important reality of the classroom: The outcomes the teacher intends are not necessarily what the students take away from the experience. This should come as no surprise to you, as it has likely happened even in your own college experience. This situation, however, directed us to a consideration of children's science and how it differs from scientists' science. The common theme is that children and scientists construct knowledge from the materials available to them. Scientists typically have better tools available and approach the task in a more objective and systematic way, but the process of building knowledge in order to explain things in a personally satisfying way is characteristic of both scientists and children.

With that in mind, we moved to a discussion of constructivism as a referent to educational theory and strategy. If children construct knowledge, then it is the teacher's responsibility to provide opportunities for appropriate experiences for the development of desired concepts. The teacher cannot give experience or knowledge to the student. Any stimulus that a child, a scientist, or *you,* receive, only becomes knowledge after it has been considered in light of your own preexisting knowledge.

Finally, having established that people construct their own knowledge and that there are ways for teachers to impact upon that process, we have tried to make it plain to you that misconceptions are to be expected. However, by assessing your students' knowledge and identifying misconceptions and partial understanding, you are prepared to design lessons that will effectively address their needs. No matter what grade level you teach, your students will come to you with a host of background experiences. And no matter how familiar or different your topics, all of those experiences will influence the way in which your students interpret and internalize the new experiences under your guidance. It is an awesome and exciting responsibility to be a teacher. The next section of this chapter weaves together all that has been presented thus far into a model for understanding conceptual development.

FACILITATING CONCEPTUAL DEVELOPMENT

We have discussed constructivism as a philosophy and as a referent to educational theory. Along the way, it has become evident that children, as well as adults, learn as a function of what they already know. Such a situation can easily lead to misconceptions and/or incomplete understandings. In the previous section, we tried to characterize all of this as being fantastically dynamic, though at this point you might be thinking that "confusing" would be a better term. In this section, we try to bring order to that confusion by representing what has been discussed as a model. In that way, you might better appreciate just how you can monitor childrens' learning, and even direct their conceptual development.

The Conceptual Development Model

By interviewing large numbers of people and analyzing the responses, researchers have observed that both individual and group patterns emerge. These patterns suggest that

children go through a *progressive development* of understanding of topics of study rather than changing from a primitive explanation to the acceptance of the scientific explanation in one step. Consider the variety of responses in a discussion among a group of children.

> **Mark:** A shadow is something that appears when I go outside.
> **Sarah:** When I go outside and the sun is shining, I see my shadow.
> **Brenton:** If you have a light, like a flashlight, and you shine it on something, it will make a shadow.
> **Angel:** If you hold something up in front of a light, you will see a shadow on the wall. If you move the object closer to or farther away from the wall, you change the size of the shadow.

The quotations above are actual responses given by children to the question, "What can you tell me about shadows?" While the responses vary considerably, they all reflect the same thing: the individual's understanding of the concept of shadows. The differences in the explanations and complexity of the responses are due to the individuals' unique sets of experiences. Each child has constructed his or her own explanation, and from those explanations, it is possible to infer some differences in those experiences. From their responses, we can infer that the first two children have probably had experiences limited to firsthand observations of shadows in outdoor settings. The other two children have probably had additional experiences when they manipulated light sources and observed the resulting production of shadows.

As a teacher planning an instructional unit on light and the production of shadows, it is important to understand the diversity of explanations that children have for shadows. It is also important for the teacher to be aware of the complexity of the concept to be taught—in this case, shadows—and the

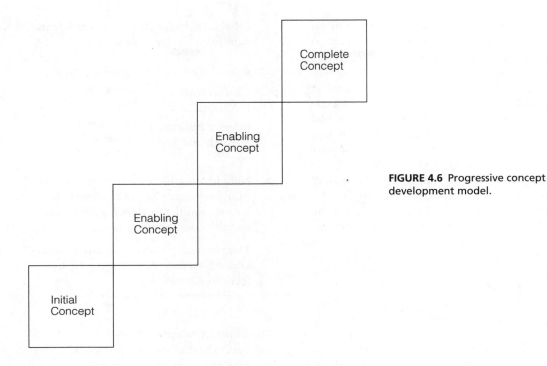

FIGURE 4.6 Progressive concept development model.

progressive development of that concept. In fact, most concepts are too complex for a person to proceed from no understanding of a concept to a complete understanding of the concept in one step. And based on peoples' constructions, the concept can frequently be subdivided into progressive steps of development. A generalizable model of this progressive development devised by Ebert and Ebert (1993) is illustrated in Figure 4.6.

The first (lower left) cell in Figure 4.6 represents *initial conceptualization* of the concept, which may simply be word recognition. This entry level acquaintance with the concept frequently, but not always, occurs prior to formal instruction. For example, by the time children reach your first-grade classroom, they will have experienced shadows. They may not understand shadows or be able to describe how they occur, but they know what you are talking about when you say shadows.

The last (upper right) cell in Figure 4.6 represents the *complete understanding* of the

concept and would be in agreement with accepted scientific explanations. This, of course, represents the goal of any course of study. However, given our earlier suggestions that science is tentative and subject to change, it is possible that greater understanding serves to increase the sophistication of the concept and thereby extend the model. In essence, this begs the question of whether anyone could ever know everything about anything. But setting the philosophical questions aside, it is still the case that the path to increased understanding is built upon the current level of understanding.

Figure 4.6 shows just two steps between Initial Concept and Complete Concept. It is important that you understand that this is done only to save paper. Depending on the sophistication, there could be many, perhaps dozens or hundreds, of steps between the first cell and the last. For instance, a young girl who has an interest in how long it would take for an M&M to reach the ground from her bedroom window will progress through many, many levels of formal education on her way to becoming a recognized expert on astrophysics. However, and this is an important "however," strings of enabling objectives represent educational experiences at various levels. For instance, if you are teaching first grade, the first series of enabling objectives after the Initial Concept cell would be the concepts that you will teach to your first-graders. At the end of first grade, the young girl that we mentioned above, will not have a complete understanding of the concept of gravitational acceleration, but she will be at a higher level in her progressive development of that concept. Her next teacher will begin with her further development from that higher level. Even now, you have heard that education seeks to develop "lifelong" learners. The Conceptual Development Model exemplifies how you are involved in putting students on that path.

Though the model can be taken to represent the overall picture of conceptual development, our concern now is focused on the strings of enabling concepts that you would be responsible for as a classroom teacher at any given grade level. So, as we continue with this discussion, consider the first cell of the model as representing the conceptual understanding that your student brings to the classroom. Similarly, consider the final cell, no matter how many enabling concept cells separate it from the first cell, to represent the desired conceptual understanding that should result from the educational experiences you provide.

ACTIVITY 4.4

Building a Conceptual Development Model: Seasons

In this activity, you will build a representation of a Conceptual Development Model. In order to complete the activity, you will need a stack of index cards.

- Label each index card with a different item from the list below:

Annual Events	Understanding Causes for Seasons
Characteristics of Seasons	
Relative Position of Earth and Sun	Recurrence of Personal Events

- Now identify the card that you believe would represent an initial conceptualization, and the card that would represent the concept being taught.

- The remaining cards represent Enabling Objectives, and we will come back to them in Activity 4.6.

Enabling Concepts The cells between initial conceptualization and complete understanding represent the sequentially arranged subconcepts which enable the progressive development of the concept. These *enabling concepts* are small, vital parts of the whole explanation of the concept. Although Figure 4.6 indicates two enabling concept cells, *the actual number varies depending on the complexity of the specific topic or concept.* Sequencing the enabling objectives so that one concept provides the foundation for the next is called instructional planning. Providing opportunities for experiences that exemplify those concepts is called . . . teaching.

Let us focus on the concept of shadows as our discussion example, and use the reasons for the seasons as your practice example as we have begun in Activity 4.4. The model of progressive concept development, illustrated in Figure 4.7 and based on research data of people's explanations for shadows (Kuehn & McKenzie, 1988), may help to clarify this important issue. An analysis of many explanations allows for the emergence of patterns of responses. The patterns from responses to questions about light and shadows have re-

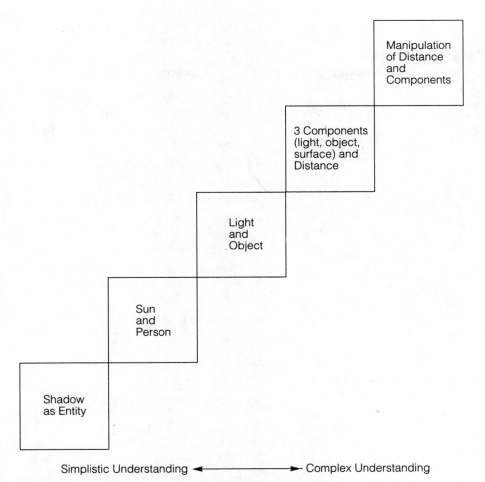

FIGURE 4.7 Progressive concept development for the topic "Shadows."

sulted in the development of this conceptual model.

From the responses people have given during interviews, the authors have found that some children perceive shadows to be entities in and of themselves. The explanations sound very much like the portrayal of shadows in the story of Peter Pan. As in Mark's explanation on page 80, a shadow is something that is observable, sometimes, and can be "put away" at other times.

Other explanations, such as Sarah's response on page 80, suggest a need for the presence of the individual person and the sun. The shadow is something that belongs to or is a part of an individual and is observable only when the sun is shining. A slight variation of this explanation requires the presence of the individual and the sun, but the sun is considered to be the source of the shadow.

Children like Brenton (see page 80), who have had opportunities to study or experience shadows in a more objective manner, generalize the light source and the object. No longer is the sun the only source of light nor is the person required. Any object can cast a shadow.

Chen Long

PHOTO 4.3 Understanding that they are the objects, these children explore changing the shadows they can form.

The more opportunities children have for manipulation of shadows, the more complete the explanations for shadows become. The responses include various light sources, objects, and surfaces upon which the shadow appears. In addition, the explanations, as seen in Angel's response (see page 80), involve the changing of shape, size, and location. The explanations become quite elaborate, as indeed, the concept is very complex.

ACTIVITY 4.5

Progressive Concept Development

Try answering these questions:

- What can you tell me about shadows?
- Where does a shadow come from?

- Can you make a shadow disappear? How or why not?
- Can you make a shadow appear where you want it? How or why not?
- Can you make your own shadow smaller? How or why not?
- Can you make your own shadow larger? How or why not?
- What is the largest shadow you have ever seen?

Now consider the following questions:

- Where on the progressive concept development for shadows does your overall response appear to be?
- Compare your answers with some of your classmates or ask some friends to answer the questions.
- How much diversity did you find?

ACTIVITY 4.6

Arranging the Enabling Objectives

When you have completed Activity 4.5, return to the cards you prepared in Activity 4.4. Consider again which you believe would represent the initial understanding and which the complete concept. Now arrange the remaining cards in a stepwise sequence to demonstrate the progression from initial understanding to complete concept. Compare your representation with the models developed by other students in your class. Can you come to a consensus of the proper order?

Facilitating Concepts It is important for teachers to recognize the significance of the enabling steps to the concept as illustrated in the model. Instructionally, however, identification of the *facilitating concepts* is crucial to the development of the concept. In order for students to move from one step to the next, something has to happen. A simple analogy would be a regular staircase. Just because you find yourself facing a set of stairs, you do not automatically move from one step to the next. There must be some reason or motivating force that gets you to move. Similarly, facilitating concepts are the ideas or pieces of information that are required in order for children's conceptualizations to move from one level on the progressive development of the concept to the next higher level. Without awareness of the facilitating concepts, the process is left up to chance; the development of the concept may be incomplete. The result is that the students' conceptualization may be inaccurate.

Let us focus again on the topic of shadows. For a child to advance an understanding of the concept from the notion that a shadow is an entity to the idea that a shadow is the result of the sun shining on a person, the child will recognize two things: (1) the need for the sun and oneself, and (2) that any person can produce a shadow. The order in which these two facilitating concepts occur is not as important as the necessity for both before progress can be made. In order for the child to advance to the third step in the model, he or she must understand two other facilitating concepts: (1) Not only the sun, but any light source will do, and (2) any object, not just a person, can cast a shadow.

Advancement to the next step in the model requires two more facilitating concepts: (1) Shadows have three components: a light source, an object, and a surface upon which the shadow will appear, and (2) the distance between the components is important. Progression to the fourth level where a child understands that shadows can vary in size and shape is dependent on these facilitating concepts: (1) Varying the distance between the components will change the size of the shadows, and (2) manipulating the components will alter the shape of the shadows. Figure 4.8 indicates the enabling concepts

in solid blocks, and the necessary facilitating concepts in dotted blocks. A scientifically accurate development of the concept requires that a child acquire an understanding of all facilitating concepts as the progress is made. If, for instance, the child's explanation for shadows allows for the manipulation of only two components—light and an object—for the production of shadows and the distance between those components, the predictions for changing shadow size and shape will be incomplete or inaccurate. An inaccurate explanation, or misconception, is due to the omission of an important facilitating concept. It is necessary that the child have the opportunity to recognize the importance of the surface upon which the shadow is formed. Providing opportunities for experiences that focus the child's attention on the various surfaces and the manipulation of the surfaces will facilitate the complete understanding of the concept of shadows.

Using the various explanations for any topic, a model can be drawn to illustrate the progressive development of that concept. A model appears in Figure 4.9.

ACTIVITY 4.7

Adding In the Facilitating Concepts

No doubt, you could see this activity coming all along. Label additional index cards with the facilitating concepts listed below. Now arrange them in the model. When completed, you will have a representation of not only the lesson you want to teach, but a means of getting there. Consider each of your facilitating concepts in terms of activities you might have the students complete in order to gain experience with the concept.

12 Months	Angle of Sun's Rays
General Holidays and Events	Weather Patterns
Distance between Sun and Earth	Orientation of Earth on Its Axis

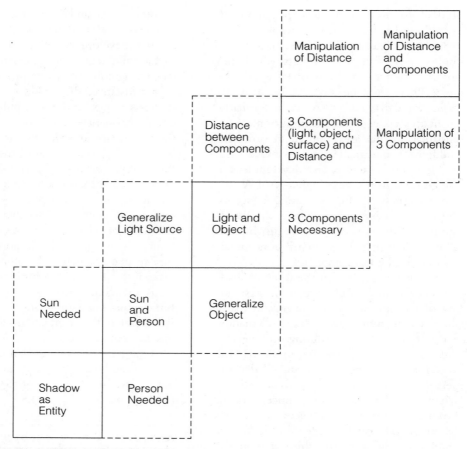

FIGURE 4.8 Relationship between Enabling Concepts and Facilitating Concepts.

Duration of
Daylight

Plant and Animal
Behavior

Instructional Implications of the Conceptual Development Model

An awareness of the enabling concepts that lead to the progressive development of a concept will help teachers identify long-term and short-term goals and instructional objectives. However, the facilitating concepts are the ones that identify the information necessary for children's development of the concept. Once the necessary information has been identified, teachers can design appropriate experiences that facilitate learning. The facilitating concepts are therefore particularly useful in curriculum development.

Where can curriculum designers find these facilitating concepts? Much of it is to be found through experience. Since curricula differ from region to region, it is almost impossible to provide a detailed set of materials. And since textbooks are typically written to be adopted throughout the country, they tend to be stronger on the enabling concepts and weaker on regionally appropriate facilitators of those concepts. However, facilitating concepts and the materials for

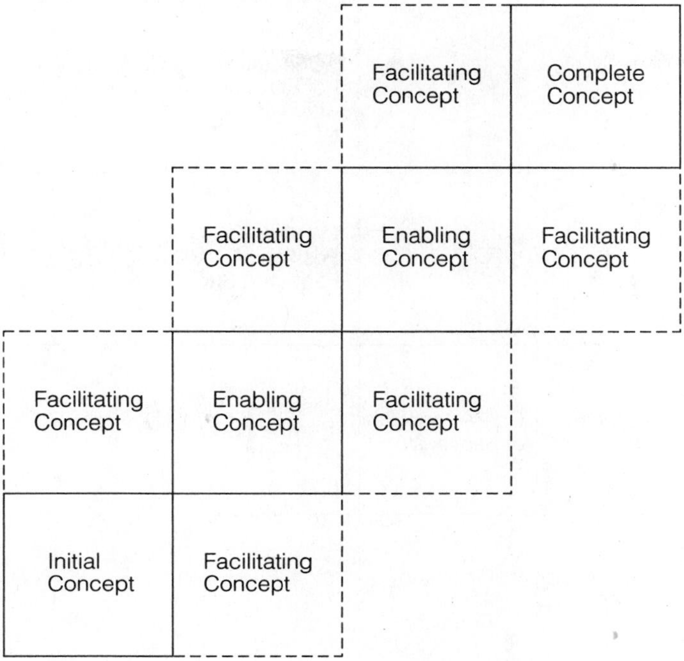

FIGURE 4.9 Conceptual development model.

presenting them can be collected by teachers themselves. Each year, select a few topics, develop sets of questions (see chapter 5 for directions), and interview children. It may take several years to collect enough information for the entire curriculum, but the process of collecting the information is well worth the time and effort. If the aid of other teachers in collecting this information is enlisted, the process will be faster. It is essential that you understand that your students are the best source of information. Talk to them, and more important, *listen* to them. Activity 4.8 provides some practice with this idea.

ACTIVITY 4.8

Matching Responses to the Conceptual Development Model

It is time for you to try analyzing children's responses to questions in order to identify where their explanations are in respect to the progressive development of a concept. Enabling and facilitating concepts for the topic "seasons" are presented in Figure 4.10. Does your index card model match Figure 4.10?

Read the six children's responses to the question "Why do seasons change?" Compare their explanations with the given concepts related to the understanding of seasons. Where along the progressive development of the concept do they appear to be? And identify each as representative of

initial concept,

enabling concept,

facilitating concept, or

complete concept.

For example, Jack's response is representative of the facilitating concept, general holidays and events.

Why do seasons change?

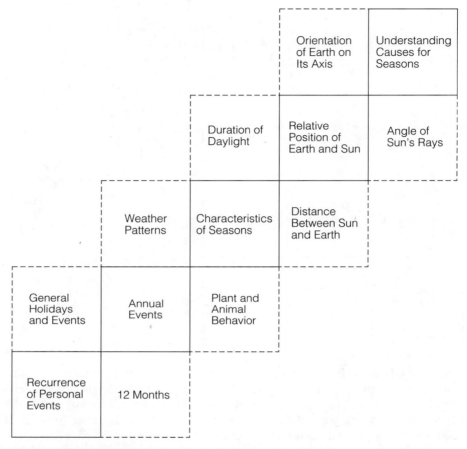

FIGURE 4.10 Progressive concept development for the topic "Seasons."

Jack: So at Christmas it snows and on the Fourth of July it's hot and we can go to the beach.

Sonya: So we don't get bored.

Tyrone: The earth revolves around the sun and is tilted on its axis.

Juan: Because they help the earth grow its plants and help us in certain ways with food. Just the way it is so we can live in the environment.

Joel: The reason the seasons change is because plants and animals and we need it to change because if there wasn't spring the plants wouldn't grow. If it wasn't for winter, the animals wouldn't hibernate. If it wasn't for summer, we wouldn't be able to cool ourselves off by going swimming.

Gina: Because of the weather.

Quick Review

Although the model represents the complete development of a concept, it should be noted that incomplete understanding of concepts is what occurs most often in children's science and is to be expected at the elementary and middle school level. As children continue to construct knowledge by revisiting the topics of study in science throughout their schooling and through new personal experiences, their understanding of any given concept will change, progressively becoming more complete.

As a classroom teacher, the particular concepts or topics that you teach in any given subject represent the steps in some strand of enabling concepts that lead from an initial understanding to a complete understanding. If you use the interviewing techniques discussed in chapter 5 to find out exactly what your students know about a concept, you will be able to establish just where along the strand each student is functioning. From there, it is your job to present the facilitating concepts that will allow each student to take the step from one level to the next. If all of the information seems overwhelming to you, take some time to align it with the Conceptual Development Model. The result will be a virtual blueprint of teaching for conceptual change.

CONCLUSION

As teachers working with children, incomplete understanding and misconceptions related to the topics of study in science are to be expected. Through our examination of "children's science," we know that children construct their own explanations for the world around them based on experiences in formal and informal educational settings. They use their unaided senses to make observations, and their perspectives are often humanistically centered. The "informational pieces" are individually selected and applied. Consequently, the explanations vary from one person to another and are not necessarily in agreement with the explanations espoused by scientists.

The explanations constructed by the children, whether or not they are aligned with others, are personally satisfying. At the very least, they work well for the time being, and until the children are willing to give up or modify the explanations, they will remain intact. Unless children become dissatisfied with their own explanations and find intelligible alternatives that are plausible and fruitful, conceptual changes will not occur.

It is important to keep in mind that adults also hold fast to many misconceptions. Some adults think that clouds are responsible for the phases of the moon and that the seasons result from the earth's varying distance from the sun. However, in the educational setting where conceptual change is of primary importance, the Conceptual Development Model provides a means of monitoring progress, that is moving from a level of misconception or incomplete understanding of the concept to an appropriate level of understanding. The model illustrates workable, logical increments that facilitate gradual change. Of key importance to teachers is knowing where each child is in relation to the progression of the concept. In the final analysis, it may be best summarized by Ausubel (1968): "If I had to reduce all of educational psychology to just one principle I would say this: the most important single factor influencing learning is what the learner already knows."

Once a teacher understands what children's science is and how it compares with scientists' science, then the problem of the discrepancy between intended learning outcomes and actual learning outcomes becomes clear. The problem is that children do not have blank minds waiting to be filled with ideas presented by the teacher. They come into the instructional setting with ideas and explanations that have been individually constructed from experience and interaction with many people. The solution to the problem, at least in part, and the educational implications of children's science may be found in Ausubel's insightful observation.

What children already know has a tremendous impact on what they will learn. Therefore, it is important, if not imperative, for teachers to determine what children know prior to instruction. Chapter 5, "Eliciting Children's Conceptions about Science," presents a direct and effective means of assessing children's knowledge for this purpose.

5 | | Eliciting Children's Conceptions about Science

The Purpose of Interviews

The Dynamics of Interviews

Conducting Interviews

Analyzing Interview Responses

Finding Time for Interviewing

Conclusion

Your Academic Roadmap

Study of this chapter should help you to understand the following concepts:

- The interview, a tool for designing lessons, is a noninstructional experience in which the student is the expert.

- Interviewing will provide you with information about individual beliefs and classwide conceptual tendencies.

- Effective time management will allow you to interview your students and, as a result, design more appropriate lessons and classroom experiences.

Where does a shadow come from?
It comes from your body, because your body makes it when it gets dark. A glow comes from your body, a dark glow.

—Jessica, six years old

THE PURPOSE OF INTERVIEWS

The classroom teacher is responsible for both presenting material that is appropriate for the intellectual level of the students and presenting it in a manner that the students can understand. The specific content of any particular class or subject area is usually determined by people outside of the classroom, such as school board members, state legislators, and authors of textbooks. Most of it is beyond the control of the teacher.

The method of presentation, however, is very much the teacher's concern. Consequently, it would seem reasonable that a teacher would need to be aware of what the students already know in order to design effective instruction. If you want to know what your students think or know about a particular topic, who would you ask? Would you check the teacher's edition of the science textbook? Would you look in your human growth and development book? Each of these could provide you with information about children in general, but not specifically about the children in your classroom.

Each classroom of children is different because the individuals are different. Nobody knows your students like you know your students . . . and only they know what they think. A textbook cannot tell you what is on your students' minds. The only way to find out is to ask. And more often than not, given the chance, they will tell you. The interview saves you from assuming that everybody has the same understanding, and allows you to find out what your students "know" in order to design instruction that will be most effective for them.

Teachers need to get information from the students they will teach in order to design effective instruction, just as physicians need to get information from their patients in order to prescribe effective and appropriate treatment. However, typical paper-and-pencil tests do not allow students to elaborate and explain what they know and want to express. The interview is an effective means for obtaining an understanding of your students' ideas about a concept because it allows them to verbalize what they know in a low-anxiety environment.

This chapter discusses the nature and design of the interview; conducting interviews; analyzing the responses and identifying their practical implications; and modifying the interview technique to meet your specific needs and situation.

THE DYNAMICS OF INTERVIEWS

Interviews are conversations initiated by one person to find out what another person knows about a particular topic or concept. Only recently has interviewing been used by teachers as a method to elicit information. You may not think of interviewing as a teaching method, but we consider it to be vital to the instructional process. After having conducted years of interviews with children and college students, we have validated the importance of this nongraded, noninstructional approach to finding out what students know. By the time you finish reading this chapter, you will be amazed at what children have to say, if only you are willing to ask.

The Nature of Interviews

Like scientists, children are curious about the world around them. In their struggle to understand the world, children construct their own explanations for how and why things behave as they do. These ideas are called children's science. The differences and similarities between children's science and scientists' science is of great importance to the teaching of science.

The interview is a technique specifically designed to elicit information and, in this context, elicit children's science. The interview is an informal conversation between adult and child that takes place in an accepting environment. It is intended to be nonjudgmental. The focus is not on right or wrong answers but to determine the child's understanding of the subject matter. The child's beliefs about the topic are acceptable responses, whatever they may be. The interview is noninstructional in the sense that the set of questions, although carefully planned, does not lead the child to a predetermined explanation of the concept or topic. The child's knowledge and logic are not directed or judged but elicited and accepted as they are.

The interview provides both the teacher and the student with a new awareness of the child's understanding of a concept. From the teacher's perspective, information is obtained that can be of critical value in the preparation of instructional opportunities. The student benefits from the fact that the teacher has a better idea of what needs to be addressed through instruction. In addition, the student may come to a clearer appreciation of his or her understanding of a topic or concept and may find that other students share the same or varying ideas.

These informal discussions between student and teacher will plainly delineate students' understanding into the categories of incomplete understanding, misconception, or scientifically correct understanding of the concept. This basic and easily obtained information can radically affect a teacher's science program with regard to class time, emphasis, and instructional methods.

Chen Long

PHOTO 5.1 Interviewing allows the teacher to understand each child's view of science concepts.

Challenges on Many Levels

The task of eliciting children's understanding can become very challenging. Two factors may contribute to this situation: (1) how receptive or unreceptive the students are to your questions, and (2) the sophistication of the concept or topic with which you are concerned.

Children for the most part are receptive to the interview and enjoy the opportunity to talk one-on-one with someone about their thoughts and ideas. Often, their explanations become quite lengthy. Even children who tend to be somewhat reticent in the classroom willingly accept the opportunity to engage individually in a conversation with the teacher. An environment open to the expression of ideas encourages and allows students to elaborate on their responses, providing much detail. The responses given in this setting are strikingly different from the usual clipped and concise responses so often heard in the classroom.

It can be expected, however, that some children will be reluctant to share their thoughts, or to take the chance of expressing an idea that might be considered incorrect. These children will attempt to elicit from the interviewer some kind of verbal or nonverbal cue to determine whether they are doing what the interviewer "wants" or that their answers are correct. Such reluctance may become evident to the interviewer when the child asks "Is that right?" or states his or her response with the inflection of a question. Still other children may avoid answering questions by saying "I don't know" or "Just because." This sort of response occurs more frequently with probing questions as opposed to information-based questions, which are discussed in the next section of this chapter.

Another response form that may indicate a child's reluctance to continue is the use of religious or supernatural explanations, for instance, "Because God made it so" or "That's the way Mother Nature works." There is not much more that an interviewer can do given a response of this sort if the accepting environment of the interview is going to be maintained. Finally, some children may be uncomfortable discussing the answers because they are unfamiliar with the topic of the interview. For example, "Where does the darkness come from?" is a question that the child may never have considered before or been asked. Given the constraints of the interview situation, coming up with an answer right away may be somewhat intimidating. As you will see as you practice with interviewing, this is true of adults as well as children.

The sophistication of the topic may also make eliciting children's beliefs a difficult challenge. An examination of the concept of living and nonliving illustrates this point. Living and nonliving initially appears to be a relatively simple concept. For the past several decades, it has typically been addressed in the elementary science textbooks three or four times in a kindergarten-through-sixth-grade series, and often was initially presented in the kindergarten- or first-grade-level books. Recent textbook series, however, have avoided the early presentation of the concept. Instead, the books present chapters on animals *as* living things, and plants *as* living things. The actual comparison of living versus nonliving is avoided. Upon closer examination of living and nonliving, the complexity of the concept becomes apparent. You can find this out for yourself by completing Activity 5.1.

ACTIVITY 5.1

Living versus Nonliving

Write down your answers to the following questions.

Is the sun alive?

Is a candle alive?

Is a fire alive?

Is a horse alive?

Is a bicycle alive?

Is wind alive?

Is a tree alive?

Is a leaf alive?

Is an apple alive?

Is a seed alive?

Is lightning alive?

Is a volcano alive?

Is a bird alive?

Is a feather alive?

Is an egg alive?

Now go back through the questions and your answers and ask yourself "why or why not?" for each of them. Finally, consider this question: How can you tell if something is alive or not? Did you find it difficult to answer some of the questions? Which ones provoked the most thought? Why?

If you were to compare your answers with others in your class, you would probably discover quite a variety of responses. That is because people use different criteria for making their decisions and supporting their responses. In this case, the variations may be due to different operational definitions of living and nonliving. For instance, does nonliving mean "dead" or does it refer to things that never were alive? Even in your own answers you may have found that you used different criteria when responding to different items. Did you use the same criteria for leaf as you did for feather? How about for fire and horse?

In order to get a better appreciation for the variety of responses that could be elicited, try answering each of the questions from an opposite perspective to that which you took the first time. If, for instance, you said that the sun is not alive, this time say the sun is alive and try to support your answer. Think of different criteria or additional information that, when used, could justify your response. Here's an example:

First Time: No, the sun is not alive. It is a burning ball of gases—a source of energy.

Second Time: Yes, the sun is alive. Scientists say it is not a new star or a really old star, but it is changing and will die someday.

ACTIVITY 5.2

A Second Look at Living versus Nonliving

In order to get a better appreciation for the variety of responses that could be elicited, try answering each of the questions from an opposite perspective to that which you took the first time. Write down your answers to the following questions.

Is the sun alive?

Is a candle alive?

Is a fire alive?

Is a horse alive?

Is a bicycle alive?

Is wind alive?

Is a tree alive?

Is a leaf alive?

Is an apple alive?

Is a seed alive?

Is lightning alive?

Is a volcano alive?

Is a bird alive?

Is a feather alive?

Is an egg alive?

Now go back through the questions and your answers and ask yourself "why or why not?" for each of them. Finally, consider this question: How can you tell if something is alive? Did you find it difficult to answer some of the questions? Which ones provoked the most thought? Why?

Activity 5.2 may help you appreciate the different kinds of "logic" used to explain naturally occurring phenomena. Whether the logic that your students use is correct or incorrect, according to scientists or other adults, it is nonetheless what they think, and therefore determines the point from which you, as the teacher, must design the instruction you will provide.

Perhaps the difficulty lies with the fact that specific characteristics of living things are often taught; there are from three to five characteristics typically presented in elementary science textbooks. However, no specific set of criteria for nonliving things is presented. In fact, many of the criteria for living things seem to exist in things generally considered to be nonliving. For example, try applying these characteristics of living things to *fire:*

1. All living things grow and reproduce.
2. All living things need oxygen and food.
3. All living things move and/or respond to stimuli.

So, is fire alive? Fire does start small and get larger. One fire can certainly cause other fires. It must have oxygen and does consume wood and other materials. Fire can move, sometimes very rapidly, and even jump roads. Fortunately, fire will respond to water and various chemicals and eventually die. So, alive or not alive?

It is also possible that the complexity of language affects the concept of living and nonliving. Many people use the word "living" as if it were synonymous with "alive," which varies in meaning from active, full of emotion and energy, sensitive, and teeming with life, to "not dead." Some would operationally define living as organic matter and nonliving as inorganic matter. That definition is helpful because "dead," which might be classified by others as a third category, can be distinguished from nonliving.

Children sometimes use the word living as if it were applicable to humans or anything that has humanlike characteristics such as facial features, vocal abilities, and appendages for movement. This conception of living is illustrated in the responses given by seven-year-old Tony.

> Is the sun alive?
> *No, it can't breathe. It can't talk. It has no arms or legs. If it were alive, it couldn't live in outer space.*
>
> Is a dog alive?
> *Yes, it moves its body, makes sounds, runs, smells, and plays.*

The word living, as used by biologists, involves characteristics in addition to those presented in elementary science texts, characteristics based on cellular structure. Biologists talk about the homeostatic internal environment and the highly organized structures within organisms. These characteristics are not directly observable, however, and are therefore not included in typical elementary science curricula. Once again, we return to the idea of children's understanding of science being a function of observable events.

The previous information may have helped develop an appreciation for the complexity of the concept of living and nonliving, but that does not explain why the complexity of the concept causes difficulty in eliciting an individual's understanding of the concept. The difficulty lies in the diversity of characteristics that may be used to make the decision of whether something is living or nonliving. The information presented thus far has provided a sampling of the possible characteristics. Perhaps during Activities 5.1 and 5.2, you and your classmates thought of other characteristics or information that allows for different perspectives of the concept.

Component Questions for Designing Interviews

It is fairly easy to elicit children's ideas about specific science concepts. Once you have selected a topic, identify a few questions related to the basic concepts involved. For ex-

ample, suppose that you want to find out what children know about night and day. You would probably want to ask these questions:

> What is day?
>
> What is night?

At this time you are looking for each child's own operational definition of the basic components of day and night. You may anticipate that the two will be distinguished based on light and darkness. Therefore, include questions addressing that basic criteria, such as the following:

> Where does the light of day come from?
>
> Where does the darkness of night come from?

Finally, ask a question eliciting an understanding of the relationship that exists between the components:

> What causes day to change to night?

In actual practice, all five of these questions would comprise the interview. As shown, the interview progresses from basic to more complex, though always allowing the student to take each step at his or her own level. The judgment of correct or incorrect does not enter the picture.

Now suppose that you are interviewing upper elementary/middle school students and want to extend the interview to elicit what they know about the changes in duration of night and day. You may want to add the following questions:

> How long is a day?
>
> How long is a night?
>
> Are all days the same length? Why or why not?
>
> Are all nights the same length? Why or why not?

You will notice that the interview includes a combination of questions with varying degrees of difficulty and probing. Questions such as "Are all days the same length?"

are simple, *information-based questions* and can be answered by a response of yes or no. Information-based questions are ones that elicit responses that provide specific information but do not address causation or relationships. Since an information-based question can often be answered with a yes or a no, the child has an equal chance of answering correctly or incorrectly, regardless of whether he or she knows the answer. You can probe and clarify the students' meaningful level of understanding by following up an information-based question with the questions "Why?" or "Why not?" For instance, in an interview about shadows, suppose you want to know whether the student understands how to manipulate the size and shape of shadows. The information-based question might be "Can you make your shadow smaller?" After the child responds "Yes" or "No," you ask the following appropriate *probing question,* "Why?" or "Why not?" This style of questioning elicits the student's ideas better than using a leading question such as "What would happen if you moved the light source?"

Questions such as "What causes day to change to night?" are more difficult and provoke more thought. These probing questions require that a student consider cause and effect, relationships, or justifications for a response. Probing questions are those which tend to get at the student's understanding of a concept rather than simply their knowledge of it.

Questions may also be classified as *convergent* and *divergent,* based on the kinds of responses elicited. Convergent answers seem to focus on one generally accepted idea. "Where does the light of day come from?" tends to be convergent since many children respond that the sun is the source of daylight. "Where does the darkness of night come from?", however, tends to be much more divergent, as evidenced by the responses that it elicits. In this case, many children will respond first with "I don't know." Then, when

encouraged and given time to think, they will say that it comes from, for example, the moon, the clouds, the other side of the world, outer space, or God. The range of answers expands rather than narrows, as there are many possible responses. As you might expect, the time needed for a child to respond to these divergent questions is greater than that required for the convergent type of question. Using a balance of the various types of questions helps children maintain their confidence and willingness to converse. The interviewer can then ascertain a clearer understanding of just what the child knows about the concept.

Seeking Generalizations and Operational Definitions

Since the perspectives are numerous, the development of the set of questions to be used during the interview needs careful attention. A closer look at the set of questions used in Activities 5.1 and 5.2 and those used to interview the children referenced in this chapter may be helpful.

The living and nonliving interview is composed of a series of specifically selected objects, some living and some nonliving. Among the living objects are plants and animals, whole organisms (tree, horse, bird) and parts of organisms (leaf, feather), as well as propagative structures (apple, seed, egg). The nonliving objects in the interview include naturally occurring and man-made objects. The naturally occurring phenomena exhibit various forms of energy that can be observed by children. Because children sometimes reply, "Bicycles are not alive; they are just something people ride," horse was selected as a mammal to be included in the set of questions.

The concluding question—"How can you tell if something is alive or not?"—asks for a generalizing statement and attempts to elicit the individual's operational definition of living. Once the definition has been stated, the interviewer can compare that definition to the responses given to the other questions. Sometimes the operational definitions, even though very simplistic or naive, are consistent with the responses to the other questions. For example, five-year-old Aline responds to an abbreviated version of the interview:

> Is the sun alive?
> *Yes, because it makes the flowers and plants grow.*
>
> Is a bicycle alive?
> *Yes, because it moves.*
>
> Is a tree alive?
> *Yes, because the sun helped it grow.*
>
> Is a candle alive?
> *I don't know.*
>
> What does it mean to be alive?
> *To be able to move and grow.*

Aline's operational definition based on movement and growth are supported in all of her responses. Admittedly, adults may distinguish between "making flowers grow" and "growing," but Aline does not. She is, however, consistent in her explanation of the concept.

An examination of ten-year-old Jeremy's responses to an abbreviated version of the living and nonliving interview, however, reveals a discrepancy between his operational definition and the specific object responses:

> Is the sun alive?
> *Yes, it shines and is yellow.*
>
> Is a candle alive?
> *Yes, when it keeps burning; no when not burning.*
>
> Is a bicycle alive?
> *No. It can't grow and doesn't eat.*
>
> What does it mean to be alive?
> *When your heart beats and your brain works.*

You may have thought that the older child's responses would have been more consistent with one another or with the operational definition, but that is not substantiated

here. In order to determine a child's understanding of this sophisticated concept, it requires asking a series of questions about specific objects in order to identify a pattern being used, and asking for an operational definition in order to make a comparison between the pattern and the generalizing statement.

Thus far, the construction of interviews has been examined, piece by piece, including an in-depth look at the concept of living and nonliving. You have even had personal experience with the interview on living and nonliving in Activities 5.1 and 5.2. The following is a transcribed interview, on the same topic, with Thomas L. It is included here to provide an example of an interview in its entirety. Notice the conversational flow and interchange between Thomas and the interviewer.

The Thomas L. Interview

Thomas, I want to ask you some questions. I want to know what you think about some things. First of all, can you tell me, is the sun alive?
No, I think it is dead. It is just floating. It is dead. The moon darkens it . . . Yes, it is alive. I think it knows when to cut on and off. Yes, I think it is alive.

Is a candle alive?
No.

Why not?
It is just made. I just think somebody made it.

Is fire alive?
It is just hot stuff that burns. It is very dangerous.

Is a dog alive?
Yes, definitely, a dog and a cat are alive.

Why do you say that a dog and a cat are alive?
They move and they talk in their own language. Let me see if I can imitate them. (He barks like a dog and meows like a cat.) *They run and they have got to be alive.*

Is a bicycle alive?
It runs but it is not alive. It will run. Its wheels are alive. Its steering is alive, but the rest of it isn't. Nothing is alive but the wheels.

Why do you think the wheels are alive?
Because it runs but the rest of it isn't alive.

Do you think the wind is alive?
This is a hard one. Let me think on this one. I am a fast thinker. (He thinks for a short time.) *The wind goes but it is not alive . . . a wind takes another one to blow it. I think that God sends it out of the tip of his little finger and blows it with his middle finger. That is what I think.*

Is water alive?
(He chuckles.) *This is a hard one; you're getting harder. I'll tell you something about water. When you jump in it, it splashes up to the top. I think that water spouts. It just runs and runs when you take a bath. When you put something in it, it splashes up and is full. Yes, I think.*

Do you think it is alive because of being fuller?
No, I think half of it is real and half is not. There has got to be a difference between it. Some water can do that and some cannot do that and some can.

What can it do?
I think that swamp water and sulphur water in West Virginia will not do it, but I think that some water is alive. It is alive because it moves.

Is a tree alive?
Let me tell you a story. Sometimes in commercials they make a tree alive with eyes that can see and they can talk. The trees outside are dead but they live. They are asleep everyday. They want to walk, and move, and talk, and see but they cannot because they are stiff. It is a living thing. I would be sad if someone stuck a nail in the tree.

Is a leaf alive?
I think a leaf is dead.

Why?
I think the wind blows it. It is just a leaf you can crush.

Is an apple alive?
Let me start a story. A little boy's mother asked him what is red and has four babies in it. He went for a walk to think about it. He asked the mailman and he could not tell him what was red and has four, five red things in it. Then he asked a farmer and he said he didn't know but gave him an apple. The boy went home eating the apple. He told his mother he didn't know the answer to the riddle. She said, "You're eating it." She cut the apple open and inside showed him the five seeds and how they looked like a star. It is round and red. The one with seeds is the mother and the one without the seeds is the daddy. They are parents. A daddy apple and a momma apple were started when the world started and I guess it just kept going.

Is a seed alive?
Yes, I think God placed a little star with seeds in it in a momma apple.

Is lightning alive?
That is a tough question. I am afraid I can't help you on that but I know what the noise of it is. The noise is the angels bowling and angels moving furniture.

Is a volcano alive?
That is very easy. I am glad you asked that. Dinosaurs have a place where they lived and I think the volcano killed the dinosaur. I think the fire killed the dinosaurs. The dinosaurs came from South Carolina, North Carolina, and different parts. The volcano killed the dinosaurs. The volcano is arrested so they can't do nothing. The dinosaur would break the volcano and if a dinosaur smashes it, it is dead but if it doesn't, it is alive.

Is a bird alive?
Are these all dinosaur questions? Yes, I think the bird is alive.

Why?
He has to be alive because he moves. Some

are dangerous and some are not. If he lies and does not move, he is dead.

Is a feather alive?
They move in action to make them fly. If a dog had feathers on his ears, he could fly. It is moving to an action so if it is on the wing, it is alive, but if it isn't, it is dead.

What does it mean to be alive?
This is getting tiring. This is the last question. The world spins around real fast so I think civilization and everything is alive.

What does it mean to be alive?
You're living, you're talking, you're walking, you're feeling. You can do anything you want to do as long as your mother and daddy agrees with it.

Although Thomas L. was only six years old at the time of the interview and not yet enrolled in first grade, he already has many ideas. Just as many children are quite willing to do, he eagerly shares his ideas, often in elaborate detail. Some of his ideas represent explanations he has been given by others and has accepted. Many of the explanations are the result of his synthesis of personal knowledge and experiences. It is important to realize that children, even very young ones, think and construct their own reality as they try to understand the world around them. Take some time to discuss the Thomas L. interview with some of your classmates. As a teacher, what would be the implications of Thomas's explanations? Which of Thomas' ideas would you say are consistent with scientific notions of living and nonliving?

Quick Review

The classroom interview is a very specialized instructional tool. It is based on a relaxed and accepting dialogue between the student and the interviewer. That nonjudgmental atmosphere must be established by the interviewer, and can often be difficult to maintain because children will inevitably offer some

sort of idea or delightful explanation that simply takes the interviewer completely by surprise.

The challenge when interviewing children is to keep the interview conversational and noninstructional. *The student is the expert when answering your interview questions.* We highly recommend that you practice interviewing classmates and friends before you interview children. Even your friends will reveal ideas (often misconceptions) that you would not have expected to hear. Practice will prepare you for what children will have to say.

The question types to use are information-based, probing, convergent, and divergent. These four types will enable you to elicit an astounding variety of conceptualizations. As you conclude an interview, always try to include a question that is intended to allow the student to draw a conclusion based on his or her own thinking. Having elicited an operational definition or generalization of the concept, do not turn right around and challenge the student with any inconsistencies that may be apparent. Remember, the interview is a tool by which you gather information to design instruction. Using the interview as a testing strategy will ultimately erode the accepting atmosphere that is so necessary to a conversational exchange of ideas.

CONDUCTING INTERVIEWS

As we have emphasized, the environment established by the interviewer is important. Since the interview is not an instructional opportunity or an evaluation situation for which grades will be assigned, it is important that the interviewer communicate that same idea to the person being interviewed. The purpose of the interview should be communicated in such a way that anxiety is reduced and the interview is seen as a conversational

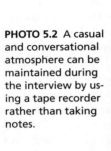

PHOTO 5.2 A casual and conversational atmosphere can be maintained during the interview by using a tape recorder rather than taking notes.

setting. Also, particularly if you are going to interview children as part of your pre-service teacher education program, be sure to discuss your plans with your cooperating teacher and/or principal. Take the necessary precautions to ensure the students' rights of privacy. With that in mind, here are some guidelines to help you as you begin interviewing children.

1. Begin the interview with an explanation of purpose; for example, "This is not a test. I am not looking for right or wrong answers. I am just interested in your ideas about some things."

2. Record the interview with a tape recorder so that you are not preoccupied with writing down the responses.

3. Be a good listener. Use nonverbal and brief verbal cues to indicate that you are listening and following the person's thoughts. Nod your head, smile, and make simple statements such as, "hmmm . . . ," "interesting," "okay!"

4. If the child responds, "I don't know," ask the following question: "If you were going to guess, what would you say?"

This statement from the interviewer communicates a willingness to accept any answer and is very effective in eliciting a response from the child being interviewed. The child has been given license to "try out" an answer even if he or she has never verbalized it before this situation. *Note:* this suggestion communicates a very different message than if you had said, "Take a guess," which is not a suggested probe.

5. When a child gives a response that does not seem clear to you, use a spontaneous probing question (a probing question that was not written into the original interview). Instead of restating the explanation in your own words, which may actually influence the child's thinking, ask for clarification. Examples of spontaneous probing questions might include "Tell me more," "Can you explain that to me?" and "What do you mean by . . . ?"

6. Remember, this is not an instructional situation. (As teachers, we are naturally inclined to "teach.") Refrain from pointing out or labeling inconsistencies in the

responses. For example, if a child during an interview on living and nonliving uses the characteristic of breathing as the main criteria for decisions about the sun, candle, fire, dog, bicycle, water, and tree, but says that a volcano is alive ". . . because it erupts," do not say, "You said that things are alive because they breathe and other things are not alive because they do not breathe. Now you say that a volcano is alive because it erupts." This type of response shows that you are being judgmental of the ideas expressed; you are implying that there are correct and incorrect answers. Instead, try responding in a nonjudgmental manner but allowing the child to recognize his or her own inconsistency. Say, "Does a volcano breathe?" After the child has responded with a yes or a no, then ask, "Is a volcano alive?" Do not insert the word "then" in the last question. If you do, you are imposing your logic to the response, not allowing the child to use his or her own logic. Often, the child will not recognize the adult-perceived inconsistency, because that is part of the difference between children's science and adult's science.

ACTIVITY 5.3

Practice Interview

Now that you have read about interviews, their nature and design, it is time for you to try interviewing. Select one of the sets of sample interview questions in chapter 14, "A Compendium of Resources for Teaching Science" (see page 299), and interview one of your classmates, a roommate, or a friend. Tape-record the interview. Listen to the recording and reflect on the effectiveness of the interview. The purpose of this activity is to allow you the opportunity to

ask the questions in a manner that establishes an environment that is conducive to the expression of ideas. What dimensions of the interview went well for you? What changes will you make before interviewing children?

ANALYZING INTERVIEW RESPONSES

Once the interviews are conducted and transcribed, it is time to analyze the responses. The teacher must consider the patterns of responses that emerge as well as the specific answers. Planning instruction for the group will require attention to classwide conceptual tendencies. Individual needs, however, must not be ignored when a lack of understanding is clearly indicated, even though it may not reflect the overall belief of the class. When analyzing the responses, you, as the teacher, need to look for (1) individual *and* group patterns of understanding, and (2) categories of responses relative to conceptual development.

Individual and Group Patterns of Understanding

How you analyze the responses depends on your purpose for the interviews. You may be searching for a particular child's understanding of a topic or concept, in which case you need only one child. As a means of developing a better appreciation for children's science, you may be interested in knowing what youngsters think about things. If this is your purpose, you need to talk with many children of differing ages, backgrounds, and experiences. Perhaps you are looking for the diversity of beliefs held by the students in your classroom. This diversity may apply to your students' ideas regarding very specific questions, such as "How can you tell if it is spring?" or very broad concepts, such as "Why do the seasons change?"

On the other hand, you may be interested in the progressive development of a topic or concept, in which case you are comparing responses of many children of differing ages. The interviews with six-year-old Shawn and eleven-year-old Jody, transcribed below, are two examples that could be used for comparison to facilitate the progressive development of the concept of day and night. (Keep in mind that for a satisfactory understanding of the progressive development of a concept, you would need to look at many students' responses.)

Shawn, six years old

What is day?
Day is when the sun is out and I get up and eat and I go to school.

What is night?
It gets dark. The moon comes out and people sleep.

Where does the light of day come from?
The sun.

Where does the darkness of night come from?
Clouds. Clouds cover up the sun and the moon comes out.

What causes the day to change to night?
The clouds.

Why does the day change to night?
So people can sleep.

This child explains day and night in terms of personal activities conducted during daylight hours and nighttime hours. There is nothing to suggest that the child has any knowledge of the earth's rotation. Instead, the movement of clouds is used to suggest the changing of day to night as well as the source of darkness. The last response suggests that naturally occurring phenomena exist for the benefit of humans. The expla-

nations may be said to reflect the use of directly observable events and personal experience to explain phenomena.

Jody, eleven years old

What is day?
Day is when the sun comes up. It's light outside.

What is night?
Night is after the sun goes down. It gets dark and the moon is in the sky.

Where does the light of day come from?
The sun.

Where does the darkness of night come from?
I don't know. I guess it's just that the sun isn't there. The darkness is just in the sky.

What causes the day to change to night?
The earth rotates. It turns. When we are having day, it's night on the other side. And when it turns we have night and it's day there.

Why does the day change to night?
Because the earth rotates.

This child explains day and night in terms of light or darkness but avoids personal involvement. Darkness is attributed to the absence of light. The change between day and night is related to the earth's rotation. These explanations are much closer to the scientific explanation for day and night. Since Jody is much older than Shawn, perhaps it would be appropriate to assume that she has studied the concept of day and night.

Children, in their struggle to understand the world around them, construct explanations for naturally occurring phenomena. The concepts constructed reflect perspectives that range from very naive views, due to limited experiences, to very complicated views, resulting from the combining of many diverse experiences. Whatever the perspective may be, the responses are quite interesting and often entertaining. For example, seven-year-old Marie has a unique explanation for day and night:

> What is night?
> *When it gets dark and the stars and moon come out.*
>
> Why is it dark at night?
> *Because you can't go to sleep in the daytime.*
>
> Where does the darkness come from?
> *Black paper.*
>
> What is day?
> *White paper and when the sky is clear, it's blue paper.*
>
> What makes the day change to night?
> *They change the paper.*

Marie presents an interesting explanation of day and night. The "they" she refers to is left vague but may be the same "they" as adults refer to when saying, "You know what they say . . ." Important to this interview is the child's use of paper to explain the difference between night and day. If we consider the age of the child and the experiences she is likely to encounter in school, it is reasonable to assume she has constructed pictures using different colors of paper or has changed white paper using coloring markers to represent daytime and nighttime scenes. Transferring information that has been useful in one situation to another is a frequent means of constructing personal explanations for natural phenomena.

Personal experiences are reflected in the following interviews related to the topic of weather. As the age of the children increases, we see a broadening of the perspectives, perhaps of the environment, and of the experiences themselves.

Katie, three years old

> What is thunder?
> *Thunder is a warning to all of the animals in the park that it's going to rain.*
>
> Where does this noise come from?
> *From God so all of the animals won't get wet.*

> What is lightning?
> *That is when the lights in heaven need to be changed.*
>
> What is rain?
> *When the water pipes in heaven break, like they did at my grandma's.*

Katie's world probably is limited to her home, her neighborhood, and her extended family. The explanations she uses in response to the questions are based on directly observable events from her own small world.

Renee, five years old

> What is thunder?
> *Thunder is when God becomes mad at all of the angels.*
>
> Where does this noise come from?
> *This noise comes from God.*
>
> What is lightning?
> *The noise that the angels make when they are crying after God has yelled at them, like my mom does to me.*
>
> What is rain?
> *The tears of God and the angels crying after they have made friends again.*

Renee, as many, very young children do, uses religious explanations for the source of or cause for natural phenomena. However, the analogies she uses, relating the emotions and interactions of angels and God to herself and experiences with her mother, are quite endearing.

Jeremy, eight years old

> What is thunder?
> *Noise when it rains.*
>
> Where does it come from?
> *From God.*
>
> Why does it make that noise?
> *From the lightning, because God's in the sky.*
>
> What is lightning?
> *The sky.*

What makes the lightning?
The clouds because God's there.

What is rain?
It comes down.

Where does it come from?
When the cars and houses get washed.

Is there water in the sky?
Yes.

How does it get to the sky?
When we use our sink, it goes up in the sky so our houses and cars can get washed.

Jeremy has his own version of the water cycle. Experiences from his daily or weekly routines have been incorporated into his explanation. While Katie's and Renee's responses use a very personal reference when explaining natural phenomena, Jeremy's responses reflect the philosophy that the world exists for the benefit of humans.

Todd, fifteen years old

What is thunder?
When two clouds crash. Deals also with voltage and current.

Where does it come from?
Turbulence in the air and particles collide.

Why does it make that noise?
From static electricity.

What is lightning?
Static electricity.

What makes lightning?
Electrical currents crashing into each other.

What is rain?
Rain is caused by high pressure causing humidity.

Where does it come from?
The sky.

Is there water in the sky?
Yes. The humidity.

How does it get into the sky?
Through transpiration.

Where does the rain go?
To the ground and some evaporates.

In this case, Todd's experience is his study of weather and electricity and his acquisition of vocabulary. The interview responses are filled with "scientific vocabulary," words such as voltage, current, high pressure, and transpiration. Todd has learned the words and knows, for the most part, the topics to which the words are related, but unfortunately, his responses do not suggest that he understands the concepts.

In each of these situations, the child has constructed his or her own explanations for natural phenomena. There may be some similarity in the explanations, but the differences in children's explanations are of great importance. On the other hand, the following responses from interviews on shadows provide an example of the diversity that might exist within a single classroom. All of the following were given by seven-year-old children while responding to the question, "What can you tell me about shadows?" The question attempted to elicit very general information about the topic and was used to begin the interview.

Raynard: They are black. Sometimes it gets scary. When you move in the light, they move.
Melanie: Yes, they can scare you and become ghosts.
Julian: They're not alive.
Albert: Wherever you go and the sun is shining on you, your shadow follows you.
Mandi: Shadows are what people make when they walk in the dark.
Louis: You can make a shadow in the light but you can't make a shadow in the dark.
Steven: You look at shadows and they can be longer or shorter, skinnier or fatter, and sometimes you don't see

anything at all. And shadows, when you spread your legs, it looks like you spread your legs farther. And when you go to Kmart, you take your shadow. And when the sun and the dark's put together, it makes shadows.

These seven children present quite a variety of perspectives. Some responses suggest that shadows are objects that exist constantly, while others suggest that shadows are created under precise conditions. The conditions for the appearance of the shadows vary and even contradict one another. Most of the responses mention the sun as the light source and do not generalize beyond that particular source. Only one child talks about the shadows varying in size and shape. Does this bring into question the typical assumption that all the children entering your classroom share the same level of conceptual understanding? Certainly, knowing that such a disparity exists would affect the instructional planning that a teacher might do.

By looking at the responses given by older children, different patterns emerge and other comparisons can be made.

> **Dayna (eight years old):** They aren't real; they are just a reflection of yourself.
>
> **Stephanie (eight years old):** Shadows are pictures of you that you can't touch.
>
> **Bruce (eight years old):** Shadows are dark and they only come out at night when the lightbulb is on.
>
> **José (nine years old):** Well, you and light make it and it's the way the light shines on you. It's the empty spot where there isn't any light.
>
> **Toby (ten years old):** The sun is in front of you and the shadow is in back of you. It is an image of yourself.

> **Erin (ten years old):** A shadow is a light or a dark light that is covering over something that makes a black or gray spot.
>
> **Meghan (ten years old):** They are dark and they float. They can block you from the light.

The variety of explanations equals the number of people being interviewed. Although one child still refers to shadows as a product of the sun and oneself, many others have not restricted the light source to the sun. The words they use when describing shadows—"reflections," "images," and "pictures" of oneself—are much more sophisticated. They also speak of "empty spots," "gray spots," and "dark light" in attempts to describe the absence of light. None of these children mentions in the first question of the interview a surface upon which the shadows appears; in fact, one child describes shadows as floating. Of course, finding out that a multitude of perspectives exists within your classroom is not enough. You need to do something with that information. As the next section explains, categorizing those various responses may be your next step.

Categorizing Responses Relative to Conceptual Development

Up to this point, the interviews have been analyzed in terms of patterns of responses. The differences and similarities that have emerged represent important information for teachers when designing instruction to fit the needs of individuals as well as entire classes. In this section, the focus shifts to the classification of responses according to accepted explanations for natural phenomena; in other words, comparing children's science to scientists' science.

When analyzing interviews, the responses may be classified relative to the conceptual development of the topic. The responses given by children will tend to fall into one of three categories:

1. *Misconception:* The belief expressed by the student is not supported by scientific information. The student's response is incorrect or undeveloped.
2. *Incomplete understanding:* The explanation given by the student is partially correct but incomplete. In this case, the student understands part of the concept but is not able to apply his or her understanding correctly in all situations.
3. *Complete understanding:* The student's explanation of the concept matches with the accepted, scientific views.

To illustrate the three different categories, the following explanations are answers to the question, "Is a leaf alive?"

Sammy: No, it's just part of a tree.

Sammy does not recognize the leaf as a living object. Without examining responses to additional questions, it is difficult to tell whether or not he even knows that trees are living. As is, the response is an example of a *misconception.*

Deborah: Well, it grows, but it doesn't reproduce, so no.

The explanation given by Deborah indicates that she knows, correctly, that living things grow and reproduce. She fails, however, to apply the second criteria correctly. She applies "the ability to reproduce" to a part of the living organism rather than to the entire organism, which, in this case, is a tree. Her response is an example of an *incomplete understanding* of the concept.

Sidney: When it is green and on the tree, it is. When it is brown and has fallen to the ground, it isn't.

Sidney has used observable characteristics associated with leaves and given consideration to the possibility of death of a living thing. His response, although limited to an isolated object, illustrates a complete understanding of the concept. How would you categorize the responses to Activities 5.1, 5.2, and 5.3?

As we continue to emphasize, children constantly attempt to make sense of the world by constructing explanations based on personal knowledge and experiences. In view of this, it is rare that a young person would have a complete understanding when it comes to many naturally occurring phenomena and it would be inappropriate to expect them to do so. Textbooks often try to supply the scientific basis for natural phenomena; however, they are unable to account for each child's personal experiences. The classroom teacher who interviews his or her own students can determine the degree to which each student has developed an understanding of a given concept or topic. Combining this information with textbooks and other educational materials allows the teacher to design and present the most appropriate instruction for his or her students.

ACTIVITY 5.4

Interviewing Children

It is time for you to interview some children. Select one of the sets of interview questions found in chapter 14. Following the guidelines that have been presented in this chapter, interview three children. You might want to talk with children of approximately the same age, in which case you can examine the diversity of beliefs that might be found in a single classroom. Perhaps you would prefer to talk with children of various ages and compare their diversity of explanations. Either way, you will have the opportunity to collect your own data. Transcribe the interviews, categorize the responses, and share them with others in your class. The exchange of responses can be entertaining and help you broaden your perspective with regard to the way children perceive the world around them.

Identifying Instructional Implications

So far we have described the interview, examined the construction of the interview, discussed and practiced conducting the interview, and analyzed the responses obtained. Now it is time to examine the educational implications of the interview.

If you were to build a house without paying attention to the condition of the ground or the strength of the foundation, it would be a tricky business. The possibility exists that everything would work out just right and the building would stand. Chances are better, however, that the structure would shift and settle, and perhaps even collapse. Interviewing students is an effective means of avoiding this situation when helping students "build" an understanding of a concept. By first determining just what the students know about a topic, a teacher can use such an awareness to design instruction that enables a student to add to an incomplete understanding or to correct a misconception.

The premise of this strategy is that the teacher can present a far more effective lesson when it is based on what the children in a particular classroom actually know about a topic. As an example of this practical application, look at an account of the preparation for a unit on weather done by a Wyoming teacher, Ms. Russell:

A Wyoming Teacher's Story

It is a typical winter day in Wyoming, cold and a bit windy, but sunny. Evidence of the fourteen-inch snowfall from two days ago remains, much of it in huge snowdrifts around buildings, trees, and fences. But the streets and sidewalks are clean and dry. Weather is an intense reminder of the ever present natural phenomena: change. In particular, changes in weather occur rapidly and often dramatically. It is definitely a major factor which influences everyone's lives on a daily basis. It is not so much the northern latitude that affects the weather patterns here as it is the high altitude and mountain ranges.

The children respond noticeably to weather changes, especially on stormy days like two days ago. But today the barometric measure is steady and the atmosphere within the school is back to normal. I am planning to start a new unit of study on weather in a few weeks and now would be a good time to find out what my second-graders already know about the topic.

The first-grade science textbook that my students used last year has a chapter on seasons and seasonal weather. Wyoming's seasons do not match what is typically presented in the textbooks, and I know that their teacher spent some time talking about local seasonal change. However, that does not tell me what the children individually learned then, or know now, about weather. In order to find that out, I need to talk with the children.

By interviewing the children individually, I cannot only find out their responses to specific questions, such as "Where does the wind come from?" but I can follow up the responses with appropriate probing questions which help to elicit their understandings of the concepts. I can use their responses to become aware of individual misunderstandings as well as to identify patterns of misunderstanding that the students have as a group. Using the information from these conversations, I can plan instruction so that it is appropriate for my students.

So far, many of the interviews have revealed supernatural explanations associated with the weather. Thunder, for instance, is "God, shouting at the angels" or "God, bowling." Rain is "Mother Nature's way of cleaning things." Animistic explanations frequently use phrases such as "Thunder is the clouds clapping hands," and "Rain falls out of the clouds when the clouds want it to."

Occasionally, I receive explanations that are almost poetic, such as Marie's response to the question, "Where does snow come from?"

There are white mountains where white bears live and they cut out snowflakes and they spread them all over.

It is not surprising that many of the students agree that "snow comes from the mountains." Their personal experiences seem to corroborate that view. Visits to the mountains provide evidence that the snow falls in the mountains earlier in the fall than it does here in town. Also, more snow is present in the mountains during winter, and roads through the mountains often close due to snow, some remaining closed until the middle of June.

Wind is another prevalent, and often dramatic, weather phenomenon in Wyoming. Children often associate it with the mountains also, at least as its source. However, the question, "Where does the wind go on a calm day?" produces more individualized and personalized responses. Janie suggests, "It goes to three little towns and then to Sheridan and then to Cheyenne."

The diversity that I found in the students' responses is interesting and challenging. Their explanations seem to be based on observable events and religious causes. That seems appropriate for second-graders. As I develop the unit on weather, I will have to include many opportunities for collecting data. The students will have to make daily observations of the sky and record observations regarding clouds, the shape and color of the clouds as well as the amount of cloud cover. They can also make daily records for temperature, precipitation, and wind.

I know that some students will be reluctant to give up their beliefs when it comes to certain aspects of weather. For example, thunder, although observable, is very abstract in it's source and therefore difficult for young children to comprehend. It is not appropriate for me to explain to these children that the sound is caused by the rapid expansion and contraction of air as lightning passes through. It will be satisfactory to help students make the association between thunder and lightning.

Yes, daily observation and data collection will be good for my students!

It is important to notice that Ms. Russell talks about identifying students' misunderstandings but acknowledges that these beliefs are appropriate for the children she is teaching. It is not necessary that second-graders have a complete understanding of weather phenomena. Some of the concepts associated with weather are difficult even for adults to understand. However, Ms. Russell now knows where to begin instruction so that each child can advance his or her understanding of the related concepts. Knowing that the students' explanations are based on their experiences, Ms. Russell realizes the importance of providing new and different educational experiences that allow children to reconstruct and further develop their own understandings of the topic.

The interview, when used as an instructional strategy, provides both the teacher and the student with a new awareness of the child's understanding of a concept. From the teacher's perspective, information is obtained that can be of critical value in the preparation of an instructional unit. The student benefits from the fact that the teacher has a better idea of what needs to be addressed through instruction. In addition, the student may come to a clearer appreciation of his or her understanding and find that other students may share the same or varying ideas.

When using interviews as an instructional strategy, there are six basic components to the overall design and preparation of an instructional unit. The first step in the instructional design is to develop the questions to be used in the pre-instruction interviews. With the concept-related questions prepared, the second step is to conduct the interviews to obtain an indication of the students' understandings of the topic. The information is used to enhance awareness from two perspectives. In the first, and most obvious, the teacher utilizes the information to determine whether the students involved understand the topic. Their responses should fall into the categories of incomplete understanding, misconceptions, or correct understanding as described earlier. The second perspective is that of the student. Feedback from the teacher, after the interviewing process is complete, may show the students that many of them share the same understanding of a particular topic. Moreover, the students may find that there are several, if not many, variations of conceptual understanding among their classmates.

At this point, the teacher is prepared for the third step, matching the results of the interviews to the text or other materials to be presented. It may be found that some material requires more emphasis than others. It may even be the case that previous material must be retaught before the newer concept can be addressed. In any case, the teacher has the information necessary to match the particular group of children in a class with the materials available.

Development of appropriate questions and activities to guide students through an exploration of the concept is the fourth step. The teacher can now tailor activities to meet the specific needs of the students, needs that may not have otherwise been identified. For instance, it may become obvious that some students feel that the sun is alive because it is so often rendered in cartoons and advertisements with a face. In such case, the teacher will do well to avoid using anthropomorphic representations in any of the instructional materials that will be used.

With appropriate guiding questions and activities designed, the fifth step is to allow the students to explore the concept under consideration. The course of their explorations should provide them the opportunity to confirm their understanding, to add to an incomplete understanding, or to replace a misconception.

Finally, some sort of assessment is in order to determine the conceptual development progress that has taken place. In general, the assessment could take one of three forms: The teacher could provide a formal test of the material; the students could apply their knowledge in the form of a project or report; or the teacher could conduct post-instruction interviews.

The use of these steps provides a unit that allows the teacher to maximize class time by concentrating only on those areas identified through the interviews. With the information obtained through interviewing, the teacher need not waste time on concepts children already know. And just as important, he or she won't begin teaching lessons on a level that is too far above the students' understanding. Further, students have a clearer understanding of their own perceptions having verbalized them, and can now explore

FIGURE 5.1 The six steps for interviewing students for understanding

1. Construct the interview.
2. Conduct the interview.
3. Compare the responses to curricular materials.
4. Design activities and probing questions.
5. Allow students time for exploration.
6. Assess student understanding.

the concept in a more meaningful way with appropriate guidance from the teacher.

Quick Review

Teachers have little chance of making any impact unless they know what children think and why they think that way. In order to design appropriate instruction, teachers need to get information from their students. The interview is an effective means for eliciting that information. The teacher must consider the patterns of responses that emerge as well as the specific answers. Planning instruction for the group requires attention to classwide conceptual tendencies. Individual needs, however, must not be ignored when a lack of understanding is clearly indicated, even though it may not reflect the overall belief of the class.

ACTIVITY 5.5

Putting Together Your Own Interview

Now that you have had the opportunity to practice establishing the appropriate environment for interviewing (Activity 5.3) and actually interviewed children using given sets of questions (Activity 5.4), you are ready to try constructing your own interviews. Begin by selecting a topic for the interview, then identify the basic concepts or components that relate to the topic. Next, develop questions that elicit the child's operational definition, or what the

child knows, of those basic components. You need not develop a lengthy list, but attempt to develop a representative list. The next series of questions you need to write should ask about the relationship that exists among the components. In addition, you might wish to include questions that require the child to extend the concept or manipulate the components. It may be helpful, the first time through this activity, to work with a fellow classmate. Whether you work alone on this assignment or with one of your peers, it would be beneficial to have someone else review your set of questions and provide feedback. Keep in mind that the interview is not meant to be instructional and that the questions should avoid leading the child to some predetermined explanation of the topic.

FINDING TIME FOR INTERVIEWING

You might think that interviewing students sounds like a wonderful strategy, and you might realize its importance in designing appropriate instruction, but you do not have time to interview all of your students every time you want to start a new unit. And your point is well taken. Time is valuable. However, according to teachers who have used the interviewing technique with their students, the interview questions encouraged higher-level thinking and the students gave more complex and lengthy responses than are presented during usual class discussions (Kuehn & McKenzie, 1989).

Resource Personnel

Ideally, interviewing all of your students at the beginning of the school year as part of your diagnostic assessment program would be a plausible task. Admittedly, however, you may need to work with your school's science curriculum for a year in order to develop a strong set of interview questions. With that in mind, try to schedule interviews with four or five of your students each day. During the time that you are interviewing one student, you will have to have other tasks available for the rest of the class. If you are fortunate enough to have an aide, this would be a great time to utilize that person. If you have been assigned a student teacher, you may want to provide that individual with plans to implement while you conduct interviews. Of course, in either of these situations, it would be best to set up a quiet area in the classroom for interviewing the students. We are not suggesting that you leave the classroom. This can all be handled right there where the rest of the school year will be taking place.

Since many of those who use this textbook are pre-service teachers, we would like to make another suggestion. When you enter your student teaching semester, ask the cooperating teacher if you could conduct interviews with the students during those first weeks of the semester. In collaboration with the teacher, select a topic. After developing a set of questions, review them along with the cooperating teacher. Then, arrange to interview four or five students per day. The information that you collect will of course be valuable to the teacher. However, it will also provide you with an opportunity to practice interviewing an entire class in a setting that you will never have available again. Take note of what the rest of the class is doing. Look for ideas about what you could have students doing at this time. And certainly, if this is a school district in which you hope to teach, use the information you gather to prepare for your own classroom.

If none of the scenarios just described fit your particular reality, there are ways of effectively modifying the interview to maintain some of the benefits while not consuming as much class time. These modifications include sampling the class and modifying class discussion.

Sampling the Class

Interviewing each child in the classroom can be a very time-consuming task, especially if you have twenty-five to thirty children to interview. Though it may not be possible to interview each one, a wealth of information can be gained by interviewing four or five of the students. Select children with varying backgrounds and ability levels. Keep in mind that children construct their own explanations based on personal experiences and their own knowledge, and that informal education makes as much, if not more, of an impact as does formal education. Do not allow the identified differences among the children to influence the information you gain from the interviews. It is not always the academically able or academically successful students who have the best understanding of natural phenomena. Interviewing four or five students should present enough diversity to provide the teacher with a basis from which to work. The similarities and differences in the patterns that emerge will facilitate instructional planning.

In order to provide for the other benefits of the interview situation, the ones related to higher-level thinking and improved responses, the teacher needs to establish a system to assure that every child gets the individual attention that is inherent in the interview situation. Therefore, the sample of students interviewed for each instructional unit needs to vary.

Modifying Class Discussion

Another means of eliciting students' understanding of a topic prior to instruction is by beginning a class discussion with a question

Christine Ebert

PHOTO 5.3 What can you tell me about shadows?

that might be used to initiate an interview or that asks for a generalization. For example, a teacher might ask the entire class an open-ended question, "What can you tell me about shadows?" or "How can you tell if something is living or nonliving?" All students are encouraged to respond, and all responses are accepted as worthy contributions. No judgments regarding correctness are made by the teacher or by other students. The responses might be recorded, for the teacher's purpose of planning instruction, or for the students' purpose of providing a framework to which each student may individually add or subtract information as he or she deems appropriate. The alterations to the framework, of course, accompany instruction related to the topic.

This technique of questioning the entire class is suggested in addition to interviewing all students or a sampling of students because it serves as good feedback to the students. The children become aware of the similarities and differences among the explanations for how and why things behave as they do. Consequently, children have a personal need to reconcile these differences and are more open to instruction related to the topic. This technique may replace individual interviews,

if done in advance, because the situation will reveal much of the diversity present among the students and patterns will emerge that can be used to facilitate planning and instruction.

ACTIVITY 5.6

Topics for Class Questioning

For each of the topics listed below, write a question that could be used to elicit children's understanding in a class discussion format.

rocks and minerals	light
magnetism	energy
animal adaptations	cloud formation
plants	the solar system

Quick Review

It will be easy to identify time as the culprit that prevents you from interviewing your students. There are, however, ways to accommodate the already full schedule that you will face. It really goes back to an old saying, "There's never time to do things right, but always time to do them over." Avoid being caught in that trap. Use resource personnel to good educational advantage, plan your interviewing schedule carefully, or if necessary modify the interview as has been described here. We can tell you, from years of experience at the elementary, middle school, high school, and college levels, that making assumptions about what your students know (or, as discussed in chapter 4, have "learned") can be the first step toward a lot of lost instructional time. Sampling the class will provide you with some idea of the common experiences that students share and how those experiences have affected learning. Alternatively, questioning the class as a whole, allowing responses from a number of children, and using the same accepting attitude that we discussed earlier in the chapter, will provide you with valuable insights for use in your instructional planning.

CONCLUSION

Like scientists, children are curious about the world around them. In their struggle to understand the world, children construct their own explanations for how and why things behave as they do. It is these ideas that are called children's science. The interview technique that we have described here is specifically designed to elicit children's science when conducted in a comfortable and accepting environment. The interview is a combination of information-based questions and probing questions, and is intended to be nonjudgmental and noninstructional.

Two factors affect how challenging the task of eliciting children's understanding can become: (1) the receptivity of the students, and (2) the sophistication of the concept. Children, for the most part, enjoy the opportunity to talk one-on-one with someone about their thoughts and ideas. The receptivity of the students will be a function of the atmosphere you establish. You will have to monitor the progress of the interview. If a child feels overly challenged or threatened, you will find it virtually impossible to continue. The sophistication of the concept is one of those factors that can affect how challenged the child feels. Study your curriculum carefully so that the questions you design for the interview are indeed representative of a conceptual level appropriate for your students.

Once the interviews are conducted, teachers can analyze the responses, looking for the individual and group patterns that emerge. The responses can also be analyzed relative to conceptual development and categorized as one of the following: misconception, incomplete understanding, or complete understanding of the concept. Remember that instructional planning requires attention to classwide conceptual tendencies without ignoring individual needs when a lack of understanding is clearly indicated.

By using interviews, teachers can plan and design instruction that enables students to add to, change, and develop appropriate explanations for natural phenomena. Teachers have little chance of making any impact unless they know what children think and why they think that way. The scientific explanations—children's science—that your children will provide are going to astound, startle, and delight you.

Section III Methods of Science Teaching for the Elementary and Middle School Grades

The four chapters in this section represent methods and techniques that characterize a teacher's interaction with students in the teaching of science. More than a dozen activities are presented throughout these chapters that may be used with students. It is important, however, to understand that our goals are that the reader be able to develop activities, to select strategies, and to determine the best course of instruction for the students in a particular classroom situation. We can make generalizations about students, but as a teacher you will not face generalizations—you will face real children. *It is imperative to know how to take a topic and fashion a lesson, rather than looking for an activity written by someone who never met your students.*

Chapter 6, "Developing the Skills of the Natural Investigator," demonstrates that the children who enter the classroom do so with a natural inclination to explain the world around them. This inclination works to the teacher's advantage, because the work of the scientist is motivated by this same inquisitive nature. Further, both children and scientists utilize many of the same skills to answer their questions. Developing these skills to the point of proficiency is a primary focus of the science program.

The skills discussed in chapter 6 become the basis for conducting scientific inquiry as detailed in chapter 7, "Investigations in Science." A common misconception held by many people is that anything done in science is an experiment. Rather, experimenting is just one of at least eight investigative approaches that scientists, as well as students, put to use in their work. Each approach is appropriate for a particular circumstance. Choosing the type of investigation that is best suited to what you want your students to experience is a crucial step in conceptualizing your science lessons.

Taken together, chapters 6 and 7 provide the means to (1) help students formulate questions into something that can be explored, (2) develop the skills necessary for that exploration, and (3) identify the format that would be best for the investigation. In essence, these represent the tools with which a teacher constructs a lesson. Chapter 8, "Designing Science Lessons," will help you in selecting and organizing the particular tools and materials needed to meet the demands of the science concepts to be presented. Two lesson formats that provide a dynamic and interactive approach to teaching are discussed.

Education does not end at the close of the school day. The school day represents only a small proportion of the time children spend learning. Chapter 9, "Making Real-World Connections," offers the opportunity to see that what happens in school makes relevant connections in the minds of students to the world outside of school. Some of these experiences bring the world to the classroom, and others extend the classroom to the world. This is a step that is often overlooked in formal systems of education, yet it is the one that makes learning meaningful.

6 | | Developing the Skills of the Natural Investigator

Children's Questions

Inquiry

Science Process Skills

Conclusion

Your Academic Roadmap

Study of this chapter should help you to understand the following concepts:

- Children are natural investigators, and naturally ask questions about the world around them.

- The inquiry approach as a teaching technique is the planned use of questions to initiate activity.

- Children who know how to conduct investigations and understand the value of the inquiry process are well prepared to independently find answers to their own questions in the future.

- Effective science lessons are planned to allow the use of multiple skills.

What I wonder about is why sometimes dogs are
wild and some not? And why do dogs chase cats?

—Ashley, six years old

CHILDREN'S QUESTIONS

Young children are fascinated by the world around them. They are curious about worms, caterpillars, ants, and other crawling things; about crickets, frogs, rabbits, and other creatures that hop; and about birds, butterflies, lightning bugs, and other animals and insects that fly. They collect pretty and not-so-pretty rocks, shells, and assorted man-made objects. They study the components of the world in order to make sense of it all—to construct for themselves an explanation of their world. And they do all of this without being instructed to do so. They do this naturally.

Youngsters frequently ask questions in attempts to clarify their own observations or to gain additional information. This inclina-tion toward inquiry is indicative of the nature of the learner. They do not yet have the skills to systematically investigate their environment even though the desire is there. But that is the purpose of science education—to help children acquire the skills necessary to investigate more thoroughly and systematically. So, in this chapter we examine some strategies for inquiry development: from formulating questions to transforming questions into investigative opportunities. Following that, we discuss each of the basic science process skills. These skills that are characteristic of the work done by scientists are the same skills that children use in what we have already referred to as children's science. The difference is that while children do not need instruction to be curious, they do need instruction and guided practice in order to develop these skills and use them in more systematic ways.

Most of us are familiar with the phase that young children go through at about age four when curiosity blossoms into questioning. With the advent of developing language skills, they question almost everything. Some of the questions are interesting or cute, perhaps because of the child's naivete or because the questions are the same ones we thought about as a child and haven't thought about since: "Why do dogs chase cats?" "Why do balls bounce?" "Why don't chickens fly?" Some of the questions can be irritating when it seems that time is short and many tasks need to be accomplished: "Why do I have to take a bath?" "Why do I have to go to bed now?" "But why do I have to go to sleep?" Often, these questions are perceived to be delay tactics and they might be just that. However, the child is also attempting to formulate an explanation for recurring events. The child knows what a bath is or what sleep is but does not yet understand the reasons for them. And some questions are intellectually challenging for the adults who are recipients of the questions: "Why do giraffes have long necks?" "Why does it thunder when it rains?" "Why do people die?" "Why" questions seek out explanations. The person asking the question expects the person listening to the question to answer it.

Questions such as "Why do we have to go to Grandma's house?" are reflective of the child's social-emotional personality development. In early childhood, children are working to establish their own identity and a sense of autonomy (Erikson, 1950). Many of their questions test the limits of that autonomy. Other questions such as "Why do worms wiggle?" are indicative of intellectual development. Children seek to make sense of their world by constructing plausible explanations based on their observations (Piaget, 1929). Due to limited experiences children often seek missing information by asking questions of others. Typically, these questions are in the form of "why?", expecting the person asked to supply missing information. As educators, however, this presents oppor-

tunities to channel that curiosity into constructive investigations.

Our examination of the science process skills later in this chapter will show that an "inference" is a statement that attempts to explain objects or interpret events based on observations. Those observations could have been made recently or sometime in the past. For example, suppose we observe holes in the leaves of a raspberry bush. In the past when we saw holes in the leaves, we also found Japanese beetles on the plant. Even though we have not yet seen any insects, we infer that beetles have been on the bush eating the leaves. We observe more carefully now, looking for the beetles, and sure enough, we find them. This further observation has verified our inference but was not necessary for the construction of the inference. The inference was constructed on the basis of our first observation combined with past experience.

The "why" question is an attempt by one person to request another person to use past experience, perhaps an accumulation of many experiences, to construct an explanation (inference) for the object or event in question. Using the same scenario, a novice gardener may ask someone with more expertise, "Why are there all these holes in the leaves of the raspberry bush?" The questioner does not have the information or experience with past observations, or does not recognize the past experiences as being related to the current situation, and therefore asks someone else to help generate an explanation for the event. Situations such as these are naturally prevalent with young children who have limited experiences or little practice at constructing inferences for themselves. They frequently ask "why?" in an attempt to gain information from others who have a broader experience base and more knowledge.

It is important to keep in mind that inferences may or may not match or be consistent with the actual situation. For instance, a closer examination of the raspberry bush may not have revealed the presence of Japanese beetles. They may have been there in the past but are not there now. It might have been a different insect that ate the leaves and left. We may never know for sure. The inference is acceptable in that it is based on observation. It just is not verifiable at this time.

The same applies to answers to questions. The explanation makes use of information available to that person at the time. The actual information necessary to answer the question and be consistent with scientific explanations may not yet be available to the person. For example, suppose the question is "Where do sunflower seeds come from?" A person who has seen sunflowers growing may answer the question by saying, "Sunflowers are very tall plants with large blossoms. In the center of the blossom are many dark seeds. If you cut down the flower after it blossoms, you can get the seeds from it." Someone else who has studied anatomy of flowering plants may go into a detailed explanation involving stamens and pistils and maturing ovaries. Another person, who has a very limited experience with sunflower seeds, may say, "They come from Wal-Mart and other stores." Each explanation is based on personal experience and is therefore a reasonable answer . . . for that person at that time.

Answers to "why" questions are even more difficult to verify. For instance, "Why do sunflowers have seeds?" The answer "So that sunflowers can reproduce" may come to our minds rather quickly. That answer is a result of our ability to understand cause-and-effect relationships and our generalized understanding of reproduction. What about the question "Why do birds lay eggs?" Is the answer "So that they can reproduce"? Or is the answer "The eggs are individually too large for three or four to incubate internally." The answer "Because God made it that way" may seem just as reasonable. The answer may depend on how much informa-

tion a person has to work with when constructing an explanation.

In some cases the answer to "why" questions may never be verifiable. For example, "Why do birds fly?" Does the answer involve structures particular to birds, such as feathers, wings, and hollow bones? Or do those things just list some required components for flight? Do the principles of aerodynamics need to be involved in the answer? Even with all this information, do we really know *why* the bird flies? Do birds have a choice in the matter? Do birds fly because they *want* to fly?

As teachers, we need to remember that science is not a collection of answers to questions, but the *search* for information that answers questions. Instructionally speaking, science helps students learn to answer their own questions. It is an opportunity to help children make observations and build knowledge bases from which they can construct their own explanations. The more opportunities they have for exploration and discovery, the more sophisticated their answers become. For instance, "Why is the sky blue?" would have different answers depending on the information that has been accumulated. Children might say,

> "Because God made it that way."
>
> "That's just the way it is. My dad said so."
>
> "As the sunshine comes through the sky to earth, it makes the sky blue."
>
> "Because light bends and reflects as it goes from space into our atmosphere."

The cartoon in Figure 6.1 exemplifies the nature of children to ask questions, and to answer them as well.

In actuality, scientists do not investigate the "why" questions. In pursuit of the answer to the "why" question, they transform it into questions that can be investigated. They break it down into questions such as

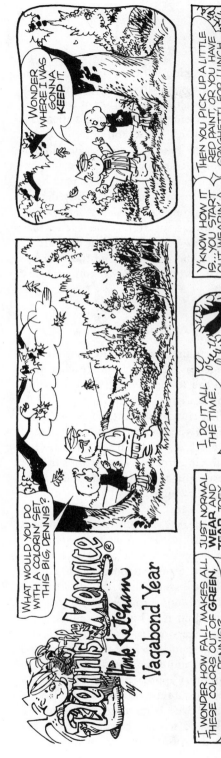

FIGURE 6.1 Dennis the Menace®. Used by permission of Hank Ketcham and © by North America Syndicate.

Christine Ebert

PHOTO 6.1 The variety of colors, textures, and shapes of seashells easily stimulate the inquisitive nature of children.

"what . . . ?" "how . . . ?" and "where . . . ?" In the example of why do birds fly, the questions become "What is necessary for flight?" and "How do birds fly?" These questions can be answered based on observation and evidence. Once the information is collected, then the investigator is no longer dependent on someone else to construct an explanation. The investigator can construct his or her own explanation for "why." And in many cases, the explanation remains an inference.

Children are natural investigators and naturally ask questions. As teachers, we have the opportunity to help children transform those questions into investigations. The inquiry approach to the teaching of science is just that: a means for transforming questions so that children can discover how to find answers through their own investigations.

INQUIRY

Inquiry is seeking information by questioning. An inquiry initiated by a child is usually expressed with the expectation of an oral response. For example, a child might ask a parent or a teacher, "What kind of bird is that?" or "What do bluebirds eat?" The child is hoping for information from someone perceived to be more knowledgeable than he or she. Or the inquiry may be initiated by a teacher. For example, to elicit what students already know about a topic, the teacher may ask, "What do you know about bluebirds?" Channeling the power of questions for instructional purposes is known as the inquiry approach.

The Inquiry Approach

After the children have shared their current knowledge of the topic, the teacher may continue the lesson begun in the previous paragraph using the inquiry approach, asking, "What else can we find out about bluebirds?" Following the question is a discussion during which a set of plans for discovering the missing information evolves. It is the use of a question to initiate activity that makes this an inquiry approach to the teaching of science.

The inquiry approach is quite different from the traditional lecture approach. The traditional approach is selected all too frequently as the teacher tells the children what they need to know, lists the information on the board, and provides verification by having children read books. Essentially, the teacher, in response to guidelines, chooses what is important, provides all of the missing information, and is done with the topic.

The inquiry approach is developmentally more appropriate for children than a lecture approach. In the beginning, the inquiry is guided by the teacher because the teacher asked the question. The goal, however, is to teach children how to direct their own inquiry, and this is done through practice. For this reason, it is important to teach children to phrase questions in a way that can be investigated. These questions will be used to initiate activities that in turn will provide new information. The activities for answering these questions may be characterized as investigation, research, or both.

Investigation Investigation is the search for information or solutions to problems by means of discovery. There are many forms of investigation, and those mentioned here are discussed in detail in chapter 7. Documenting, prediction testing, product testing, trial and error, reflecting, and experimenting are investigative means that pursue *information*. Modeling and inventing result in *products* of a slightly different nature. In each of these forms of investigations, the investigator is actively involved in the collection of data.

If the question were, "Which is the best paper towel?" a product test could be used to help children discover information necessary to answer the question. After establishing the criteria to determine what "best" means, (i.e., absorbency, strength, quantity, cost), the children can conduct tests to measure each brand of paper towel. The results can be compared and decisions can be made.

In order to answer the question, "Which color of M&M's candies do people prefer?" a different investigative form would be used: documenting. The children could create a questionnaire and conduct a survey to collect the information. Another documentation activity involves separating the M&M's by color and placing each color in a separate bowl. Then when people are asked to select ten M&M's, a record of which ones are chosen can be recorded. By having children predict the preferences in a subsequent round of collecting the information based on the observations from the first round, the investigation form becomes prediction testing. In any case, the question leads to activity that generates information and results in answers to the question.

Research Often times, research is used as a component of an investigation. To a great extent, scientists depend on research. They do not want to take the time to personally discover every scientific principle germane to their investigations. They are in pursuit of new information, and use the information obtained by research as a tool to facilitate that pursuit.

Research, then, is the pursuit of information previously discovered. Literally, the word research means to search again. Since it is often unlikely that as researchers we can go to the original source of information, we have to depend on documentation of the original search and any follow-up research. For example, suppose the topic is penicillin. Penicillin is a derivative of *Penicillium notatum,* a mold discovered by Alexander Fleming in 1928. It was later concentrated and studied by British scientists Ernst Chain and Sir Howard Florey. Although it is not possible to talk with any of these British scientists, much information can be found about penicillin by searching in secondary sources such as books or computers. Searching for information that has already been discovered, the product of previously conducted investigations, is research.

The advantage of research is obvious. Written information transforms human endeavor. Scientific research creates a body of knowledge common to a given culture and provides a means by which diverse cultures can come to understand one another. Rather than making it necessary that all scientific principles be discovered and rediscovered, research makes information readily available to investigators who seek to broaden that body of knowledge. One can learn from others rather than discovering everything for oneself.

There is also a disadvantage to research. The value of original thought or creative thinking of the general population is diminished as the value of researchers' ideas assumes the greatest recognition. People tend to put more confidence in what is read in a book than in their own ability to conduct meaningful and productive investigations. Frequently, people will say, "I know it is true because I read it in a book" or ". . . because I saw it in the newspaper" or ". . . because my teacher said so." Rarely do you hear, "I know it is true because I investigated it myself" or ". . . because I collected my own evidence and thought about it."

Combining Investigation and Research

A combination of investigation and research is as appropriate for young children as it is for the work of scientists. Revisiting the bluebird example, the search for answers to the question may take various forms but will likely include both investigation and research. Plans might involve observations of bluebirds as they nest and eat (investigation). Some time might be spent pursuing information that others have already discovered about bluebirds and has since been written in books or encyclopedias, found in the school library or a computer system (research).

Often, a combination of investigation and research yields the best information. In this situation, some research needs to be done in order to successfully conduct the investigation. Building or using the appropriate size and style of birdhouse and feeder will facilitate data collection, whereas using inappropriate materials will result in observations of different kinds of birds. (Of course, there is something to be learned from that, too.)

Let's identify another question to examine the various options for inquiry: "Why do some objects sink while others float?" If a child were asking the question of a teacher or another adult, the recipient of the question could simply give a personally constructed explanation for the concept: "Some things are made of materials that are less dense than water and they will float. Other things will sink." This response may be easily assimilated into the child's existing construct and satisfy the child's curiosity. On the other hand, the reference to density might have been more confusing than satisfying. It is also possible that the child could have asked someone who really does not understand the concept and so received an incorrect explanation. "Things that are lightweight float, and heavy ones sink." Nonetheless, this explanation could have satisfied the child's curiosity despite the fact that some very heavy objects (such as cruise ships) float quite nicely.

Another way of answering the question is to research the topic. The child, perhaps with the guidance of an adult, could look for scientific explanations in books. In which case, Archimedes' principle of buoyancy and definitions of such terms as density, surface tension, and water displacement may be presented. Such information may be believed and memorized because of the faith and respect the child has for written information. It is also quite likely that the information is too abstract to successfully alter the child's understanding of the concept. The child's curiosity may be satisfied or stifled.

An investigative approach to the question would allow the child to personally discover an explanation of the concept through the manipulation of objects in water. By predicting the behavior of various objects placed in a container of water, based on the child's current understanding of the concept, and by testing those predictions and then modifying those explanations to account for the actual results, the child is constructing a new and personally satisfying explanation. By being in control of the investigation, the child can stop when his or her curiosity has been satisfied. The explanation may not completely match the scientific explanation, but it is more sophisticated than the child's previous level of understanding. More important, to the child, it is plausible and can therefore be useful and modified in the future.

The most powerful learning experience is a combination of investigation and research. First, the children get the opportunity to conduct an investigation and construct personal explanations for the concept. The activity is then followed by some reading (from the textbook or another source) that verifies this newly discovered information. The children feel good about themselves and confident about their ability to learn. In this way, research becomes a tool, even a necessary tool, rather than simply an isolated assignment.

Inquiry Development

For those who know how to ask questions, the inquiry approach is a process to which one can easily adjust. For those who have not yet developed the language skills involved in formulating questions, it is a process that can be taught.

The "I wonder . . ." Model One of the first ways to facilitate the development of the information-seeking process is to model the process. The teacher creates opportunities to verbalize some of the thinking that takes place and is not observable otherwise. The teacher can frequently use the following sentence starters:

> "I've been thinking about . . . (what you said about . . .)"
>
> "I've noticed (or observed) something just now . . ."
>
> "I wonder about . . ."

Here's an example of how this process could be verbalized in front of the children:

> *"This morning I looked outside and noticed that it wasn't very sunny. I observed lots of*

gray clouds. I wondered if it was going to rain today. I could have just carried an umbrella in case it did rain and not thought about it anymore. However, I was planning to wear my new shoes, and I really didn't want to get them wet and dirty the first time I wore them. So I checked the newspaper and the weather channel. The paper predicted . . ."

By listening to the teacher think out loud, verbalizing the sequence of thoughts, the children are exposed to the strategy called wondering. Wonderings arise as people become aware that there is a gap between a particular experience and their ability to explain it. As we get older, these gaps often seem to appear when challenged to explain something we thought we knew. Think back to the living versus nonliving interview assignment in chapter 5. Does that help you understand what we mean?

As the teacher models and repeats this process in the classroom (see Figure 6.2), the children begin to recognize the pattern and learn to imitate it. And perhaps even more important, they learn that verbalizing a question and finding a way to answer it is a valuable experience.

An examination of the weather scenario reveals these observations: (1) not very sunny and lots of gray clouds; (2) the question, stated in the form of "I wonder . . . is it going to rain?" and (3) the sources of information used to seek answers to the question (the newspaper and the weather station on the television). In one brief paragraph, the teacher has demonstrated how to go from wondering to a plan of action.

The possibilities for inquiry scenarios is only as limited as one's imagination. The

FIGURE 6.2 The "I wonder . . ." model.

1. List observations.
2. Formulate question.
3. Identify possible sources of information.

topics might reflect personal experiences or hobbies, such as travel, fishing, or gardening, or might be related to children's problems and interests, such as dentistry, bicycling, or pets. After listening to the teacher model the "I wonder . . ." process on several different occasions, children can begin to participate in the last part of the scenario by suggesting possible sources of information and collecting that information. With additional practice or a slight bit of encouragement, the children will actually generate their own scenarios by identifying situations for the application of the "I wonder . . ." model.

You want to eventually create situations for which the sources of information are not so easy to find and for which personal investigation would be the most appropriate means of acquiring the information. For example, "I noticed that the wild bird seed that I bought has a variety of seeds. I wonder which seeds birds prefer or if different birds eat different seeds. What do you think we could do to find the answers to these questions?"

Why not give this model a try for yourself? Follow the directions in Activity 6.1 and, if possible, verbalize your scenario with young children.

ACTIVITY 6.1

"I Wonder . . ."

Create your own scenario that could be used to model the information-seeking process, "I wonder . . .". After writing the scenario, identify the vital components: observations, question, and possible answer source.

Formulating Questions Some children are more inclined than others to ask questions. Others come to school not yet having devel-

oped the verbal skills of questioning. For example, suppose a veterinarian visits the classroom, making a presentation on the knowledge and skills involved in the practice of veterinary medicine. Perhaps a few animals are brought for the purpose of demonstration and to stimulate interest. At some point, the children get an opportunity to ask questions. Most young children are eager to talk but may say, "I have a German shepherd dog, too. Her name is Mandy" or "One time, a skunk came into our yard and I was afraid." They want to participate but do not understand the question format for conversation. The skill for formulating questions can be taught through inquiry development.

Inquiry development is a pre-investigation approach that focuses on wondering about things based on what the child already knows. And this is where investigations begin. As David Ausubel (1968) says, "If I had to reduce all of educational psychology to just one principle I would say this: the most important single factor influencing learning is what the learner already knows." It is an excellent place to begin when working with most children in the elementary school setting. However, for very young children, who have a limited knowledge base, an even more appropriate place to begin is with their wonderings. They have to know something about a subject before they can tell you what they know. But even if they know nothing about a topic, they can learn to wonder about it. In either case, the teacher's challenge is to turn curiosity into appropriate questions.

To do this, the teacher starts with some object of interest. It could be something that the teacher planned in advance, something brought to school by one of the children, or something that the children discover on the playground. Suppose that the object is a cricket. The teacher places it in a container designed to accommodate live animals. The container is large enough for the cricket to move around freely, and clear enough to allow the children to observe it easily. In small groups, the children are allowed plenty of time to observe the cricket. As the children describe the cricket, the teacher makes a list of what the children know about the cricket. Next, the teacher asks the children what they wonder about the cricket. The first several times this approach is used, the teacher provides an example of what is meant by wondering. In this case, the teacher may say, "I wonder . . . what do crickets eat?" For the next several days, the children will observe and learn more about crickets. While the observations are very important, it is also appropriate to look at other sources of information to acquire additional information.

If the approach is used in an environment filled with enthusiasm and where the individual's ideas are *valued,* the children will become very interested in the topic. And the more the children learn, the more they will want to learn. As the list of what children know increases, the list of things to wonder about also increases. It is the formation of the wonderings that is the beginning of formulating questions. Once the children are comfortable expressing what they wonder about, it takes very little to change to the questioning format. The statements of children, such as "I wonder about what ants do" and "I wonder what turtles eat" become "What do ants do?" and "What do turtles eat?" These are questions that can be answered through investigation and research. The teacher, while helping the young children make these verbal adjustments, has also prepared them for initiating their own inquiry.

Concept Mapping Rather than just making a list of the things that the children wonder about, you, as the teacher, may want to use concept mapping as a more visual representation of the information. You have seen numerous examples of concept maps throughout this book. The topic is represented as a

Chen Long

PHOTO 6.2 Children observing a classroom cricket.

circle in the center of the paper or board. Circles representing major subheadings are connected to the main circle. Finally, more detailed information is written around and connected to the subheadings. This technique graphically demonstrates how concepts relate to one another.

Concept maps can be done individually and become very sophisticated organizational and learning techniques (Novak & Gowin, 1986). However, in this situation, it is suggested as a simple, visual means for representing known information. As a map, it is useful in showing where one has been as well as where one wants to go. The concept map in Figure 6.3 shows what is known and provides direction for additional inquiry. Activity 6.2 will help you create your own concept map.

FIGURE 6.3 Example of a small group concept map indicating what children have learned about insects. The following questions are things that children wonder about:

Do insects live in water?

What do insects eat?

Where do insects come from?

Do insects have blood?

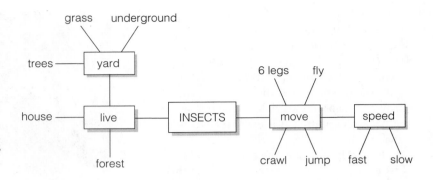

ACTIVITY 6.2

Creating a Concept Map

Try creating your own concept map. Begin by selecting one of the following topics or one of your own.

rainbows	salamanders	pine cones
clouds	magnets	rocks
peanuts	respiration	the brain

Place the word representing the topic in the center of a blank page. Next, add words for major subtopics and, finally, fill in the appropriate details. Remember that lines indicate connections or relationships. Sometimes one word will have more than one connection. That is okay. Draw the lines as you deem appropriate. This is your map. When you have completed the concept map, make a list of at least five things related to the topic that you wonder about.

Using Questioning Games The asking of questions can be encouraged through game strategies. Twenty Questions is a game whereby participants ask questions that can be answered yes or no. The purpose of the questioning is to identify an unknown object by asking twenty or fewer questions. This type of game fosters critical thinking, emphasizing logical deduction.

Children can also learn to formulate different kinds of questions. An alternative type of questioning game using open-ended questions can be employed to identify an unknown object. The purpose of the game is to learn to generate useful questions when solving problems. This inductive approach emphasizes creative or divergent thinking rather than critical or convergent thinking. Figure 6.4 gives examples of questions that might be appropriate for use in each of the two types of questioning games.

It is important to avoid an overemphasis on convergent or deductive questions that provide only yes or no answers. It is true that deductive questions are helpful in the process of eliminating possibilities. This is appropriate for adults who have a broad knowledge base. Young children, however, do not bring an extensive background of experiences to the problem-solving situation. It is more important for them to increase the range of experiences. The inductive approach is more conducive to accomplishing this. The answers to questions from the Superquestions list go beyond yes or no and provide the person with descriptive information. Questions that reflect that open-

Twenty Questions	Superquestions
Is it blue?	What color is it?
Does it make a noise?	What kind of noise does it make?
Does it have moving parts?	How does it work?
Is it bigger than my shoe?	How big is it?
Is it heavy?	How much does it weigh?
Is it made of wood?	What is it made of?
Could I use it?	How could I use it?
Is it usually found outside?	Where might I find it?

FIGURE 6.4 Examples for twenty questions and superquestions.

ended or divergent nature better facilitate transforming children's curiosity to questions that can be investigated.

ACTIVITY 6.3

Generating Questions

Try your hand at generating questions appropriate for both Twenty Questions and Superquestions. Make a list of twenty questions that can be answered with yes or no responses. Then transform each of the convergent questions into open-ended ones.

Integrating the Curriculum through Inquiry Inquiry development serves well as a basis for integrating the curriculum. As the children seek additional information—that is, find answers to their wonderings—curriculum subjects other than science become important. Information and skills involved in language arts, mathematics, social studies, art, music, and physical education serve a genuine purpose. An example of this integration of the curriculum can be seen as we expand on the inquiry about crickets.

The language arts connections are quite obvious. Fiction and nonfiction books may be accessed for interest and information.

These books can be read to the class during regular story time or as a special addition to the curriculum. Books can be taken home by the children to look at or read, or to be read to the children by parents and siblings. Many possibilities for writing activities also exist whether children use invented or traditional spelling. The children can maintain individual journals recording their observations of the cricket. The journals might also include personal wonderings or information deemed personally significant. Children could write fantastic or factual stories about crickets, such as "One Day in the Life of a Cricket." Artwork may accompany the stories or journal entries. The children might try drawing objects (e.g., grass, worms, and sidewalks) as they think they would appear to a cricket. Measurement and counting activities make mathematical connections. The children could estimate and measure the distance and height of cricket hops, as well as the size and number of body parts. Through a social studies investigation into folklore, different cultural perspectives of the cricket can be revealed. There are also several songs involving crickets that would be appropriate for young children. Imitating the movement of the cricket is a kinesthetic activity that is fun and appropriate for young children. In summary, as young children's wonderings are not content specific, an inquiry approach provides the means to address their curiosity through many disciplines.

Chen Long

PHOTO 6.3 Children imitating a cricket.

Quick Review

Science in particular lends itself to a discussion of questioning in that a question initiates investigation and that new questions arise as a result of investigation. Given that children bring a natural curiosity with them, science education provides an outstanding opportunity to develop the skills of both asking and answering questions. The inquiry approach as a teaching technique is the planned use of questions to initiate activity. The questions may be generated by the teacher, the students, or as a collaborative effort. When using an inquiry approach, there are actually two educational dynamics at work. First of all, children involved in inquiry are interested in the answers to their questions. Second, the teacher's primary concern is that the children learn the process and construct appropriate conceptions.

Investigation, the discovery of information new to the children but not necessarily new to the rest of the world, is the basis for the inquiry process. The "why" questions that children have can be rephrased by the teacher in a form that facilitates investigation. This forms the basis for an inquiry approach

to education. Once children know how to conduct investigations and understand the value of the inquiry process, they are well prepared to independently find answers to their own questions in the future. Particularly appropriate for young children is the "I wonder . . ." model, which is easily demonstrated by the teacher and provides a three-step format for dealing with questions.

Concept maps visually represent what children know about a topic and give guidance for future inquiry. As the maps expand, greater opportunities for integrating the curriculum through an inquiry approach present themselves. Children are well prepared to find answers to their own questions when they know how to conduct investigations and understand the value of the inquiry process.

SCIENCE PROCESS SKILLS

We have established now that children are prone to inquiry. And as shown in this next section, they tend to engage in many of the processes that scientists utilize in their attempts to answer questions. In fact, we all use the skills that will be described here throughout our daily lives. As you read about inferences, predictions, classification, and the like, you will see that they are skills for life and living. The educational challenge is to help develop and refine these skills in our students.

Basic Science Process Skills

In the early 1960s, when considerable effort went into science education reform, the science process skills were generated as a way of describing what scientists do. *Science: A Process Approach (SAPA),* the elementary curriculum developed by the American Association for the Advancement of Science (1975), led the way. We will discuss a number of the major reform efforts in chapter 11, but for now we will just say that since that time of reform programs, the list of process skills have changed slightly. The following descriptions are common to most lists of the basic science process skills: observation, inference, classification, communication, measurement, and prediction.

Observation Observation is using all five senses to perceive objects and events, their properties, and their behavior.

Children learn about the world through observation. Using the five senses—taste, smell, sight, touch, and hearing—people collect bits of information that can be combined to give understanding to what is perceived. Observation begins the construction of knowledge.

The following observations could be generated by a group of children examining a lime:

> It is green on the outside.
>
> It's juicy on the inside.
>
> It tastes sour.
>
> It smells like jello.
>
> It makes no noise when I shake it.
>
> It is about as big as my fist.

> It has six seeds.
>
> The inside part of the peel is white and mushy.

These observations involve all five senses. Yet, people tend to make mostly visual observations and seldom use the other senses. Children need to be encouraged to use the senses of hearing, smell, and touch. As a teacher, you may want to establish a class rule that says the sense of taste is not to be used for making observations unless the children are told specifically that it is safe and appropriate.

Qualitative Observations Observations can be classified into two categories: qualitative and quantitative. Most observations made by children are qualitative in nature, such as "It is green on the outside" or "The inside part of the peel is white and mushy." Children observing the same object would be likely to use the same color descriptions (green and white) but would be less likely to use the same texture description (mushy). Because of the nature of language, people use different descriptive terms. While this is reflective of the different ways people perceive things, it can lead to confusing descriptions when communicating observations. For instance, if a friend were to say that she bought a blue car, the blue you picture may not match the blue of your friend's automobile.

Quantitative Observations On the other hand, quantitative observations, ones that include numbers and comparisons, use a standard unit and tend to be more precise than qualitative observations. If a child reports that a lime has six seeds, it is likely that other children observing the same lime would make the same quantitative observation. Observations using comparisons, such as "It is about as big as my fist," are considered quantitative because the child has used a unit (a fist) as a standard to which the object (the lime) is compared.

Michael Bentley

PHOTO 6.4 Children using hand lenses to look at the pattern of veins on coleus leaves.

Providing children with hand lenses, rulers, and thermometers enhances their ability to make observations. These simple products of technology enable children to make more detailed and precise observations and become better investigators.

Inference Inference is making statements that attempt to explain or interpret objects or events based on observations.

Children need help distinguishing between observations and inferences. Suppose that while observing a plant, one child reported, "There are two leaves that are dying." The child may think that he was making an observation, while he was actually making an inference. He is attempting to explain the difference in leaf color. The actual observation is that two of the leaves are mostly yellow and the other leaves are green. The inference is that the two yellow leaves are dying. Other attempts to explain the difference in leaf color might be "Part of the plant doesn't get any sunshine" or "This type of plant has a mixture of leaves" (variegated leaf color). Each of these explanations is a plausible inference. The variations reflect observations from differing past experiences.

It is very important for teachers to recognize that more than one reasonable inference may exist for any given set of observations. While an inference is an attempt to explain a set of observations, it may also reflect observations from past experiences. Since every individual has a unique set of past experiences, children are quite likely to include similar, current observations and some diverse, past observations, resulting in the generation of inferences. By encouraging children to find several plausible inferences, the teacher is stimulating higher-level thinking.

One more distinction regarding inferences is necessary. Inferences are frequently not verifiable. An observation by one person can be verified by another, or a prediction made before an event can be compared to the results after the event. However, inferences are made after the event, and sometimes there is no way of reconstructing the actual occurrence. For example, suppose that observations of a set of animal tracks (shape, size, location, distance between prints, etc.) leads one to infer that the tracks were made by a dog. The person may have seen many dog tracks before and feel very confident with the inference that was made. The fact that the animal is no longer present and was not seen at the time the tracks were made means that the inference cannot be verified.

ACTIVITY 6.4

Observation and Inference

Be sure to complete all four parts of this activity.

1. Select an object to observe. Perhaps choose something that is common because it is used occasionally but that you have not paid much attention to, for instance, a peanut in the shell, a safety pin, or nail clippers. Generate a list of at least six observations.

2. Read through your list of observations. Indicate which of the senses you used to make each observation. Also indicate whether each observation was qualitative or quantitative. Now add to your list of observations. Pay particular attention to the senses you used least frequently and be sure to add more quantitative observations.

3. Next, try observing an event rather than an object. Select an event that takes a relatively short time to occur. A candle burning, an ice cube melting, or an Alka-Seltzer dissolving in water would be examples of simple events appropriate for this activity. Make a list of at least five observations at each of these times: *before, during,* and *after* the changes occur.

4. Finally, write four inferences that attempt to explain what happened in the event you just observed.

Classification Classification is grouping objects or events into categories based on specified characteristics or attributes.

Given the tremendous number of objects and events in the world, it is impossible for a child to comprehend each one if studied individually. However, by forming groups of objects and events, the diversity becomes manageable. By studying the characteristics and attributes of groups, and by looking for similarities, differences, and patterns, generalizations can be made that serve as the basis of concept development. The ability to classify, therefore, is very important. Two kinds of classification are used in the context of science: binary classification and multistage classification.

Binary Classification Binary classification is the simplest form of classification. All objects are separated into two groups, or subsets, based on a given characteristic. Asking children to get into two lines, one for boys and one for girls, is a form of binary classification. One group would be "boys" and the other group would be "not boys," which would later be labeled "girls." They could be separated into two groups based on other characteristics such as eye color (those with brown eyes and those with eyes that are not brown) or the type of clothing worn (those wearing shoes with shoe strings and those wearing shoes without strings). Binary classification is the most basic and appropriate form of classification for young children to use. Almost any set of objects can be used to practice binary classification. Leaves, rocks, shells, buttons, and pictures are common and easily accessible objects that can be provided for manipulation and classification.

Multistage Classification Multistage classification is a more advanced type of classification and should be used only after children have had considerable practice with binary classification. Multistage classification is a succession of binary classifications (see Figure 6.5). Suppose that a set of blocks is separated into two groups based on a characteristic of shape; some are rectangular and others

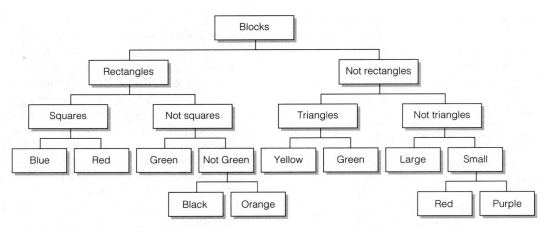

FIGURE 6.5 Multistage classification.

are not. The group of blocks that are rectangular can be subdivided into a group that is square (or cubic) and another group that is not square. Other characteristics, such as color and size, can be used to continue the subdividing. Each time, the remaining objects are placed into two categories until all objects in the group are identical.

Taxonomic Keys A taxonomic key is essentially a multistage classification system that is written out in a list format. By following the key and answering questions, you are led to the identity of the item that has been classified. Figure 6.6 demonstrates how each level of the classification scheme is numbered. Note that for each level there is an "a" and a "b." The "a" side represents the particular attribute, while the "b" side represents the absence of that attribute.

The multistage classification scheme that we have just described would be written out as a taxonomic key as in Figure 6.7. By selecting an object and then reading down the taxonomic key, you can identify just what that object is. Of course, this might be

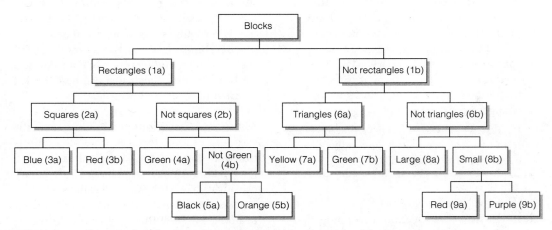

FIGURE 6.6 Multistage classification scheme numbered for a taxonomic key.

FIGURE 6.7 Taxonomic key for colored blocks.

1a. rectangle . . . . go to 2

1b. not a rectangle . . . . go to 6

2a. square . . . . go to 3

2b. not a square . . . . go to 4

3a. blue . . . . Blue Square

3b. not blue . . . . Red Square

4a. green . . . . Green Rectangle

4b. not green . . . . go to 5

5a. black . . . . Black Rectangle

5b. not black . . . . Orange Rectangle

6a. triangle . . . . go to 7

6b. not triangle . . . . go to 8

7a. yellow . . . . Yellow Triangle

7b. not yellow . . . . Green Triangle

8a. large . . . . go to 9

8b. not large . . . . Small Trapezoid

9a. red . . . . Red Trapezoid

9b. not red . . . . Purple Trapezoid

pretty easy when working with little colored blocks. But taxonomic keys are often used for field guides. So when you are out there collecting leaves, you can read down the key, answering questions (the shape of the leaf, venation, color) and ultimately identify that indeed that is poison ivy that you are handling.

ACTIVITY 6.5

Classification

This activity has three parts. Begin by selecting some items to classify. You might choose your CD collection, your wardrobe, your laundry, or a collection of action figures, for example. Whatever you decide choose, it must have at least fifteen different items.

1. This particular activity works best if you have a classmate or friend with whom to work. Begin by classifying all of the

objects into just two groups. Then have your friend look at the two groups and try to identify the characteristic or attribute that you used to separate the two groups. Try it again using a different set of characteristics.

2. Now classify your fifteen or so objects using a multistage system. Keep in mind that a multistage system simply begins as a binary classification (one group possesses the characteristic and the other does not) and then continues subdividing the remaining groups of objects until only one item is left in each category (assuming that there are no identical items in your initial group of stuff).

3. With item 2 completed, write out your multistage classification scheme as a taxonomic key. Use the numbering scheme illustrated in Figure 6.6 as a guide to numbering your classification scheme. When properly completed, you should be able to select an item from the group and identify it based on reading through your taxonomic key.

Communication Communication is transferring information from one person to another by verbal and/or nonverbal means.

Communication is basic to the interactions of people and the sharing of ideas. Although it can take many forms, the use of the spoken and written word are the most obvious. In the earlier classification example using blocks, the drawn diagram would represent written communication. If children had done the classification of blocks by describing the characteristics to one another, they would be using a form of oral communication.

Other forms of communication that are especially important in science include charts, graphs, maps, and drawings. These forms provide information or data important to the sharing process. Charts are a means of

Daily High and Low Temperatures (degrees Farenheit)

FIGURE 6.8 Temperature chart.

	Monday	Tuesday	Wednesday	Thursday	Friday
High Temp.	63	62	55	50	42
Low Temp.	47	49	48	32	26

organizing information such as temperature observations made over a period of time (Figure 6.8) or the number of seeds germinated under various conditions.

Graphs are used to visually show patterns that may exist in the collected data. For instance, a line graph may be used to show how the temperature of a closed container of water placed in sunlight increased over a period of time (Figure 6.9). Line graphs are used to display the change in only one variable over time.

A bar graph may be used to indicate the number of seeds that germinated under a damp paper towel, on top of a damp paper towel, under a dry paper towel, and on top of a dry paper towel (Figure 6.10). Bar graphs compare discrete variables against a common measure, for instance, frequency of occurrence. An example would be graphing the number (vertical axis) of students in your class who prefer apples, to those who prefer oranges, to those who prefer bananas (variables on the horizontal axis).

Maps and drawings are used to indicate important components and the relative position of the components (Figure 6.11). Maps are used when distance is an important factor. Drawings are usually used to provide details of objects.

ACTIVITY 6.6

Communications

Try your communication skills with this activity. Choose a location some distance from your house—the college or univer-

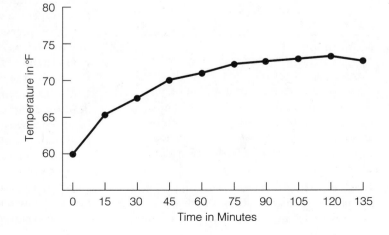

FIGURE 6.9 Graph of water temperature inside a glass jar.

Water Temperature Inside Glass Jar

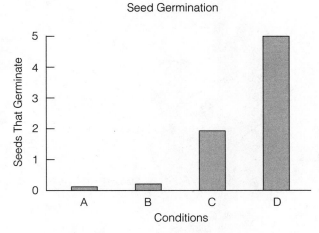

FIGURE 6.10 Bar graph of seed germination.

Key for Conditions

A = on top of dry paper towel
B = under dry paper towel
C = on top of damp paper towel
D = under damp paper towel

sity, the school where you are doing your field studies, a friend's house, or another location of your choosing. Prepare two sets of directions that tell how to get from one place to the other. Write one set of directions in a narrative format. Draw another set as a map. Give both forms of communication to one or more of your fellow classmates without any additional comments from you. Which form of communication do they prefer? Which do you prefer? Why?

Measurement Measurement is using numbers to describe objects or events.

Because numbers are so ingrained in our society, measurement, a specific form of observation called quantitative observation, is recognized as its own category of science process skills. The importance of numbers is obvious to adults. Imagine spending just one day without numbers. You might oversleep because you have no clock to measure time.

You might run out of gas on the way to school because you have no gas gauge. Of course you couldn't get a ticket for speeding, because there are no speed limits or speedometers! This is good, because you also have no money. Your schedule for the day would be confusing since you have no calendar to indicate the date. You wouldn't know when classes begin or end. And without dials or numbers, how would you set the microwave to cook your frozen dinner?

The importance of numbers for children is not so obvious. In order for children to understand measurement as a process, they must learn to recognize attributes that are measurable, such as time, temperature, length, area, weight, and volume. Children need to have firsthand experience through a variety of activities to develop an understanding of and appreciation for standardization of measurement, estimation, and the use of tools for collecting precise observations.

For young children in particular, understanding standardization of measurement is

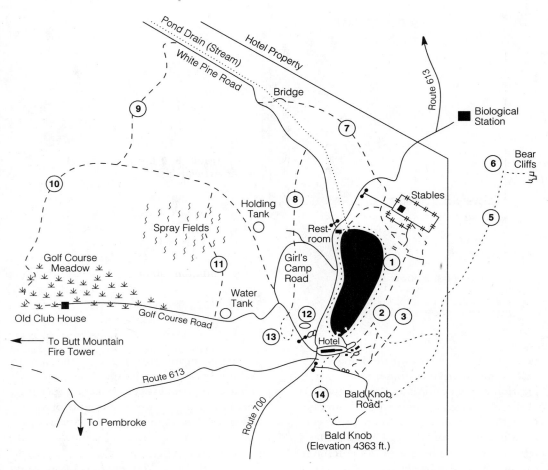

FIGURE 6.11 Sample map.

an important lesson. We can select any unit to use as our measurement device, and as long as we all agree on it, it can be used as a standard. At some point, our "standard" measures were new ideas. Horses are measured in hands, the speed of ships in knots, and computer operations in nanoseconds. So, allow your students to identify nonstandard units of measure, such as pencils or shoes, as practice with the use of measurement devices. When that has been done, it will be easier to introduce standard measures, such as the metric system, and to indicate the increased degree of precision that they offer.

ACTIVITY 6.7

Standard and Nonstandard Units of Measure

Rulers and meter bars represent standard units of measure, rather than the actual concept of measurement. Measurement is the quantification of an object or event with reference to an agreed–upon standard. In order for you, and your students, to understand the concept, it is helpful to measure objects using nonstandard units. Though you can measure time, distance, volume, weight, or speed, you will likely find it easiest to confine this activity to distance (or length).

1. Select three items to use as your nonstandard unit of measure, and one standard unit. For instance, you might select a watchband, a page of notebook paper, and a convenient stick as your nonstandard units, and a metric ruler as the standard unit. In order to make this activity most enjoyable, be creative! Select three nonstandard units that you are certain no one else will think of using.

2. Now go out and measure ten objects using each of the four units of measure. Do not confine yourself to small items. Accept the challenge.

3. It would be helpful to construct a data table for this activity. Across the top of your table, list the four different units of measure. Down the left side, list the ten objects that you will measure.

4. After you have completed the measurements, consider each of the units that you used. What were the advantages and disadvantages of each?

Prediction Prediction is forecasting future events based on a previously developed model.

Predictions are based on models, and the models used to make predictions are based on experience. A model is a visual or cognitive representation that includes essential components and their relationship to one another. A guess, rather than a prediction, is the result of no experience and no model related to the situation. A well-developed model, based on numerous activities and opportunities to discuss a concept, allows a person to feel very confident when making predictions related to that concept. Experience is therefore important to the development of future

models and should be the primary consideration in the teaching of the basic skills of investigation.

Children make predictions every day. If they enter the classroom and see seeds, bags of potting soil, and containers on the tables, they may predict that during science they will be planting seeds. If, on the other hand, they see seeds, glue, and construction paper, they may predict that during art they will be making collages. The children are able to make these predictions because they have past experience with these materials and have formulated a model concerning the use of the materials in a classroom setting.

Predictions, unlike inferences, are verifiable. Children can be asked to predict which pendulum will swing slower, which plant will grow taller, or what color will result from a combination of given colors. After the predictions are made, they can be tested through appropriate actions, such as the mixing of colors or the swinging of pendulums. The testing of some predictions, such as plant growth, involves an extended period of time, but can eventually be verified. Verification of predictions contributes to the conceptual model by strengthening or modifying it and is therefore an important part of the process.

ACTIVITY 6.8

Prediction

Practice your prediction skills with one of the following:

1. Fill a glass with water. Fill it as full as you can without it overflowing. Now predict how many paper clips can be placed carefully into the glass of water before the water spills over the edge. After you have written down that number, gently drop paper clips into the water. Compare your prediction with the results. Explain any differences.

2. Gather a collection of fifteen objects that are metal or partially metal, such as various coins, pens, pencils, tableware, rulers, nails, screws, and the like. Make a list of your objects and indicate which ones you think will be attracted to a magnet. Test each object by placing a magnet near it. Record your results. Explain any differences between your predictions and the results. Write one sentence that explains what type of objects are attracted to magnets. Next, collect eight different objects that are metal or partially metal. Again list the objects and indicate your predictions. Test each prediction and record the results. Were your predictions more accurate the second time?

Integrated Science Process Skills

The integrated science process skills incorporate the basic process skills in combination to facilitate various investigative activities. The most commonly listed integrated science process skills are shown in Figure 6.12.

As you can see from this list, the integrated skills are simply a more sophisticated version of the basic skills. In addition, they tend to be organized for particular investigative pursuits. Elementary school science focuses on the basic skills. So, rather than examine the integrated skills in isolation, we will explain them in context as they apply to

FIGURE 6.12 Integrated science process skills.

- Identifying and controlling variables
- Defining terms operationally
- Formulating hypotheses
- Collecting and recording data
- Interpreting data
- Drawing conclusions

the various forms of investigation discussed in chapter 7.

Quick Review

Clearly, the basic science process skills are not some secret list of scientific activities that require years of graduate work to learn. They are, however, skills, and skills require very directed practice in order to refine and then apply effectively. You can put your students in situations throughout the school day and across all of the subject areas that will facilitate the development of these six skills. And you may be surprised to find that your students will not have as much difficulty understanding these skills as perhaps you or some of your classmates have had. Early instruction and practice is the key.

The integrated process skills are a higher-level application of the basic skills. We have emphasized the basic skills because they are most appropriate to elementary school science education. However, students with a solid foundation with the basic skills will be able to understand and apply the integrated skills. We discuss this in chapter 7, "Investigations in Science."

CONCLUSION

With all of the challenges that face organized education and teachers, one aspect that is a distinct advantage is that children come to school with a natural inclination to ask questions and seek answers. Too often, however, the school curriculum fails to seize the opportunity that exists. The result is that by the middle school and high school years, students wait to be told what they are supposed to know, and have failed to develop the skills that would allow them to keep asking questions and finding ways to solve problems. The inquiry approach represents a perspective of education that recognizes natural curiosity as a very valuable starting point for educational pursuits.

The basic science process skills represent the tools that enable an inquisitive mind to discover answers. Whenever you fashion a lesson for your class, you should ask yourself which of the science process skills can be utilized. Rarely is it the case that only one of the skills would apply to a given investigation. So challenge yourself to incorporate as many as possible. The result will be a classroom of actively engaged students who are developing valuable skills while learning science. Is there more that you can ask for?

Actually, at this point, there might be more. Chapter 7 provides you with a discussion of eight investigative formats. As you work with each of them, look for the possibilities for using the process skills. Chapter 8 then provides you with specific lesson-planning formats that match the inquisitive nature of the learner with a discovery-based nature of instruction that seeks to maximize the science learning that will take place in your classroom.

7 | Investigations in Science

There Is More Than One Way to Investigate

Types of Investigations

Conclusion

Your Academic Roadmap

Study of this chapter should help you to understand the following concepts:

- There is more than just one scientific approach.

- Scientists (and your students) use a variety of investigations that are suited to different purposes.

- There are at least eight investigative techniques that are appropriate for elementary/middle school science.

- Understanding how to conduct an investigation and knowing when to use which form of investigation are fundamental to scientific endeavor.

THERE IS MORE THAN ONE WAY TO INVESTIGATE

As described in chapter 6, there are important science process skills that facilitate the pursuit of understanding. But science is more than process skills in isolation. As a way of knowing, a means for understanding the world around us, the essence of science is investigation.

Children, with their natural curiosity and wonder, eagerly seek to understand their surroundings but lack the skills for the investigative process. They need appropriate guidance and encouragement from teachers to become better, more systematic investigators. To foster this development, children must become aware of the importance and value of the process.

A common misconception is that there is only one scientific approach, the scientific method. Traditionally, people think of experimentation as being synonymous with the scientific method. This misconception often occurs as a result of work done on science projects using specific steps. Experimentation is certainly a very important form of investigation that is critical to scientific endeavors, but it is not the only form of scientific investigation. Scientists use a variety of investigations that are suited to different purposes. This chapter helps to overcome that misconception by examining various types of scientific investigation. In addition, suggestions for appropriate investigative activities are provided.

TYPES OF INVESTIGATIONS

Eight different types of investigations used in the world of scientific endeavors and appropriate for the science curriculum are presented here, beginning with what might be considered the least sophisticated and

FIGURE 7.1 Eight types of investigations.

1. Trial and error
2. Documenting
3. Prediction testing
4. Product testing
5. Experimenting
6. Reflecting
7. Generating models
8. Inventing

proceeding to perhaps the most sophisticated type, requiring the highest level of thinking (see Figure 7.1). Although the goals of some of the investigations are similar, each has a distinctive strategy and meets a particular need.

Trial and Error

Trial and error, an arbitrary search for solutions, is the least sophisticated form of scientific investigation. It is the type of investigation often used by very young children as they try to understand the world around them. However, there is a difference between children's trial and error and scientists' trial and error. With children, it is a random search for patterns that will in turn be used to solve problems or satisfy needs. When young children have problems, such as how to pack all the things they want for lunch into small lunch boxes or how to retrieve objects that have fallen into holes deeper than the children are tall, one attempt to solve the problem is followed by another without any particular logic involved.

Trial and error, as used by scientists, is systematic. One attempt to solve the problem is followed by another, but records of the attempts are kept, which facilitate the search for the necessary or desired pattern. For example, Thomas Edison, in his search for the best filament for the lightbulb, tried nearly six hundred different possibilities before reaching the desired solution.

Children can be taught to systematize trial and error so that it becomes a more efficient form of investigation. The teacher can facilitate the process by asking questions and encouraging the use of record keeping. But the process of record keeping, itself, does not mean that the children will use the information to develop a logical approach to solving the problem. The teacher needs to model the utilization of the information in logical ways by thinking out loud as she or he processes the information and determines what to try next or what to avoid. The purpose of the teacher thinking out loud is not to impose a particular kind of logic but to help children learn to keep track of previous attempts and avoid repeating them.

ACTIVITY 7.1

The Egg Drop

Packaging a raw egg to withstand a drop of 3–4 meters (10–13 feet) is a good activity for trial and error. Each child is given an egg and asked to package it using any common materials. The only stipulation is that the package itself cannot be larger than 20 centimeters (8 inches) in any direction.

Before dropping the packages from a second-story window, the top of some playground equipment, or any other safe place above an easily washed surface, the students are asked to explain what type of packaging was used and why.

After the egg packages have been dropped, the children are asked to report the results of their packaging, telling whether their eggs survived and what about the packaging helped the egg survive.

For those whose eggs did not survive, they are given another opportunity to package and drop an egg. Ideally, the children have as many opportunities as it takes to meet the challenge, and they should document and use whatever information they gain from the results of the previous egg drops. The sharing of the information is very important because it adds to each child's storehouse of knowledge.

You will likely find in this trial-and-error approach, either with your students or among your own classmates, that the solutions are arbitrary. This is reflected in comments such as the following from children who have addressed this challenge:

"I wrapped it in toilet paper because it is advertised as soft."

"I wrapped it tight with tape to hold the shell together, and then put it inside a paper towel tube."

"I put the egg inside a cup of popcorn because mom put popcorn in a box around presents when sending them to my brother."

As an investigation, it is extremely important that your students verbalize the thinking behind their approach to the task. This not only allows them to form a clearer picture of what they are doing, but also allows other students to consider ideas that had not come to mind. Encouraging your students to document their intentions and their results will serve to make this a more systematic approach that focuses on trial and error more so than on error and repeat.

ACTIVITY 7.2

The Egg Launch

As if dropping an egg to the ground is not enough, this activity provides a means for extending an activity on trial and error to another experience that may involve study of simple machines, creative thinking, and certainly more problem solving.

The same packaging requirements apply. However, in this activity students are to find a way to launch an egg at least 3 meters (10 feet) into the air and have the egg survive the fall back down.

Construction of the launching device represents another exercise in trial and error. The devices may be some form of slingshot fired while lying on the ground (don't fire straight up!) or perhaps a simple board-and-fulcrum catapult.

You might want to use a length of PVC pipe (white plastic pipe) cut to a length of 3 meters (10 feet) as your standard during the launching activities.

As with Activity 7.1, it is important that children verbalize the thinking behind their launching system. And documenting the process and the results once again makes this a systematic investigation.

Documenting

Observation, the most basic science process skill, is using the five senses to perceive objects and events. Extended observations, those recorded over a period of time, can actually become a form of scientific investigation, referred to here as documenting. Scientists conduct extended observations while studying things such as volcanoes, rain forests, and endangered animals, making and recording their observations as a means of documentation.

There are many classroom activities that lend themselves well to documenting. Having an animal in the room can be fascinating for children. They enjoy assuming part of the responsibility for caring for animals. The children can be taught to also make and record observations on a chart, in a class journal, or in individual journals. The information can then be reviewed periodically to identify patterns of behavior and growth changes if they exist. The animals can vary from the common cricket or guinea pig to the more unusual snake or family of finches. The purpose of this type of investigation is to encourage children to be detailed observers rather than superficial ones and to use their observations to identify naturally occurring patterns.

Documenting plant growth can also be an interesting school-based activity. The children can select a particular tree on the school grounds and begin documenting in September and finish in May. The changes over eight months will go unnoticed by most children when the observations are not guided. However, the changes will be quite noticeable, if the children document the observations and review the evidence collected. Planting and caring for wildflowers or butterfly gardens are also interesting challenges for children.

Other types of activities that are appropriate for documenting include constructing and maintaining bird feeders, charting local weather conditions, and monitoring neighborhood growth and development. Once children have participated in a few documenting investigations, they can easily be encouraged to identify their own topics of interest and conduct documenting activities independently. And if the teacher saves the data from these activities from year to year, students will have an even richer source of information to add to their own observations. Activity 7.3 is organized around documenting the growth of a tree during the school year. You can use the same format to practice with documenting change (e.g., weather patterns) or events (e.g., variety of foods served in the dining hall) during your science methods semester.

PHOTO 7.1 Documenting tree growth

ACTIVITY 7.3

Documenting Change or Events

Use the data collection page provided in Figure 7.2 for this documenting activity. Students will need one page for every two weeks of available observation time.

Select a fast-growing variety of tree somewhere on the school grounds to use for this activity. You may want to have your students select several trees, and let several groups each document the growth of a different type of tree. With just a dab of paint, mark a spot on the trunk where the measurements are to be made throughout the year.

Following the directions on the data page, students will make observations of the weather conditions each day. Every two weeks, they are to measure the tree's circumference and calculate its diameter.

As changes are documented on the charts, discuss with your students the factors that can be contributing to the changes they have documented.

Documenting Tree Growth   Page _____ of _____

Month: _____   Type of tree: _____

Weather Documentation:

In each cell, record the daily temperature (be sure to take your readings at the same time each day), enter the total rainfall (if any) for the 24-hour period between making weather observations, and include a general statement of the weather conditions for the day (e.g., cloudy, unseasonably hot or cold). In the final cell for each week, enter the average temperature and total rainfall.

	Monday	Tuesday	Wednesday	Thursday	Friday	Averages
Week of:						
Week of:						

Record the following information about the tree every two weeks:

Date: _____   Diameter: _____   Circumference: _____

General Observations of the Condition of the Tree (e.g., leaves are changing color, branches are beginning to bud, etc.)

FIGURE 7.2 Documenting the growth of a tree and accompanying weather patterns.

Prediction Testing

Prediction testing is similar to experimenting in that statements that serve to focus the direction of the investigation are generated. However, prediction testing is a much less complicated form of investigation than is experimenting. Rather than controlling variables and identifying cause-and-effect relationships, prediction testing emphasizes developing a model based on accumulated observations. While predictions are statements based on models that forecast future events, prediction testing requires an additional step of verifying the prediction. Whether the prediction turns out to be accurate or false, the information gained through the verification process serves to further develop the model.

Scientists frequently use prediction testing as a form of investigation and continue the development of models by finding evidence to support or modify existing models. An obvious use of prediction testing in the scientific community is found in the field of meteorology. Scientists, for decades, have collected and recorded daily weather observations. Based on those observations, meteorologists have identified numerous patterns related to the movement of air masses and the sequence of weather phenomena. The weather forecasts we hear on the news are actually predictions based on highly sophisticated and well-developed scientific models (even if the occasional missed forecast makes that difficult to believe). Scientists, in pursuit of understanding, use prediction testing in investigations ranging from the vastness of space to the infinitesimal atom. In either situation, mathematical formulae constructed on scientific evidence predicted the existence of objects before the objects themselves were discovered.

Robert Ballard's expedition to locate the sunken *Titanic* provides a good example of prediction testing as an investigative endeavor. Based on the historical information relating to the sinking of the vessel, information obtained from other expeditions, and oceanographic information, a model was constructed of where the *Titanic* should have come to rest. Using sophisticated tools, those predictions were tested. As increasingly precise information was obtained, thus strengthening the developing model, increasingly accurate predictions could be made. Ultimately, Ballard and his colleagues were able to use ALVIN and JASON, deep-ocean submersibles, to test and verify their prediction. Once located, the investigation to find the *Titanic* was completed. No attempts were made to raise the *Titanic* or recover items from the wreckage. The entire investigation, which focused on making and testing a prediction, was complete when the prediction was verified. Subsequent study of the wreckage in order to understand what caused the vessel to sink as it did represents a separate and new investigation.

Classroom investigations that use prediction testing begin with questions or challenges such as Which pendulum will swing faster? or Where in the room do you think the temperature will be the highest or the lowest? or Which objects will sink and which will float? The students are then asked to make predictions before observing the actual events, such as the swinging of pendulums, the measurement of air temperature, or the placement of objects in water. The predictions can be written down by individuals on their own papers, or a class tally of predictions can be recorded on a chart, a transparency, or the chalkboard.

The purpose of asking children to make predictions is to encourage them to think about their understanding of the concept and any related information prior to the collection of new data. If the children are asked to share their predictions and their explanations for those predictions, as in the second phase of the model Planning for Conceptual Change (see chapter 8), they become aware of the diversity of explanations. At that point, they are more likely to question the validity of their own explanations, make purposeful observations, and subsequently change their beliefs related to the concept.

Data collection sheets can be used to help children systematize this form of investigation. The following example may serve to clarify the simple structure involved in prediction testing. Suppose we use the challenge Which objects will sink and which will float? to help children understand such concepts as water displacement, density, surface tension, and buoyancy. The level of understanding of the concept and the terminology introduced during the lesson depend on the grade level and experience of the children involved. If the lesson is conducted in fifth or sixth grade, all of the terms may be appropriate. If the lesson is conducted in first grade, none of the terms would be appropriate. The activity without any emphasis on terminology, however, is still helpful to the growth of the knowledge base of the young children. In grades 2–4, some terminology may be appropriate. Water displacement, for example, is directly observable and does not require abstract or formal reasoning to be useful.

ACTIVITY 7.4

Sink or Float

To proceed with the Sink-or-Float activity, the teacher provides each group of students with a set of common objects: a container

Sink and Float

Directions:
1. For each item listed below, predict whether the object will sink or float in water. Give a reason for each of your predictions.

Object	Prediction Sink/Float	Reason for Prediction	Observation Sink/Float	Explanation
plastic pen				
pencil				
straight pin				
aluminum foil				
clay ball				
jar lid				
an orange				

2. After writing your predictions and reasons for predictions, test the predictions and record your observations on the chart above. If your observations do not match your predictions, write your explanations for the discrepancy.

3. Summarize your findings on what makes some objects sink and others float.

FIGURE 7.3 Sample Sink-or-Float data sheet.

of water, and a data sheet, such as the one in Figure 7.3. The challenge is then presented: Which of these objects will sink in water, and which will float?

Follow the directions on the data sheet. Be sure that a prediction is listed and a reason provided before the item is placed in the water! Remember, this is an investigation, not a test of knowledge.

The children independently write their own predictions and reasons for the predictions. The teacher encourages the children to share their predictions with others in the small group. Then, in small groups, the children test the predictions. While placing each object in a container of water, they make and record observations. They are encouraged to compare the observations to their predictions and discuss any discrepancies. The children are also encouraged to manipulate the objects, if possible, and the placement of the objects within the container, noting any differences discovered. The discussion of results and resolution of discrepancies, along with the teacher's insertion of appropriate terminology, will lead to a generalization of the concept of sinking and floating. The entire process of making and testing predictions and then discussing them

PHOTO 7.2 The Sink-or-Float activity

facilitates conceptual growth of each child's personal model. As shown in chapter 8, what has been described here follows the Planning for Conceptual Change model step-by-step.

Many other topics that lend themselves to prediction testing exist in the curriculum. Children enjoy making daily weather observations, and they can use the collected information to predict the weather for the next twelve to twenty-four hours. During the study of sound, children can be asked to predict which substances either facilitate or prevent the transmission of sound. While studying heat energy, they can predict hot spots and cold spots in the classroom or on the school grounds. They can also predict the interactions of magnets with various objects or the changes in plant and animal behavior as environmental changes occur.

Children who have experienced many challenging prediction-testing situations can become good problem solvers even when given incomplete information. This particular form of investigation requires that they (1) draw upon what they do know about the concept and any related information to formulate a prediction and (2) test the predic-

tion, thereby collecting additional information. The new evidence serves to strengthen or modify the original model of the concept. While this form of investigation is less complex than experimenting, it is more appropriate for elementary-age children. It is a powerful teaching strategy because it is an integral part of the Planning for Conceptual Change model and it can be used by teachers to effectively build self-confidence and self-esteem among children.

Product Testing

Product testing may initially seem to be an unfamiliar form of investigation. But it is easily recognized when considered in the context of advertising and commercials. For instance, suppose we want to determine which paper towel is the quicker picker-upper. We could listen to the television commercial and accept the claims that it makes. Another option would be to perform our own test on a variety of paper towels, measuring the length of time it takes each brand of paper towel to absorb water. This second option is called product testing—the process of identifying and using criteria to make decisions.

Suppose we really do want to determine which is the best paper towel. We would not want to limit the investigation to just the time it takes to absorb water, since absorption is just one characteristic of paper towels. We would want to test many factors. The first step of product testing is to generate a list of criteria that might affect the final decision. Possible criteria for deciding which is the best paper towel might include size, thickness, absorbency, color, smell, type of paper (recycled versus new).

Different criteria are important to different people, and individual lists will therefore vary. For example, when it comes time to purchase a roll of paper towels, additional criteria may come to mind and influence the decision. The cost of the paper towel may be an important criteria for some people. Others may say it depends on the use for the paper towel. Paper towels used in the garage may be very different from paper towels used in the kitchen. The more people you have involved in the generation of the criteria list, the more detailed the list is likely to become.

Children will enjoy testing products for which they have seen advertising claims, such as paper towels. They are even more interested in product testing when the products are child oriented. They especially enjoy testing food. Activity 7.5 involves a favorite of many children: chocolate chip cookies.

The question that drives the investigation is, Which is the best mini–chocolate chip cookie? Once the teacher presents the question and the children discuss some of the possibilities, the focus of the discussion should switch to the various criteria being suggested by the children. A brief explanation of product testing and its purpose will set the stage for conducting the test. It is also important to point out that product testing is a way of eliciting personal preferences. There is no one correct answer to the question. If

that were the case, only one brand of the product would exist. Instead, the grocery stores are filled with many brands of products to provide customers with choices based on personal preferences.

ACTIVITY 7.5

Product Testing

The data collection sheet in Figure 7.4 is based on four criteria that provide a good introduction to product testing. Provide a copy of the data collection sheet to each student.

Though you can use the full-size cookies, it is handy to buy three different brands of mini–chocolate chip cookies. Label three paper plates A, B, and C, respectively. Since the students are not to know which brand is represented, be sure that you label the boxes as A, B, and C so that you will know which cookie was which brand later on. Then place a quantity of cookies on the respective plates—these will be presented to the class.

Provide each of your students with three paper towels, and have them label the towels as A, B, and C. When they select two or three cookies from plate A, they should place them on towel A, and so on. Now let them conduct the test in accordance with the steps on the data collection sheet.

After conducting the product test, the class should discuss the results and what the impact would be if the criteria were changed. For example, the cost of the cookies might make a difference in selection when it came time to purchase the product. The brand name, fat content, or number of calories also makes a difference to some people. The important concepts that the children should learn as a result of

THE MINI–CHOCOLATE CHIP COOKIE TASTE TEST

Directions: Cookies should be on coded trays. Take two cookies from each tray. Be sure to label each cookie's code so that the brands don't get confused. Test each brand doing the test in order from 1 to 4.

Test 1: Appearance of the Cookie
Award 1st place to the cookie that looks the most delicious and 3rd place to the one that looks least appetizing. Explain why the cookie looks good or bad under "Reason."

	Cookie Code	Reason
1st place (3 points)	———	——————
2nd place (2 points)	———	——————
3rd place (1 point)	———	——————

Test 2: Number of Chips
Carefully break up one cookie of each brand and count the number of chips found. Award 1st place to the cookie with the most chips and 3rd place to the cookie with the fewest chips. Save the chips for the next test.

	Cookie Code
1st place (3 points)	——————
2nd place (2 points)	——————
3rd place (1 point)	——————

Test 3: Taste of the Chocolate
Taste the chocolate chips you separated from each of the cookies. Award 1st place to the cookie that has the best-tasting chips and 3rd place to the cookie whose chips you least like.

	Cookie Code	Reason
1st place (3 points)	———	——————
2nd place (2 points)	———	——————
3rd place (1 point)	———	——————

Test 4: Taste of the Cookie
Now taste the second cookie of each brand. Think about the texture. Is it chewy or crispy enough? Do you like the flavor of the cookie? Is it sweet enough? Award 1st place to the cookie you like the best and 3rd place to the cookie you like the least.

	Cookie Code	Reason
1st place (6 points)	———	——————
2nd place (4 points)	———	——————
3rd place (2 point)	———	——————

MY PREFERENCE IS...
This is it! It is time to determine which of the three brands you liked the best. Total the number of points each cookie received in tests 1, 2, 3, and 4. Put the total points in the Total Score column.

Cookie Code	Total Score
A	——————
B	——————
C	——————

FIGURE 7.4 Data collection sheet for product testing activity.

this form of investigation are that conducting product tests determines personal and group preferences and that the criteria selected for testing affects the results of the test. The decisions made as a result of product testing vary as the criteria change.

Experimenting

Experimentation is probably the best-known form of investigation associated with science. Historically, the lists of science process skills were generated through a process of analyzing experimentation with the purpose of identifying its discrete components. Today,

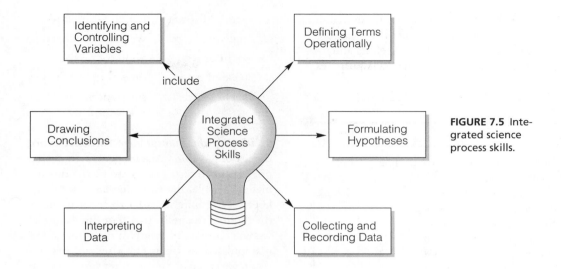

FIGURE 7.5 Integrated science process skills.

most textbooks and science curriculum guidelines include a list of integrated science process skills in addition to the basic science process skills (see chapter 6). The list typically includes those listed in Figure 7.5.

Sometimes experimenting itself is included on the list. Experimenting, however, is not a skill but an investigative form that combines all of the integrated science process skills. Having identified the integrated science process skills helps one understand the steps involved in experimentation. An examination of an experimental design may help clarify each of the integrated science process skills and their relationship to one another.

Experimenting is the most rigorous of all the investigative forms in terms of its procedural structure. This is due to the numerous steps and precise sequencing involved. In addition, the design of the experiment must include sufficient detail to allow another person to conduct the same experiment, thereby testing the results of the first experiment.

Figure 7.6 is a list of the steps involved in experimenting. The list is divided into two sections: designing an experiment and conducting an experiment.

FIGURE 7.6 Steps for experimenting.

**EXPERIMENTING
(GIVEN THE TOPIC)**

Designing an Experiment
1. Phrase the general question related to topic.
2. List many variables.
3. Identify the manipulated variable.
4. Identify the responding variable.
5. Control all other variables.
6. Write the hypothesis.
7. Define terms operationally.
8. Write procedures.
9. Prepare the data table (optional).

Conducting an Experiment
10. Collect data.
11. Analyze data (graph results).
12. Draw a conclusion.
13. Compare conclusion and hypothesis.

Designing an Experiment Usually the purpose of an experiment is to find out what factors affect a particular natural phenomenon. For example, we might be interested in knowing what factors affect plant growth, the bounce of a ball, the absorption of heat, or the flight of paper airplanes. By designing and conducting an experiment, we can discover the information we are seeking and use the information to suit our own purposes.

ACTIVITY 7.6

The Paper Helicopter

Enlarge the drawing on the right to approximately 4cm × 11cm. Cut on all the solid lines and fold on the dotted lines. Fold A away from you. Fold B away from you. Fold C up and also away from you. Fold D toward you but do not bend it more than 90° and bend E away from you, also not more than 90°. Stand on a chair and drop the paper. What do you observe? Try it again. What does it remind you of? We call it a paper helicopter, with rotors and a long skinny fuselage hanging down.

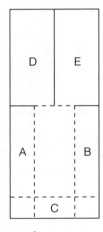

Now use the paper helicopters from Activity 7.6 as an example for designing and conducting an experiment. The first step is to state the problem in the form of a general question.

1. Phrase question. Our question is What factors affect the flight of paper helicopters?

2. List many variables. Once we have identified the problem or the general question that we want to investigate, we must then generate a list of possible factors. Though our list could be much longer, it might include the following variables:

length of rotors	length of fuselage
angle of rotors	weight of helicopter
width of rotors	width of fuselage
shape of rotors	type/weight of paper
height of release	surrounding air movement

3. Identify the manipulated variable. From the list of possible variables generated in step one, we need to select one to be the manipulated variable, the variable that we will deliberately change in order to see if it affects the flight of the helicopter. For this example, we will choose the length of the rotors as the manipulated variable. For a second experiment, we could choose another variable from the list. Each experiment, however, can have only one manipulated variable.

It is important to have at least three variations of the attribute selected. With only two, the data may indicate a difference between those two specific objects or events, but a pattern cannot be determined. With three or more variations of the attribute, the data will be more likely to reflect an existing pattern. Suppose we make five helicopters, each with different rotor lengths: 2 cm, 4 cm, 6 cm, 8 cm, and 10 cm.

4. Identify the responding variable. The next step is to decide how to determine if there is some affect on the paper helicopters. How will we observe the differences, if they exist? In this case, we will observe the flight of the helicopter. We could see whether it flies in a straighter line, or flies faster, or flies for a longer period of time. We select the length of time it flies as our responding variable, because that can be quantitatively measured using a stopwatch.

5. Control all other variables. At this point, we must address all the other variables listed in step two. Based on our previous assumptions, we can say that all five helicopters will be constructed out of the same paper and have the same overall shape and size, except for the length of the rotors. The rotors will be bent the same amount so that the angle remains the same. The helicopters will be launched from the same place, out of any draft or wind, and from the same height.

6. *Write the hypothesis.* A hypothesis is a very precise statement used in experimenting. The statement indicates an anticipated relationship between the manipulated and the responding variables and the direction of that relationship. In this experiment, the hypothesis could be as follows:

> As the length of the rotors increases, the length of flight time increases.

The manipulated variable is the length of rotors. The responding variable is the length of flight time. The direction of the relationship in both cases is increase.

Keep in mind that more than one hypothesis could be written. The hypothesis could just as easily have been "As the length of the rotors decreases, the length of flight time increases." The hypothesis does not have to match the outcome of the experiment. If we knew the outcome, we would not need to conduct the experiment. The hypothesis is a statement that we can test. By conducting the experiment, we will find out if the results support or do not support the hypothesis.

7. *Define terms operationally.* Defining terms operationally is not the same as using definitions that are found in a dictionary. Defining operationally means explaining how the term is used in the context of the experiment. For example, suppose we were conducting an experiment on factors that affect plant growth. The term "plant growth" would have to be operationally defined because plant growth can be measured in a va-

riety of ways. It could be the number of leaves, the number of flowers, the height of the plant, and so on. Without an operational definition of the term plant growth, other people could not replicate the experiment and be sure they were measuring the same type of plant growth.

All terms that might not be explicitly clear need to be defined. In addition, the responding variable must be defined. Also, the definition must include how the variable will be measured and in what units.

In terms of the helicopter experiment, then, the term "length of flight time" must be operationally defined. The following statement would satisfy the criteria of an operational definition:

> The length of flight time will be the amount of time from release of the helicopter to the moment it touches the floor. It will be measured to the nearest hundredth of a second using a stopwatch.

8. *Write procedures.* The procedures are a written explanation of the experiment. The purpose of the procedures is to convey information so that other people, should they choose to do so, could repeat the experiment exactly. The following paragraph serves as procedures for the helicopter experiment.

> Five helicopters will be constructed from plain white copy paper as indicated in Activity 7.6 except that the length of the rotors will vary, one each at 2 cm, 4 cm, 6 cm, 8 cm, and 10 cm. They will be individually launched from a height of 3 meters in a room with no circulating air from heater, fan, open window, or air conditioner. The flight of the helicopters will be timed with a stopwatch from the moment they are released to the instant they touch the floor.

FIGURE 7.7 Flight time in seconds.

	Length of Rotors				
	2 cm	4 cm	6 cm	8 cm	10 cm
Time in Seconds					

FIGURE 7.8 Flight time in seconds for each trial.

	Length of Rotors				
	2 cm	4 cm	6 cm	8 cm	10 cm
Flight #1					
Flight #2					
Flight #3					
Average Time					

9. Prepare the data table. A table is a helpful way of organizing the observations to be collected. For our helicopter experiment, the one in Figure 7.7 would be sufficient for recording the data.

If we intended to replicate the flights, releasing and timing each helicopter three times and averaging the flight times, then the one in Figure 7.8 would be more appropriate. Replication, or the repeating of the experiment, is a way of collecting more data. It adds strength to the conclusion and therefore to the support or nonsupport of the hypothesis.

With the data table prepared, the design phase of the experiment is completed. If written properly, the design should be clear enough for anyone wishing to conduct the same experiment to do so without confusion. At this point, all we have left to do is construct the helicopters as indicated in the design and see what happens!

Conducting an Experiment With the design written and the helicopters constructed,

we can complete the experiment. Here are the remaining steps:

10. Collect data. Knowing the procedures and having a table to collect the data, we are ready to conduct the investigation and have some fun. One member of the team can launch the helicopters while other members can observe and record the flight times. The information collected can be entered into the table as seen in Figure 7.9.

11. Analyze data. Next, analyze the data for patterns that may exist, patterns that may help answer the original question that was the basis for the experiment. Examination of the data can be facilitated by using graphs to represent the data (see Figure 7.10). For this experiment, a line graph is appropriate for displaying the flight times for each rotor length.

12. Draw a conclusion. The conclusion is a statement, based on the analysis of the data, that indicates the observed relationship between the manipulated and the responding

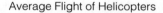

	Length of Rotors				
	2 cm	4 cm	6 cm	8 cm	10 cm
Flight #1	2.50	2.69	3.18	3.35	5.41
Flight #2	2.41	2.65	3.28	3.35	5.75
Flight #3	1.90	2.90	3.21	3.41	5.78
Average Time	2.27	2.75	3.23	3.37	5.65

FIGURE 7.9 Sample flight time in seconds for each trial.

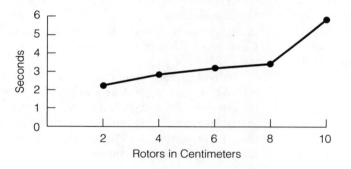

FIGURE 7.10 Graph for analyzing helicopter flight data.

variables. In this experiment, the conclusion is

> Helicopters with longer rotors fly for longer periods of time than helicopters with shorter rotors. The longer the rotor, the longer the flight time.

13. Compare conclusion and hypothesis. The last step of experimenting is to compare the conclusion that was drawn from observation to the hypothesis that was written during the design stages. The conclusion may or may not support the hypothesis. In our example, the conclusion does support the hypothesis.

It is a misconception to think that conclusions of experiments prove hypotheses. The conclusion is an expression of the results of just one experiment. To replicate an experiment, that is, to conduct the same experiment collecting additional data, adds more support to the hypothesis and strengthens the conclusion. As the number of replications increases, the support for the hypothesis increases. However, there is always the chance that the experiment could be conducted one more time and that those results might not support the previous conclusions and the hypothesis. Therefore, the hypothesis is not *proven* to be true. What usually happens is that after extensive experimentation, the hypothesis has been supported so many times that it is accepted by the scientific community as a scientific principle.

Experimenting is the most structured form of investigation. It involves many detailed steps that must occur in a specific order. In terms of levels of thinking and abstractness, it is very demanding. Elementary-age children are often not capable of designing a science experiment on their own or without considerable practice. But they are capable of conducting an experiment once it has been designed. They are also able to understand and even enjoy designing an experiment when the teacher guides the class through the steps of design. Some children, when given enough practice, are capable of designing and conducting their own experiments. The important point is that since the process is cognitively challenging, children need much supervised practice before proceeding on their own. Unfortunately, as you are probably aware, the science curriculum tends to give children "experiments" to do, and does not make the transition to allowing students to design experiments, despite their increasing cognitive ability.

Reflecting

Perhaps least likely to appear on a list of investigative approaches is reflecting. You are probably familiar with the process but have not associated it with science. It is, however, an important part of scientific endeavors. This form of investigation is not really product or information driven. Instead, scientists use this as a means of collecting thoughts about a topic of concern. The collection will include the scientist's own thoughts as well as the thoughts of others who have been studying the same or related topics. Reflection may occur in large groups such as conventions sponsored by professional organizations, in small groups at project meetings, or individually. The reflection process may occur in writing by maintaining a journal for individual reflection or by corresponding with others through regular or electronic mail. The end result of reflection is often a question for extending the study or clarification of the direction of the current pursuit.

Children can participate in their own forms of reflection and should be encouraged to do so. Reflection, unlike assessment, provides them the opportunity to consider what they have done and to organize it in a manner that facilitates cognitive adaptation. Near the end of a formal unit of study, the teacher may ask the children to share what they know about the topic. They can be encouraged to express what aspects of the topic they do not yet understand or ones they want to pursue further. The teacher can help them form questions that will serve as a guide for the remainder of the unit of study.

A second option is to allow the children to use the questions and pursue their own interests as an extension to the unit, as in "Pursuing Questions," step six of the Planning for Conceptual Change model (see chapter 8, page 185).

Individual reflection can be facilitated through the use of student journals. Maintaining journals, a great feature in an integrated curriculum, also encourages the children to recognize the importance of skills and strategies across disciplines.

ACTIVITY 7.7

Class Journal

A journal can be a formal requirement, utilizing a bound book of blank pages with specific instructions for formatting. Or, a journal can be a simple collection of pages in a notebook. The important part is that it provides people with a way of recording their thoughts about a topic.

For your science students, or for practice as a part of your science methods course, a journal can be made from several sheets of folded 8.5 × 11 paper. If you want to get fancy about it and use a computer to print cover pages, go to it. Otherwise, decorate or label your journal cover any way you'd like.

With five pages folded in half and stapled along the crease, your book will contain nine two-page entry areas. On the top of each left-hand page, write the heading "Class Observations." On the right-hand page, write the heading "Reflections." After each science class (or methods class), students should write down what actually happened. Then, on the page labeled "Reflections," they are to write down their thoughts about that class. In particular, consider the following:

- The purpose of today's lesson was . . .
- I learned . . .
- The question that I have is . . .

Generating Models

Most people are visual learners, and yet elementary curricula typically include very few specific activities and teaching strategies that facilitate visual thinking. Visual thinking has been separated into several different skills or components (Arnheim, 1969). These can be simplified and grouped into three categories: perceptual, mental, and graphic visual thinking (Kuehn, 1985). Perceptual visual thinking occurs first as the person observes an object or event. Mental visual thinking occurs as the brain attempts to manipulate the mental images and various shapes. People sometimes shut their eyes because it helps them form an image in the "mind's eye." Graphic visual thinking occurs as the person attempts to draw the visual concept that is forming in the mind. The drawing helps clarify the visual image, its components and their relationships. As a result of graphic visual thinking, a model is produced. The model is a representation that can then be used to communicate the idea with others. Often, the first drawing will indicate to the drawer that something would not work as drawn. So corrections are made, perhaps returning to

perceptual visual thinking as well as mental visual thinking. It is fascinating to watch students involved in this process!

The use of models in science is familiar to most people. Models are visual or cognitive representations that include the essential components of the construct and their relationship to one another. Models demonstrate how the parts of a given system interact. Three-dimensional models of the solar system, molecules, cross sections of plants, torsos of the human body, and other subjects often decorate the classroom. Two-dimensional models found in textbooks attempt to clarify complex phenomena, such as the water cycle, the food web, and the conservation of matter and energy.

Models themselves are not a form of investigation but the products of investigations conducted by others. *Generating* models is a form of investigation. Rather than searching for new information, as was the purpose of the investigations presented earlier, the purpose of generating models is to create a product. The product is a visual representation showing the relationship between essential components, and it communicates that relationship to others.

An example of a model generating activity may help clarify this particular form of investigation and the visual thinking involved in the process. The machine in Photo 7.3 is reportedly a "prize selector." The person demonstrating the machine collects numbered disks, placing them one at a time into a slot on the side of the box in the center of the machine. The slot holder is pushed back into the side of the box and locked shut with a tiny key. After a lot of bell ringing and water siphoning on the left side of the machine, a clock on the right side, "set" to run for twenty minutes, is eventually turned on automatically. The students are told that when the timer goes off, they will hear a marching band play music as a cue that the machine is selecting the winning number. Soon, a sign

Christine Ebert

PHOTO 7.3 The automatic door prize machine (ADPM)

will appear at the top of the box announcing the winning number. The students are then asked to draw on a piece of paper what they think is inside the box that will somehow select the winning number. They have twenty minutes to complete the task.

Perceptual visual thinking is active as they watch and listen to the person explaining the "prize selector." They see the outer shape of the box and its visible outer components. They watch as the person places the disks into the box and locks it. They observe the machine in action up until the clock begins to move. For the next twenty minutes the box is silent.

When the students are challenged to draw what is inside the mysterious box, they engage in mental visual thinking. They begin to formulate various shapes that must connect one to another. Questions may come to mind, such as "What do the disks fall into?" "Where will the music come from?" "What is the timer attached to?" No doubt they draw on previous knowledge to solve this problem, but words themselves are not helpful. They have to form mental images of the various possibilities as they occur to them.

Graphic visual thinking begins to take place as the students start to draw a possible solution. The important thing about graphic visual thinking is that it helps to clarify the concept as they generate it. As they draw the initial shapes and begin to connect them, no doubt they discover a few errors. They may erase or draw over their first attempts as they realize that the positions of certain objects need to be slightly altered in order for the solution that they have created to work.

The model or product of this type of activity is useful in communicating ideas with one another. But it is the process of generating the model that is very beneficial for young children. It allows them to apply what they have learned from previous experiences in an open-ended way. Since many possible solutions could be generated to solve the mystery, it encourages divergent, creative thinking. In fact, all students' ideas in an activity such as this are valuable and worthy of consideration, so everybody can have a successful experience. In addition, the teacher learns a great deal about what the children know and can apply. The inclusion of levers and switches or simple electrical circuits shows a

Christine Ebert

PHOTO 7.4 A mysterious mystery box and a mystery box revealed.

certain amount of understanding of such concepts. If some of the drawings rely on magical solutions, that also tells the teacher something. Perhaps some students are unfamiliar with or uncomfortable applying certain concepts. The sharing of possible solutions provides students with a larger repertoire of ideas from which they may draw in the future. Besides, generating models is fun!

The use of "mystery boxes" for the purpose of generating models is especially effective when the teacher wants to stimulate creative thinking. Because it is an unfamiliar object, there are few, if any, preconceptions associated with the object. People feel less inhibited to explain something that does not have a predetermined usefulness. And these are much easier to prepare than an ADPM!

As described here, mystery boxes are closed cardboard boxes of various sizes and shapes. Shoe boxes work well for this. Inside are mazes or obstacles made of cardboard that have been glued or taped in place. With the top open, a marble is placed inside. Of course with the top off it is no trick to see how to work the marble through the maze. But if you've never seen inside and the top is on, visualizing the path that the marble takes be-

comes a whole different story. As students manipulate the box and make observations about the movement of the marble, they try to draw out what the maze looks like.

As you can imagine, these boxes can range from the very easy to the extremely complex. Allow your students to work up to the complex after they have gotten some practice with the easy versions. And don't be afraid to decorate the boxes to add to the mystique. Wrapping paper, contact paper, or a collage following a suitable theme will add an interesting dimension to the activity. Of course, you will very likely find yourself with a class full of students who also want to construct their own mystery boxes. So you might want to practice visualizing some of these yourself before one of your students comes in and says, "Try this one!"

ACTIVITY 7.8

Mystery Boxes

You will need a shoe box, some cardboard, glue or tape, and a marble. Decorations for the outside of the box are advantageous, though optional.

Cut the cardboard into strips that are about 2 cm (1/4 in.) taller than the inside of the shoebox. Now fold the strips along the long edge so that there is a 2-cm "base" to each strip. Using your own imagination, arrange the cardboard strips inside the box to form a maze. Use glue or tape on the 2-cm base in order to fasten it to the box. The maze need not be an intricate one. However, if you make several mystery boxes you may want to make the mazes increasingly sophisticated to challenge your students. Be sure to remember to put the marble inside of the box before taping or gluing the top in place.

You need not limit yourself to mazes in the box. Make cardboard ramps or barriers. Include a bell that the marble could strike. Be creative!

When your students (or classmates) use the mystery box, encourage them to draw a picture of what they believe is inside. And resist the temptation to expose the answer. The point of mystery boxes is to provide opportunities to generate models, not to know what happens to be in a particular box.

Generating models is not limited to mysterious objects. Many common objects are quite useful for the purpose of generating models. Objects such as fire extinguishers, parking meters, and soft drink dispensers are commonplace, but the inside workings are rarely visible. What happens when you press a key on a piano that ultimately results in playing a note? These and other such items are great for this type of investigation. Keep in mind that the purpose of this type of investigation is not to see who can come up with the correct model, but to generate numerous possible solutions in order to develop the skill of combining knowledge to explain phenomena.

Inventing

In the real world, a mutually beneficial relationship exists between science and technology. That relationship is very important in the teaching of science. Briefly, science is a way of generating knowledge. Inventing, the active process of technology, is a way of applying the knowledge generated through science. Allowing children to invent serves to demystify the world of technology. At the same time, children are actively engaged in the construction of their own understanding of how things work and the scientific principles underlying those workings (Ebert & Ebert, 1998).

Inventing therefore becomes an exciting possibility for scientific investigation in the classroom. Although, traditionally, it may not be considered a form of investigation, children's inventing, as described in this chapter, is a form of investigation with tremendous instructional implications. Inventing is another form of investigation that is product driven rather than being a search for information. It is the process of selecting and combining previously existing ideas and/or objects to form new and unique entities.

Of all the approaches we have discussed, inventing may well be the most sophisticated form of investigation because the inventing process often incorporates various forms of scientific investigation (Figure 7.11). Rarely do scientists have all the information needed to invent a new product. More often, during the inventing process, additional information is needed. In order to acquire, clarify, verify, or refine information used in the inventing process, other investigative forms are utilized.

The foundation steps contribute the background work for inventing. The inventing process begins with identifying a problem or a specific need, which may come from personal experience or, in a classroom set-

FIGURE 7.11 Steps for inventing.

INVENTING

Foundation steps
1. Identifying a problem or need
2. Researching former solutions to the problem

Process steps
3. Generating ideas toward a new solution
4. Designing the invention
5. Constructing the invention

Concluding step
6. Patenting the invention

ting, may be provided by the teacher. Researching former solutions, that is, looking up the results of previous inventive endeavors or other scientific investigations, provides information for the investigator. The information about prior solutions may reference important scientific principles employed in the process as well as identify the advantages and disadvantages of that solution to the problem.

The process steps are the exciting part of inventing, the steps that actually develop the product. Creative thinking is emphasized during these steps, especially during generating ideas. While designing a model for the invention is a cognitive process resulting in a mental image, children should be encouraged to draw the design on paper. The visual thinking that occurs as the conceptual idea is drawn facilitates the clarification of the idea. Constructing the invention begins with collecting and assembling parts. As the invention is being designed or constructed, often using the trial-and-error investigative approach, difficulties may occur that had not been apparent during the generation of the idea. The inventor may return to the first of the process steps and generate additional possibilities. The three process steps may be repeated many times before the inventor is satisfied with the invention.

The concluding step, patenting, is conducted as a means of claiming ownership of the invention. This step is quite involved, requires the assistance of attorneys, and can be expensive. Yet, it is the safeguard of creative enterprise. Students sometimes do design an invention with potential beyond the classroom, so a basic understanding of patents is very useful.

Children's Inventing We know that children's science is in many ways similar to scientists' science, but that it also has very important, distinct differences. And those differences are vital to the teaching of science. Likewise, inventing for children is similar to and yet different from the inventing done by adults. Inventing, for all people, is dependent on what knowledge is available. For example, only if one knows that heat makes things expand, or that cellophane tape on an inflated balloon will allow for the penetration of a pin without popping the balloon, can those principles be incorporated in the inventing process. In the adult world, inventors typically have a large, if not comprehensive, knowledge base from which they draw information. Inventors combine that information with newly acquired information and create an idea or product that is unique and previously unknown. Children's knowledge is quite limited. For them, inventing accompanies the acquisition of knowledge. They develop a real understanding of the information as they apply it. Therefore, inventing for children is an investigation rather than a pure application process.

Levels of Inventing Having examined the various steps involved in the inventing process and identified the differences between children's inventing and inventor's inventing, it is time to focus on the instructional applications of inventing and, consequently, the demystification of the world of technology.

Instructionally speaking, there are three levels of inventing:

Level 1—How Things Work

Level 2—Inventing with Humor

Level 3—Practical Inventing

The levels reflect the sophistication of the activities. They can be used either as a sequencing technique for an in-depth use of the inventing approach or as activities that are age-appropriate for primary-, intermediate-, and upper-level students. Each level, with its particular focus, facilitates success at the next higher level.

How Things Work The first level of inventing focuses on discovering how things work. We often use objects without paying much attention to how they do whatever it is that they are supposed to do. Doorknobs, for example, are used by everyone many times in a single day, and yet how many people understand how the doorknob mechanism really works? Children can learn a great deal of information by closely examining objects, observing their component parts and seeing how they interact. For instance, children might investigate the mechanism of a simple, hand-cranked pencil sharpener, which could be found on a wall in almost any classroom. Items such as can openers, egg beaters, scissors, and tire pumps effectively serve as challenges to students to discover the scientific relationships and principles underlying the function of common objects.

A great way to begin an inventing investigation is to observe simple objects with multiple components. Start with the all-familiar pencil. Using the data collection sheet, Figure 7.12, you would first write in *pencil* for the object. Next, you would examine the characteristics of the object, writing down observations using a variety of your senses. For example, you might say:

Bright yellow mostly wooden object, about 6 inches long, skinny, gray piece is in the wood, rubberlike tip fastened to the wood by a metal piece, grey part is sharply pointed, etc.

Next, you look for the attributes of the object; that is, you examine the parts to see if and how they move. You check to see how it behaves. Does it bend, roll, or change shape? Does it make noise(s) as it moves? In this case, you might find that the pencil is

A single object with components that do not separate without breaking, rigid enough to form a "bridge" between two separate objects, grey part breaks when pressure is exerted, small rubber eraser is somewhat flexible, rolls on flat surface making a slight noise, when dropped on table the pencil makes a small clunking sound unless it hits on the eraser and then it makes a muffled sound, the metal part makes a dull tapping sound when struck, the grey stuff makes a mark on paper and other surfaces, and the eraser when moved over the grey marks removes them.

Having made a close examination there may be some "tests" you might like to try. With the pencil you might want to

- check for reaction to magnet,
- see if it floats,
- find out if it conducts electricity (using a simple battery circuit), and
- see if pins or thumbtacks stick when pressed into the various pencil parts.

The types of tests done by children would depend on their previous experiences and knowledge base. If they have not done this type of investigation before, the teacher may want to suggest appropriate activities. As much as possible, the teacher should allow the children to conduct the tests and record the results. The information collected will add to the knowledge base and be useful in future inventing activities.

ACTIVITY 7.9

Attribute Finding

Make a version of the data collection sheet in Figure 7.12. Identify a common object and try completing the form. Spring clothespins are super for this activity.

FIGURE 7.12 Attribute Finding data sheet.

How Things Work—Attribute Finding

Object: _____

Characteristics:

_____

_____

_____

_____

Attributes:

_____

_____

_____

_____

Testing the Object: Results:

_____   _____

_____   _____

_____   _____

_____   _____

After having spent some time examining various objects, the children are ready to design and construct their own versions. The flashlight is a good example of an object that first can be examined to see how it works and then constructed by children using simple materials. If they have had experience with simple battery–operated electrical circuits, they are probably ready to do this activity. If not, they may need some of those experiences before beginning this activity. Another approach is to interject the electric circuit activities during the flashlight activity, after attribute finding and before construction.

Directions for inventing the objects, in this case a flashlight, are not provided, and so guidance on the part of the teacher is important. The teacher and the use of data collection sheets can ensure a systematic approach to inventing investigations that might not otherwise occur to the children.

It is very important to recognize the difference between (1) providing instructions to assemble a flashlight and (2) allowing children to discover how to design and construct their own version of a flashlight. In the first situation, someone other than the children has done the thinking necessary to understand how flashlights work and how the parts can be assembled to make one. That defeats the purpose of this activity. The reason for conducting inventing investigations is for children to do the discovering and the think-

ing that is needed to produce a working object such as the flashlight.

Each small group of children should have their own store-bought, inexpensive, hand-held flashlight. The children should first examine the flashlight, its component parts, and the interactions of those parts, disassembling the flashlight in the process. Documenting their observations by using something like the Attribute Finding data sheet is very helpful for systematizing the investigation. Rather than have the children identify "tests" they would like to perform, as indicated on the Attribute Finding sheet, the teacher should encourage them to identify systems and subsystems.

A *system* is a group of components that are assembled to accomplish a task that individual components alone cannot accomplish. A flashlight is an example of a system that is designed to generate and focus a beam of

FIGURE 7.13 Inventor's recycle bin.

string	wooden dowels	balloons
toothpicks	paper bags	magnets
nails	milk containers	yarn
foil	pipe cleaners	straws
pulleys	mousetraps	buttons
candles	sandwich bags	feathers
wire	film cans	newspaper
tape	rubber bands	mirrors
spools	coat hangers	marbles

FIGURE 7.14 Flashlight investigation.

**HOW THINGS WORK—
FLASHLIGHT INVESTIGATION**

Pursuit of information
1. Examine flashlight.
2. Identify components and systems.

Application of information
3. Identify materials for components and systems.
4. Assemble parts.
5. Test product.
6. Refine systems as necessary.

light. A *subsystem* is an assembly of components, a feature added to the system that enhances its function. The switch on the flashlight is an example of a subsystem. The flashlight could generate and focus light without a switch, but the switch prevents a constant drain on the batteries.

Once children have discovered how flashlights work and have identified the important components, they are ready to construct their own flashlights. They may use whatever materials are available to assemble a working flashlight that looks very much like the one they took apart or a modification of that design. If children have access to some batteries (D cells), plastic-coated wire, cardboard tubes, flashlight bulbs, aluminum foil or muffin cups, paper clips and duct tape, they have the necessities for constructing the flashlights. However, they may design flashlights that require other materials. Teachers should try to anticipate items that might be requested as the children invent their own designs, and should have them available, if possible. For example, children may realize that a metal funnel or a plastic funnel lined with aluminum foil would make a sturdier reflector than just a piece of aluminum foil surrounding the lightbulb. Children may invent switches that need something other than a paper clip, or something in addition to a paper clip. A "recycle bin" containing an assort-

ment of useful objects is almost a necessity when inventing. An example of the contents of such a box is provided in Figure 7.13. A summary of the flashlight activity in a generalizable format is presented in Figure 7.14.

Children's inventing is a form of investigation that, in turn, incorporates more than one type of investigation. The first part of the activity focuses on the pursuit of information. Examining the object and writing down the identified characteristics, attributes, components, and systems is a form of the investigation called documenting. The second part of the flashlight activity focuses on applying what was learned in the first part of the activity. Trial and error is the investigative form used during this construction process.

The knowledge gained from such activities serves to broaden the knowledge base that students can bring to more sophisticated activities. For young children who depend on observations and tangible experiences to help understand the world around them, this type of inventing—How Things Work—is a valuable form of investigation.

Inventing with Humor Humor, as an educational strategy, serves to motivate students, relieve tension, and reduce anxiety when they are asked to generate a science project. Inventing in the Rube Goldberg fashion is

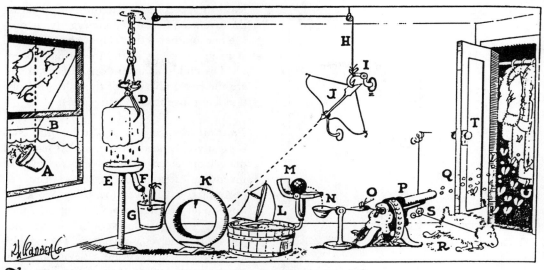

THE PROFESSOR EMERGES FROM THE GOOFY BOOTH WITH A DEVICE FOR THE EXTERMINATION OF MOTHS.
START SINGING. LADY UPSTAIRS, WHEN SUFFICIENTLY ANNOYED, THROWS FLOWER POT (A) THROUGH AWNING (B). HOLE (C) ALLOWS SUN TO COMB THROUGH AND MELT CAKE OF ICE (D). WATER DRIPS INTO PAN (E) RUNNING THROUGH PIPE (F) INTO PAIL (G). WEIGHT OF PAIL CAUSES CORD (H) TO RELEASE HOOK (I) AND ALLOW ARROW (J) TO SHOOT INTO TIRE (K). ESCAPING AIR BLOWS AGAINST TOY SAILBOAT (L) DRIVING IT AGAINST LEVER (M) AND CAUSING BALL TO ROLL INTO SPOON (N) AND PULL STRING (O) WHICH SETS OFF MACHINE GUN (P) DISCHARGING CAMPHOR BALLS (Q).
REPORT OF GUN FRIGHTENS LAMB (R) WHICH RUNS AND PULLS CORD (S), OPENING CLOSET DOOR (T). AS MOTHS (U) FLY OUT TO EAT WOOL FROM LAMB'S BACK THEY ARE KILLED BY THE BARRAGE OF MOTH BALLS.
IF ANY OF THE MOTHS ESCAPE AND THERE IS DANGER OF THEIR RETURNING, YOU CAN FOOL THEM BY MOVING.

FIGURE 7.15 Rube Goldberg. Reprinted by permission of United Feature Syndicate, Inc.

an especially appropriate way to capitalize on humor. Rube Goldberg (1883–1970) was an American cartoonist who published many comic strips about Professor Lucifer Gorganzola Butts, an absentminded professor who came up with ideas for preposterous inventions. Typically, the cartoons illustrated a wildly complex and humorous solution to accomplish a very simple task (see Figure 7.15). The phrase "a Rube Goldberg" is commonly used to describe any device or method that uses an extremely complex and roundabout way to do a job that could be done simply.

When involved in this type of inventing, teachers challenge students to invent devices that, for example, automatically pop a balloon, make the bed, wash the chalkboard, or water houseplants while the family is away on vacation. The products of such inventing may take the form of ideas or drawings on paper. Eventually, the products should take the form of actual working devices. The wonderful part about this type of inventing is that the supplies used for construction are inexpensive, common materials. Paper towel tubes make excellent troughs for rolling marbles. Strips of aluminum foil or paper clips are terrific switches for simple battery-operated electrical circuits. Spools that hold ribbon or thread make great pulleys. And mousetraps are fantastic because they can be used to pull strings and plugs, move something from here to there, or serve as electrical switches opening and closing battery-operated circuits. With a box of discarded objects (the inventor's recycle bin), a few scraps of lumber, and lots of duct tape, Rube

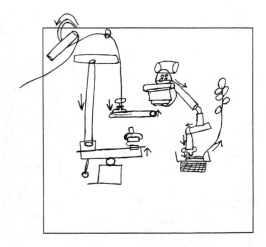

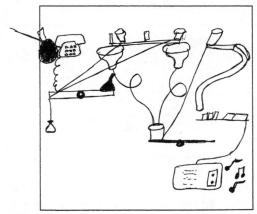

FIGURE 7.16 Initial drawings such as this balloon releaser (top) and automatic music player (bottom) represent a major step in turning students' invention ideas into realities. Used by permission.

Goldberg inventions can really take shape. Creative thinking is stimulated as children combine an odd assortment of common objects to perform a task not at all similar to the originally intended use.

Students who have previously been reluctant to participate in science fair projects because they fear possible humiliating responses from peers, are no longer hesitant. Laughter becomes a measure of success when doing Rube Goldberg inventing. Children

learn to appreciate the tension of preparing the invention for display and eagerly encourage one another as they achieve minor as well as major successes in the inventing process.

The children's inventions and comments are the best indicators of the value of Rube Goldberg inventing (Figure 7.16).

Practical Inventing Success at the third level is greatly enhanced when students have had many experiences with the first two levels of inventing. After children have had many opportunities to discover how things work and how to create humorous inventions, they develop strong feelings of self-confidence and see themselves as inventors. Then, when asked to tackle inventing a device that has practical applications in their own lives, they are not overwhelmed by all of the steps of inventing, or at least by the first five steps. Without having experienced the fun of inventing with humor, which focuses on the process steps of inventing, and without the knowledge gained through discovering how things work, they are reluctant to undertake the foundation steps. Too often, curriculum projects that address inventing place too much emphasis on the very first steps. Those foundation steps are quite intimidating for many children, and without proper motivation, the research can be difficult and uninteresting.

Practical inventing in the classroom involves all of the inventing steps, with the likely exception of patenting. Since identifying a personal need may be difficult for some children, a transitional approach to practical inventing might be helpful. Rather than expect the children to assume the total responsibility for the identification step, suggest some categories for them to pursue, but avoid actually providing the problem to be solved. For example, the teacher may suggest that the inventions could be something to help with chores at home, games that can be played at school, or ways to organize or secure their personal items. By narrowing the options, but not limiting them to the categories suggested, the first step of inventing is not difficult for the children. In fact, they are probably anxious to get started with it.

Practical inventing can be a highly individual matter. Each person accesses a unique knowledge base and processes new ideas in a very personal way. Teachers, however, can facilitate the process. While the teacher wants to avoid overstructuring the thinking process, guidelines can be provided in the form of daily activity suggestions. For example, on the first day or two, the teacher may have the children spend some time individually thinking about possible needs or problems and some time discussing possibilities in small groups. The goal is for each child to identify and state a personal need or problem to be solved. The next couple of days, the teacher may suggest that the children access books and other resources as a means of researching former solutions and recording helpful information. Then, the children should be encouraged to generate lists of ideas, as many as they can, and to sketch some possibilities if appropriate. Once students begin to design the inventions, the teacher's interventions will be on an individual basis, helping children to overcome obstacles by asking questions, or steering a child to appropriate, helpful resources.

If this is the first time the children have attempted practical inventing, extra assistance for researching former solutions may be necessary. It is very helpful to have available books and other resources that focus on how things work, science and inventions references, and historical developments of technology. Perhaps more important the first time is showing students how to look for something in a book and how to briefly record significant information. If the teacher models the process of researching former solutions rather than merely telling students what to do, the children will be better pre-

FIGURE 7.17 Questions to facilitate the inventing process.

What is the problem you need to solve?

What information have you found on former solutions?

What about checking other sources of information?

What are some ideas you have come up with so far?

Have you talked about your ideas with anyone?

Has that been helpful?

Have you been writing questions in your journal, such as:

> What do I need to know now?
>
> What is another way?
>
> What else could I use?

pared to conduct their own research. Modeling the process should involve searching for relevant resources, locating pertinent information, and recording helpful information, accompanied all the while by the verbalization of the thinking that occurs.

In addition, inventor's journals can be used to help children become more systematic during the inventing process. The journals are an excellent means of recording the inventing process, somewhat like a chronicle of the development of the invention. Children can record any pertinent information collected from the various resources and their own ideas. Those records can then be reviewed by the child at any time, and they are especially useful when the child decides to redesign the invention or pursue another alternative.

Asking questions is one of the most helpful strategies teachers can use to encourage children's thinking. The questions in Figure 7.17, and other similar questions, would be appropriate at various points within the inventing process.

Figures 7.18, 7.19, and 7.20 represent a sixth-grader's inventing experience. What Hattie has done to invent a burglar alarm is

Hattie's Journal

Day 1

Problem: My sister tries to read my diary all the time.
I don't like that.
I want to protect my diary. I need to invent a burglar alarm for diaries.

Day 2

I looked through the books on burglar alarms that the teacher got from the public library.

Notes: Security Systems Simplified by Steven Hampton
        pages 3-5   History of Intruder Alarm Systems

1. Ancient Egyptians invented pin tumbler lock made of wooden pegs and used large wooden key to raise pegs
2. Egyptians made mazes and deadly traps in pyramids to protect pharaohs and stuff
3. Watch dogs to make noise - no date or people for this
4. First true intruder alarm system was patented by Edwin Homes in 1889 breaking of electrical circuit with a switch alarm was usually a bell or loud noise
5. 1930's vibration detectors, floor-mat pressure switches, and tight-wire devices
6. 1940's photoelectric systems, glass break detectors
7. 1960's infrared and ultrasonic things
8. 1970's microwave and computers
9. 1980's pyroelectric systems sensed body heat

page 12

I like this idea!!

page 17 - The book says to think like an intruder. I've never thought like an intruder. I need to work on this.

Day 3

I need to think like an intruder.
Where would I look for a hidden diary?
Possible hiding places???
        Not   Maybe
        under pillow   in closet
        in drawers   book case
        under bed   in bed

If I were an intruder I would look under things - inside things - high and low places. What about middle places?

I like the name Intruder Alert, I will invent:

        Hattie's Intruder Alert

FIGURE 7.18 Hattie's Journal, Day 1–Day 3

---

an example of the process of practical inventing. In addition, it illustrates the value of maintaining an inventor's journal.

ACTIVITY 7.10

An Inventing Activity

The best way to understand practical inventing is to try it yourself. Invent your own form of intruder alert or burglar alarm or something else. Keep a written record of your progress. Include sketches and photographs, if possible. Also, keep your materials simple. Use materials that are readily available. Let the questions in Figure 7.17 guide you as you begin.

Summary of Inventing Inventing serves a variety of purposes in the elementary classroom. The classroom is a unique place and very different from the adult world. Some phenomena that seem so common in the school environment are not found outside of schools. For example, adults are not expected,

Hattie's Journal

Day 4

Just some ideas for: Hattie's Intruder Alert

Put string around bed or inside bedroom door to trip intruder
Something to scare intruder
Noise makers - buzzer - horn - radio - bell - balloon pop - drum
Watch dog - Brownie won't bark at my sister

Books in school library <u>Fun with Science - Electricity and Magnets</u> by Terry Cash

    Notes: page 17 shows how to make a Burglar Alarm. It uses a battery, wire, cardboard, aluminum foil, tape, and a small buzzer. It says a light bulb works too. The switch made of cardboard and wire is hidden under a rug. It makes noise when somebody steps on it. That must be like floor-mat pressure switches in 1930's.
    page 21 Another neat thing is Electronic Quiz Game. A bulb lights up when you touch the right numbers with two wires. Maybe I can use numbers for a secret code.

Day 5
    Hattie's Intruder Alert
floor mats with numbers - use secret code
step on the right numbers is OK
step on wrong numbers makes a big noise

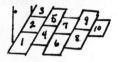

It might be a problem when my friends or mom come into my room.

Day 6
    Notes <u>Fun with Science - Sound</u> by Terry Cash
    pages 10-13 shows stuff on making sounds louder
           megaphone and ear trumpet
           tube telephone and string telephone

A tube telephone would let me hear when someone was near the diary but only if they make noise. I would also have to drag around the tube.

Day 7
    A new design
    The burglar alarm on page 17 hides the switch under a rug.
    That's low
    What else could push it together? in a middle place?

What about book in the book case? When they come together, that could set off the alarm

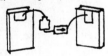

diary

The wires, buzzer, and battery are hidden behind the books on the shelf.
One wire goes to aluminum foil on one book.
The other wire goes to aluminum foil taped to the back of another book.
The diary is between the 2 books. If my sister, or some other intruder, takes my diary off the shelf, the 2 book fall together and ring the buzzer.

FIGURE 7.19 Hattie's Journal, Day 4–Day 7

Hattie's Journal

Day 8
    Made the intruder alert and it worked but it had problems.
  Problems:
        1 The books don't always fall.
        2 The books don't always touch in the right place.

Day 9
    Made new and improved Hattie's Intruder Alert

Make sure the books lean against one another.
Put foil at top of short book and a long piece on the other book

Day 10
    Invention Fair Day - Demonstrated Hattie's Intruder Alert

      It worked great !

FIGURE 7.20 Hattie's Journal, Day 8– Day 10

FIGURE 7.21 Investigation types, strategies, and results.

Type	Strategy	Result
Trial and error	Arbitrary search for solutions	Product/Information
Documenting	Making and recording observations	Information
Prediction testing	Making and testing predictions	Information
Product testing	Identifying and using criteria	Information
Experimenting	Identifying and controlling variables	Information
Generating models	Creating visual constructs	Product
Inventing	Selecting and combining ideas/objects	Product
Reflecting	Contemplating ideas	Question/Guide for future pursuit/Summary of what has been accomplished

on a regular basis, to account for what they have learned. And scientists choose whether or not to apply the information they have generated. Often, they leave the application of that information to someone else. Children, however, are routinely required to demonstrate their mastery of information. And those who have weak verbal skills are automatically at a disadvantage in a written test situation. Inventing, however, is a vehicle that allows children to apply what they have learned in science, and to do so in a way that is not verbally dependent. In addition, children develop a sense of accomplishment and self-esteem while inventing. They are proud of their inventions and, most important, of the thinking that took place while inventing. At the same time, they are becoming a part of the real world of science and technology and are enjoying themselves. You can find information about several excellent books about inventing in the classroom in chapter 14.

CONCLUSION

An investigation is a search or inquiry done systematically. The information in Figure 7.21 helps to compare the various forms of investigation presented in this chapter.

Each form of investigation serves a different purpose and can be thought of as a different system. The strategies for each investigative form represent the guidelines that distinguish one system from another. On the other hand, the type of results of the investigations are not as varied. The results can be in the form of information, products, or questions that guide additional inquiry.

It is important to note that while Figure 7.21 reports the type of results of each of the forms of investigation, those results are products of investigation from the perspective of the investigator. That is, the person conducting a product test or an experiment is in pursuit of information. And the outcome for a person who is involved in generating models or inventing is a product. However, for the teacher who has established an investigative approach to the teaching of science, the focus is not the same as the focus of the investigator. The process of investigation rather than the product of the investigation is the primary concern. Students are often proud of the results of investigations and rightfully so. The teacher's goal, however, is to provide students with the opportunity to engage in the thinking-and-doing process. Understanding how to conduct an investigation and knowing when to use which form of investigation is a tremendous accomplishment. Students and teachers alike should be proud of that accomplishment, and they will be if the emphasis is on the process—the thinking and doing.

ACTIVITY 7.11

Reflecting on the Investigative Approaches

This might be a good time to reflect on your understanding of the various forms of investigations in science. Think about the information you have recently acquired through your readings, discussions, and activities. Summarize your thoughts about the various forms of investigation. Which of the investigative approaches strike you as most interesting? What questions do you have at this time for your instructor? Make a list of questions that could be asked of your peers, experienced classroom teachers, and scientists that would help you better understand teaching science using an investigative approach.

Designing
Science Lessons

**The Three Components of
Science Education**

Discovery Learning

Conclusion

Your Academic Roadmap

Study of this chapter should help you to understand
the following concepts:

- The product of science is knowledge gained
  through having a curious attitude and using an
  investigative process.

- The Discovery Approach, though more time-
  consuming than other approaches, yields more
  meaningful learning.

- The Learning Cycle and the Planning for Conceptual Change model are lesson formats that
  highlight the nature of the learner as an inquirer.

- High-quality learning takes time for doing and
  time for thinking.

Science is different things for different people.
Science, for me, is learning about rocks and
minerals and different kinds of scientific facts.

—Jamie, twelve years old

THE THREE COMPONENTS OF SCIENCE EDUCATION

As discussed in earlier chapters, children are curious, and what they do naturally—construct meaning for the world around them—is really what science is all about. Therefore, if children do not enjoy their science experience in school, it is probably a result of the way the two, science and children, are brought together. And that is the major focus of this chapter: to present ways to design and teach science lessons so that experiences are enjoyable and positive for all. This chapter considers the three essential components of science education, two models for the presentation of science lessons, and several strategies for teacher-student interaction that will help facilitate a discovery learning approach.

Content, Attitude, and Process

Over the past several decades, the definition of science as it relates to elementary school curricula has changed from "a body of knowledge" to "science is what scientists do." With the recent recognition that attitude is an important aspect of science because it relates to both the nature of science and the impact of attitude on the learner, it has also been incorporated into the definition of science. As a result, science curricula for grades 1–8 often reflect the historical changes in science as such:

Science = Content + Process + Attitude

This formula, however, is just the opposite of what scientists really do. The scientist starts with curiosity, a question that needs answering or a problem that needs solving. Through some form of investigation, in which the science process skills are of primary importance, information is gained. Content or knowledge, typically the starting point in the design of the curriculum, is not the beginning but the end of scientific endeavor. Knowledge is the product of scientific investigation. A more appropriate representation of the three aspects of science would be

Science = Attitude + Process → Knowledge

Survival Values

Researchers have found that retention rates differ for various kinds of learning. The information gained from these studies provides an empirical basis for identifying the most appropriate method for teaching science or any other subject. You may find it helpful to complete Activities 8.1 and 8.2 before continuing to read the text.

ACTIVITY 8.1

Rating Survival Values

Read through the chart below and rank the various categories of learning.

Survival Values of Learning

Task: Predict which of the following categories of learning was found to be retained at the highest level after one year. (1 = highest, 6 = lowest)

Ranking   **Learning Category**

_____ **Factual Material:** (Example) The population of the United States in 1998 was 270,496,300. Oxygen has six protons in its nucleus.

_____ **Attitudes about Yourself in Relation to Subject, Studies, and Other:** (Example) I enjoy the outdoors. I feel comfortable around environmentalists. Math is super.

_____ **Motor Skills:** (Example) Printing, typing, riding a bike, sewing, skiing, putting (golf).

_____ **Conceptual Schemes:** (Example) Man is a product of hereditary and environmental factors. For every action, there is an opposite and equal reaction.

_____ **Nonsense Syllables:** (Example) alad, busky, rab, stul, nol, dut, etc.

_____ **Thinking Skills and Processes:** (Example) How to solve problems. How to observe, infer, form a hypothesis, communicate, and so on.

ACTIVITY 8.2

Educational Implications of the Survival Values

Upon completion of Activity 8.1, examine the graph in Figure 8.1, which shows the actual results of the study. What are the educational implications of these findings?

The graph in Figure 8.1 indicates what the research found. Do any of the results surprise you? Most notable for the challenge of teaching is the "Attitudes" category. Since attitude has 100 percent retention after one year, it has the greatest impact on the learner. Think back to the time when you were in elementary school. Can you think of a grade or subject you especially liked? What about a grade or subject you especially disliked? It comes back to you almost instantaneously, doesn't it? It may be that you really liked fifth grade because you did "neat things" and the teacher made you feel good about what you had accomplished. On the other hand, you may not have liked spelling because you were never any good at it or you felt inadequate. Your attitudes regarding spelling or other experiences may have changed, but you can easily recall those feelings, even after many years.

If science is enjoyable and the students have successful experiences that build self-confidence, then positive attitudes toward science will be established. The teacher can foster that positive attitude toward science with a positive attitude of his or her own. If the teacher is curious about the world and finds pleasure in pursuing the answers to questions and solving problems, then the students will also very likely enjoy these pursuits. On the other hand, if the teacher has a negative attitude about science, the students are more likely to perceive science as an unpleasant portion of the curriculum.

Attitude is also the starting point in science. Scientists begin with a curious attitude, the need to understand the world around them, or questions that need answering. They want to answer these questions, rather than be told to answer them (see chapter 6).

The category "Thinking Skills and Processes" is essentially the same as the science process skills identified in chapter 6. That these processes are retained at a level of 80 percent underscores the significance of the science process skills in the teaching of science. Once these skills and processes are understood by the students, they can be applied to any problem-solving situation, both in and out of school. Once children have learned to classify, they can classify numbers in math, types of stories in language arts, artifacts in social studies, as well as objects in science, such as shells, leaves, and rocks. They can even classify objects at home, such as stamps, stuffed animals, baseball cards, and clothing. Because the skills and processes are so useful and not dependent on subject-specific content, they become a meaningful part of everyday life.

The "Motor Skills" are also highly significant to learning. In science, these are referred to as "hands-on" activities. It is the physical contact with the components of the concept, the personal manipulation of the objects, that facilitates learning. The construction of knowledge begins with di-rectly observable, tangible experiences, is followed by verbal discussion of the concept, and eventually evolves into an abstract level of understanding.

"Conceptual Schemes," which is used to organize many textbooks, has only a 50 percent retention. As much is forgotten as is retained. And "Factual Material" is retained at a dreadfully low 35 percent—twice as much is forgotten as is retained!

You should also take notice of the drop-off rate. The loss, in all five categories, is rapid during the first three months. What is retained after three months seems to be retained over the entire year.

The educational implications of this research are tremendous. If the approach to teaching emphasizes memorization of factual information, the quality of learning is very poor. And yet, the real world of teaching is greatly influenced by the use of standardized tests. Accountability for teachers is a real issue. Pressure to assure that students know the appropriate conceptual schemes and factual information still exits. These are issues that go far beyond a science methods textbook, but we think the information described here provides you with some valuable educational insight.

DISCOVERY LEARNING

Science is a way of explaining how things work and a means for understanding the world around us. Children, filled with their natural curiosity and eagerness, attempt to understand the world around them, but in ways that vary from those used by the scientific community. (See chapter 4 for a discussion of children's science versus scientist's science.) Scientists use a variety of investigative approaches in their pursuit of understanding the world, but it is very important to note that all the scientists' approaches are systematic. Children lack that structure in their natural pursuits. Science education

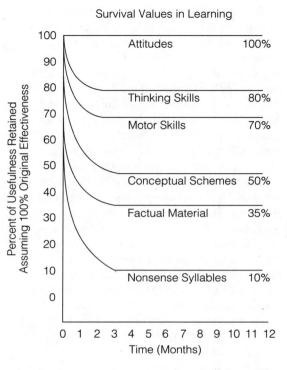

FIGURE 8.1

Survival values results. (An interpretation from Cronbach, 1963)

can provide the necessary experiences that will add a systematic perspective to children's science.

Chapter 6 discussed inquiry as reflecting the nature of the learner; that is, the child who comes into your classroom is naturally inquisitive. On the other hand, *discovery learning* addresses the nature of *instruction*. Discovery learning is an approach to the teaching of science that emphasizes students' personal experiences with information and materials as a foundation for conceptual development, and thus it makes best use of the child's inquisitive nature. Children are provided materials to manipulate. The science process skills, which are an important part of systematic investigations, are emphasized. Children make firsthand observations rather than depend only on observations reported in textbooks or other authoritative sources. They are encouraged to ask their own questions and are given problems to solve rather than answers to memorize! The minds and hands of the

children are active. Discovery learning is an extension of the natural way that children learn and is a reliable way of coping with the day-to-day problems of the real world.

Effective teachers of science can use the discovery learning approach, which emphasizes (1) a positive attitude, (2) the science process skills, and (3) a hands-on approach. These teachers can be confident that pertinent information is learned to a higher level of understanding and retention than with other teaching approaches that emphasize memorization of facts and schemes.

Something else that supports the discovery learning approach is the ancient Chinese proverb shown in Figure 8.2.

If students listen to a lecture, they are likely to forget what was said. A demonstration will have a greater impact. They may not understand the concept, but they will remember seeing the event that demonstrated the concept. But if the students are active in the process, manipulating the com-

FIGURE 8.2 Chinese proverb.

I hear and I forget . . .
I see and I remember . . .
I do and I understand.

ponents of the concept, they establish an ownership of the concepts discovered and they understand.

The following two models for designing and presenting science lessons each capitalize on the process of science and building positive attitudes toward science.

The Learning Cycle

The Learning Cycle (Figure 8.3) is a model for designing science lessons that ensures a successful, positive experience for students. Originally, it was a three-stage model developed by Atkins and Karplus (1962). It was incorporated into the Science Curriculum Improvement Study (SCIS Program) created during the 1960s. Since that time, it has been used and sometimes modified by many science educators. The model presented here is a four-phase model. The first phase was not present in the Atkins and Karplus model.

Introduction The purpose of Introduction is to motivate students. At this time, the teacher captures the students' interest through the use of discrepant event demonstrations, interesting materials, or challenging questions and problems to solve. Most likely, you know what interesting materials are (animals, plants, an aquarium, simple machines, etc.) and are familiar with the concept of challenging questions or problems to solve, but what about discrepant events? Discrepant events are situations in which things do not happen as you would expect them to happen. For example, what would you expect to happen if you press a 12-inch steel needle through a balloon? Well, when you do that, and the result is the same as in the photo

FIGURE 8.3 The Learning Cycle.

THE FOUR-PHASE LEARNING CYCLE

Phase 1	Introduction: Motivating student interest
Phase 2	Exploration: Working with manipulatives to discover the concept
Phase 3	Concept Development: Verbalizing the concept
Phase 4	Application: Applying the newly learned concept

on page 182, then you have a discrepant event on your hands. Do you think that would capture the interest of your students?

Exploration Exploration is a very active phase for the students. Independently or in small groups, they work with manipulatives investigating the concept to be learned. The science process skills are important and obvious during this phase. The teacher's role at this time is one of guidance. Having previously established a conducive learning environment and designed one or more activities that include directions and questions, the teacher now challenges students and encourages independent thinking as they investigate. The purpose of exploration, therefore, is to provide children with an experience-based opportunity to construct their own understanding of the concept.

Concept Development This phase provides an opportunity for students to report their findings and share what they discovered with one another. While eliciting information and ideas generated by the students during Exploration, the teacher directs the discussion and provides appropriate terminology. Also, as necessary, the teacher helps students resolve differences in their findings. All the while, he or she is guiding the students as they develop a new understanding of the concept. The purpose of the Concept Development step is to allow opportunities

Chen Long

PHOTO 8.1 Needle through the balloon—this discrepant event is sure to capture a student's attention.

for verbalizing and clarifying the concept. If there is information in a written format that might help in the verbalization or clarification of the concept, from a textbook or other source, it is read at this time, not before Exploration.

Application If the students understand the new concept, they will be able to apply it to a new, but closely related, situation. The Application phase provides that opportunity. It may take the form of another activity, or it may be a problem-solving or a question-answering discussion. The application of the concept may also serve as a means of evaluation. The purpose of this phase of the learning cycle is to assess student understanding of the concept.

The Learning Cycle is not a linear progression but a cyclic one, as the name implies. The teacher may choose to extend the study of the topic by using the Application phase to begin a new cycle. The question or challenge of the Application becomes a challenge for a new Introduction, encouraging interest in further study of the topic.

An Example In order to help clarify the model, consider an example of a teacher who wants to begin a study of magnetism.

Introduction: The teacher, displaying an interesting assortment of materials and a magnet, begins by saying that she tipped over a box of things on her desk yesterday and noticed that some of the objects were attracted to a magnet she happened to be holding at the time. She says that some of the objects practically jumped up to the magnet, but not all the objects responded to it. She then presents the following question as a challenge to the students: What kinds of objects could be picked up or moved by a magnet?

Exploration: The students, working in small groups, are given magnets and boxes of assorted objects. They are asked to observe the interactions between the objects and the magnet and to classify the objects into one of two categories: (1) objects attracted by the magnet and (2) objects not attracted by the magnet.

Concept Development: Students are asked to share their findings from Exploration. If discrepancies in the classification occurred, further discussion would help to resolve the differences. The teacher helps students identify patterns that exist within the classification and formulate a generalization. Quite likely, the students will generate and agree on a statement such as "Magnets attract metal objects and do not attract objects that are not made of metal." Although much remains for the children to learn, the statement is appropriate at this time and is accepted. The teacher has facilitated the verbalization of the concept rather than making the "scientific statement" for the students.

Application: The teacher provides an opportunity for students to apply what they have learned by asking them to predict whether or not a displayed object (which is only part metal, such as a spring clothespin made of wood and metal) would be attracted by the magnet. If the students understand the concept at this point, they should be able to make a prediction that accounts for magnetic interactions with the different parts of the object.

Extending the Cycle The teacher will probably want to continue to develop the concept of magnetism. In that case, the Application challenge could involve a discrepant event. The teacher could ask the students to predict the magnetic behavior of another set of objects, some of which are metal but are not composed of iron (or large concentrations of nickel or cobalt) and therefore not attracted to magnets. Through additional exploration, the students would have an op-

portunity to distinguish between magnetically attractive and nonmagnetically attractive metals. In Concept Development, the students would verbalize that distinction. The cycle is very effective for gradually increasing the level of understanding of the topic under consideration.

As mentioned, the Application phase can also be used to assess student understanding. For example, if the teacher felt the need to record student progress at this point, the students could be given a set of objects to classify. A check for understanding or points to be recorded in a grade book could be assigned to the activity.

ACTIVITY 8.3

The Learning Cycle Format

Choose one of the topics below, and then write a lesson plan using the Learning Cycle (see Figure 8.3). Pay particular attention to the challenge that you will provide in the Introduction, and the activities in which the students will engage in the Exploration phase. Keep in mind that you want to have the children use as many of the basic science process skills as possible during this time.

weather	magnetism	solar energy
simple machines	germination	adaptive coloration

Teaching for Conceptual Change

While the Learning Cycle is a truly effective model for designing science lessons, or lessons for any other subject area, it does not explicitly consider children's preconceptions— that is, what children already know about a topic prior to instruction. Teaching for conceptual change is an approach that extends the Learning Cycle model by not only revealing to the teacher the students' level of understanding prior to instruction but, very

FIGURE 8.4 Conceptual Change model.

PLANNING FOR CONCEPTUAL CHANGE

1. Being Challenged: In response to a challenge, students become aware of their own beliefs about the topic.
2. Sharing Ideas: Students expose their personal beliefs by sharing them with members of the class.
3. Exploring Concepts: Students work with manipulatives, testing their ideas and exploring the concept.
4. Resolving Conflicts: Students work to resolve conflicts between what they discovered during exploration and their previous beliefs.
5. Making Connections: Students make connections between the newly learned concepts and other parts of their lives.
6. Pursuing Questions: Students raise and pursue their own questions reflecting individual interest.

importantly, allowing each child to acknowledge personal beliefs. At the same time, students discover that classmates have different ways of explaining the same phenomena. It is much easier for students to recognize the need to reassess their own explanations if differences exist among peers, rather than if the only acknowledged difference is between their unexpressed explanations and those espoused by the book or teacher. The following model makes children aware of their own level of conceptual understanding prior to instruction and provides experiences for individuals to question current beliefs, test those beliefs, and change to a new level of understanding.

The Planning for Conceptual Change model presented here (Figure 8.4) is a modification of Stepans' (1994) Teaching for Conceptual Change. The brief description of each step included in the planning model states what is to happen to the student. But what is the teacher's role? The teacher's job, obviously, is to facilitate the process of conceptual change. By extending the study of

magnetism, the example used for the Learning Cycle, we can more closely examine the roles of the teacher and students.

Being Challenged Suppose the teacher has continued with a series of activities and is working on the concept of magnetic fields. The teacher asks the students to predict whether magnets will attract objects if something, such as a piece of paper or aluminum foil, is between the magnet and the objects.

Sharing Ideas The students are encouraged to think about the question first and then share their own ideas with others in small groups. They are encouraged to give reasons for their predictions. The teacher then asks for an oral report of the prediction by small groups. For example, one group might report that two people think that it will make no difference, that the objects with iron metal will still be attracted to the magnet. One person thinks that the objects will no longer be attracted to the magnet, even if they are made of metal with iron, and that "metals can't work through other stuff." Another child thinks that it will depend on what kind of material is placed between the magnet and the objects, that "magnets can work through some stuff but not all stuff." The teacher writes the prediction explanations on the board without rewording the statements. If two or more children give the same explanation, tally marks can be used to indicate the frequency of responses. Everybody's ideas are shared, although not necessarily individually.

Exploring the Concept Once the predictions are made, the children are provided materials to investigate the concept. In this situation, each group would receive a magnet, an assortment of objects, and a variety of materials such as paper, wood, plastic wrap, and aluminum foil. Children are encouraged to investigate other materials if they so desire. The students may be provided with or allowed to design their own data collection sheet. They record the observations made as they manipulate the magnets and other materials. (*Note:* The suggested items would not interfere with the magnetic attraction. If the students place a piece of metal containing iron between the magnet and the object, the metal plate will interrupt the magnetic attraction.)

Resolving Conflicts The class as a whole discusses the information discovered during the exploration. If some groups have different results, or additional information, they share it with everyone. The teacher helps students resolve any discrepancies or conflicts between what was predicted and what was discovered. The teacher facilitates the students' verbalization of the concept rather than making the "scientific statement" that explains the concept.

Making Connections The lesson is extended by the teacher by asking students how the concept is important to them or how what they have learned impacts on their daily lives. This is just a bit more involved than one might think. Too often, teachers try to make the new information relevant for the students; that is, as if by pointing out why something is relevant, they could convince students to simply accept it as so. Sometimes, however, the connections make sense to the children and sometimes they do not. It is better if the students themselves recognize the relevancy of the concept. If the teacher asks the children to make the connections, even if it is after one example from the teacher's perspective, then the teacher can be assured the connections are taking place and that the concept is relevant from the students' perspective. In this example, children may see the connection between what they have just learned and using magnets to hold messages or school papers on refrigerator doors. That is not exactly the first step in de-

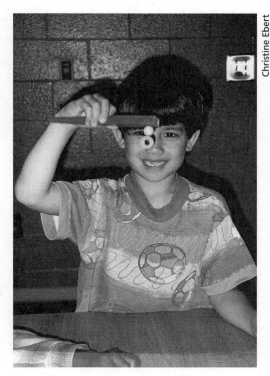

Christine Ebert

PHOTO 8.2 The exploration phase provides a tangible experience for students to discuss.

signing rockets to distant galaxies, but it is the start of seeing how what is done in class applies to life outside of school.

Pursuing Questions The students have ownership of the new concept if they have been able to make connections between what was recently learned and their daily lives. The ownership becomes more personal if each child is encouraged to raise and pursue his or her own question regarding the concept. Not everyone will have the same interests or the same "next question." For that matter, not everyone will want to pursue the topic; some students will be satisfied with the new information. To allow for the individual differences, the teacher should create opportunities for open-ended investigations and provide guidance only as requested or needed.

For example, one student may want to find out about the strength of magnets and ask, "Are bigger magnets stronger magnets?" Another student who has discovered magnets in old radio speakers may ask, "Why are there magnets in speakers and what do they do?" The students should also be encouraged to pursue their own interests on their own time. Not everyone should be expected to pursue the concept.

ACTIVITY 8.4

The Planning for Conceptual Change Model Format

For this activity, choose a topic other than the one you chose for Activity 8.3. Write out a lesson plan using the Planning for Conceptual Change model format (see Figure 8.4). Which of the two models fits your "style" best? Do your classmates show a preference for one over the other?

Weather	Magnetism	Solar Energy
Simple Machines	Germination	Adaptive Coloration

ACTIVITY 8.5
INFOTRAC COLLEGE EDITION
INVESTIGATION:

Pursuing Questions

A particular feature of the Planning for Conceptual Change model is that students are specifically encouraged to formulate their own questions and pursue those interests. What is a possible question that might arise from the lesson as you have designed it in Activity 8.4? Use InfoTrac College Edition to locate additional information that would help to answer that question. An activity such as this allows you (or your students) to answer questions and to practice using electronic access to information as a meaningful tool.

Interactive Strategies That Facilitate the Discovery Approach

As you can see, both models are dynamic lesson formats because student thinking is integrally involved in the progress of the lesson. The inherent dynamism of the lesson models is enhanced when the teacher incorporates strategies that facilitate the discovery approach. Strategies for sharing information can take many forms. Each has advantages as well as limitations. Three such strategies are presented in this chapter: discussion, demonstration, and the Socratic method.

Discussion Discussions are used to promote the verbal exchange of ideas. Both the teacher and the students are verbally active. Unlike the sharing of objects where one person gives some possessions to another person, thus diminishing the giver's resources, the sharing of ideas increases one's storehouse of knowledge. The ideas shared are not lost from the warehouse, but are added to the ideas gained from experience and others.

To demonstrate this difference, consider the following. You and a study partner decide to share some snacks after a study session. You brought four chocolate chip cookies and your partner brought two apples. If the sharing is done equally, the result is each person has two cookies and one apple. While you have gained an apple that you did not have before, you have traded away half of your cookies.

Now you and your partner decide to share some ideas, and the topic of conversation is eating habits. You share the following with your partner: "I think that if I eat a snack, such as crackers and peanut butter, just before studying by myself, that it helps me focus on the content and think better." In turn, your partner says, "I find that if I eat a snack right before I go to sleep, that I have more vivid dreams." While sharing ideas, you have gained some insight from your partner and she or he has gained from you. But neither person has lost anything. Your ideas remain whole and intact. The sharing of ideas in a discussion always leaves all participants with more than they had to begin with.

The advantages of discussions extend beyond the sharing of ideas. Equally important, individuals learn multiple perspectives related to the topic of discussion as others share ideas from various points of view. The consideration of multiple perspectives, along with seeking patterns and relationships, is at the heart of creative thinking (Ebert, 1994).

Depending on the position of the discussion relative to the overall unit of instruction, discussions can serve different purposes. Those that occur at the beginning of a unit of study may engage student interest. Students can contribute what they already know about the subject and be encouraged to identify what they would like to find out as a result of the study. Following an investigation or other common science activity, such as a walk through the woods next to the school, small group discussions are purposeful activities. Besides discussions facilitating the sharing of observations and inferences, they often help clarify thinking. In addition, discussions are useful when drawing closure to a topic of study. The whole class can participate while summarizing the concepts explored.

Discussions allow for verbal participation on the part of children and so enhance social interaction skills. However, it is important to recognize that discussions by themselves do not contribute to children's further conceptualization of the concept (Good, 1977). Discussions are most effective when used as one complementary component of the design for science instruction.

Demonstration Occasionally, it is appropriate for the teacher to be the one who manipulates the objects as the children observe, a teaching approach that is called demonstration. Sometimes the events occur so quickly or subtly that the children would not make the necessary observations unless the teacher conducted the activity, stopped at the appropriate times, and cued the children.

For example, an activity that helps children understand air pressure involves getting an egg that is larger than the opening of a jar into the jar (see Activity 8.6). The activity is best done as a demonstration. The teacher handles the burning materials and can direct student attention to the bobbing of the egg on the mouth of the jar just prior to its dropping into the jar. The final part of the activity, blowing into the bottle to get the egg back out, is also best done by the teacher, at least the first time. The teacher, knowing what is going to happen, can perform the activity and make it visible to the students. Students trying the activity without having first seen it done, and not knowing what to expect, often interfere with the action of the egg.

There are other situations that call for the use of demonstration. If an activity involves the use of hazardous materials, the teacher should handle the materials and guide the observations. It is also appropriate for teachers to demonstrate the correct use of delicate or expensive equipment. Once the children become familiar with the proper use of the equipment and know the guidelines for handling the objects, it should not be necessary to confine the teaching approach to demonstration.

ACTIVITY 8.6

Another Egg Activity

It is essential that a demonstration not be a new experience for the demonstrator. Use this activity as a means for practicing the skill of demonstration, that is, continuing your discussion with the observers while conducting the demonstration.

The Egg Activity

How can you put an egg into a glass bottle without breaking it?

Materials needed:

Glass bottle, a 1–quart milk bottle or something similar

A piece of paper

Matches

Hard-boiled egg with shell removed

Procedures:

1. Place the egg on the mouth of the glass bottle, showing the students that the egg will not fit into the bottle without being crushed.

2. Remove the egg. Wad up the paper, light it with a match, and insert it into the bottle.

3. Immediately place the egg on the mouth of the bottle.

4. Have students observe the results.

Results:

The egg will bob up and down on the mouth of the bottle and then slowly descend into the neck of the bottle. Finally, the egg will plop into the bottle.

Background information:

The air in the bottle is heating and expanding. The air escaping from the bottle causes the egg to bob up and down. When the paper stops burning, the air inside the bottle cools and the pressure decreases. The normal air pressure on the top and sides of the egg remains unchanged. Therefore, the egg is forced into the bottle. It is important that the size of the egg be comparable to the size of the mouth of the bottle. Large eggs can be used with large-mouth bottles and small eggs can be used with small-mouth bottles.

Additional challenge:

How can you get the egg back out of the bottle without breaking it?

This can be accomplished by inverting the bottle and blowing hard into its mouth. Increasing the air pressure inside the bottle will force the egg out.

Socratic or Maieutic Method What is typically referred to as the Socratic method is actually the maieutic method, a particular approach to teaching based on the famous technique Socrates used to educate his students: questioning. Other than being an interesting collection of vowels, the word maieutic refers to midwifery. In the context of intellect and teaching, it refers to the idea that people know more than they think they know, and by proper questioning that knowledge can be brought to the surface. Socrates believed that men were "pregnant with knowledge," and that his task was to assist in the birth of that knowledge by having people answer appropriate questions. Don't let the fact that Socrates was executed for asking all of these pesky questions intimidate you.

In the classroom, the teacher uses questions to draw from the children what they already know about the topic, and to guide their thinking as they share and synthesize new ideas. The teacher prepares a series of questions that will lead the thinking to the desired outcome. But the teacher must also be prepared to make adjustments. Even with great thought given to anticipating what children might think and say, you need to be flexible and able to accommodate the spontaneous responses of the students.

Questioning, when used correctly, is an effective teaching technique that encourages children to think for themselves. If teachers formulate and ask high-level questions (according to Bloom's taxonomy of the cognitive domain), students' responses will match teacher expectations. By asking many divergent questions rather than convergent questions, teachers can encourage students to consider more than one perspective before responding and to seek multiple solutions to problems. The amount of thinking as well as the level of thinking is greatly improved.

While questioning is appropriate for the teaching of all subject matters, good questioning is the essence of guided discovery learning in science. Specific kinds of questions effectively facilitate science activities:

Invitation to investigation

Creative thinking opportunities

Reflection for understanding

Invitation to Investigation The first part of teaching is to motivate students. Learning is more easily facilitated when students are interested in the topic and anxious to get involved in the investigation. A good question or challenge helps to pique curiosity. The following questions help to encourage children to get involved and manipulate materials in order to discover answers.

1. What could you do to find out which factors affect the bounce of tennis balls?

2. What would happen to the flight of the paper gliders if you changed the shape of the wings?

3. How many pennies could we drop into this glassful of water before the water would spill out?

Creative Thinking Opportunities Divergent questions are especially appropriate for encouraging creative thinking. The students are expected to consider multiple perspectives and acknowledge the usefulness of multiple solutions. When students are not accustomed to this type of questioning, they may be reluctant to share some of their ideas. However, with practice and given an accepting environment, answers to these types of questions will become prolific and range from practical to almost bizarre. New and exciting ideas

come as a result of creative thinking, which can be stimulated with questions such as the following:

1. How could you find out how many M&M's are in the bag without opening it?

2. How could we use an M&M to determine the height of our building?

3. How could you package an egg so that it could survive a drop of 10 meters (33 feet)?

Reflection for Understanding Questions that require reflection may be used to summarize and personalize the learning for the students at the end of a lesson or the end of a unit of study. The students are encouraged to identify and use criteria while making decisions. The following questions may serve as examples for this category.

1. What do you think is the best solution to the noise problem in our community? Why?

2. What have you learned about fire safety that will make a difference in your home?

3. If camouflage helps animals blend in and not be seen, how could we use coloration so that we can be seen? What are some examples that you have seen?

ACTIVITY 8.7

Generating Questions

This is a good time for you to try generating your own questions. Select a topic in science and write at least three questions for each category:

Invitation to investigation

Creative thinking opportunities

Reflection for understanding

Strategies in Combination As mentioned in chapter 7, there is not "one scientific method." Nor is there only one way to teach science. Science is a way of pursuing knowledge that involves many forms of investigation and a variety of perspectives. Just one teaching strategy cannot facilitate that kind of pursuit. Only the use of a combination of strategies that effectively supports your teaching style and the needs of your students will result in an enjoyable experience. Select strategies and use them when and where they are appropriate rather than deciding to use one for one lesson and a different one for another lesson.

Quick Review

The discovery approach to teaching science may be more time-consuming, but the learning is more meaningful. In this approach, children are encouraged to construct their own understanding of the world and make personal connections between what they already know and the new information.

As you consider the models presented in this discussion of the discovery approach, it is important that you understand the distinction between the teaching process and learning process. You cannot learn for the student, but the student does come to you with an inclination to learn. You can arrange experiences that will capitalize on that inclination.

Both the Learning Cycle and the Planning for Conceptual Change model are lesson formats that highlight the nature of the learner as an inquirer in a manner that directs that inquiry toward scientific investigation. The Planning for Conceptual Change model is really an extension of the Learning Cycle model for designing science lessons. The four steps of the Learning Cycle, with slight changes in the wording, are found in the Planning for Conceptual Change. The major addition found in the Planning for Conceptual Change is in explicitly addressing what children know and don't know. A teacher can best facilitate conceptual change when both the teacher and the individual students are aware of the beliefs related to the concept prior to instruction.

Some children may be unwilling to give up their previous beliefs even though there is evidence to support conceptual change. Forcing children to repeat "scientific explanations" does not make for meaningful changes in understanding (see chapter 4). Instead, it often results in children developing dualistic perspectives that suggest that there is a "school-related explanation" and personal belief that works outside of school. Some children need time and additional experiences, opportunities to struggle with the concept, before adopting a more sophisticated explanation of it.

CONCLUSION

If a teacher covers all the material in the book or the curriculum guidelines by the end of the school year, is she or he to be congratulated? Some people may think so. However, if the effectiveness is measured according to how well the children learned the material, then chances are very good that the teacher is not to be congratulated. Most science textbooks and curriculum guides have too much information stuffed in them. The phrase aptly used by Project 2061 to describe the science curriculum of the 1990s is "overstuffed and undernourished." Too much is involved for learning to take place effectively. High-quality learning takes time for doing and time for thinking. Rushing the process results in inferior learning.

The level of understanding and the retention of science learning is greatly increased if science lessons (1) capitalize on the natural curiosity of children and encourage a positive attitude toward science and learning, (2) emphasize the science process skills as children conduct investigations, and (3) use manipulatives so that children are physically active and have firsthand experiences while discovering the concept. With this in mind, science lessons can be designed in such a way that everyone involved has a pleasant and rewarding experience. A science program that accomplishes this incorporates a variety of additional approaches to the teaching of science, including discussion, demonstration, and the Socratic method. The basic science process skills are essential to that process and include observation, inference, classification, communication, measurement, and prediction.

The two lesson formats discussed in this chapter specifically address the discovery learning approach to science education. The Learning Cycle is a model for designing science lessons that assures success for all students and fosters a positive attitude toward science. Planning for Conceptual Change is a way of planning instruction that adds another dimension to the Learning Cycle by allowing teachers to elicit what children know and do not know about a topic and to accommodate appropriately. In either case, planning a science lesson is focused squarely on the matter of *what the children will do,* rather than what the teacher will do. If you find yourself writing lesson plans that include a lot of "the teacher will," then you are very likely losing the dynamic opportunities that a discovery approach would afford to you and your students.

ACTIVITY 8.8

A Discovery Learning Lesson Design

It is time to bring together all that has been discussed through chapters 6, 7, and 8. The topics considered in these chapters should allow you to construct a sound science lesson from any topic. To complete this activity, select a chapter or unit from a science textbook. Look through the material that you have selected, and then complete each of these items:

1. Write out five questions that you have about the material, or that you believe students studying that chapter would have *prior* to instruction.

2. Assuming that you are planning one science lesson (rather than a series to complete an entire unit), which of the basic science process skills would be most appropriate to utilize? Explain your choices.

3. Of the eight types of investigations, which one would you use for this lesson? Explain your answer.

4. Now, choose either the Learning Cycle or the Planning for Conceptual Change model as the format for your lesson. Explain what will happen during each phase of the model you have selected.

9 | Making Real-World Connections

Relevancy and the Teaching of Science

Approaches for Relevant Connections

Nontraditional Educational Opportunities

Conclusion

Your Academic Roadmap

Study of this chapter should help you to understand the following concepts:

- Children need opportunities to use science to investigate questions within the context of their own worlds.

- Real-world demonstrations, relevant documentation, and individual investigations are three techniques for helping children understand science beyond the classroom.

- Opportunities for making real-world connections abound if the teacher is willing to coordinate the efforts of valuable community resources.

Imagination is more important than knowledge. Knowledge is limited, whereas imagination embraces the entire world—stimulating progress, giving birth to evolution.

—Albert Einstein

RELEVANCY AND THE TEACHING OF SCIENCE

Many educators agree that the main purpose of education is not just to prepare for college. Though more people attend colleges now than in decades past, there are many more who do not attend college. In any case, education is a means for providing all individuals with lifelong skills that in turn may lead to an improved quality of life. A great deal of emphasis has therefore been placed on making learning relevant. Teachers and curriculum resource guides have made accommodations just for this purpose. Authors of textbooks make concerted efforts to include examples or stories that capitalize on experiences common in the lives of young people. School-to-work transition, a more recent educational concern, focuses on drawing attention to possible connections between the information being learned and the occupational needs and applications.

The various attempts to make learning relevant for students have had an impact on what happens in the classroom. But does that assure pertinent connections between school-based education and the real world from the perspective of the children? Keep in mind that the teacher cannot actually make the learning relevant. The child is the only one who can do that. Just as each child constructs his or her own reality, relevancy is something that one must establish for oneself. The teacher can only create opportunities and experiences that are more likely to be seen by the students as relevant through connections to the world in which they live.

Thus far, our approach to the teaching of science has been directed toward what can be done in the classroom setting. We have described science very broadly as a way of finding answers to questions or solutions to problems. We have stated that it is a search— an investigation—that leads to an understanding of the world around us. Investigations come in many forms: trial and error, documenting, prediction testing, product testing, experimenting, modeling, inventing, and reflecting. Each of these investigative forms has its appropriate place in the search for understanding. The skills required to do the investigations, the science process skills, are the tools we use to accomplish the investigation.

Regarding how to teach science, we have employed the Learning Cycle as a way of designing science lessons. This design promotes a positive attitude toward science, uses manipulatives in a hands–on approach, and encourages discovery learning by providing exploration activities prior to verbalizing the concept. Using the Planning for Conceptual Change model accounts for the constructivist perspective by eliciting children's prior experiences, what they already know about the topic, as the starting point for instructional designs. In addition, children are encouraged to pursue more detailed study of topics that are of particular interest to them.

With all of this preparation and understanding of the teaching of science, it is to be hoped that the children see the connections between the science they are doing in school and the world in which they live. However, through our research, in which we have used interviews and examined the results, we have found that children do not always learn what teachers intend; instead, they construct their own explanations and levels of understanding of the concepts addressed. It would be as inappropriate to assume that all of the children perceive the relevancy of science as it would be to assume that all children have the same conceptions prior to or following instruction. In order to assist students in discovering the relevance of scientific principles, teachers can allow them the opportunity to consider those concepts in situations that reflect their own worlds.

Homework typically has been used to provide students with opportunities to practice newly acquired concepts, principles, and, more often, vocabulary. Most homework assignments, however, involve contrived situations that do not make direct connections to the environment outside of school. This approach to practice perpetuates what Moravcsik (1981) calls the sterile manipulation of a set of rules. In order to be consistent with an investigative approach to science and to assure that children have learned to use science as a process for understanding the world around them, they must be given opportunities to investigate within the context of their own worlds.

APPROACHES FOR RELEVANT CONNECTIONS

Three approaches can be used to better assure the making of relevant connections: (1) real-world demonstrations, (2) relevant documenting; and (3) individual investigations. Using real-world demonstrations, the teacher brings something commonly found in the home environment into the classroom for the purpose of investigation. The second approach would require the teacher to challenge the students to use documenting of specified observations for the purpose of collecting data that children identify as relevant. This relevant documentation might take the form of listing the frequency of specified occurrences in the home environment (see Figure 9.4); for example, counting the number of objects that use electricity. It could also take the form of maintaining individual journals that record observations in the home setting. An example might be keeping a record of all the food personally consumed in twenty-four hours or the names of TV programs watched during a specific period of time. Using the third alternative, a teacher would ask children to conduct investigations at home and then report the results to the class. These individual investigations might take the form of experiments, inventions, product tests, or any of the other investigative forms discussed in chapter 7.

Keep in mind that the appropriateness of each of the approaches is justifiable because each option has advantages as well as limitations. Real-world demonstration requires the most direction by the teacher. Individual investigation allows for the highest degree of input and direction from the individual child. It is to be hoped that given sufficient opportunities, the last alternative will become the most frequently used, since it fosters the highest degree of relevancy. Let's consider each in more detail.

Real-World Demonstrations

Real-world demonstration is the most teacher-directed approach to making practice relevant, because the only person typically involved in manipulating the materials is the teacher. In general, there are three situations in which it is advantageous for the teacher to do a demonstration. When the activity involves special precautions or when hazardous materials are used, the teacher ought to ensure the safety of everyone by conducting the activity. A second situation involves those times when expensive pieces of equipment are involved. Under these circumstances, the teacher needs to provide special directions and demonstrate the appropriate use of such equipment before children use it (e.g., the first time microscopes are used). Finally, sometimes children are likely to miss important observations during an event. The teacher can facilitate those observations by conducting the demonstration and stopping when appropriate to ask pertinent questions.

In the case of real-world demonstrations, the teacher may choose to demonstrate an activity because of limitations in the home setting. For example, to illustrate the frequently overlooked occurrences of chemical and physical changes in the home, the teacher might want children to bake a cake. In some home environments, that request would be met with support and encouragement. In others, however, the necessary materials, equipment, or adult support to conduct such an investigation would not be available. In order to overcome these limitations, the teacher may decide to bake a cake right at school. Opportunities for student interaction exist, and at the same time, the teacher can employ high-quality questioning techniques to facilitate distinctly important observations. Here is an example.

Let's suppose that you are fortunate enough to have some sort of access to an oven in your school, perhaps through the good graces of the cafeteria personnel. The purpose of the demonstration would be to examine physical and chemical changes in events that are common in the home environment. You'll need the following materials (in addition to the oven, of course):

cake recipe or cake mix

ingredients as listed (*Note:* Because of the possibility of bacterial contamination, do not allow students to taste the raw egg or the batter with the raw egg.)

bowl and mixer

mixing spoons and spatula

measuring cups and spoons

baking pan, pot holders, cooling rack

toothpicks

measuring stick (in cm/mm if possible)

many plastic spoons (to be used for individual observations) (*Note:* For safety, each child must use a *new* spoon to taste each ingredient. No "second tastes" are allowed.)

Whether you use a cake mix or a recipe involving basic ingredients, there will be many opportunities for observing chemical and physical changes. In either case, and depending on the intended level of sophistication, you might want to provide extra demonstrations in order for the students to better understand the chemical reactions that occur. For example, leavening is what causes the cake to rise, and it is based on the production of carbon dioxide. This process may be better understood by the children through an isolated examination of the reaction of baking powder. See Activity 9.1 for an investigation of a variety of baking powders. It may provide a greater appreciation of the chemical reaction.

ACTIVITY 9.1

Baking Powder Investigation

The Speed of Reaction of Baking Powder

Materials needed: 3 egg whites; 3 types of baking powder: double-acting with phosphate, double-acting with alum, and a combination of baking soda and cream of tartar; 1 tablespoon; 3 beakers; metric ruler; stopwatch

Procedures:

1. Place 1 tablespoon of each type of baking powder into separate *dry* beakers. Note the time as you add the egg white to the dry mixture. Stir gently until powder is moistened, and then stop.

2. At the end of every minute for five minutes, measure the height of the foam in the beaker.

3. At the end of five minutes, place the beaker in a pan containing very hot water (near boiling), and for the next five minutes, again measure the rate of rise.

4. Record your results.

5. Answer the following questions:

   Which type of baking powder produced the most carbon dioxide (foam)?

   What did you notice when the beakers were placed in hot water?

For Your Information: Because it was not always convenient to bake the cake batter immediately, double-acting baking powder was developed. Alum (sodium aluminum sulphate) is the acidic ingredient. It will not react with the baking powder ingredient until it is heated. Therefore, leavening does not begin until the batter is in the oven.

Early double-acting powders with alum had the disadvantages of having a bitter taste and producing a heavy baked product. Consequently, double-acting powders with two acid ingredients were developed. Cream of tartar, a fast-acting ingredient, starts forming carbon dioxide as soon as it mixes with liquids. It begins to change the texture of the cake before being placed in the oven and therefore overcomes the heaviness. Alum, a slow-acting ingredient, does not react until placed in the heat of the oven. It can be used in lesser amounts now that two leavening ingredients are used, thereby avoiding the bitter taste. (Adapted from Eby and Tatum, 1977)

While following the directions for making the cake, allow children plenty of opportunities to make observations of each ingredient before and after it is combined with others. Ask each student to observe each item and respond to the following questions: How does it feel? taste? smell? look? Be sure to use transparent bowls so that children can

FIGURE 9.1 Observation form for the cake baking activity.

CAKE BAKING ACTIVITY

Ingredients	Amount	Observations
flour	1½ cups	Looks white and grainy; smells like flour; feels soft and gritty at the same time; doesn't have much taste
salt	½ tsp	Looks white and granular; no smell; feels rough and grainy; tastes salty
baking soda	3 tsp	Looks white and powdery; feels smooth; tastes salty and bitter
sugar	1 cup	Looks white and granular; feels gritty; tastes sweet
margarine	2 Tbsp	Looks yellow, feels slippery, tastes salty and creamy
egg	1	
milk	¾ cup	
vanilla extract	1 tsp	
cake batter		
baked cake		

(*Note:* Because of the possibility of bacterial contamination, do not allow students to taste the raw egg or the batter with the raw egg.)

Identify changes. (Note whether you think the change is chemical or physical.):

1. Physical change—eggs broken when stirred up and added to shortening and sugar.
2. Physical change—shortening and sugar stirred together changes texture; when eggs and milk are added, it gets creamy.
3. Physical change—dry ingredients added to creamy mixture makes moist, thicker batter.
4. Physical change—mixer adds air to batter and volume increases.
5. _____
6. _____
7. _____

see through the sides. Transparent bowls are important when making visual observations and when making relative measurements of the volume of batter before and after beating with an electric mixer.

Depending on your particular circumstances, the baking may have to take place somewhere else and at a time when the class is occupied doing something else. The other obvious alternative is to do what the TV gourmets do: Set aside the batter that you have just mixed (and observed) and take out the cake that you baked at home ahead of time. Making observations of the baked cake involves everyone. And while the comparison of observations before and after baking

are vital to the lesson, from the children's perspective, the observations made after baking are more tasty!

Figure 9.1 is a partially completed observation form used for the cake baking activity. Similar forms are helpful when students are conducting any relevant documentation activities. The forms are meant to facilitate the learning by directing the students' observations. Having made the necessary observations, the students then have sufficient information from which to construct their own explanations (inferences) for the demonstrated event. This approach transforms the demonstration technique into a discovery learning experience rather than a direct

FIGURE 9.2 A documentation journal.

transmission of information approach more typical of demonstrations.

Relevant Documentation

Topics in the school curriculum are often related to students in a general sense, but opportunities for personal connections are not explicit. For example, nutritional studies address the need for consuming a variety of foods within specific groups. Occasionally, the school lunch menu is examined to identify the appropriate balance. Since the children supposedly eat what is on the menu, the activity may be considered a good attempt at linking learning with the real world. Realistically, though, what children eat outside of school, which is probably more reflective of personal choice, is more relevant to them. If they maintained records of what was actually consumed in a period of twenty-four to seventy-two hours, as in Figure 9.2, the data would be truly relevant.

In another context, perhaps you are familiar with the following investigation, which may be associated with the study of heat energy, air, or weather. The students are given thermometers to predict and measure air temperature in various locations around the room or outside on the school grounds. From this investigation, they may learn that the temperature outside when taken in the sunshine is much greater than when taken in the shade, or they may learn that the air near the ceiling of the classroom is warmer than the air near the floor. The activity is a good one and the information acquired is quite useful. However, through relevant documentation, the children can easily make connections between the information gained in the school settings and at home. The teacher, providing the same thermometers, can ask children to measure different locations in their homes. Record sheets such as the one in Activity 9.2 can be sent home with the children to facilitate documentation. The children also may be encouraged to record similar information in their own journals. Because children have actually collected data in personal settings, the real world connections are explicit. The questions are no longer contrived or hypothetical but instead ask children to make individual decisions related to their personal surroundings.

ACTIVITY 9.2

Temperature Investigation

Temperatures in My Home

1. Placing the thermometer on your bed, measure the temperature of the air in the room where you sleep.
   The temperature of the air just above my bed is _____.

2. Predict what the temperature will be in other parts of your room. Do you think it will be warmer (W) or cooler (C) than the air just above your bed? Once you have recorded your predictions by placing a W or a C in the appropriate box, use the thermometer to measure the temperature. Be sure to leave the thermometer in each place several minutes to allow the reading to change. Use the table below to record your predictions and measurements.

Based on the information you collected about temperature variations in your home, answer the following questions:

1. Where in your home is the warmest temperature?

2. Where in your home is the coldest temperature?

3. In the summer, would it be more comfortable, temperature-wise, to watch TV sitting on the floor or on the furniture? Why?

Temperatures in My Home

Prediction				
Measure				

| Location: | Bedroom Floor | Bedroom Ceiling | Bedroom Window | Bedroom Door |

3. Identify other areas of your home, such as the kitchen, stairways, and TV area, to measure temperature and record the data in the table below.

4. In the winter, would it be more comfortable, temperature-wise, to watch TV sitting on the floor or on the furniture? Why?

More Temperatures in My Home

Prediction						
Measure						

Location: _____

Most topics in the science curriculum have connections to the home environment of the children and consequently may involve relevant documentation. With the study of sound, children can document examples in the home where sounds are enhanced (stereo speakers and doorbells) and where sounds are suppressed (headphones and closed doors).

With the study of energy, they can document the various types of frequencies used in the home. They can also document the frequency of living things (plants, animals, and fungi), the various applications of magnets (latches on cabinet doors, stereo speakers, note holders, etc.), or examples of controlled use of light (lamps, cameras, TV, etc.).

Individual Investigation Form

Name _____ Date _____

FIGURE 9.3 Individual investigation form.

Investigation: (circle one)	Trial and Error	Prediction Testing
	Inventing	Experimenting
	Reflecting	Documenting
	Modeling	Product Testing

| Outcome: (circle one) | Information | Product | Question |

Procedures:

Results:

Individual Investigations

You will eventually want students to conduct their own investigations in the context of their world. Having been taught the skills necessary for investigating and having conducted various types of investigations in school, with a little encouragement, students are capable of applying these skills and processes on their own. Individual investigations are the most independent of the three approaches to relevant activities. The students identify, design, and conduct their own investigations. The teacher may provide guidance by asking students to do a particular type of investigation at home, such as a product test. The students are given the freedom to select the type of product and thereby choose for themselves something that is relevant to them. On the other hand, the assignment might be extremely open-ended and the type of investigation can be determined entirely by the student. A form such as the one in Figure 9.3 might be used to facilitate the documentation of the investigation. It provides opportunities to identify the type of investigation selected by the student. By having students identify the intended outcome in terms of information, product, or question, the teacher can monitor their understanding of the purpose of each investigative process.

A sample of a completed form, Figure 9.4, shows how a student kept a record of a personally relevant individual investigation while at home. The form is designed to provide guidance without telling the student how to plan and conduct an investigation or which investigation to choose. The teacher may, however, want to approve investigations before they begin. Though you can certainly check to see that the student has identified an appropriate investigative technique and put together a plan of action, you should definitely check to see that the proposal is appropriate and safe. You may also wish to monitor an individual student's attempts to investigate, and encourage diversity if appropriate.

ACTIVITY 9.3

An Individual Investigation

- Using a form such as the one provided in Figure 9.3, conduct your own individual investigation. Since you are not beginning from the context of a science lesson (as your students would be), you might want to begin with an "I wonder . . ." question, as discussed in chapter 6.

- Select the type of investigation you will use, identify the outcome that you seek, and then describe your investigation. Finally, detail your results.

Individual Investigation Form

Name: Alex   Date   10 / 24

Type of Investigation: Prediction Testing

Desired Outcome: Information

Procedures:

I predict that when ice cubes are added to a refrigerated soft drink it will get colder faster than when ice cubes are added to a soft drink stored at room temperature.

I got 2 glasses just alike and put 4 ice cubes in each one. Next I poured the cold soda in one and the room temperature soda in the other. I put thermometers in each glass and recorded the temperatures in degrees Fahrenheit. I measured the temperatures every two minutes.

FIGURE 9.4 Example of an individual investigation.

temperatures measured

refrigerated	42	39	39	36	32	32
room temp	62	46	44	40	40	40
minutes	0	2	4	6	8	10	12	14

Results: The cold soda did get colder but the warmer soda got cold faster.

- Share your results with your classmates as part of an "Investigation Festival" in class.

Quick Review

The three approaches to real-world connections can be utilized in a wide variety of ways. Each of the techniques can stand alone as a lesson or an assignment. It is also possible to combine approaches, such as doing the cake demonstration in class and allowing your students to design individual investigations to apply or extend what has been learned from the demonstration. Relevant documentation is a technique that can be started early in a lesson sequence (or school year) and continued for an appropriate period of time to collect data for subsequent use. For example, a brief discussion of weather patterns in September could start data collection that would provide the basis for meteorology lessons in March or April. Keep in mind that if you do engage in long-term projects such as this, you will need to keep the motivation going. An occasional review of what has been collected, or talk of a particular event (a big local storm, for example), as well as reference to the students' work when a particular event happens for a wider region (a hurricane in the Southeast, drought in the Midwest, extensive rains on the West Coast, etc.) will reinforce the real-world connections that you are trying to establish.

NONTRADITIONAL EDUCATIONAL OPPORTUNITIES

In addition to the three approaches to making relevant connections to the home environment, other educational settings can be used to facilitate the teaching of science: (1) at play, (2) on excursions, and (3) facing environmental issues. The playful setting can be found on the school grounds, but the focus here is on children's natural settings outside the school hours. Typically, we are referring to the yard around the home, the local park,

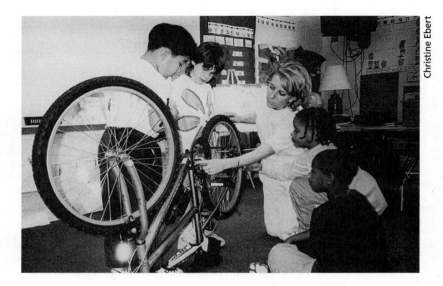

Christine Ebert

PHOTO 9.1 The familiar bicycle is a collection of many simple machines.

and the neighborhood in general—places where children play ball, ride bikes, skate, and the like. Another type of nontraditional setting for studying science would be places where children might go on "field trips," either with a class or with a group of personal friends and relatives—places such as museums, zoos, planetariums, aquariums, state and national parks, and wildlife refuges. Many other possibilities for science excursions exist, some of which are discussed later in this chapter—places such as amusement parks, farms, airports, manufacturing plants, professional ballparks, and marinas. The third opportunity for nontraditional experiences with science is through the examination of and involvement in environmental issues. This option helps children see not only the relevancy between science and their own worlds, but the connections to society and the world at large. The scope of these issues can be as narrowly focused as the concerns relevant to the local community and neighborhoods, such as waste disposal, noise pollution, and traffic congestion. On the other hand, the scope can expand to encompass national and global issues, such as acid rain, global warming, and deforestation.

At Play

Children obviously enjoy spending time playing with their toys, games, and sporting equipment. Not so obvious are the possibilities for learning; however, many opportunities for the study and application of science exist in playful settings such as playing ball, skating, swimming, surfing, skiing, or even building snow forts. Examples to illustrate relevant science in playful settings will be presented in each of the three approaches to making learning relevant.

Real-World Demonstration Suppose a class has been studying simple machines. From the adult perspective, the connections between simple machines and their occurrences in everyday life is quite obvious. To help children recognize the frequency of simple machines, a teacher could ask children to do a relevant documentation activity. They could record as many examples of simple machines as they can find in their own homes. Simple machines, however, rarely exist in isolation. Most often, they are in combination with other simple machines. It is this complexity of the combination that makes identifying them difficult for children. A

FIGURE 9.5 Learning Cycle lesson plan for a real-world demonstration activity.

BICYCLE ACTIVITY
(A REAL-WORLD DEMONSTRATION)
Purpose: To examine a child-relevant, common object of medium complexity to identify its subsystems and component parts as a way of looking for simple machines in our daily lives.

Introduction
Having a bicycle in the classroom will probably get the attention of the students. In addition, a question or challenge to focus the intent of the lesson would be an appropriate beginning to the lesson. "Many of you have probably used a bicycle as a means of transportation or just for fun but probably not closely examined the component parts of a bicycle to see how it works. Let's see how many simple machines we can find as we examine this bicycle." If possible, the instructor should "dress in costume of early bicyclists" by wearing elastic bands such as garters over pants legs to keep clothing from getting tangled in bicycle gears.

Exploration
Since student participation is limited during any demonstration, it is important to keep the children mentally involved. Have each student use a data collection sheet, such as the one in Figure 9.6, to record observations and inferences. If several bikes are available, the students can work in small groups and be more closely involved in the exploration.

Concept Development
Ask students to discuss the various subsystems found within the bicycle. The following questions could be used to guide discussion: What parts are involved? How are they connected? What force and motion are transferred within the system? Ask students to discuss any historical developments or changes in bicycles with which they are familiar.

Application
Challenge students to compare tricycles or unicycles with bicycles. Another possible challenge is to ask students how they would construct the gear system for a tandem bicycle.

---

real-world demonstration can be used to increase student awareness of the frequency of simple machines and, at the same time, demystify the process of identification.

For example, a bicycle is something with which children are familiar. Yet they have probably never taken one apart or even examined each component to see how the parts interact and make the bicycle work. The lesson plan in Figure 9.5 illustrates how the real-world demonstration better prepares students to do a relevant documentation activity of identifying simple machines around the home. Figure 9.6 shows a suggested data sheet as a student may have completed it during the demonstration.

Relevant Documentation at Play Having participated in the bicycle activity, the students have had practice finding simple machines within other machines. It is appropri-

ate now to ask them to conduct a relevant documentation activity identifying simple machines in the play environment. The assignment could be specifically related to the bicycle activity, whereby the children are asked to document simple machines in their own bikes or in other bikes in the neighborhood. As a separate activity, they can look for simple machines that are not associated with bicycles. These searches for simple machines may occur in the children's backyards, neighborhood parks, or other places in the neighborhood.

Many topics within the science curriculum can be connected to play through documentation. Children could be asked to document examples of toys or sporting activities that involve topics such as friction or the reduction of it (roller blades, sledding, air hockey, etc.), air or its movement (whistling, blowing bubbles, kites, balls, etc.), or

FIGURE 9.6 Data collection sheet for the bicycle activity.

Bicycle Data Sheet

Name: *Kimberly*

Subsystems	Parts	Simple Machines
Forward Motion	back wheel	wheel & axle
	pedals	lever, inclined plane
	gears	wheel & axle
	chain	
	derailleur	lever
	cable	
	frame	
Steering	handlebar	lever
	front wheel	wheel & axle
Braking	hand grips	lever
	cables	
	brake pads	lever
Comfort & Safety	seat	
	grips	
	fenders	
	lights	
	basket	

What simple machines did you find?
5 levers, 3 wheel & axles, 1 inclined plane

transfer of energy (slinky, trampoline, balls, bicycling, etc.).

The first time an assignment of this sort is given, the lists may not be very lengthy. Children are not used to looking for these connections between school studies and playing. With a little practice and some encouragement, however, they begin to recognize the relationships and even enjoy making these relevant connections.

Individual Investigations at Play Children can be challenged to conduct individual investigations while playing. The partially completed investigation form in Figure 9.7 is an example of an experiment conducted by a child interested in paper gliders. And

FIGURE 9.7 Individual investigation.

Gliders
(Individual Investigation)

Name: *Toby*   **Date:** *October 15*

Type of Investigation: *Experiment*

Desired Outcome: *Information about the flight of paper gliders*

Procedures: *I thought about the various things that might affect the flight of my paper glider and decided to try changing the weight—how much and where it was located. First I launched the glider with no paper clips (weights) and measured how far it flew. Next I added 1, then 2, then 3 paper clips and measured how far it flew each time. Finally I added only 1 paper clip first under the nose of the glider and measured how far it flew. Then I moved the paper clip under the front part of the wings, and finally just behind the wings. Each time I flew the glider, I measured how far it flew.*

Distance of Flight

1 paper clip _____
2 paper clips _____
3 paper clips _____
front _____
under wings _____
behind wings _____

Results: *I found out that . . .*

while experimenting may not be a frequently employed form of investigation, since it requires special considerations for controlling variables, other forms such as prediction testing, trial and error, and product testing may often be applicable for children in this type of setting.

Children may wish to study and improve their own efforts related to sports, such as golf swings, batting baseballs, throwing footballs, and shooting basketballs. These movements can also be documented. For example, a child could vary his or her stance, hand position, or amount of follow-through and observe the effects on the direction of the thrown or hit ball. Other children may be interested in studying the effects of tails on kites or types of soap used in making bubbles. These studies may not be precise from the perspective of a scientist, but they allow children to study some things of personal interest.

ACTIVITY 9.4

Relevant Connections at Play

Now it is your turn to create a relevant learning opportunity. Select one of the following playful activities. Explain how it could be used by children for a science investigation. Identify the activity as real-world demonstration, relevant documentation, or individual investigation.

archery	badminton	baseball
basketball	tennis	football
soccer	flying kites	horseshoes
throwing	throwing	riding
a Frisbee	a boomerang	skateboards
ice-skating	roller-blading	

Science Excursions

Science excursions refer to nontraditional science activities or "field trips" that take the children outside the regular classroom setting and away from the school. The specific intent is educational. Real–world connections, planned in advance of the excursion, help to keep a scientific focus without diminishing the novelty of the trip. This section suggests ways that facilitate discussing the experience at a later date.

Real-world Demonstrations for a Science Excursion
Occasionally, an idea for a visit to a workplace gets complicated due to a limited amount of observation space on site. The number of students in your class just may not fit comfortably into the room. In these situations, it may be better to ask the expert to first visit your classroom. Then, after some preliminary information and guided observation, a site visit would be much more

FIGURE 9.8 Sample observation sheet for a science excursion.

CRIMINAL INVESTIGATIONS

Test Conducted	Equipment and Materials Used	Evidence Collected
1. fingerprints		
lifting prints		
matching prints		
2. blood tests		
types		
substance analysis		
3. fiber identification		
4. _____		

beneficial. An example of such a situation might be a visit to a local law enforcement crime laboratory. If you were to ask a crime scene specialist, or technician, to first visit the classroom, he or she would be able to explain the various types of laboratory techniques used during investigations. The specialist could demonstrate specific techniques used to collect or examine evidence, while focusing the students' observations. In addition to answering students' questions, the specialist could also make suggestions for specific observations of on–site equipment or techniques to look for while visiting the laboratory. An observation sheet such as the one in Figure 9.8 would also facilitate student observation.

Relevant Documentation while on a Science Excursion
A trip to an amusement park or local fair provides a wonderful opportunity for making relevant connections to the world of children. Little do they suspect that science is closely related to the "feelings" they experience while on the amusement rides. But a study of force and motion becomes much more meaningful when experienced firsthand and while having fun. The incomplete form in Figure 9.9 illustrates the type of information students can collect

AMUSEMENT PARK

Amusement Ride	Direction of Force	Gravitational Force	Resultant Force
Tilt-a-Whirl	counterclockwise	downward	strong
	circles within circle		outward
			counterclockwise
			pressed down
Roller Coaster			
Ferris Wheel			

FIGURE 9.9 Data collection sheet for science excursion.

while visiting the amusement park. The information can be discussed when the students get back to the classroom.

Individual Investigations while on a Science Excursion We like to think that science excursions result in all-around high-quality experiences for everyone involved. Good planning is very important, but it tends to focus on the logistics and recruitment of volunteers to ensure that the excursion is not only safe but pleasant and well organized. Advanced planning can also ensure academic quality by challenging each student to conduct an individual investigation while on the excursion. Each student, in advance of the trip, identifies a particular topic of interest and formulates an appropriate question. Providing simple data sheets such as the one in Figure 9.10 will help guide the students' observation. In the example shown, the children are making a visit to the zoo. Questions such as the following would be appropriate: In what ways do young monkeys behave differently than adult monkeys? or What special conditions are necessary for reptiles, and how is this environment controlled? When the class returns to school, the information can then be used to share with peers. The results greatly enhance the overall impact of the excursion. The final entry on the data sheet can be used to guide individual research as a follow-up activity to the science excursion. Thereby, relevant connections are made before and after the trips.

Facing Environmental Issues

Environmental issues are generally thought to be "big problems" that belong to the adults of the world, those people who caused the problems or who have the power to make decisions about dealing with the problems. Facing the environmental issues, however, is something that children as well as adults can do. Facing the issues is a way of becoming aware of the environment and the impact people have on it. It also involves finding ways that individuals, no matter how old, can do something to preserve the environment.

Science experiences designed at the appropriate level do not frighten or overwhelm children. Nuclear waste disposal problems or worldwide disasters, such as global climate change, might be too big to tackle at a young age. But there are many other issues of local concern and smaller problems that are good experiences for the novice. These experiences help children see themselves not only as good problem solvers but also as important people in the community.

Real-World Demonstrations while Facing Environmental Issues Opportunities exist for people to attend open forums or meetings intended to inform the local citizenry. Children rarely get to attend these meetings nor do they naturally have the inclination to do so. However, interest can be fostered through real-world demonstrations in the classroom. Rather than take children to such a meeting, bring a meeting to the

FIGURE 9.10 Individual investigation form.

**VISIT TO THE ZOO
(AN INDIVIDUAL INVESTIGATION)**

My question is . . .

I observed . . .

I asked . . .

I found out that . . .

I want to find out more about . . .

classroom. Invite people who represent opposing sides of local issues to visit the classroom. Prepare the children in advance by collecting some information from such easily accessible sources as the local newspaper. Then help them prepare a few questions to interview the experts or representatives who come for a visit. Also prepare children for the possibility of debate of the ideas, if appropriate. This preparation will provide advance focus of observations.

Relevant Documentation Related to Environmental Issues Numerous conditions, known and unknown to the local citizens, have daily impacts on their lives. Children need to become aware of at least some of these issues. They also need to recognize the degree to which the adults in the community are or are not informed. Children can conduct a survey of people in their neighborhoods, and it will reveal something about the number of local issues and the frequency with which people express concerns.

Littering is a concern to at least some degree in every neighborhood. Children can easily make relevant documentation of the amount and location of the litter where they live. Rather than collect the litter, which if done unsupervised may be hazardous to the health of the children, they can make lists of

what is found, using a form such as the one in Activity 9.5. Having documented the information and discussed the findings with others in the class, the children can now make informed decisions. And they can decide what to do next. For example, they may decide that there is a need for more trash receptacles. The location of these containers could be determined on the basis of the information already collected or on information yet to be collected. Particular strategies for preventing litter (e.g., removing outdated campaign signs) could be generated. Other decisions about cleaning up the environment can be made while also attending to important safety and health precautions.

ACTIVITY 9.5

Environmental Issues Documentation Form

LOCAL LITTER LIST
(A Relevant Documentation Activity)

Type of Object   Amount of Stuff   Location

How much litter did you find between your home and school?

Which things could be reused?

Which things could be recycled?

Individual Investigations with Environmental Issues A particularly interesting activity from Project WILD, Dragon Fly Pond, allows students to assume the roles of people representing various business interests and community groups. Students play the roles of farmers, manufacturers, townspeople, directors of water purification and waste disposal plants, and so on. All of the people and businesses depend on Dragon Fly Pond as a vital source of water. In turn, they also use the water and create waste that

Michael Bentley

PHOTO 9.2 Constructing and using one's own checklist leads to greater ownership of the investigation.

impacts on the quality of the water. The object of the activity is for class members to assume the roles of council members who must consider the needs of all the community members and create an informed solution to their environmental problem. Simply put, they must decide who has access to the water source and in what order.

Similar activities can be found in other sourcebooks and in computer software. These activities provide opportunities for students to assume different perspectives and lobby for those interests. A variety of questions can be added to these scenarios, such as the following:

- If you were to build a new house in your community, where would you locate it? Why?

- If the population continues to increase at this new higher rate, additional subdivisions and elementary schools will need to be built. Where would you locate them?

These questions may change the focus of the activity but they maintain the importance of community decision making. If this activity were used for the Exploration and Concept Development phases of a Learning Cycle lesson plan, an appropriate Application phase would be to relate the activity to the students' immediate environment. Locate several community maps, and challenge students to identify the locations of businesses, food producers, water sources, sources of pollution, residential areas, and the like. Ask students to contact local representatives and ask about local environmental concerns. Encourage the children to become informed citizens of their neighborhoods.

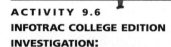

ACTIVITY 9.6
INFOTRAC COLLEGE EDITION
INVESTIGATION:

Environmental Initiatives for the Classroom

There are many ongoing environmental initiatives with which elementary students can become involved. Some are local, others national, and still others are global in nature. Use InfoTrac College Edition to locate information about environmental programs that can become a part of your school's science program. You might want to develop a file of different possibilities. If you and your classmates work in groups, each searching information for one of the three categories mentioned above, the group effort could yield a substantial portfolio of environmental project possibilities.

Quick Review

We hope that you can see from this discussion that making real-world connections between science in your classroom and science in the students' lives is not a difficult prospect. Possibilities are all around, but these experiences do not just materialize. You will have to do considerable planning. Yet, imagine what your class lessons will be like with a roomful of children eager to connect the outside world with the classroom world. And by all means, make use of the considerable community resources at your disposal. The newspaper alone can be a wonderful resource. Students can track the newspaper to see how often stories about a particular issue, or issues, are reported (relevant documentation). From there, plans for excursions or individual investigations can blossom.

CONCLUSION

This chapter has shown that many opportunities exist for making classroom instruction relevant in the lives of children outside the classroom. Though these opportunities allow children to make connections between science and the real world, the responsibility for structuring those opportunities still rests with the educator. The challenge is to provide enough guidance so that the task is within the cognitive abilities of the student without providing so much guidance that the activity becomes just another school assignment.

As a guide for educators, we have identified three approaches to making relevant connections—real-world demonstrations, relevant documentation, and individual investigations—which integrate well with the investigative approaches discussed in chapter 7. Since each of the three reflect different levels of student involvement, they should not be seen as mutually exclusive when designing lessons. That is, the use of one may set the stage for using another.

Each of the three approaches may be applied in any of the three nontraditional educational settings discussed in this chapter: making connections at play, on science excursions, and when facing environmental issues. By incorporating activities designed to help relate classroom experiences to experiences outside the classroom, you can expect a new dimension of interest and involvement from your students.

Section IV Aligning Curriculum, Instruction, and Assessment

The four chapters of this section represent the structuring of science education as a curricular issue. The reader will find a discussion of the integration of science with other subject areas, descriptions of formal programs in science education that can be adopted or adapted by schools or districts, techniques for managing a science program, and techniques for assessing the progress of students.

Chapter 10, "Science, Technology, and Society: Connections," focuses on the increasingly important STS triad in our increasingly technology-oriented world. Much of technology today has an almost mystical nature. Yet, the mutually beneficial relationship between science and technology, of which scientists and technologists are aware, need not represent mysterious territory to the users of technology. The key to understanding lies in demonstrating, as a regular part of science education, the relationship between science and technology, and its impact on social problems.

Chapter 11, "Developing the School Science Program," provides a closer look at many of the science education programs that were first referred to in Section I. At that time, the focus was on the events that led to the development of programs. We held this particular chapter for

Section IV in order to give the reader an opportunity to develop an understanding of what science teaching is all about. With this accomplished, it should be easier, and a more meaningful exercise, for the reader to evaluate the advantages and disadvantages of "packaged" programs and their goals.

Effective science education, perhaps more so than any other discipline, requires the appropriate use of many different resources. Chapter 12, "Planning and Managing Science in the Classroom," is concerned with identifying and organizing those resources. The chapter discusses individual and group work strategies, as well as arranging experiences outside of the classroom.

Finally, chapter 13, "Assessment of Student Learning," addresses those important questions of accountability. Though the standardized, selected response test continues its tenacious hold on school districts as a tool for policy decisions, there are alternative forms of assessment that allow the teacher to determine what the students understand, how they have changed their thinking, and how they have grown in a cognitive sense over the course of the instruction provided. The emphasis of this chapter is on demonstrating understanding, rather than allowing for one's best guess.

10 | | Science, Technology, and Society: Connections

What Is STS?

Science and Technology as a Social Issue

STS in the Classroom

Conclusion

Your Academic Roadmap

Study of this chapter should help you to understand the following concepts:

- The people who will solve the "people problems" of the future may be the children in your classroom.

- STS activities provide dynamic and thought-provoking ways of integrating the subject areas.

- An STS approach to education engages children in personal, local, national, and global issues in which science, technology, and society interact.

It suddenly struck me that that tiny pea, pretty and blue, was the earth. I put up my thumb and shut one eye, and my thumb blotted out the planet Earth. I didn't feel like a giant. I felt very, very small.

—Neil Armstrong (returning to Earth on *Apollo 11*)

WHAT IS STS?

This chapter is about science, technology, and society (STS), a topic that refers to both content and method. Therefore, this chapter relates back to Section I, which was about the content of the elementary curriculum. It also relates to the chapters of Section III, which focused on the methods of teaching science. So why is this chapter here in Section IV? It is because STS represents a very particular context for the teaching of science. Though STS refers to three distinct areas of endeavor, the relationship between them is so intimate that to talk of one necessarily brings the other into play.

Veteran science educators recognize that STS refers to the nature of science and technology and to the connection of science and technology to our lives as social beings. STS also refers to an approach to teaching science, which can effectively utilize particular methods. The approach involves trying to engage children in problem-solving and decision-making activities set in real-world contexts. Through such activities, children also have opportunities to learn the "pure science" part of the curriculum.

STS education is closely linked with social studies and environmental education. And the focus in this chapter is on the environmental aspect of the relationship (note, however, that STS does not necessarily refer to environmental concerns). An STS approach also offers many opportunities to link science with language arts and mathematics. Integration of subjects across the curriculum is a natural result of instruction focused on the social and environmental problems and issues relevant to children's lives.

The STS approach to science education has been gaining ground among practitioners since the 1970s. STS education, according to Dennis Cheek (1992), embraces two distinct educational goals:

1. Teaching students about the nature and culture of science and technology as experienced by practitioners and understood through the conceptual lenses of sociology, history, psychology, anthropology, and philosophy.

2. Introducing students to personal, local, national, and/or global issues at the interface between science, technology and society . . . [which] entails personal decision making and informed, premeditated action. (p. 199)

The first of these two areas, the nature of science, was the focus in chapter 1. In this chapter, we explore the second area, the issues at the interface between science, technology, and society.

The national curriculum frameworks for several subject areas support STS education. "Science, technology, and society" and "global connections" are two of the ten themes identified as social studies content in the National Social Studies Standards (NCSS, 1994, p. 28). The National Geography Standards identify "physical and human systems" and "environment and society" as two of six clusters of content for geography in the curriculum (Geography Education Standards Project, 1994). The latter states that a "geographically informed person" is one who understands how human actions modify the physical environment, how physical systems affect human systems, and how changes occur in the meaning, use, distribution, and importance of resources.

The National Science Education Standards (NRC, 1996) affirm that an STS approach is appropriate for the science program. In the science standards, content is clustered into eight areas, each of which is recommended to be taught in some form from kindergarten to grade 12. Here are two of the eight content strands:

Science and Technology

Science in Personal and Social Perspectives

Science and Technology is about the first STS education goal identified by Dennis Cheek. The subtopics for Science in Personal and Social Perspectives are the following:

Personal Health (for grades K-4 and 5−8)

Characteristics and Changes in Populations (K−4)

Types of Resources (K−4)

Changes in Environments (K−4)

Science and Technology in Local Challenges (K−4)

Populations, Resources, and Environments (5−8)

Natural Hazards (5−8)

Risks and Benefits (5−8)

Science and Technology in Society (5−8) (NRC, 1996, 138, 166)

A long list of problems and issues can be related to these topics. To which of the subtopics above can you link items in the list in Figure 10.1? As you can see from the list, the STS issues connect to many aspects of human endeavor. Science provides information that technologists use to extend the capabilities of scientists. The work of both necessarily have some impact on the society at large. If you are looking for a way to make what goes on in school meaningful and relevant to your students, you should look at the STS issues in your school's community and use one or more of those issues as a conceptual framework for your classroom science program.

FIGURE 10.1 Some STS topics related to the standards' content "Science in Personal and Social Perspectives."

Science, technology, and society: Some problems, issues, and topics

Populations and population growth

Pollution

Social issues related to science/technology (e.g., cloning humans, fetal tissue transplants, freedom and surveillance)

Lifespan extension

Green revolution and projected future needs

World hunger and poverty

Toxic substances in food chains

Dam construction for hydroelectric power

Solar energy

Wind as an energy source

Biomass as an energy source

Mineral resource reserves and depletion

Resource exploration and exploitation (e.g., offshore drilling)

Renewable and nonrenewable resources

Toxic waste disposal

Radiation exposure (e.g., UV, microwave, power plant leaks)

Ground and surface water use and depletion

Weather/climate modification

Surface mining

Deforestation

Soil erosion

Wildlife extinctions

Weapons and preparations for war

The Human Genome Project

Science and technology in foreign policy

Global resource reserves

Quality of life

Fossil fuels

Food and agricultural policies

Use of oceanic resources

Aquaculture

Nuclear energy

Geothermal energy

Tidal energy

Synthetic fuels

Aquifer management

Air pollution

Solid waste disposal

Noise pollution

Ozone depletion

Land use

Forest use

Soil pollution

Desertification

Wildlife habitat destruction

Health care policies

Housing policies

Transportation policies

SCIENCE AND TECHNOLOGY AS A SOCIAL ISSUE

Science and technology connect with the environment in at least two ways. First, they may cause or influence particular environmental situations. For example, had it not been for the work of physicists and engineers, there would be no nuclear power, and thus no problem of having to safely dispose of nu-clear waste. This problem must be weighed against the benefits of nuclear technology. Second, one role of science and technology in society is to understand and solve environmental problems. In relation to the example of nuclear waste, scientists and engineers continue to work on solutions to this problem.

As a result of education, children should develop an ecological understanding of the environment and how human activities interact with the environment. This includes understanding local, regional, and global environmental conditions, how conditions have changed over time and are changing now, what is causing the changes, and what responsible citizens should do in response. Activity 10.1 encourages you to think about other problems faced by society. What trends do you perceive? What social role does science and technology play?

ACTIVITY 10.1

Thinking about the Future

---

1. Make a list of ten problems faced by humankind today that you consider to be most important.

   After you have made your list, go over the list and put an asterisk in front of every item that you could link in some way to science and technology.

2. After placing asterisks, go back over your list and put a second asterisk next to each item you think might continue to be a problem through the year 2025, when today's schoolchildren are adults.

3. Compare and discuss your list with those of a classmate. What kind of education does society need for the world you envision from now until c.e. 2025?

Social Change: The Big Picture

The transforming possibilities of new discoveries and inventions became manifest during the Industrial Revolution. By the nineteenth century, industrial society the world over was enamored with technological change. While people were eager for the benefits, most tended to ignore the negative effects, and yet the consequences of scientific and technical changes have often been surprising and frequently troublesome (Winner, 1989).

Moreover, sociologists have found that most people are uninformed and ill prepared for the outcomes of new developments (Dean & Shayon, 1989).

The social situation in industrial society around the globe has been particularly unsettled since the end of the Vietnam War in the early 1970s. Leonard Waks (1995) has pointed out four dimensions of social changes since that period. First, people have become increasingly aware of the environmental impacts of industrial production. Second, there has been a rapid development of new technologies of communication and information processing. Third, international competition for markets has led to the rise of multinational corporations. And fourth, changing social situations relate to global security systems. Extranational organizations such as the North Atlantic Treaty Organization (NATO) and the United Nations have accepted expanded roles in peacekeeping and global policing.

These four dimensions of social change have changed the nature of citizenship. The trend toward global institutions has not been matched by the development of a concomitant institution of world citizenship. Waks (1995) concludes that a characteristic of postindustrial society is social polarization and the deterioration of citizenship as it was understood in the past, including the eventual diminishing of social, political, and even civil rights. If our job as educators is to help children come to understand the world situation as well as their options as social actors, then this situation clearly presents a challenge to us. Let's explore this issue further in order to better understand that challenge.

Carrying Capacity: The Crunch Is Here

Understanding the world situation today, and our own situation as a species, involves grasping several ecological and economic concepts, the most important of which may be

FIGURE 10.2 A concrete demonstration of the finite nature of Earth's land resources.

A CLASSROOM DEMONSTRATION: THE EARTH AS AN APPLE

Consider the earth as an apple. Slice the apple into quarters. Set aside three of the quarters, which represent the oceans of the world. The fourth quarter roughly represents the total land area.

Slice this land quarter in half, which yields two $\frac{1}{8}$ world pieces. Set aside one of the pieces to represent land inhospitable to people—the polar areas, deserts, swamps, very high or rocky mountainous areas. The other $\frac{1}{8}$ piece is the land area where people live, but don't necessarily grow the foods needed for life.

Now slice this $\frac{1}{8}$ piece into four sections, yielding four $\frac{1}{32}$ pieces. Set aside three of these pieces, which represent areas too rocky, too wet, too cold, too steep, or with soil too poor to actually produce food. These pieces also represent the areas of land that could produce food but are buried under cities, highways, suburban developments, shopping centers, and other human-made structures.

This leaves one $\frac{1}{32}$ slice. Carefully peel the skin off this slice. The piece of apple peel represents the soil layer, the very thin skin of the earth's crust upon which humankind depends for food. On average less than two meters (6.5 feet) deep, the soil represents the limited amount of food-producing land available to humanity.

With a fixed land resource base and an ever increasing number of people trying to feed themselves from the fixed base, this demonstration illustrates that each person's portion becomes smaller and smaller.

carrying capacity. A sustainable society is one that "satisfies its needs without jeopardizing the prospects of future generations" (Brown et al., 1990, pp. 12–13). Carrying capacity is the maximum number of organisms that a particular ecosystem can sustain indefinitely, given a set of environmental conditions.

No one really knows for sure what the earth's carrying capacity is for Homo sapiens. And there are no existing models of sustainable societies. The world's industrial societies have created automobile-centered, fossil fuel–driven economies that are clearly unsustainable, yet most developing nations are aspiring to the same resource-consumptive systems.

Land availability is one of many factors involved in calculating carrying capacity. In Figure 10.2, an apple is used as a model representing the earth. The apple activity concretely demonstrates the finite nature of the earth's land resources. The rate at which these resources are being consumed can be used to guage changes in the carrying capacity. Experts may disagree on how much of a given resource remains, but it is widely recognized that as resources are consumed and environmental quality declines, the carrying

capacity is decreased—the environment is able to sustain fewer inhabitants.

From the perspective of ecology, the world at the beginning of the twenty-first century is at an historic watershed. Future historians may look back with wonder regarding our current exuberant, if not profligate, lifestyles. The bottom line is that the earth's remaining resources simply are not sufficient to indefinitely sustain the level of consumption to which we in the developed countries have become so accustomed. Yet our economic system is structured such that growth in consumption is promoted by most economists and politicians. Advertisements urge us to consume more of every product. Yet, in the words of Robert Louis Stevenson, "Sooner or later, every man [sic] must sit down to a banquet of consequences."

The Nature of Exponential Change Ecologists tell us that every organism has its limits to growth. For one thing, growth is limited because natural systems can buffer only so much waste. For another, growth is limited because material resources in any ecosystem are limited. In 1798, Thomas Malthus recognized the fundamental principle that population growth is limited when resources are finite (Whittaker, 1975). Except for meteorites from space, no new materials are being added to the ecosystem. We must make do with our present supply.

The phenomena of exponential human population growth is a major obstacle to the creation of a sustainable society due to its effect on carrying capacity. One of the major principles of ecology elucidated by Garrett Hardin (1985) is that "the sanctity of the carrying capacity" should take precedence over the sanctity of life. A look at the ramifications of exponential growth against the finite resources of the ecosystem will help make the problem clearer.

Any quantity that increases (or decreases) by a percentage over a unit of time is said to grow (or become depleted) exponentially. When something is growing exponentially, its quantity will double in an amount of time that is easy to determine mathematically. The doubling time of any quantity increasing at some percentage is found by the equation:

$$T_2 = 70/p$$
T_2 = doubling time   P = % increase

An everyday example of exponential arithmetic is how money accumulates in a savings account. Even a modest savings account can accrue a large sum when enough time passes. An example illustrating how the doubling-time relation works is found in Activity 10.2.

deemed by some descendant of yours. Assume the interest rate is 5 percent per year.

How much would your relative inherit? Here is how to calculate the answer. In our example, the doubling time would be

$T_2 = 70/p$ (p = the interest rate
$T_2 = 70/5$ as a percentage)
$T_2 = 14$ years

How many doublings can take place in 500 years?

$$500/14 = 35.7 \text{ doublings}$$

With almost 36 doublings, your relative could pick up $55.8 billion! If he or she waited fourteen more years, the bundle would be twice that, or $111.6 billion. After the 500 years, the interest on the two dollars would be rolling in at the rate of $7,586 per minute, $455,000 per hour, almost $11 million a day!

Now try using the doubling-time relation in the following examples.

1. Suppose Metropolis has a population of 30,000 people and is growing at 3.5 percent. In how many years will it have a population of 60,000?

2. Assume Centerville's 2.5 million inhabitants will double in thirty-five years at its current rate of growth. What is Centerville's growth rate?

(You will find the answers to these problems at the end of the chapter.)

ACTIVITY 10.2

Practice Using the Mathematics of Doubling Time

The Exponential Growth of a Savings Account

Suppose you took $2.00 and put it into a 500-year certificate of deposit, to be re-

Human Population Growth over Time

No one knows the date when our species, Homo sapiens, first appeared. Paleontologists figure our particular ancestors appeared somewhere between half a million and a million years ago. And then our population began growing.

During the first century C.E., the global human population was about 250 million.

(Figures may not add to totals due to rounding)

FIGURE 10.3 World vital events per time unit: 1998.

Time Unit	Births	Deaths	Increase
Year	133,009,117	54,291,659	78,717,458
Month	11,084,093	4,524,305	6,559,788
Day	364,409	148,744	215,664
Hour	15,184	6,198	8,986
Minute	253	103	150
Second	4.2	1.7	2.5

World POPClock (1998)

About eighteen centuries later (C.E. 1830), our population was a thousand million—a billion. After that, the second billion was attained in only 100 more years, or about 1930. Only 30 years were needed to add the third billion, which occurred about 1960. The fourth billion came 15 years later, in 1975; and the fifth only 11 years after that, in 1986. As we enter the twenty-first century, the world's human population will be over 6 billion. The net addition of a billion people now takes place in less than the time it takes a child to complete his or her schooling. If you would like to keep up with the growth of the world's population, http://www.census.gov/cgi-bin/ipc/pcwe on the Internet will keep you up to date.

The successively shorter periods between each unit of quantity is the significant characteristic of exponential growth. The populations of most species are held in check by predators and other limiting factors. However, having eliminated many of our own natural competitors and limiting factors, humankind now must deal with the consequences of exceeding the earth's carrying capacity.

The current annual net population gain of the world is over 90 million people, more than the population of Great Britain or France. The number of humans is increasing at a rate of 1.7 percent (Population Reference Bureau, 1995). At that rate, world population will *double* in about forty-two years, yielding a population of 12 billion early in the twenty-first century, about the time today's elementary-age children are parents themselves. Figure 10.3 shows the global figures for population changes by different spans of time.

Population is just one part of the problem. "First-worlders" often view the high reproductive rates of the poor countries as the source of our global problems, but that is not the case. More fundamental is the problem of resource consumption. The world's industrial societies consume the most resources and produce the most waste. The impact of population on the carrying capacity is greatest where consumption is highest. If the fundamental global problem is overconsumption of resources, we Americans, among others, have a lot of soul-searching to do.

Everything Is Recycled A key principle in ecology is that everything must go somewhere, everything has to end up somewhere else on the earth. Natural systems use energy from the sun and from inside the earth to continually break down and circulate matter. The waste produced by living things, including humans, is recycled through natural buffer systems in the atmosphere, the hydrosphere, and the biosphere. These buffer systems handle the excretory wastes of our bodily processes, including solid and liquid wastes and the carbon dioxide we exhale and also exhaust from our vehicles. Waste gases such as carbon dioxide and methane enter the atmosphere. Solid and liquid wastes may be buried in landfills but ultimately may leak into the hydrosphere through groundwater.

The buffering capacity of the biogeochemical cycles can handle a substantial range of amounts of waste, but the capacity is not unlimited, and the systems can be overloaded and stressed. Some wastes create more of a problem than others. Many of the new chemicals that have been synthesized and produced in bulk in the last several decades have no natural agents of decomposition and tend to accumulate in the biosphere. Soil can be a reservoir for pesticides, herbicides, solvents, and plastics. Some 500 million kilograms (more than a billion pounds) of chemicals that are highly resistant to degradation are used each year in the United States. They can contaminate groundwater, topsoil, and stream sediment for decades after their initial application (Hanson, 1989). Hazardous wastes, defined as either carcinogenic (cancer-causing) or ignitable in a way that can threaten public health, are often by-products of manufacturing. They include chlorinated hydrocarbons such as PCBs, heavy metal sludges, and a whole range of acids. As part of our consumer society, each American generates between one and two tons of hazardous waste per year (Piasecki, 1989).

Some people have become very sensitive to the chemicals and toxins that are increasingly part of everyday life. A relatively new phenomenon is environmental illness (EI), also known as chemical hypersensitivity, multiple chemical sensitivity, and total allergy syndrome (Lamb, 1989). Symptoms range from fatigue and hives to severe headaches, joint pain, and hyperactivity.

Acid rain, another form of pollution, originates from the disposal of wastes into the atmosphere. It is caused by burning fossil fuels and probably causes more respiratory disease than any source besides smoking. From rocks and soil, acid rain releases toxic metals, including lead, aluminum, mercury, and cadmium. Acid rain causes distress to many tree species and is responsible for *Waldsterben,* the decline of entire forests. Recent studies document the declining health of many of America's forest ecosystems and tree species (Little, 1995).

Considerations for the Future

Without doubt, the situation that we find ourselves in at the beginning of the new century is one that has been exacerbated by a neglect for the consequences of human "enterprises" over the years. Unfortunately, the complexity of the situation is such that we cannot simply shut down, clean things up, and proceed in a more responsible manner. Instead, transition is the key term. Science and technology will be part of the new solution to the existing problems, but everyone will be part of finding alternatives to our current practices. The consequence of staying with the present trend is simply not an option. But where and when will the paradigm shift begin to take place? In all honesty, the shift could be taking place here and now as you read these words enroute to becoming a teacher. Does that give you some sense of the responsibility that teachers bear?

Extinction Is Forever The biological diversity of an ecosystem is another critical characteristic of the earth's carrying capacity. Species interact in myriad ways in an ecosystem, each dependent on others. Ecologists believe that the richness of species diversity in an ecosystem is a measure of its health, stability, and resilience to disturbances. There is a relationship between our ultimate ability to create a sustainable society and the beneficial

Biological diversity of any ecosystem is a critical characteristic of the earth's carrying capacity.

environmental functions of an unpolluted, biologically diverse ecosystem.

With all that is known about these diverse ecosystems, the fact remains that our knowledge is severely limited. The reason we know so little about so much of the biosphere is that most of the species are too tiny to see without aid. Ecologists recognize a phenomenon called the pyramid of diversity, meaning that the species that consist of very small individuals have a greater diversity of numbers of species. The reason for this is that small organisms can divide the environment into smaller niches than large organisms can. Because of this, most species on the earth remain completely unknown to science. Of

Michael Bentley

Michael Bentley

the species we know about, over 99 percent are known only by a scientific name (Wilson, 1992).

Though we do not know much about what really is "out there," biologists warn us that species are becoming extinct at the fastest pace since the extinction of the dinosaurs 65 million years ago, and that most of the current extinctions are caused by human activities. E. O. Wilson, an expert on biodiversity at Harvard University, reports that in the past two thousand years, 20 percent of the species of birds worldwide have been eliminated and that about 20 percent of the world's freshwater fish species are either extinct or in a serious state of decline (Wilson, 1992).

The message from scientists is that biological diversity contributes to the health of the global ecosystem and that human activities can harm other species. One responsible reaction is to work to reduce one's own impact on the biosphere by reducing consumption, recycling, and the like (see Figure 10.4). Another is to work for a society that preserves significantly large areas as

FIGURE 10.4 Conserving planetary resources.

WHAT YOU CAN DO TO CONSERVE PLANETARY RESOURCES

- Use energy-efficient compact-fluorescent lightbulbs (six times more efficient than incandescent bulbs).

- Set the water heater thermostat to 120°F and wrap the tank with insulation.

- Fill unused parts of the refrigerator with jugs of water.

- Clean the refrigerator gaskets; make sure they seal tightly.

- When your power gadgets wear out, revert to hand-powered substitutes, e.g., alarm clock, food mill, lawn mower, snow-blower, etc.

- Get a solar recharger for rechargeable battery devices.

- Think about what you can live without.

wilderness. Also, as teachers, we can do much to educate children to value species diversity. Children can learn that their own personal happiness and security depends less on possessions and more on the quality of their environment.

The Global Commons Everyone depends upon a commons of resources, the most basic of which are the atmosphere (for oxygen and light), the hydrosphere (for water, food, and minerals), and the geosphere (for food and minerals). The dynamic interactive processes within and among the atmosphere, hydrosphere, geosphere, and biosphere provide a generative structure for the development of all life.

The carrying capacity of the earth depends on the quantity and quality of resources of the commons, the "bottom line" for our individual and corporate well-being. Years ago, insightful thinkers such as Henry David Thoreau, John Muir, Lewis Mum-

ford, and Aldo Leopold recognized the need to protect and preserve this commons.

One early alarm was sounded by marine ecologist Rachel Carson. Her best-seller, *Silent Spring,* originally published in 1962, alerted the public to the damage being done to the commons by the pesticide DDT. The first Earth Day was celebrated not long after, on April 22, 1970. On that day over 20 million Americans took part in demonstrations, teach-ins, neighborhood cleanup projects, and other activities in communities of every size. Grassroots concern for the environment was communicated to public officials, and legislation soon followed, including the Endangered Species Act and the act creating the U.S. Environmental Protection Agency (EPA).

Learning from History In particular localities, overpopulation and degradation of the carrying capacity have occurred in the past. In fact, the depletion or destruction of natural resources has been cited as the chief cause for the decline of many ancient civilizations. The shift from hunting-gathering to agriculture some ten thousand years ago brought about a rapid increase in human population and led to permanent dwellings in villages and cities (Dubos, 1974). Thereafter, local carrying capacity was frequently exceeded. The classic study *Topsoil and Civilization,* by Dale and Carter (1955), documented the fates of societies that cut down or burned their forests, overgrazed their grasslands, hunted wildlife and waterlife to extinction, wasted metals and other necessary minerals, and overcropped, allowing their topsoil to erode away.

Since the first Earth Day, people's awareness of being interrelated with natural systems has grown, and progress has been made in solving many environmental problems. Nonetheless, some problems have grown worse. Our planet faces an array of new ills, such as ozone holes, climate change, ocean pollution, acid rain, and dying forests. The essential fact, however, is that these are all "people" problems.

Quick Review

Perhaps the most promising notion from all of this is that people are of sufficient intelligence to face and resolve the problems that have been created. But it must be mentioned that solutions come with consequences as well. Not all of the consequences of reversing a self-destructive trend may be appealing to all people. Significant changes in lifestyle may be required. But the lessons of biological existence, of common needs for sustenance, and the record of history could not be more in accord with the fact that people must solve the problems that people have, and will, develop. The people who will one day be at the forefront of finding those solutions may well be students in your classroom in the next few years. So with that in mind, turn your attention to some of the things that can be done in the classroom to address STS concerns.

STS IN THE CLASSROOM

Education has an important role in any approach to solving a problem or issue. As the old industrial society fades away and a post-industrial society emerges, economic development that is sustainable will require that today's use of resources not leave future generations with less. Narrow conceptions of economic self-interest have to be replaced by the understanding that prosperity built on environmental degradation is foolish and will ultimately impoverish us all. "Anticipate and prevent" will have to become the operational phrase for society, replacing "Live for today, pay for it tomorrow."

ACTIVITY 10.3
INFOTRAC COLLEGE EDITION INVESTIGATION:

Identifying Environmental Problems

Environmental issues are among the most dynamic that we can consider in science. Select one of the topics below and use InfoTrac College Edition to find the most current information about that particular environmental issue. It would be useful if students in your class could each select a different topic. This one assignment could give you a much greater idea of impact of such issues.

acid rain	air pollution
noise pollution	deforestation
ozone depletion	toxic waste disposal

Try to answer the following questions through your research:

1. What was your conceptualization of the problem before researching the topic?

2. Has the particular issue gotten worse, or is the situation improving?

3. What could you do in a classroom to address this issue?

Infusing STS Education into the Curriculum

We hope that the information provided in this chapter has served to inspire you to action. Though the present situation is disturbing, it is not hopeless. It is appropriate that young children be spared the doom and gloom of the statistics you have been reading; however, children need to become empowered by believing that they can make a difference.

As a teacher, you can engage children in learning about ecosystems and their components from activities such as creating a classroom terrarium to conducting field studies in the neighborhoods, fields, forests, streams, and ponds of your locality. The U.S. Fish and Wildlife Service has identified fifty-two major ecosystems in the United States, mainly on the basis of watersheds (Chadwick, 1994). Your classroom will be located in one of them. You can help children assess environmental quality and identify problems in your locality and its regional ecosystem. With experience and knowledge of the local ecosystem, children can compare different ecosystems and seek patterns of similarity and difference. By the end of their elementary years, children can understand many basic ecological concepts and principles involved in environmental problems and can learn much about the role human actions play in the environment. They also can develop an appreciation for nature and a commitment to environmental values. Some important concepts include the following:

carrying capacity	limiting factors
the food pyramid	finite resources
biogeochemical cycles	the commons
agricultural efficiency	tolerance limits
exponential change (growth and depletion)	sustainability
	buffers
environmental monitoring/ futures reconnaissance	

Children also can learn to judge the relative importance of environmental problems. Public perceptions of the seriousness of problems can be very different from the perceptions of knowledgeable scientists. In one study, two-thirds of adult respondents ranked hazardous waste sites as the most serious problem but ranked the climate alteration due to the greenhouse effect as twenty-third. In contrast, EPA scientists ranked the greenhouse effect high and hazardous waste sites as low-to-medium in health risk (Smith, 1989).

Find out what children in your own classroom think is most serious. Do a "think-pair-share" (T-P-S) activity with the class. Make a list of environmental problems and ask the class to rank them in order, with "1" being the most serious. Next, have each child compare his or her responses with those of a classmate. Finally, ask children to share their observations and the results of their discussion with the class. The T-P-S format is a good way to conduct STS discussions because every child gets involved.

Using Simulations/ Role-Playing/Projects

Simulations and role-play activities enable children to interact with each other over issues related to the environment and society. Playing a role helps a child see the world from another's perspective and gain insight into a situation. Children can be creative in interpreting their roles, as long as they stick to the "givens" provided in the activity guide. A debriefing should follow the activity. During the discussion, your observations and questions can challenge children to further thought. You can lead children to compare the make-believe to real-world situations and engage them in follow-up research and project work.

An example of a simulation activity is provided in Activity 10.4. Notice that it includes several key considerations, such as group structure, roles, tasks, and background information. There are many sources of other simulations and role-plays. See chapter 14 for sources of materials described here. The Population Reference Bureau (PRB) makes available to teachers the "Food for Thought" kit for intermediate to secondary children. Activities in the packet integrate science, math, and social studies (economics and geography) and focus on concepts such as population distribution, density, and resource allocation. Also available from PRB is a student's book of activities and a teacher's guide, *Making Connections: Linking Population and the Environment* (Crews, 1992).

ZPG is another organization that produces population-environment education materials, including simulation activities. Available are two guides, *Earth Matters: Studies for Our Global Future* and *Elementary Population Activities Kit*. Edmark publishes the Imagination Express series of CD-ROMS that provide different simulated environments for children to explore. Current titles in the series include *Destination: Rain Forest; Destination: Ocean;* and *Destination: Neighborhood.* STS issues can also be found in MECC's Oregon Trail and in the SIM series—*Simcity, Sim-earth, Sim-town, Sim-farm,* and so on. Publisher of the SIM series of CD-ROMs is Maxis, Inc. Go to http://www.maxis.com/index.html to contact them.

ACTIVITY 10.4

"Star City" Land-Use Simulation

Here is the situation: One hundred fifty hectares (1 ha = 10,000 m^2 = 2.5 acres) of valuable land were inherited by Star City according to the will of former mayor and philanthropist J. F. Richmore. The land had been used as a "gentleman's farm" and is about half forested and half in pasture. The southwest quadrant of the property borders Star River. The property includes an historic brick farmhouse (ca. 1860) and a large, 1960s outbuilding used to board horses.

The teacher should randomly assign students to groups according to the number of students in the class and the roles as listed below. It is not necessary that every role be filled.

Local Government Planning Commission:
  Retired person (has banking interests)
  Local business leader (owns chain of building supply stores)

Clergyperson
USDA Forest Service Superintendent (of the Burnt Ewart National Forest nearby)
Lawyer (former state senator)

Note: While the players (below) are preparing, your group will

- Elect a chairperson to conduct the hearing to answer the question: "How will Star City use its newly acquired property?"
- Discuss and list priorities for Star City
- Complete the additional task(s) assigned by the instructor

Industry:
CEO and corporate officers of (one of the following) Steel Co., Concrete Plant, Recycling Plant, Construction Co., Limestone Quarry, Chemical Co., Refinery, Auto and Truck Plant, Timber Co.

Not-for-Profit Cultural Group:
Executive Director and associates of (one of the following) civic center, science museum, concert hall and theater complex, art museum, sports arena and outdoor recreation facilities

Not-for-Profit Educational Institution:
President and officers of (one of the following) Community College, State University, Consortium Research Park, County Library Authority

Public/Social Service Agency:
Executive Director and associates of (one of the following) hospital, nursing home/hospice, state adolescent psychiatric hospital and drug treatment center, regional correctional facility (prison), sewage treatment plant

NGO (nongovernment organization):
Executive Director and associates of (one of the following) Star River Valley Association (environmental/preservationist group; local affiliate of the Wilderness Society),

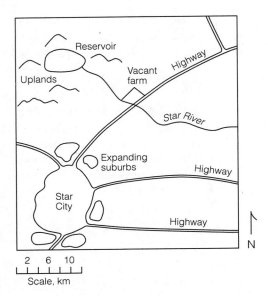

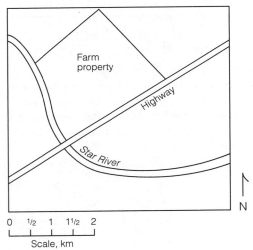

FIGURE 10.5 Star City map.

Heritage Foundation (regional historical society), White Water Club (regional canoeists group), Star City Chapter, Audubon Society

Each group is to prepare a five-minute presentation to the Star City Planning Commission advocating the position of the group on the use of the land.

Materials Available

- Flip charts
- Markers

In order to complete the simulation, here is some background information about Star City (see also Figure 10.5): With a population of 250,000, it is the third largest city in East State. The population has been rapidly increasing and the suburban fringe has been expanding even more rapidly (both residential and commercial use). This growth has been accompanied by demands for more housing, jobs, services, and recreational areas. The city has the available electric power for industrial uses, adequate public transportation, and a skilled labor force. There is a national forest to the north. Land surrounding the city is devoted mainly to farming. The Star River is unpolluted and is the source of irrigation water as well as the city's water source. The river is too shallow for freight transportation, but logs can float on it and it is valued for its white water (class 2 and class 3 rapids) and fishing. The gravel bed of the river is appropriate raw material for concrete manufacture. The present sewage treatment plant and landfill are at maximum capacity.

STS projects can take many forms: individual, team, or whole-class projects. For older elementary children, STS issues and problems can be the focus of research projects. Refer back to the list of STS topics in Figure 10.1. Which would appeal to children for further investigation?

Another worthwhile STS investigation is for children to study their own personal impact on the environment. Activity 10.5 addresses the use of water in the home. Children can learn where water is used most and find ways to save water at home. A similar investigation can be devised for other topics, such as energy use.

ACTIVITY 10.5

Investigating Water Consumption in the Home

Directions for students: Cut out and post the data tables in your bathroom and kitchen at home, and ask your family members to place a tally mark in the appropriate column each time the following activities are performed over two days.

For posting in the bathroom:

Activity	Gallons per Use	Day 1	Day 2
Toilet flush	5		
Tub bath	36		
Shower	25		
Teeth brushing			
water running	5		
water off	½		

For posting in the kitchen:

Activity	Gallons per Use	Day 1	Day 2
Hand washing dishes:			
water running	30		
in basin	10		
Dishwasher use	20		
Clothes washer use	30		
Meal preparation	5		

Work with a classmate to calculate the following:

- The average amount of water used per day for each activity on the charts.
- The total water used in a day.
- The average amount of water used per person per day.
- The total amount of water used per person in a year.

Another kind of STS project that a class can undertake is a habitat restoration. Whatever the type of habitat—woodland, pond, or prairie—such a project would require students to learn how to identify both native and alien plant species for that locale. Your local 4-H Extension Agent or state or national forester would be helpful resources. The project would entail systematically removing the alien species by pulling them up or cutting them down, and methodically seeding the area with seeds of desirable native plants. Depending on the size of the tract of land, this project might involve classes for several years. See Figure 10.6 for a list of other outdoor projects.

ACTIVITY 10.6

Environmental Restoration Project

Consider the following project if you have a group of students with which to work (for instance, in a field experience or practicum placement). Alternatively, go through as many of the following steps as you can in terms of planning a restoration project for a class.

What restoration projects are needed in your area? Obtain a map of your city or county, and identify areas where natural habitats have been disturbed or degraded by human activities. From this list, find one or more sites that are accessible to where you will be teaching and where permission to conduct the student project can be obtained (public lands are usually your best bet). Scout the site, making notes about restoration potential and safety concerns. If possible, visit the site with a naturalist who can help you plan your restoration project. Enlist community volunteers and parents to work with you and your students. Plan the project with input from your students and the volunteers. One possibility is

FIGURE 10.6 STS outdoor projects

- Plant street trees in areas such as historic districts, parking lots, and around public buildings.

- Inventory street trees. A tree inventory can provide the community with valuable information about the condition of the urban forest, which can be used to develop a maintenance and replacement plan.

- Plant a living snow fence or windbreak, for example, along a road to prevent snowdrifts, or on the southern side of buildings (deciduous trees) and on the northern side (evergreens) to help moderate building temperatures in summer and winter.

- Create an arboretum of native trees (which are hardier and more durable than many exotics) on the school grounds.

- Plant a garden or park for people who are elderly or who have disabilities. A "scent" or "touch" garden would be for persons who are blind. Make raised garden beds and accessible walkways.

- Plant a heritage garden to preserve genetic diversity. A heritage garden is made of traditional varieties of fruits, vegetables, and flowers.

- If your school community has a strong ethnic heritage, plant an ethnic garden featuring traditional food plants, garden styles, and traditions.

- Restore or preserve an old cemetery.

- Adopt a neglected urban park.

- Plant colorful bulbs, annuals, and shrubs on traffic islands and in other public spaces. Good project sites include the grounds of public buildings, hospitals, community centers, post offices, schools, churches, and libraries.

- Transform a vacant lot into a park or garden.

- Preserve an important natural area such as a wetland, grove of virgin timber, or habitat for an endangered species.

- Identify and preserve remnants of native prairie.

- Plant wildflower yards. Wildflowers in public areas require little maintenance and water, and are thus economical and energy conserving.

- Use all available media and communication outlets to publicize your project (Paschall, 1992).

to stake out parcels of an area that can be assigned to small groups of students, each led by a parent or community volunteer. Groups might post their progress reports on a bulletin board or class web page. Take photographs or videotape the "before" conditions so you can chronicle your progress. You might want to promote your efforts by notifying the local newspaper or TV news.

The Worldwatch Institute has published an authoritative annual report on the state of the environment entitled *State of the World* (Brown et al., 1998). All of the data from the scientific studies consulted each year is published in a database diskette for both Macintosh and Wintel computers (Worldwatch Institute, 1996). Population Reference Bureau annually publishes U.S. and world population statistics (PRB, 1995). Apple Computer produces the earth explorer CD-ROM, a multimedia encyclopedia of the environment. Satellite photos of the United States and the world provide concrete evidence of human-caused environmental change. These are available on CD-ROMs in the Small Blue Planet series from Now What Software.

Yet another excellent resource is a software package called EnviroAccount 10, which enables children to see in detail the impact of their lifestyle on the environment. It is a tool to monitor one's progress in achieving a lower-impact lifestyle. In addition, see Figure 10.7.

Helping Children Analyze and Discuss Issues

As a teacher using the STS approach, you can set up situations for children to think about environmental issues. Children's thinking becomes more sophisticated as they participate in activities that allow them to express their ideas and feelings, listen to what others think, and present a position. As the discussion facilitator, the teacher can help by modeling active listening, posing questions, and giving feedback at appropriate times.

One or more of the ecological concepts and principles discussed earlier in the chapter can be useful to children in their analysis of an issue. Also, children's thoughts about a problem or issue can become more systematic and focused by having them address the following six questions (Enright, 1993, p. 4):

- What is happening?
- Why did it start?
- Why does it continue?
- Why don't we hear more about it?
- Why should we care?
- What can we do?

Enabling Children to Consider Consequences

Science is the only subject in the curriculum that specifically includes consideration of the future as part of its content. Children can imagine the possible consequences of an event or technology. You can start with a personal or family-related event and have children brainstorm possible results. For example, a new pet in the family might result in new caretaking responsibilities, additional expenses for food and other pet needs, a change in schedules to accommodate walks, and so forth. From such a familiar example, children can learn to speculate about the implications of new products and technologies.

FIGURE 10.7 Data for calculating environmental impact.

SOME KEY FORMULAS FOR INVESTIGATING YOUR ENVIRONMENTAL IMPACT

- Burning 1 gallon of gasoline produces about 20 pounds of CO_2.
- Using 1 kilowatt-hour of electricity produces about 2 pounds of CO_2.
- Burning 1 cubic foot of natural gas yields about 12 pounds of CO_2.
- Flying 1 mile produces about 1/2 pound of CO_2 per passenger.

One teaching strategy that can be used as a framework for children's thinking about consequences is illustrated in Activity 10.7.

ACTIVITY 10.7

The "Future Wheel" Activity (Puls & O'Brien, 1994, p. 18)

In the center oval (see Figure 10.8), write the name of an invention or event, such as genetic engineering, electric vehicles, solar power, or the extinction of the mountain lion. If the oval contains an invention, think of some of the ways the technology might be used, and list them inside the blank ovals nearest the center. Draw an arrow connecting the primary event (e.g., genetic engineering) to each potential outcome. Next, think of some of the secondary consequences of the technology. For example, what would happen if gender could be determined by genetic manipulation? Write down every secondary outcome you can think of, and connect it by two arrows to the event that produces it. Follow the same process for tertiary outcomes, using three arrows, and continue the process as far as you can imagine possible outcomes, adding additional ovals if necessary.

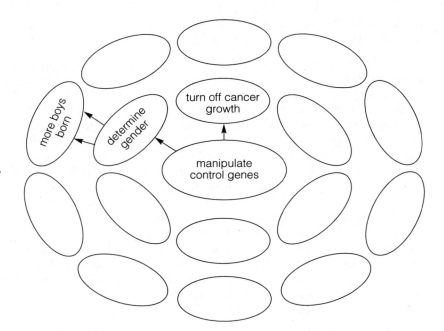

FIGURE 10.8 Sample future wheel activity sheet.

If the oval contains an event, think of some ways the event might change the environment. Draw an arrow connecting the event to each possible outcome, as before. Next, think of some of the serious consequences of the event, and connect it by arrows to the event that produces it. For example, what would happen if Congress were to repeal the Clean Water Act?

Future Wheels Activity

Suppose scientists learned how to manipulate the control genes that govern human development. Use this worksheet in pairs or groups to examine some of the ways this knowledge might affect society.

First, think of some of the ways this capability might be used, and list them inside the blank ovals nearest the center (a few examples are given). Draw an arrow connecting the primary event (manipulating control genes) to each potential outcome.

Now think of some of the secondary consequences of such manipulation. What would happen if organs could be regener-

ated, or gender determined (give one example)? Write down every secondary outcome you can think of, and connect it by two arrows to the event that produces it. Follow the same process for tertiary outcomes, using three arrows, and continue the process as far as your imagination takes you, using additional pages if necessary.

By learning to think about consequences, children learn to assess technological change and develop the concept of appropriate technology. To start, choose an invention or technology that has had or is likely to have both positive and negative social consequences, such as the automobile, television, pesticides, or nuclear energy. Here are some questions to guide thinking and discussion:

- What technology(ies) did the invention replace?

- Who benefited from the introduction of the technology?

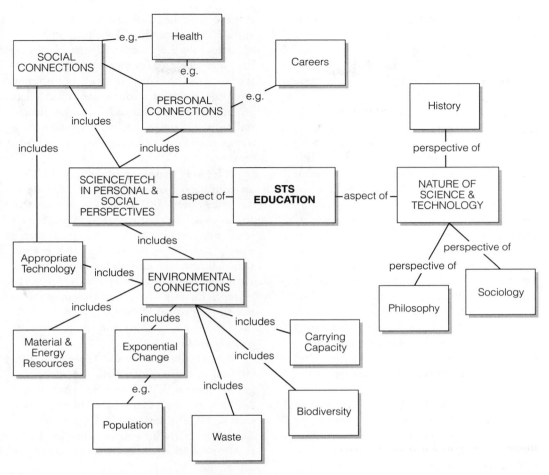

FIGURE 10.9 Concept map summarizing the content of STS education. (Dual aspects of STS education identified by Cheek, 1990)

- Who was harmed by its introduction?
- What impact did the technology have on the environment?
- What was known about the potential risks before the technology was introduced? Did anyone oppose it? Why?
- Did the government or other social influences limit or encourage the spread or application of the technology?
- Have attitudes toward the technology changed since it was introduced?

- If you had the power, would you put any constraints or limitations on the application of the technology? Why?

Quick Review

Infusing an STS component into the curriculum is an ideal method for integrating the various subject areas. All of the techniques discussed in this section are active, thought-provoking activities that have the potential for allowing your students to not only see the "big picture" but be a part of it as well. You will notice that in terms of the Taxonomy of Educational Objectives: Cognitive Domain, virtually all of the exercises that we have discussed emphasize higher levels of thinking.

CONCLUSION

An STS approach to education engages children in personal, local, national, and global issues in which science, technology, and society interact. STS education facilitates personal decision making and encourages informed and reflective action. This chapter focused upon science and technology's relationship to personal and social issues, one of two aspects of STS education. STS education is also about the nature of science and technology, which was discussed in chapter 2. A concept map of STS education is presented in Figure 10.9. Important concepts of carrying capacity, exponential change, waste and pollution, and biodiversity are mapped in the figure.

If you consider together the material of this chapter and that of chapter 1, about the nature of science and the implications for instruction of different views of science, you will have the range of STS content for the curriculum. STS education is a part of the more comprehensive changes in education and society occurring globally as industrial societies lose their industrial–manufacturing base and make the transition to postindustrial societies. As Neil Postman, a prominent educator and education writer of the late twentieth century has said, ". . . the 'future' will be a consequence of what we do now as a response to our understanding of the problems we face."

It is likely that the momentum of STS as an educational movement will continue in the years ahead. It is a paradox of sorts that the turning of a century tends to reinforce a sense of mortality at the same time that it fosters a sense of endurance and permanence. These two notions are not in conflict with each other, particularly as they relate to science, for it is the scientific endeavor in which your students will engage that will address the needs of today and the possibilities of tomorrow.

And finally, how about those questions back in Activity 10.2? Well, if Metropolis's growth rate is 3.5 percent per year, it will take just twenty years to double its population to 60,000 inhabitants. Centerville will double to 5 million inhabitants in thirty-five years with an annual growth rate of just 2 percent!

11 | | Developing the Elementary/ Middle School Science Program

Goals for Teaching Science

Reform Efforts of the 1950s–1970s:
The Alphabet Programs

Reform Efforts of the 1980s–1990s

Developing the Program at Your School

Conclusion

Your Academic Roadmap

Study of this chapter should help you to understand the following concepts:

- Your best science program will be based on the goals for your particular situation.

- Programs developed during the major science education reform movements broke new ground; however, teacher education was typically missing.

- A more effective use of technology may serve to alter the textbook-oriented approach to science that is prevalent in the schools.

- Understanding the program that exists at your school, and your role in its development and implementation, will pave the way for all that is to follow.

- The characteristics of a professional educator represent a multidimensional individual who understands the many and varied aspects involved in the delivery of a high-quality educational experience.

GOALS FOR TEACHING SCIENCE

Preceding chapters have considered science as a component of the curriculum, science content within that curriculum, and teaching strategies. This chapter is about the science program, that is, the year-long science component of what will happen in your classroom. We chose to place this chapter after Section III for a specific reason. Now that you are aware of what the activities of science instruction will be like, and how to prepare and present them, you will be able to use that knowledge as the context for organizing your particular classroom program. The chapter itself is arranged (1) to acquaint you with some of the goals to be considered in the development of a program, (2) to intro-

duce both the pioneering and contemporary formal programs of non–textbook–oriented science programs (the results of science education research and reform efforts), and (3) to have you reflect upon your role in program development at your own school.

When you become part of a school faculty, the school's science program may already be in place. If that is the case, a major task in your work will be to plan your units and lessons in a way that fits with the school or district curriculum framework. Yet even if your school already has a program guide for science, you can be sure that you and your teaching colleagues will be continually creating your school's actual science program.

Sometime in your teaching career you might find yourself in the situation of being on a team of teachers choosing curriculum materials and making decisions about the overall school or district science program.

Teachers frequently are involved in curriculum work of this kind. This collaborative effort is supported by the site-based management movement, a major trend in school administration across the United States and in many other countries. Site-based management means more autonomy for the local school, which means the local faculty and principal have more responsibility for curriculum decision making.

There is no doubt that curriculum work is demanding. For one thing, the curriculum operates on several levels, from the daily lesson all the way up to a scope and sequence of concepts, skills, and habits of mind to be developed. In most school districts, the elementary curriculum covers pre-K or K to grades 5, 6, or 8. Doing curriculum work requires not only a good grasp of the subject matter, but also a vision of what the school is about as a whole—its purposes and roles in the wider community. Such work also requires consideration of possible curriculum alternatives.

Like the curriculum as a whole, the science program can be thought of as the intended, or *explicit,* curriculum. In other words, it is the curriculum that is "written down." Alternatively, from the child's point of view, curriculum can be thought of as that which is actually experienced or learned. The experienced curriculum consists of both the explicit curriculum and the *implicit,* or hidden, curriculum. The hidden curriculum is not something devious, but rather acknowledgment that what is learned will actually depend on additional dimensions that cannot be anticipated, let alone planned. For instance, two young boys that we know were on a field trip one day. While riding on the bus, they got into an argument—not a violent argument, just a loud intellectual difference of opinion. The issue was, what would happen in a fight between a whale and a bear, which would win? Both of these animals had been discussed in class, but few teachers would

have included a discussion of relative strength as part of their plan. Yet to these children, it was an issue of considerable interest.

It should also be mentioned that there is at least one more aspect of curriculum— that of the *null* curriculum. The focus here is on what is intentionally or unintentionally left out of the curriculum. At first blush, this might seem somewhat esoteric, as if some educational theorist had nothing better to think about. Yet, particularly in a politically sensitive society such as ours, this becomes a most important concern. More likely than not, questions of the null curriculum fall to school boards to decide. Implementation, or nonimplementation as the case may be, falls to the classroom teacher. In years gone by, questions such as the teaching of evolution or sex education have been examples of the null curriculum. Can you think of some science topics that were left out of your own school experience as a science learner?

In the real world, the intended curriculum of the school rarely, if ever, equates with the learned curriculum. Despite this and because we believe the school is a public trust, we believe our intentions as educators should be made as explicit as possible. School people must be prepared to be reasonably accountable for their work. Further, it is important to understand that curriculum development is not something that is ever completed. Rather, curriculum-making is a continual process requiring individual and group deliberation.

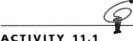

ACTIVITY 11.1
INFOTRAC COLLEGE EDITION
INVESTIGATION:

Social Issues and Education

Social issues such as the teaching of evolution, teaching abstinence versus birth control in sex education courses—if such courses are taught at all—or teaching ethics in science and technology are sensitive subjects that continue to be debated. Yet all of them impact on what is and is not included in the curriculum.

Use InfoTrac College Edition to find the latest standing of an educational debate. The topics listed above are sure to remain controversial long after the publication of this book. Other topics may include religion and education, free speech, the organization of counterculture clubs within a school.

Social pressure at any given time will affect your life as a teacher. Take this opportunity to begin staying current with what is happening, and how it might affect the programs that are part of the school curriculum.

Scientific Literacy

The level of goals or intended outcomes is a good place to begin thinking about the science program. The goals, or purposes, of a program provide a focus for the content and learning activities that you select and plan for your classroom. In the United States, the most frequently cited purpose of the school science program is to foster scientific literacy. This purpose, for example, is advocated in the new National Science Education Standards, which explain the concept as follows:

> An essential aspect of scientific literacy is greater knowledge and understanding of science subject matter, that is, the knowledge specifically associated with the physical, life, and earth sciences. Scientific literacy also includes understanding the nature of science, the scientific enterprise, and the role of science in society and personal life. (NRC, 1996, p. 21)

Jon Miller (1988) asserts that scientific literacy requires competence in three areas:

- understanding the scientific method,
- knowing the common vocabulary of science, and
- appreciating the social impact of science.

Miller has studied the scientific literacy of the adult population in the United States and in other countries. He combines his three criteria to form a single numerical index as a rating of scientific literacy. In almost twenty years of conducting his survey, Miller has found that only 5 to 7 percent of the American population qualify as scientifically literate by his criteria. The scientifically literate were mostly males, people older than thirty-five, and college graduates. Miller's general message is that the level of scientific literacy in the United States has been low for a long time and that various educational efforts have not produced any measurable improvement.

In analyzing his results, Miller identified a group that he called the "attentive public for science issues." He has estimated the size of this group to be about 18 percent of adults. This group would include the scientifically literate, but about 90 percent of this group would not qualify as scientifically literate. The attentive public includes the people (perhaps many of you reading this book) that depend on journalists and others to interpret the meaning of the science in an issue. So, with the 5 percent scientifically literate included in the 18 percent of "science attentive," that leaves some 82 percent of the adult public not only scientifically illiterate but "inattentive" as well. Statistics like these are often cited to criticize the way science is taught in the schools, and as part of the rationale for reforming science education.

Science Appreciation

But not everyone finds the idea of scientific literacy to be appropriate or useful in terms of the school science program. Morris Shamos, a physicist at New York University, says that

". . . the notion that there is a greater capability for scientific literacy is wrong." Shamos does not think people are too stupid to understand science, only that they have no incentive to learn. After all, learning science requires special effort. Shamos asks, "Why should an individual invest the time to become scientifically literate unless he [sic] has that inquiring type of mind?" (Hively, 1988, p. 443). As a goal for the school science program, Shamos suggests instead science appreciation. He contends the best we can do through teaching science is to get an audience that is not antiscience. What do you think should be the purpose of science education?

The concept of scientific literacy is difficult to grasp and even more difficult to imagine assessing. Attaining scientific literacy as Miller defines it may be too stringent for the purpose of school science. After all, many accomplished scientists are knowledgeable only in their field or in related areas. For example, there are physicists who cannot articulate a Darwinian argument for organic evolution and geneticists who are unable to explain the Standard Model for Quantum Theory. Some scientists are indeed broadminded in their knowledge of science, but many others are narrowly focused into specialty fields. Regardless, nobody knows it all these days—science is constantly changing and nobody can keep abreast of more than a few scientific fields.

Another critic of the concept of scientific literacy is Watson Laetsch, a botanist at the University of California (Hively, 1988). According to Laetsch, arguments for improving science education fall into two groups, both of which should be familiar to you from the discussions in chapter 3. The first group are utilitarian in nature and go like this: "Increasing scientific literacy will produce better workers," or "Increasing scientific literacy will make industry more competitive." Laetsch claims that there is no convincing evidence that this would be the case and that most people lead useful and happy lives without being informed about science. The other group of arguments for science education he calls "humanistic." The basic notion here is that the purpose for learning science is the enjoyment of science. According to Laetsch, the teaching of science in the schools can be defended solely on the grounds that scientific knowledge gives pleasure and enriches children's lives. *Science for All Americans* (AAAS, 1989), while drawing on the idea of scientific literacy, states that "the most powerful argument for improving the science education of all students may be its role in liberating the human intellect . . ." (p. 153).

Citizen Formation

That children should appreciate and enjoy science are certainly appropriate aims for the science program, but there are others as well. We would argue that learning science can be intellectually liberating and consequently contribute much to the child's formation as a citizen. If citizen formation is acknowledged to be a purpose of the curriculum, then the major aim of the science program would be to enable the child to become a competent social actor (Larochelle & Desautels, 1991b).

In terms of classroom practice, what does it mean to acknowledge that learning science should be related to behavior in society? It means, for one thing, that the science program should have dimensions of content other than the traditional branches of scientific knowledge—the physical, life, and earth-space sciences. It means children would learn knowledge of science as well as scientific knowledge (subject matter, or disciplinary knowledge). Thus, the nature of science has become an important content focus of the elementary science program. The foundational fields for understanding the nature of science are the history, philosophy, and sociology of science.

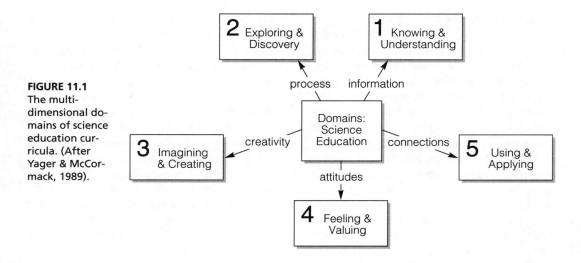

FIGURE 11.1
The multidimensional domains of science education curricula. (After Yager & McCormack, 1989).

Acknowledging the goal of citizen formation would also mean the science program would include content related to what science says about the world (refer to chapter 10). In this dimension, children would learn about their relationship to the environment and about research on such things as the decline of the ozone layer, the destruction of the rain forests, and the world's cascading loss of species. Here, science education overlaps and integrates with environmental education and also with geography and social studies education. This can be seen in the aims of geography and social studies education as proposed in the Geography Education Standards Project (1994) and the Curriculum Standards for Social Studies (National Council for the Social Studies, 1994).

If children are to become competent social actors, the content of the science program needs to be broader than what is typically found in schools today. The multiple domains of science education illustrate the kind of program breadth that is needed (see the map of the domains in Figure 11.1). In terms of content, scientific knowledge and knowledge of science are categories that span all five domains: knowing and understanding, exploring and discovering, imagining and creating, feeling and valuing, and using and applying. In order to foster the growth of children as competent social actors, the content of the science program has to be multidimensional.

The aim of helping children develop into competent social actors can be subdivided into more specific program goals. The National Science Board of the National Science Foundation (1983) states that after K–12 instruction in science and technology, students should have achieved these results:

- Knowledge of the natural environment
- Growth in natural curiosity about the physical and biological surroundings
- Ability to recognize problems, to develop procedures for addressing problems, and to recognize, evaluate, and apply solutions to problems
- Experiences with appropriate-level hands-on activities with biological and physical phenomena
- Ability to use appropriate-level mathematics in descriptions and in solving problems
- Ability to communicate, orally and in writing, observations of and experiences with phenomena

- Knowledge of scientific/technological careers and means to pursue them

Another group, the National Center for Improving Science Education (1989), identified the following goals specifically for grades K to 6:

- To develop the children's innate curiosity about the world
- To broaden children's procedural and thinking skills for investigating the world, solving problems, and making decisions
- To increase children's knowledge of the natural world
- To develop children's understanding of the nature of science and technology
- To develop children's understanding of the limits and possibilities of science and technology

Obviously, there is much overlap in these and other formulations of goals for the science program. For example, both of the lists indicate that children should develop their curiosity and their knowledge of the natural world. There also is widespread recognition that the outcomes of the science program should not be limited to scientific knowledge alone. In the United States, many states have curriculum guides for science in the curriculum. You might compare the goal statements listed here to the goals for science in your own state. You can access a Web page for all fifty state science programs at http://putwest.boces.org:80/standards.html.

Quick Review

It should be obvious to you by this point that science is a subject area like no other. The goals, content, and scope can open up discussion from many perspectives. At the same time, science—past, present, and future—is a subject that pertains to virtually every facet of our lives, and many of the issues involved

certainly are challenging. We cannot tell you that any one perspective on the goals of science is the right one. What we can tell you is that determining the goals for science in your situation is the best way to begin planning a sound program in science. With that in mind, let's consider some of the formal programs that have arisen from the considerable efforts toward meaningful science education reform.

REFORM EFFORTS OF THE 1950S–1970S: THE ALPHABET PROGRAMS

Chapter 3 provided an overview of the emergence of science in the elementary school curriculum. The period following World War II, however, was one of particularly dynamic movement for science as an elementary school subject. Since World War II, science has become increasingly prominent in curriculum reform efforts. This history is depicted in Figure 11.2. In this half-century time span, there have been two major periods of efforts to change the teaching of science. The first wave of effort began just after World War II, in the period from the mid-1950s to the early 1970s. During this time, the political motivation for change was the perceived threat to U.S. security and hegemony of the former Soviet Union. Many educators associate this period of reform with the launch of the Soviet satellite, *Sputnik,* in 1957, but the reform movement was actually spurred by the low scores U.S. troops made on their military enlistment tests.

The reform movement of the 1950s–1970s focused on creating new science program teaching materials. Millions of federal dollars were spent in financing curriculum writing committees to develop new materials. Secondary science programs, including the Physical Science Study Committee's

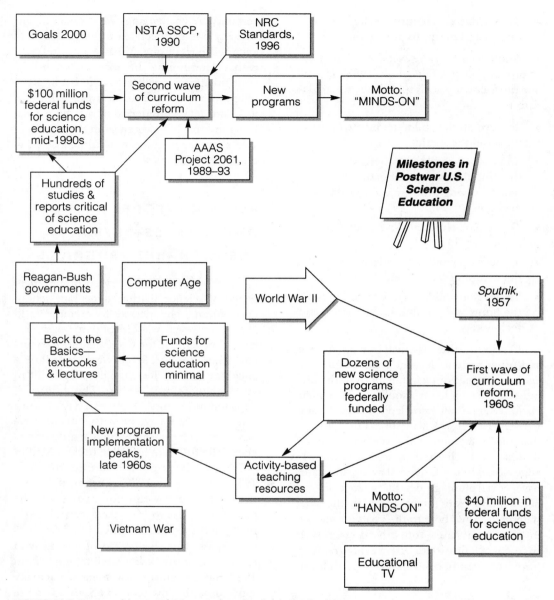

FIGURE 11.2 Postwar history of science education in the United States.

physics (PSSC), *Chem Study* chemistry, and the biology series of the Biological Science Curriculum Study (BSCS), were developed first. Many of these were in textbook format but were more laboratory-oriented than traditional texts.

More than a hundred new elementary and middle school–level science programs were developed in a similar fashion. Among the most widely used of the so-called alphabet programs were the Science Curriculum Improvement Study (SCIS), Elementary Science Study (ESS), Science—A Process Approach (SAPA), Intermediate Science Curriculum Study (ISCS), and Man—A Course of Study (MACOS). Hands-on science was the hallmark of these new programs. By the late 1960s, teachers had many new materials available for designing lesson activities.

The fundamental assumption underlying the emphasis on hands-on science in the new materials was that if children became involved firsthand with materials and phenomena, they would experience the flavor and excitement of science and would discover important science concepts as a result. Thus discovery methods were very much in favor during this reform period.

A common feature of these reform programs was their emphasis on diagnostic instruction. Many were designed so that a teacher could sequence instruction to match the learner's level. On the other hand, some programs of the period tried to be "teacher-proof." The designers wanted materials children would learn from regardless of how the teacher behaved in the classroom.

Another criticism of some of the reform programs of this period was that their content was limited. The content focus tended to be on basic science concepts, with little or no attention to applications, technology, the history or nature of science, or science-society issues.

None of the reform programs of this period were perfect, but despite their shortcomings, they were pedagogically more sound overall than the "read-about-science" textbook-centered programs they were intended to replace. Many evaluations and research studies compared the new programs with traditional textbook-based programs, and most concluded that the new programs resulted in children learning more and developing more positive attitudes (Bredderman, 1983). The names and descriptions of some of the more prominent 1950s–1970s programs follow.

Conceptually Oriented Program in Elementary Science (COPES)

This K–6 general science program focused on five major concepts: interaction and change, conservation of energy, degradation of energy, a statistical view of nature, and the structure of the universe. COPES was developed to fill the need for a sequentially arranged and highly structured approach to K–6 science education. The five concepts were considered to be among the "big ideas" with which scientific endeavor is concerned.

Elementary Science Study (ESS)

This program was developed by the Education Development Center of Newton, Massachusetts. The units can be used to enrich or form the core of a program. They come in the form of independent units with teacher guidebooks that provide the relevant background and the suggested student activities. Some "classic" units include *Kitchen Physics* for grades 5–8, *The Behavior of Mealworms* for grade 6, *Mystery Powders* for grades 3–4, *Growing Seeds* for K–3, *Gases and Airs* for grades 5–8, and *Batteries and Bulbs* for grades 4–6. Many of the original fifty-six ESS units are still in print and are available from Delta Education.

Science—A Process Approach (SAPA/SAPA II)

This process-oriented program was developed by the American Association for the Advancement of Science, an organization of scientists. The assumption behind this program was that children will retain processes longer than information. Therefore, activities focused on developing specific skills and competencies—such as for K–3, observation, classification, recognition of space-time relations, measurement, communication, inference, and prediction; and for grades 4–6, operational definition, interpretation of data, control of variables, experimentation, and the formation of hypotheses and models. That children should understand science concepts was not an emphasis in this program. Activities were specifically sequenced K–6, with the intention that they be followed in order, each skill being mastered in turn. Also, SAPA was designed to be individualized for students.

Science Curriculum Improvement Study (SCIS/SCISII/SCIIS)

This K–6 program was organized around key concepts, such as matter, interaction, relativity, ecosystems, energy, equilibrium, and evolution. The program was developed by the Lawrence Hall of Science, Berkeley, California, and units from all three of the versions are still available from Delta Education. All the units in the life and physical sciences were designed around a Learning Cycle model and stress both concept development and process skills. Student materials include record books or data logs, while the teacher guides provide background information and suggestions for using the activities.

Intermediate Science Curriculum Study (ISCS)

This program was developed for the upper elementary and junior high school grades. It was unique among the programs of the era in that, besides being entirely hands-on and laboratory-based, it was individualized and self-paced. The first and second levels focused on physical science, while the third level consisted of a number of modules from various sciences. The ISCS teacher guide strictly specified the limited teacher's role, making this program one of the best examples of the so-called teacherproof curricula of the period.

Quick Review

The programs of the 1950s–1970s were not widely implemented, despite widespread support for them in the science and science education communities. In fact, about three-fourths of U.S. elementary schools never used any of them at all (Weiss, 1987). Even where they were implemented, most schools retreated to the old textbook format when the "back to basics" movement put science on the back burner in the late 1970s and early 1980s. One reason for the failure of the reform effort was that policymakers neglected the central component of teacher education. To implement these programs in the classroom, a teacher needed a high degree of subject matter mastery as well as an ability to conduct an activity-based, discovery-oriented program. Despite many government-sponsored professional development institutes for teachers, relatively few teachers of that period had any support in making a transition to the new programs' content and methods.

The situation of failed reform of the sixties and seventies just underscores one of the most consistent patterns in the history of U.S. science education—the domination of the curriculum by the traditional science textbook. In fact, many elementary teachers still identify the science program itself with whatever textbook is being used by the school.

The curriculum projects of the 1950s and 1970s broke new ground by introducing non-textbook-based multidimensional science programs. While they were exemplary in many ways, the programs suffered from a number of shortcomings:

- More students were not attracted to elect additional secondary science courses or to pursue scientific careers.

- Applied science/technology and the social implications of science were absent or underrepresented in the content of many programs.

- Many programs were inflexible in design and were not teacher-friendly.
- There was no articulation between the elementary and secondary levels, and some programs were designed for only one year.
- Little attention was given to teacher education in program implementation.
- Little attention was devoted to assessment.
- There were few provisions for variations among learners.

Despite shortcomings such as these, the sixties reform projects are still excellent sources of hands-on activities, and many can still be found in schools. Over nine hundred science activities developed for these and other funded projects can now be accessed on *Science Helper K–8,* a CD-ROM developed by Mary Budd Rowe.

REFORM EFFORTS OF THE 1980S–1990S

A second wave of reform effort gathered steam during the 1980s as hundreds of studies and reports during those years attested to the importance of science in elementary education and criticized the level of science achievement in American schools. A culminating event occurred in 1989 when all the state governors and the president met in Charlottesville, Virginia, and ratified six national goals for education, one of which addressed the improvement of science education. As a result of all this attention, the place of science as a core subject in the elementary curriculum has gained widespread public acceptance.

In response to the many reports calling for improving science education, a number

of new national curriculum reform initiatives were undertaken. The new projects aimed to avoid the shortcomings of the earlier projects. Unlike the first-wave reform projects, which were developed primarily by academic scientists, the new curriculum projects represent the curriculum work of teams of scientists, teachers, university science educators, and commercial publishers. Many new programs are now on the market. They differ both from traditional textbook-based programs and from the last-generation hands-on programs.

One major difference in the new programs is in science content. New content for science, such as technology and environmental issues, has been incorporated. In terms of content, however, new topics have not simply been added on to the already overstuffed curriculum. As discussed in chapter 2, program developers have adopted the dictum "less is more"—a notion advanced by Theodore Sizer in his book *Horace's Compromise,* which addressed the reform of U.S. secondary schools. The "big ideas" are emphasized, and depth of understanding is the aim. Consequently, many of the new programs organize content around conceptual themes, with fewer topics treated in greater depth. The following descriptions are of some of the most significant programs to incorporate this new vision of science education.

Science and Technology for Children (STC)

This program was a joint project of the National Science Resources Center (Smithsonian Institution) and Carolina Biological Supply Company. Twenty-four eight-week units are available for grades 1–6. The units include activity books and materials. Examples of units are "Organisms" and "Weather" for grade 1; "Chemical Tests" and "Sounds" for grade 3; and "Magnets and Motors," "Experiments with Plants," and "Measuring

Christine Ebert

PHOTO 11.1 As a result of science education reform efforts, teachers have access to many science program materials.

Time" for grade 6. The units are inquiry-centered and are designed to encourage the integration of science with mathematics, language arts, social studies, and art. Children are to learn science concepts and reasoning skills through investigation, discovery, and application.

Full Option Science System (FOSS)

This K–6 program was jointly produced by the Lawrence Hall of Science of the University of California and the Encyclopedia Britannica Educational Corporation. The program consists of twenty-seven modular units containing the materials needed for the hands-on and collaborative group activities in the program. Units focus on topics in life, physical, and earth science, as well as on scientific reasoning and technology. Britannica also correlates the units to its multimedia offerings, which include videocassettes, laser discs, and interactive computer programs.

Science Alive

This K–5 program was developed by Rigby Education through an international collaboration of science educators in the United

States, Australia, New Zealand, and the United Kingdom. There are life, physical, and earth-space science units for each grade level. This core science program taps the strength of many elementary teachers—language and literacy education. Textual materials for children include one big book and four small books per unit. These are illustrated with bold graphics and photographs and focus on major science concepts. The Teacher's Resource Book contains suggestions for many hands-on activities using everyday materials, as well as activity cards and black-line masters for student logs, cooperative group work, science centers, and take-home projects. The program is supplemented by a laser disc.

Science for Life and Living and Middle School Science and Technology

These two complementary programs were jointly developed by the Biological Science Curriculum Study (BSCS) and Kendall/Hunt Publishing Company. Science for Life and Living is a K–6 program, while Middle School Science and Technology offers three levels for the middle-level grades. Science for Life and Living is a program that integrates major concepts and skills in science, technology, and health education. The components include a text for students, a teacher's guide, a kit of materials, and a school implementation guide. The program is based on a Learning Cycle instructional model and includes many hands-on and cooperative group activities. Middle School Science and Technology is a textbook-based program organized around the major conceptual themes in science and technology.

Insights

Insights is a K–6 program created by the Education Development Center, Inc. (who also produced the Elementary Science Study in the 1960s) and the Optical Data Corporation. The modules in the program also use a Learning Cycle approach and are designed to be flexibly used at more than one grade level. Laser discs rather than textbooks are the core resource.

Quick Review

As you can see, many contemporary science programs incorporate technology both as new content and, in varying degrees, as a new learning tool. The recent rapid evolution of technologies like hypercard, laser discs, CD-ROM, electronic mail, and the Internet can bring an enormous range of resources in the form of texts, sounds, and visual images for teaching science to the classroom. Young children in many schools today use these technologies with impressive skill and confidence as they conduct investigations and communicate their results in multimedia reports. Many students also have access to computers, CD-ROMs, and on-line information services in their homes. Public libraries and science museums are other places children can learn about and use these new technologies and the resources they can access.

In addition to textbooks, teachers have an abundance of resources upon which to draw in planning their classroom science programs. Such resources include posters, big books, and tradebooks (library books), as well as various media resources, including videocassettes, computer software, laser discs, and audiocassette tapes. Still among the best resources are the great variety of hands-on activities and manipulatives, as well as the school community—its grounds and nearby natural areas, and the frequently overlooked people of the school community. This variety of resources enriches the science program (see Figure 11.3).

Given the astounding rate of development of technology over the past thirty years, it seems likely that technology will influence the teaching and learning of science in most all schools, even those with limited resources. Affordability, however, is an issue that cannot just be casually dismissed in the pages of a science methods textbook. You probably noticed that the programs just described often seek to utilize up-to-date technology in their delivery systems. This of course is both a blessing and a curse. Classrooms that have access to equipment such as laser-disc players will probably use the new programs. Schools that cannot afford the electronic equipment will not be able to use such programs.

Along the lines of affordability comes the question of consumables as well. Activity-oriented science programs require materials with which to interact. Materials that get used up in the presentation of a lesson are called consumables. These must, therefore, be replaced from time to time. Though some consumables are inexpensive items, recurring expenses in days of tight budget constraints are often problematic. This, perhaps more so than any other consideration, keeps many schools tied to a textbook approach to science. However, with these concerns noted, Carin (1993) summarizes what he sees as the similarities of the new curriculum projects of the 1990s:

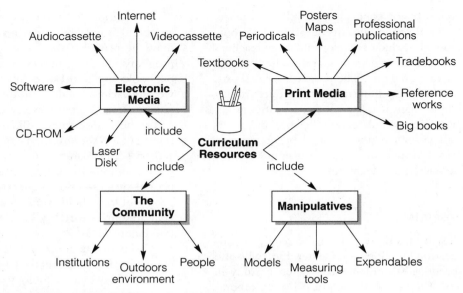

FIGURE 11.3 Today's science programs draw upon multiple instructional resources.

- A more humanistic approach with examples provided from everyday life to increase relevancy

- More emphasis on environmental and ecological issues

- Inclusion of values and social connections of science

- Integration of science across the curriculum

- More flexibility to provide for the needs of different students

- Use of more open-ended investigations and cooperative group methods, especially for problem solving (pp. 221, 231)

If you should find yourself teaching at a school that has adopted one of these programs, make full use of the resources it has to offer. If such is not the case with your assignment, investigate these programs at professional conferences and in professional journals to see whether there is an idea that can work with your situation.

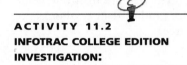

ACTIVITY 11.2
INFOTRAC COLLEGE EDITION
INVESTIGATION:

The New Programs

Any one of these new programs may well show up at the school in which you teach. Check to see whether one of them is being used in the school in which you do your field service or practicum work associated with this course.

- If the school with which you work uses one of these programs, use Info-Trac College Edition to find the pros and cons of the program. Consider what you find in light of the particular needs of the school system that is using the program.

- If your school is not using a "program," use InfoTrac College Edition to find the current pros and cons of one of the programs listed. If your classmates research other programs, you will be able to establish an anthology that will have you well acquainted with the options available for elementary science. This can be a valuable body of knowledge when you interview for a job.

DEVELOPING THE PROGRAM AT YOUR SCHOOL

There are very few circumstances under which you would start work at a school that has no science program. We do not want to discount the possibility of its happening, but the chances are slim. More likely, you will be faced with a curriculum that includes science to one degree or another. Your first task, with regard to teaching science, will be to ascertain just what is happening in terms of science at that school. Some of this will take the form of reviewing curriculum guides, as we discussed earlier. But most of your initial inquiry will be through conversation with your new colleagues.

Determine the Condition of the Science Program

Basically, there are three types of situations that you could expect to encounter as a new teacher: (1) a formal, established science education program is in place (for instance, the school has adopted and is using FOSS for their students); (2) there is no formal program, but there is a particular textbook series, perhaps curriculum guides, and expectations within the school as to how science will be presented; or (3) they are just waiting for you to walk through the door and tell them what to do. In addition, any one of these scenarios could be operating in one of at least two possible contexts: You will be working with one or more other teachers who are teaching science (and who were

there before you were hired), or you will have sole responsibility for the show.

With regard to this second set of contingencies, if you really do find yourself in a situation where you are making the recommendations and are enjoying some substantive support in that regard, then do your homework carefully and take full advantage of the tremendous opportunity to build an exemplary program. It is more likely, however, that you will be working with other teachers who already have some idea of how science should be taught. In this case, let *patience* be your watchword. Talk with your colleagues. Learn the why and the wherefores of what they are doing. If change is the obvious need, let the brightness of your ideas win the day rather than attempting to do so with the brashness of your debut.

With regard to the first set of contingencies (a formal program is in place), let's take a look at how you can plan your particular classroom science program. Following that, we will discuss three additional considerations that will enter into your work no matter which of the three contingencies characterizes your situation.

If a Formal Program Is in Place In terms of a science program being up and running, this is by far the most advantageous situation for the beginning teacher. Consult with your colleagues to find out what activities in the program seem to work and which take a bit more effort. Let them explain the sequence that they follow, the units that they include, and any science-related events (e.g., a science fair) that the school expects. And then get your own copies of the teacher's materials for the program and start studying them.

It is quite possible that you will walk into a situation in which a new program has been adopted but not yet implemented. In this case, the other teachers may not be able to provide you with a wealth of information. They can, however, tell you how and why the program that you will be using got adopted. This is valuable information to have. And again, now would be the time to get your own copies of the materials and to become as familiar as possible with the scope and sequence of the program. This involves understanding why the program is constructed as it is, along with understanding the structure and your place within it.

If an Informal Program Is in Place When we say informal program, we are referring to the use of a science textbook series, or perhaps locally developed materials, as opposed to a packaged program such as those described earlier in this chapter. In such a situation, it is essentially up to you to evaluate what is being done in terms of expectations, materials, presentation, and projected outcomes (projected based on your knowledge of science education). With that done, you will begin to develop your own classroom program. You are well equipped to do so having studied this text, so do not be overwhelmed by the task. Rather, see it for the tremendous opportunity that it presents.

This would be the situation that most beginning teachers are likely to encounter. Here are some particular questions to consider for program development:

- What has been taught to the children in previous grades?

- What are the childrens' science interests?

- What science-related issues concern the local community?

- What do teachers in succeeding grades generally teach?

- What science topics are most interesting to you, and what do you know most about?

- What special resources are available (e.g., museums, field sites, people)?

If the Place Is in Need of a Program In the unlikely event that you are seen as the science guru who will lift the school from the depths of science nonachievement, then you truly face an exciting—and perhaps exhausting—task. All of the steps outlined in the previous section will apply. The key difference is that you have been given license to assess the situation and are expected to make recommendations. With that in mind, our discussions of the goals for science education become all the more important. You will need to find some sense of what the school and community expect of science in the school curriculum. And likely, if you were to simply ask the question, the expectation is that the children pass the tests that will be administered in the spring. Obviously, you will need to be more sophisticated in terms of the questions you ask. Should the students from your community be "scientifically literate"? Should they have a very broad understanding of science? Should they appreciate the breadth of scientific endeavor with a smattering of familiarity in several fields of inquiry? Should they be sufficiently informed of scientific endeavor in order to become competent citizens involved in community decisions? The answers to these questions, questions that you probably had not expected to be asking of people when you decided to become a teacher, will be the very foundation of the program that you develop. And by all means, include your colleagues in this curriculum development process.

The information in the following sections will help with your planning once your foundation questions are answered.

ACTIVITY 11.3

A Programmatic Interview

First and foremost, understand that this activity is not intended as an evaluation of a school's science program. With that in mind, and using all of the interviewing skills that you developed back in chapter 5, design a brief interview to learn more about the science program where you do your field service or practicum work. Interview your cooperating teacher, and if possible, arrange to interview the principal as well.

Use the questions suggested earlier in the section "If an Informal Program Is in Place" to guide the design of your brief interview. You may wish to add some questions such as the following, depending upon the particular situation you face:

- Does the district see "scientific literacy" as a goal?

- Does the district prefer to provide a broad scientific exposure or one of narrower exposure though with greater depth?

- Is science education considered as a "basic" in the district?

Being Prepared

An important element for a successful science program is being prepared—both for the activities that you plan and for the science experiences that children unexpectedly bring to your classroom. For identifying and learning about the various objects and living things children bring to school, one excellent resource to have available is a set of field guides, such as the Peterson or Audubon series. Field guides are available from any bookstore and cover insects and spiders, birds, fossils, trees, ferns and mosses, mushrooms, wildflowers, rocks and minerals, reptiles and amphibians, mammals, and the night sky. The school and local libraries should have a stock of field guides.

Various instruments are useful in investigations as well. Doublet or triplet lenses (magnifiers that have two or three lenses of different powers) are better than most other magnifiers. You should have access to microscopes and supporting supplies, such as slides, cover slips, medicine droppers, probes, scissors, and tweezers. For elementary studies, the Brock Magiscope® is a sturdy and durable microscope with superb optics. It doesn't require supplemental lighting and can be used in the field as easily as in the classroom.

Measuring devices also should be at hand. These include thermometers, rain gauges, anemometers, meter sticks, rulers, trundle wheels, balance scales, spring scales, graduated beakers or pitchers, stopwatches, cameras, and so forth. Basic tools are pen/pencil and paper, especially in the form of a science log. Children act like scientists when they make notes and measurements related to events. Accurate record-keeping can be an area of achievement for a child.

Other useful tools for the science program include a variety of containers to hold the ever developing classroom collections (e.g., dishwashing tubs, empty coffee cans, margarine tubs, 35-mm film canisters, baby food jars, and jars for caterpillars, insects, and spiders). A rock hammer and cold chisel might come in handy in looking inside rocks (and should always be used with safety goggles). An empty aquarium with a screen top should also be available to house temporary visitors from the animal kingdom. Garden trowels and other digging tools are useful for studying plants and soil organisms.

Make Room for Event-Based Science

The preparedness described in the previous section allows you to capitalize on curiosity almost whenever it arises. In the popular movie *Dead Poets Society,* the teacher captivated his students with the notion of *carpe diem,* or "seizing the day." To the science teacher, seizing the day means producing a lesson on the spot in response to a question, an expressed student interest, or a current science-related event in the outside world. Science-related events are such things as the periodic happenings in the natural world—

meteor showers and solstices, for example—as well as the less regular and predictable events of hurricanes, tornadoes, floods, earthquakes, volcanic eruptions, and human-initiated disasters such as the *Exxon Valdez* oil spill, the Chernobyl nuclear reactor meltdown, or the Bhopal chemical plant accident. Human triumphs as experienced by your students, whether personally or via the media, also stimulate students and make them eager to understand more.

Also, without advance notice to the teacher, a child may bring to class a special rock specimen, a recently discovered snake skin, or an unusual-looking beetle. These situations represent valuable teachable moments and they can occur at any time. By "seizing the day" when such events present themselves in the classroom, the teacher has the chance to model curiosity and other scientific attitudes. Taking pedagogical advantage of particular occurrences requires sensitivity and flexibility, but there are few better ways of engaging students and demonstrating the relevance of science to their lives. What's more, "seizing the day" doesn't require abandoning the curriculum, as most science-related events can be connected to key science concepts in the curriculum.

There are many ways teachers can respond to and capitalize on the learning potential of events, as well as the things and stories children bring to school (Wright, 1992). The most important factor is your own interest as a teacher in exploring the situation further. For many children in your classroom, you will be the chief model of the scientist's response to a current or novel happening.

ACTIVITY 11.4

Seize the Science Day

With all due respect to our colleagues in math, there aren't many days when a new number shows up. In science, however, new and different things are always happening. These are often reported on television and in the newspapers, and so you can well expect your students to come to class asking about it.

One way to be prepared for this is to read the newspaper and your professional journals. Another way is to practice preparedness by taking a current topic and determining how you would go about investigating it on very short notice. For example, as this book first went into production, there was debate as to whether Pluto should be considered a planet. How would you have handled the curiosity of your students if one asked how a planet could no longer be a planet?

- Select a topic of current interest from the newspaper or television news.
- If a student were to ask about that topic, what sort of investigation would you recommend?
- How might you include the entire class?
- How could you relate it to other subject areas in your classroom?

And by the way, Pluto remains a planet. For now.

Children can be encouraged to do more than just look at those special objects brought in by their peers. Depending on what the item is, children can make drawings and take measurements, for example, size and mass, that can be recorded in a science log or student notebook. Another productive strategy is to have children construct a semantic web, or concept map, showing relationships between the event or object and relevant scientific ideas, as well as the science-society connections. Figure 11.4 is an example of a concept map based on the 1995 earthquake in Kobe, Japan. The map might have been created by a middle school class following a

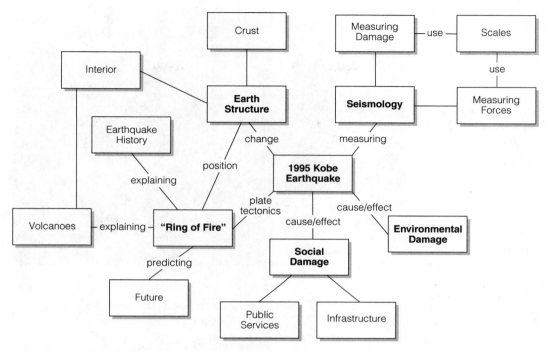

FIGURE 11.4 Concept map based upon the 1995 earthquake in Kobe, Japan.

discussion of the disaster just after it occurred. The teacher then might have used the Web to organize a study of earthquakes for her class. Concept maps can be constructed both before and after studying a topic. The post-lesson map can be compared to the children's initial map. The before and after maps can tell the teacher a lot about what the children learned and where their interests lie.

One potentially productive response to an event or special object is to invite children to express what they already know about it. Expression can be oral, but an event also is an opportunity for children to write or draw. By providing diverse contexts for expression, teachers help children more easily connect new information and the scientific concepts to their prior knowledge and experience.

What children know often can be surprising—some may know a lot about the most arcane topics (e.g., Jurassic fauna), while oth-

ers may have only rudimentary knowledge. By tapping background experiences and prior knowledge at the start (see chapter 5) as part of a science program, a teacher sets up an assessment baseline. With the child's knowledge identified, conceptual development can be tracked. And this is what "authentic assessment" is really all about.

Elementary-age children are curious about many natural events, such as earthquakes, severe weather phenomena, and natural disasters that affect people. Children frequently want to know more about underlying causes and factors related to such events, as well as the probability of future occurrences. One way students can investigate an event or phenomenon further is to work in teams to interview relatives and other local people about their recollections of similar past events or situations. Older children could use tape recorders, transcribe, and

PHOTO 11.2 Children can work in teams to interview adults about events of interest.

Chen Long

summarize their research findings. The production of oral histories like this is what led to the success of the famous *Foxfire* book project.

ACTIVITY 11.5

Interviewing Community Members

Children develop their concept of change by comparing conditions in their lives and environment with those of the past. Children can learn much from older family members and neighbors about how things have changed.

Work with a team of two or three children. Help the children identify older members of their families or communities to interview. Discuss how the prospective interviewees will be contacted and invited to participate in the activity (for example, by being invited to come to school on a special day). Prepare a list of questions; this will help children prepare for the interviews.

Here are some possible topics for focus questions:

- Famous local structures (buildings, lighthouses, bridges, dams, etc.)
- Machines of the past
- Communication in the past
- Transportation
- Timekeeping
- Printing and printmaking
- Astronomical events of the past, or earlier views of the universe
- Mining, working with metals, or making jewelry or other objects from metals
- Sailing, service in the navy, working with watercraft
- Food processing, transporting food to the market, preparing food
- People of other lands and cultures, and their customs

Children can practice their interviews by role-playing, in which one child plays the role of the adult as the other team members conduct the interview. After the interviews have been conducted, have each team summarize its findings on the board or on a chart. Reports can be presented to the class or other classes, or posted on the school's Web page.

Interviewing Worksheet

Research Team Members: _____

Date of Interview:_____

Name of Person
Interviewed: _____

Date of Birth: _____

Place of Birth: _____

Occupation(s):_____

Interview Questions:

1.

2.

3.

4.

What We Found Out: _____

_____

More Ideas to Investigate: _____

_____

_____

Integrating Science across the Curriculum

Part of your program of science, either as the teacher of a self-contained classroom or as one of several specialized grade-level teachers, should be to integrate science with the other subject areas. Deliberately planning integration related to your science program demonstrates to children the interrelationship between subject areas that they study. Events and natural objects present many opportunities for integrating the subjects. There are math links and social studies links to many science-related events. In studying storms, for example, children can chart and graph atmospheric variables, like temperature or barometric pressure, over a period before, during, and after a storm, and compare these with average figures for the period, which are usually available in the daily newspaper or on the Weather Channel. Social studies concepts often can be connected to events like natural disasters in which the normal civil routines are disrupted and transportation and communications fail.

Event-based science can be connected to reading and language arts by inviting children to locate tradebooks in the library that relate to the event or topic. Stories or particular excerpts from books can be read to the class, or the books can be used in interest centers for small group reading and discussion.

The daily newspaper is a great source of information on local and global events that might have curricular connections. A bulletin board or a vertical file could be created for news clippings about events that are brought to class. Such clippings can be useful reference for student writing and project work as well.

Events like the solstices and equinoxes, lunar and solar eclipses, and meteor showers occur on a periodic basis and easily can be the basis of a science lesson. While the local press and media may be adequate sources of information for events like local weather phenomena, reading the annual *Farmer's Almanac* is an inexpensive way to keep track of moon phases and eclipses of the sun or moon, meteor showers, and solstices, equinoxes, and cross-quarter days. For news of current events in the field of science, the teachers' magazines *Science & Children* and *Science Scope* have regular features on natural happenings. Both magazines publish monthly sky charts and announcements about events in the heavens. Other good magazine resources are periodicals such as *Science News, Discover, Scientific American,* and *National Geographic.*

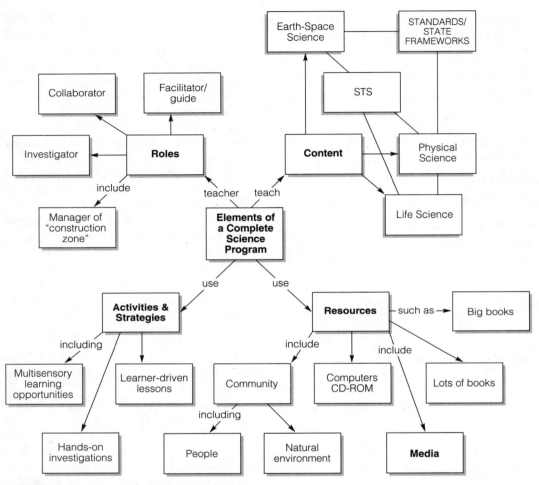

FIGURE 11.5 Elements of a complete science program.

Quick Review

In the development of the school science program, staying focused on the "big picture" pays the highest dividends. Understanding the condition of the existing science program, and your role in its development, will pave the way for all that is to follow. Whichever of the three scenarios we have discussed characterizes your teaching situation, there are ways to deal with it and there are particular tasks that need to be accomplished. The additional dimensions of preparedness, event-based science, and subject integration will extend your science program beyond the scheduled minutes of the class day.

CONCLUSION

The development of programs in science takes place on many levels. As shown in this chapter, the importance of science education to the nation has fostered two nationwide reform efforts in the last fifty years. We can only anticipate that the importance of sound programs in science will increase into the next millennium. Now is a great time to begin a teaching career. New research-based curriculum materials and new technologies have opened up multiple possibilities for developing the science program in the elementary school. One of the most exciting aspects of the development of programs and materials is the role that teachers can play. Effective curriculum development grows out of a

foundation of learning theory, a familiarity with a wide range of resources, a sensitivity to children's interests and the events of the day, and an ability to be flexible in acting out a variety of teaching roles. Taken together, these are the characteristics of a professional educator. The elements of a complete science program are illustrated in Figure 11.5. As you review these, consider each element in terms of the way that you would see that it was accommodated in the science program for your students.

12 Planning and Managing Science in the Classroom

Multiple Contexts Require Multiple Approaches

Creating Spaces That Foster Interaction

Alternative Patterns for Teaching Science

The Science Culture of the Classroom

Planning in Support of Inquiry

Conclusion

Your Academic Roadmap

Study of this chapter should help you to understand the following concepts:

- The context in which science education occurs can appropriately be expected to vary from region to region.

- An activity-rich classroom science program is facilitated by effective classroom design.

- Organization, organization, and organization are the three keys to classroom science logistics.

- Science can be the subject that launches all other subject areas.

- It is not necessary that the study of science fit on a desktop.

The point is not to cover the subject but to help uncover part of it.

**—Victor Weisskopf,
Institute Professor of Physics, MIT**

MULTIPLE CONTEXTS REQUIRE MULTIPLE APPROACHES

Earlier chapters have considered the content of the science program and many science teaching methods that develop scientific ways of thinking and help children construct scientific knowledge and knowledge of science. This chapter is about planning and managing science in the elementary and middle school classroom. Planning and management are the nuts and bolts of the science program, the processes that occur inside and outside the classroom that most directly enable children's learning.

American education is diverse because of the size and diversity of the land and because of the numbers of institutions and people in-

volved—2.5 million teachers and more than 50 million children. Florida is very different from Alaska and Hawaii is different from Boston. Children grow up in many different environments and their schools and classrooms differ, too. But in all these places, science is an important part of the curriculum. This diversity, however, is only one aspect of the task teachers face.

Classroom management is often a concern of many teachers, particularly beginning teachers. Simultaneously coping with a classroom of youngsters and the prescribed curriculum is a daunting undertaking. The first point to remember is that there is no one right way to go about your planning and management activities as a teacher. In America's 108,000 public schools you will find your 2.5 million colleagues going about these activities in many different ways, some more effective than others.

The science content of the curriculum can, and should, reflect the uniqueness of the school's location and the multiple cultures of its patrons. That is, the context in which science education occurs can appropriately be expected to vary from region to region. Fourth-graders in Illinois might be investigating the prairie, while in Naples, Florida, children at this level might be studying the Everglades. Detroit sixth-graders might study force and motion in the context of automobile transportation. Seattle sixth-graders might study the same topic, though in the context of airplanes. What is taught differs from region to region because environment and community differ.

How the content is taught, the instructional practices utilized, also might be different from place to place. The teachers who work in the nation's schools possess diverse educational backgrounds, personalities, and teaching styles. Teachers will also tell you that their classes differ each year. Most teachers recognize that the effectiveness of particular instructional practices depends on the children in their classes. Much in teaching also depends on the circumstances of the moment—lessons are nearly always planned in advance, but a lot of interactive planning can be done right on the spot in response to children's interests or needs.

Such diversity in the variables affecting classroom life illustrates the complexity of the educational enterprise. Clearly, no one formula for planning and managing science in the classroom could possibly be applicable in all or even most situations. Because of the variation, you cannot know every kind of child or every teaching situation you might have to face. Yet, despite the many different constraints and challenges, educators and children in many kinds of classrooms manage year after year to create learning communities where science flourishes. Here is one piece of advice based on our own classroom experiences: Be patient with the complexity, and keep yourself open to learning a lot on the job.

Through thoughtful planning, many of the tasks and problems of managing the science program can be anticipated ahead of time. Your fellow teachers will usually be helpful in sharing their own solutions to common management problems. For example, the first tasks each year include deciding the daily and weekly schedule and how to organize the classroom space—how to arrange the furniture and how to store and make accessible the materials and equipment for teaching science. Take a moment to consider the following questions:

- How would you place the furniture— your own desk, the children's tables and chairs, and the like?

- How would you design areas for storage and work, including one or more computer stations?

The context of your science education class cannot be described in a textbook such as this. If you become a faculty member in a school district close to where you grew up, then you may know the context already. But if you are teaching in a region that is new to you, do not dismiss the importance of finding out the values and expectations of the community in which your students live.

CREATING SPACES THAT FOSTER INTERACTION

Let's begin by considering some practical classroom management problems. Even when they are empty, America's classrooms can be all kinds of spaces. Some have high ceilings; some have low. Some are in open spaces; others are located in transportable trailers. Many have sinks and water. Some have nooks and crannies and even breakout rooms and preparation-and-storage rooms.

In some classrooms, children keep their books and belongings in their desks; in others, they use lockers or cubbies located in the classroom or hallway.

Stop and think about the different classroom arrangements you have seen. Earlier chapters considered what good, investigative, problem-oriented science teaching might look like. From your own observations, what kind of classroom setups do you think facilitate this kind of science teaching? Which do not?

Small things can make a big difference. Classroom furniture is one example. Slanted-top desks are an obstacle for many hands-on activities. Some older classrooms may even have desks bolted to the floor. Moveable classroom furniture and flat-topped desks offer more options for organizing the classroom. As you might have noticed in visiting a school, some teachers prefer each child's desk to be separate from the others. Separate desks typically are arranged in rows, which often face the front of the classroom and the chalkboard. This emphasizes individual work. An alternative plan is to group several desks together, or to use tables instead of desks as work spaces. Desks in clusters might facilitate children's conversations, cooperative learning, and the teacher's movement around the classroom. Consider, too, the location of your own desk in the classroom. A different message is sent out to the children by placing the teacher in the back versus the front of the class.

Establishing Learning Centers

Many teachers create special classroom work spaces called "centers." A center is a space in the classroom appropriately supplied with materials and directions to allow for independent or small group investigations and study. A shared responsibility for recording progress is established between the student and the teacher. A classroom might have one or more subject-designated centers, or a single center might serve different subjects at different times. A center can feature reading, writing, art, science, or anything.

One third-grade teacher has a reading area he calls "the rug," where the whole class gathers for sharing time in the morning. Sharing time is part of the important daily routine of his class. Around the edge of the rug are placed a variety of trade books in cardboard boxes and plastic bins. He also has a writing area that he uses for a variety of group work. The art center, located near the sink, includes a table, an easel, newsprint paper, recycled materials, chalk, crayons, water colors, and marking pens. Another space is used as a dramatic play area and is often the place he conducts social studies activities.

Needless to say, this teacher also has a science and math center. It consists of a large table and several shelves for storage. On one shelf is a 10-gallon aquarium. Another shelf contains math manipulatives such as Cuisenaire rods, pattern blocks, attribute blocks, Unifix cubes, number bars, chip trading materials, geoboards, and color cubes. Still another has materials used in both math and science, such as calculators, rulers, measuring cups, plastic beakers, a trundle wheel, meter sticks, spring scales, and equal-arm platform balances. Science supplies in the center also include empty containers, eyedroppers, magnifiers or jeweler's loupes, magnets, a collection of seashells and various other specimens, and reference books and data sheets for recording observations.

A science center can be created to complement an instructional unit. For example, in a unit on "minibeasts," a center could have one or more microscopes set up for children to examine insects and other small creatures close-up. Books and other items can be added during the unit so that children will want to come back and take another look. The science center can also include reference books and periodicals, posters inviting children to try particular investigations, and paper or report forms for recording observations. Alternatively, children can record observations in their science journals. Activity 12.1 can provide you with some valuable practice in conceptualizing how to set up a science learning center. Keep in mind that some children will be nonreaders or below grade level. Materials will have to be prepared to allow these children to work independently.

ACTIVITY 12.1

Conceptualizing a Science Center

Select one of the following situations, and develop an appropriate plan for your classroom.

- Design a first-grade science center to accompany a unit about animals and their characteristics.
- Design a science center for fourth-grade children for a unit on weather.
- Choose a science topic based on your own interests, and design a science center for a group of children at a level you would like to teach.

As a teacher, what would you do to guide children in their work in a science center?

Share your ideas with a practicing teacher. What recommendations for change did he or she offer?

All in all, providing learning opportunities for children involves creating an environment rich in a variety of materials and supplies, and spaces for different purposes. The "Law of Loose Parts" states that, in any environment, both the degree of inventiveness and creativity and the possibility of discovery are directly proportional to the number and kind of variables in that environment (Nicholson, 1972). Some classroom environments do not work simply because they do not have enough "loose parts" to generate learning.

One thing to remember about the classroom environment is that you and the children will spend five or six hours there on most days. You can do much to make it an interesting and stimulating place for everyone. Your aim should be to create a physical space that is both aesthetically pleasing and well organized. One approach is to have the children help you display their work around the room. This shows that their work is valued and encourages them to take ownership and contribute to making it a pleasant work environment.

Another way to enhance the classroom environment is to add plants. The same plants can also be a source of questions and investigations. Plants that can tolerate lots of water are best for the primary classrooms because young children like to care for them often. Dependable choices include coleus, impatiens, spider plants, and tradescantia. Plants suitable for intermediate grades and up include ivy, snake plants, nephthytis, pothos, Chinese evergreen, and philodendron. If the room has good sun, you might try miniature roses, sensitive plants (*Mimosa pudica*), and dwarf and scented geraniums (Pratt-Butler, 1978, p. 13). African violets and bulbs are also good classroom plants. An aquarium can house aquatic plants and animals or can be used as a terrarium for any number of organisms. Also, almost any jar or bottle can be converted into a terrarium. Figure 12.1 provides the basic plan for making a classroom terrarium.

Managing Learning Centers

Centers can be used in lots of ways in the classroom. One way is to have groups of students rotate through several centers during the same class time or on successive days.

FIGURE 12.1 Making a classroom terrarium.

HOW TO MAKE A TERRARIUM

An old aquarium would work well, though a large glass jar (thoroughly cleaned) might be easier to keep covered. Put several centimeters of small, washed gravel on the bottom of the container. Intersperse several small pieces of charcoal to absorb impurities. Over the top of this, put 5 to 10 centimeters of rich soil mixed with peat or other organic mulch (available at a pet store, nursery, or garden supply). Sprinkle the surface with water to moisten but not saturate the soil. Too much water will encourage the growth of mold and mildew.

Consult a naturalist, local agricultural extension service, or even a local garden nursery to identify plants that would be appropriate for use in your terrarium. It is important that your students understand that collecting just any plant is not safe because some may be endangered or poisonous.

After a week or two, when the plants have established themselves, introduce small animals to the terrarium. Children can be encouraged to bring organisms like isopods (sow bugs, or roly-polies) or earthworms to add to the ecosystem. One small animal such as a land turtle, salamander, or frog is suitable for your small woodland habitat. Small amounts of lettuce would feed a turtle. Frogs and salamanders, however, need small live insects.

Loosely cover the terrarium to maintain the internal humidity while permitting air circulation. Do not place it in direct sunlight, because too much heat would build up inside.

This plan is for a woodland habitat, but could be modified for desert or marshland ecosystems as well.

Here is a hassle-free procedure for moving groups of children from center to center (Novelli, 1995):

1. Divide the class into groups. Ask each group to choose a name (or color).

2. Create a master schedule-board, such as the one below, with center names or numbers going across and days (or times) going down. Write group names on cards (or use color-coded cards if you're using colors to differentiate groups). Assign one group to each center (going across) on Day 1 (or time 1) by tacking cards into place on the schedule-board.

3. Explain the rotation schedule and have students take a few practice runs. Soon, with a quick glance, they should know exactly where they are supposed to be at center time and what center is next in line for their group.

	Center 1	Center 2	Center 3	Center 4	Center 5
Day 1	Cats	Bears	Kangas	Cubbies	Ravens
Day 2	Ravens	Cats	Bears	Kangas	Cubbies
Day 3	Cubbies	Ravens	Cats	Bears	Kangas
Day 4	Kangas	Cubbies	Ravens	Cats	Bears
Day 5	Bears	Kangas	Cubbies	Ravens	Cats

"Workshop time" in the schedule might look something like this: The Kangas are working together on the computer, sending data they collected on their local weather to children in an Australian class. The Cubbies are continuing their observations of ants in an ant farm in the science center. They are recording observations in their science journals. The Ravens are working on a book they are writing together, while the Bears are constructing a model using unit blocks. Meanwhile, the Cats are painting in the art area.

Science Needs Space

You have probably noticed that we are talking about more than "take out a pencil and piece of paper, boys and girls." Science requires *stuff*. It is never too early to begin collecting your classroom science center stuff. Chapter 14 contains a list of materials frequently used in science activities. A very real consideration that arises is that science education takes up space even when it is not "science time." Some classrooms have plenty of storage space; unfortunately, many lack adequate space for storing science materials and equipment. Teachers often use cardboard boxes and plastic storage tubs and bins of different sizes to store science materials. We cannot emphasize enough that *organizing* your materials for storage is a key to making science manageable for you. And that makes it doable for your students.

In addition to space for storing materials used in science, there is a need for space in the classroom to temporarily keep children's science projects and investigations that are in progress. And then, with the increase in importance of technology throughout the curriculum, space is needed for one or more personal computers and their peripherals, for example, a printer, modem, CD-ROM drive, scanner, and external drive. Keep in mind that you would want the classroom computer station to be accessible to children working in the science and math area.

ACTIVITY 12.2

Your Ideal Classroom

Assume that you have a typical rectangular classroom that contains a teacher's desk and twenty-five student desks. You are free to add any additional items that are reasonably available.

Arrange the classroom furniture as you prefer. Be sure that your plan includes:

- learning center(s)
- storage area(s)
- individual and group work areas

What are the advantages and limitations of each component of your design?

What might be the advantages and disadvantages of placing the desks in rows versus in clusters?

What are the advantages and disadvantages of placing your desk as you have in this plan?

Quick Review

Two significant themes were prevalent in this section: (1) that the classroom science program, a program that is activity-rich, is facilitated by classroom design; and (2) that science takes up space both in its doing and in its waiting to be done. With regard to the first theme, the learning center provides a certain degree of dynamism simply by its nature. For science to be active, it is not necessarily imperative that students be scurrying around the room or calling out data across the room. Moving to a learning center—going to do science—is an activity that distinguishes what is about to happen from all other happenings. The opportunity for students to work independently or in small groups at a learning center is, in itself, an activity in autonomous investigation.

The second theme is admittedly somewhat more mundane. It relates to your ability as a teacher to handle logistics—the organizing of materials for use and for storage. By taking the proper perspective on this task, you can be prepared for science whenever it strikes. And we can assure you that a degree of preparedness like that will give you a confident feeling. Just keep in mind that there are many ways to organize. In fact, your system of organization can become a part of the decor of your classroom. Color-code your storage cartons or plastic bins. Label them clearly. You might even want to rig up an inexpensive shelving system so that each bin is accessible without removing other bins from above it. As if it is not enough that doing science is creative, here is your chance to be creative just getting prepared to do science.

ALTERNATIVE PATTERNS FOR TEACHING SCIENCE

Many different designs of the classroom's physical space can facilitate an inquiry-based science program. Also, human resources can be deployed in different ways. While the self-contained classroom under the supervision of a single teacher is still the most typical staffing pattern, teachers in many schools team-teach or work with a variety of specialists and paraprofessionals. The music teacher can contribute to your science lessons about sound. A physical education teacher might contribute with regard to forces and motion. Though a well-designed science center could be used independently by students, teachers' aides could facilitate the work that the students do when questions of procedure arise. Likewise, as you find yourself one day being asked to work with a student teacher, learning centers provide an additional advantage. For you, the advantage is that someone with a teacher education background is able to provide support for students working in a center while you are occupied with other students. The advantage for the pre-service teacher is that he or she can work with small groups of students while slowly establishing an educator-student relationship.

Prime Time for Science

Teachers in self-contained classrooms usually have some latitude in deciding details of the daily and weekly schedule and how the room is to be organized. Just as no one pattern of

furniture arrangement is necessarily the best for all purposes, children and teachers can adapt to many different staffing patterns and daily or weekly schedules. The point to keep in mind, however, is that the particular choices you make as a teacher may facilitate or, in some cases, be a barrier to students' learning science.

The professional wisdom in the matter of the schedule is that ". . . children become more engaged in their own learning when the daily routine is predictable and consistent" (Fisher, 1992, p. 57). Opening and closing routings and transitions throughout the day are especially important. The teacher discussed on page 261 for example, began the day in his third-grade class with sharing time and often ended with a journaling activity. Other teachers have developed equally effective but different routines.

Here is an example of a daily schedule a teacher created for her first-grade class:

8:40 A.M.	Settling-in time
9:10	Group meeting—community circle
9:30	Science and/or "workshop"
11:00	Snack and recess
11:20	Math
12:10 P.M.	Specialist (art, music, physical education . . .)
12:45	Lunch
1:30	Social studies and/or "workshop"
2:10	Shared reading
2:30	Independent and collaborative reading
2:55	Group meeting—community circle
3:10	Dismissal

This schedule shows that this teacher considers science as a basic. Notice that science is taught as the first subject of the day, and that a generous amount of time is allotted for effective lessons. The reading and community circle activities show that the teacher places value on both individual and group work. From this schedule, we can infer that the teacher does some subject integration in her classroom curriculum—but not a great deal—and that she probably uses methods such as projects and group work.

In elementary schools organized as self-contained classrooms, individual teachers can opt to schedule science in the morning or afternoon, though they may have to work around the schedules of others, including the specialist teachers—those who teach music, art, physical education, remediation programs, and gifted programs. This constraint aside, the teacher's personal scheme of priority of subjects—what he or she values as most important—often is the deciding factor in scheduling science and the other subjects. Unfortunately, elementary teachers too often schedule science late in the afternoon rather than during the prime morning time. Afternoon time is during children's postprandial dip—a period of low energy and attention that is part of everyone's diurnal cycle. As you know, some cultures shut down for siestas in the afternoon; it is not a time the class is likely to be most creative or to get excited about tackling a tough problem or issue.

Another unfortunate consequence of the all-too-typical afternoon scheduling for science is that science time is more subject to being cut short for assemblies, parent-teacher conferences, half-days, and so forth. Being at the end of the day sometimes even results in science getting abbreviated as preceding lessons run over. These factors may explain in part why researchers studying elementary schools have consistently found that the average time spent on science instruction in American schools is only about twenty minutes a day.

We readily admit our bias in considering science the most important subject. We believe science deserves prime billing in the daily schedule, and just about every day! To us, science and social studies should be the core content subjects in the elementary school curriculum, around and through which most other skills and content are taught. Here we recognize science and social studies as content-rich subjects in comparison with reading, language arts, and even mathematics, which are more skills-oriented subjects. Skills can be taught in the context of problems and issues, and these can be found abundantly in science and social studies.

Despite our bias, we concede that teachers may be compelled by school or district policies to divide teaching time in a particular way among the subjects—and we realize that not everyone agrees with our views about science and social studies being the "real" subjects in the curriculum. Nevertheless, you are likely to have some choices in creating the schedule for your classroom curriculum. We recommend that instead of spreading the time you have for science equally throughout the week, you bunch it together to provide longer, investigation-oriented science periods. For getting into some depth in an investigation, children usually will need an hour to an hour and a half.

Longer periods are useful not only to enable children to develop and implement their science investigations, but also to allow them time for thinking, discussion, and deliberation. A longer period allows children more opportunity to "break with everyday experience" and make the transition into an appropriate frame of mind for scientific thinking. Changing too frequently from subject to subject in a day's schedule can fragment children's thought processes, preventing them from having a coherent instructional experience. One example of how longer periods of time can be blocked for science is to designate Mondays, Wednesdays, and Thursdays as the days when science is taught for an hour and a half, while a different subject would be blocked for the same period on Tuesdays and Fridays. In our experience, most children are flexible enough to handle some daily variation in routine. The professional wisdom is to aim for a schedule that is predictable for children, but not necessarily the same routine every day.

Schedules also need to be organized within larger frames than the day. There is the weekly schedule and the "grading period," which can be six weeks, a quarter (nine weeks), or a semester. An example of a science teaching method framed in a weekly schedule is illustrated by one teacher who introduces on Monday the assignments that she expects everyone to complete by Friday. These assignments might include science observations, a commentary on a science book from the library, or a drawing or model of something related to the particular unit being studied.

Another case is presented by schools that have "bells." Some schools—especially those for the intermediate grades and above—are departmentalized. Teachers in these schools specialize in one or more subjects. Children move at the bell from place to place for instruction in particular subjects. This is the pattern typical of most secondary schools, but many middle schools also change classes, and there are many variations. For example, in one school a team of teachers is responsible for a core of several subjects, which are block scheduled. Within that large block of time, the teaching team and the children can allot the time as they choose. One advantage of this approach is that it enables science to get taught in an integrated fashion with other subjects.

The Value of Planning for Subject Integration

Elementary teachers often feel overwhelmed with the amount of subject matter in all the subjects they must teach in the curriculum. New material and programs seem to be added constantly (such as drug and alcohol abuse education or D.A.R.E. programs, sex education, domestic abuse and violence education), while nothing is ever subtracted. The only sane approach to this situation is to do as much subject integration as possible, which, in terms of scheduling, often means creating blocks of time for teaching integrated units. Some topics in science lend themselves naturally to integration with mathematics, while other topics are more naturally integrated with social studies. Language arts—or English—can nearly always be integrated with science. The bottom line is that many scheduling patterns are possible, and there are also many ways for teachers to work together with other educational professionals and paraprofessionals. Many factors are involved in determining the best approaches for the particular local situation. The sense of what fits best is something that develops with experience.

Quick Review

It would not be surprising if the teachers you speak with say that they teach math or language arts first thing in the morning because that is when the children are "fresh." As you inquire about science, you may find just what we have said—science gets "squeezed" in when and where it can. However, if you take the perspective of integrating what you do in science with the other subject areas, science can become the subject that launches everything else. What's more, there will be a definite sense of connectedness from one subject to the next. You, of course, will be quick to point that out to your students.

THE SCIENCE CULTURE OF THE CLASSROOM

So far, this chapter has considered some practical matters, like scheduling, arranging the room, and working with other professionals. Foremost to remember is that learning science is a social process. Knowledge itself is a social construct, appropriated by the child in some fashion from the culture of the classroom and the outside world. It is a mistake to think that a child in a corner reading a book is constructing knowledge in an isolated context. Rather, she is engaged in a social process; she is interacting with the authors and illustrators of the book, assimilating and accommodating as she ponders the familiar and new ideas she encounters. The learning happens in the interactions, child-to-child, child-to-adult, child-to-media, and so on, and thus it is the quality of the interactions that you will want to consider as the criteria of development of your teaching. What this means is that you will want to plan activities that optimize quality interactions. Children will demonstrate that they know particular concepts, possess particular skills, or hold particular attitudes and appreciations from what they write or say, for example, as they conduct an investigation or deliberate the merits of different ways of solving a problem.

Vygotsky (1978) has pointed out that acquiring knowledge and cognitive functions in general are internalizations of social actions. If you provide children access to appropriately nourishing experiences, such as opportunities to design and carry out investigations and to read good science books, learning will come about naturally and inevitably (Smith, 1995). The experience of a hands-on activity by itself (or of the natural environment, or of reading a book), does not produce the knowledge. Vygotsky and others suggest that knowledge does not derive directly from experience per se, that is, from the sensory data alone. The child makes sense out of the experience, and constructs scientific knowledge, through a social interaction, through inquiring in the context of a cultural setting.

As the teacher, you can do much to enhance the opportunities for science learning by attending to the cultural setting of your own classroom. Learning is the natural consequence when positive social interactions are occurring around challenging science-related problems and issues. Your task is thus to facilitate children's engagement in inquiry with one another and with the subject matter. Chaillé and Britain (1991) point out that:

> Good environments for young children permit, encourage, and even necessitate interaction with others, from simple communicative interaction to the complex negotiation of conflicts. But social interaction is important not only because it is a part of life, but also because it actively contributes to children's theory building. Unfortunately, too often the importance of the social interaction between children is neglected, while the most attention is placed upon the interaction between the teacher and the class. (p. 9)

Activity 12.3 will provide you with the opportunity to think of your classroom from a cultural perspective.

ACTIVITY 12.3

Thinking Culturally

Imagine that you have accepted a teaching position in one of the local schools. You have been assigned a specific school and classroom. Your class has twenty-six children, ages eight to ten. You begin teaching in two weeks and have a week to work in your room before the children arrive.

Consider what you already know about your local schools and the communities they serve, and answer the following questions:

- What backgrounds will the children have?

- Will there be children whose primary language is other than English?

- Will there be children who are physically or educationally challenged?

- What are the positive and negative features of the school facilities?

- What kind of furniture is likely to be in the classroom?

- Will classrooms be equipped with sinks or other access to water?

- What outdoor areas for learning will be available?

- What amount and kind of science equipment and supplies are likely to be available?

- What cultural resources, such as science museums, zoos, nature centers, public libraries, and parks, can be accessed?

- What human expertise is likely to be available to assist you in your local school community?

PLANNING IN SUPPORT OF INQUIRY

Whereas chapter 8 focused on designing lessons, the type of planning addressed here is that which you will do as you conceptualize components of a science lesson, unit, or theme that you wish to develop. Like everything else related to the classroom process, there is no one right way to plan your lessons. Teachers have different personalities and different learning styles and consequently plan in different ways (McCutcheon, 1995).

Planning can occur at any time. Albert Einstein once remarked that he could relate all of his greatest insights to the "3 Bs"—the bed, the bathroom, and the bus. Veteran teachers will tell you that the creative part of planning often occurs when they are occupied with something else—driving home from school, working in the garden, washing dishes—most any place other than school.

Experienced teachers will also tell you that they write down their plans in some fashion. Some make an outline, some create a semantic web or concept map, others write out more detailed plans. Some schools require teachers to write plans that are kept on file. You will have to find which method best fits your own style. One helpful device is to use a list of guiding questions, such as the example shown in Figure 12.2.

It is very useful in instructional planning to do some background reading on the science content you plan to teach. One of the most creative thought processes you will ever experience is modifying this content for instruction. This transformation, or "translation," as the great physicist Richard Feynman called it, creates the content in your mind that you want the children to learn. One way to make this material more concrete in your planning is to outline or web the content after you have studied it. One teacher's initial concept map for planning a physical science unit on forces is illustrated in Figure 12.3. As you can see, this teacher was not sure about using gravity as an example of a kind of force.

Using the Outdoors and Community Resources

Every community has many resources that can be tapped to enrich your science program. One of the most underutilized resources for teaching science is the great outdoors. The outdoors includes not only the school's playground, but also the neighborhood, adjacent and nearby public spaces, local public parks and forest lands, outdoor footpaths and biking trails, and resources you might never have thought about, such as the farm owned by a student's grandparents. Community resources represent an even broader category, which includes all these outdoor spaces as well as local people and institutions.

FIGURE 12.2 Guiding questions to help in planning units and lessons.

Think about the following when planning for science:

1. What is the topic/theme/issue/problem? What is its source(s)?

2. Why is this important? Why should children learn this? What, if any, influence will it have on their lives?

3. What do the children already know? How do their explanations and beliefs differ from those of the scientific community?

4. What knowledge will the children construct?
   - "big understanding"
   - concepts
   - facts

5. What processes and skills do I intend for the children to develop?
   - knowledge acquisition skills
   - thinking processes
   - social skills

6. What habits of mind do I want children to develop?
   - attitudes and dispositions
   - values

7. What other subjects in the curriculum can be naturally integrated?

8. What resources are available?

9. How will children be engaged?

10. How will I stimulate the children to investigate the topic/theme/issue/problem?

11. How will I stimulate the children to explain, clarify, and share their knowledge processes and skills, and habits of mind?

12. How can children be motivated to extend, enrich, and apply their knowledge, skills/processes, and habits of mind?

13. How will I assess the children's learning?

14. How will I evaluate my teaching?

(Powell, Needham, & Bentley, 1994)

Field Trips Field trips are often among children's most memorable school experiences. They require advance planning and attention to detail, but a good field trip can enrich back-home classroom life for days and weeks, before and after the trip. Children learn more from field trips that fit into the curriculum than from those that are unrelated. For example, a visit to an aquarium or a saltwater marsh would fit naturally into an oceanography or marine biology unit.

The first thing to do is be sure you know the community and field sites available within a school bus or charter bus ride from your school. Places where you can find out include the local library, the chamber of commerce, the science museum or park or nature center, and the science departments of the local colleges and universities.

Next, find out the school and school district policies and regulations regarding field trips. There might be a limit to the number of field trips per class per year. There also might be a school policy limiting the amount the child's caregivers can be asked to pay for transportation, admissions, or other costs. Often a request form must be submitted to the school administration for advance approval of field trips. Typical forms ask the teacher to indicate the date of the proposed trip, the site, the address, and the name of a contact at the site. Also frequently required are a written rationale for the trip that specifies its educative potential, and a statement about how the trip activities fit into the curriculum.

One tip for making an educational success of a field trip is to involve the students in planning the trip logistics and the activities that will take place. If the children have invested in the process, they will learn more and cause fewer management problems. Most children recognize that field trips are special learning opportunities and are eager to participate and cooperate. The "countdown" days before the trip can be a series of

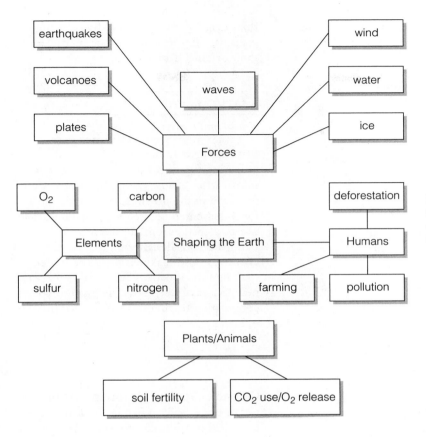

FIGURE 12.3 One teacher's initial concept map for planning a unit on forces.

deadlines for getting tasks done and everything prepared for the special event.

Usually parents are solicited to participate as chaperons on the field trip. The school might also have aides who can be available to chaperon. Often schools have "room mothers" and "room fathers" who can assist with obtaining the extra support you need. You will have to send a notice about the trip to children's homes a week or more in advance. Schools usually require that permission forms be signed by parents or guardians.

Field trip success is also enhanced if an investigative atmosphere is created, one of excitement and expectancy of multiple possibilities and discoveries. It is hard to fail if children go off on the field trip in inquiring

frames of mind, understanding and confident in their roles as observers, problem solvers, and data recorders. On the other hand, failure is almost assured if children head off on a field trip not knowing what they are responsible for doing.

The problems and/or questions that provide the focus for a field trip are established during pre-trip classroom activities. Many teachers have children keep science logs or journals, and these are often essential equipment on field trips. Art pads and colored pencils or markers are often useful to have on hand as well, so that children can sketch and record their observations. Depending on the field trip, other tools and materials might be useful. Here are some things frequently used to support children's observing and learning on science field trips:

- binoculars
- hand lenses, jewelers loupes, or magnifiers
- microscopes
- plastic bags
- bug boxes, small cages, or collection jars
- tweezers, scissors, probes—or dissecting kits
- nets (aquatic or insect)
- field guides (to insects, wildflowers, trees, birds, rocks and minerals, etc.)
- maps (road maps, topographic maps, geological maps, etc.)
- compasses
- tape recorder and blank tapes
- camera and film (35-mm color slide film gives you the most options for instruction later on)
- digital camera and disk
- a first-aid kit
- field logs or journals
- paper, pencils, colored pencils or markers

Making a field collection is an interesting, educational, and rewarding activity for children on field trips. Before collecting organisms, however, check with your county extension agent or a park agent regarding regulations that prohibit collecting particular plants or animals. Never collect any rare, threatened, or endangered species.

Here are some other planning tips. Always get a landowner's written permission to visit or collect on private property. Be sure children pick up after themselves and leave no signs of their visit behind: "Leave nothing but footprints." Encourage children to show respect for wildlife, for example, by replacing logs, rocks, and the like back into their original positions, and by releasing organisms, after examining them, back into their original habitat areas.

ACTIVITY 12.4

Field Trip Planner

It would be helpful in proposing and preparing for a field trip to have all of your information handy. Using the information provided in the previous section, design a form that could be used for planning a field trip to some appropriate site in your locale. Compare your design with that of your classmates, and make changes as required to design the most efficient and useful planner. As a final test, show the form to your cooperating teacher or principal for their opinions.

Use the School Grounds Often Less novel, but equally valuable, are learning experiences just outside the classroom, on the school grounds or in the nearby neighborhood. Sites with educative potential are within walking distance from most schools.

An elementary school in Winnetka, Illinois, is located next to a forest preserve. A fifth-grade teacher in the school used the woodland as a site for students to study local flora. She invited a local forester to help. This led to the beginning of a project for the class. The children learned to identify and remove alien plant species that had invaded the native prairie woodland. The teacher and forester trained several parent volunteers to take groups of children out on study and work expeditions periodically throughout the year. Each group was responsible for caring for a particular area in the woods. The children's enthusiasm in tackling the project to restore the native flora led to a lot of

Chen Long

PHOTO 12.1 A class garden, whether simple or elaborate, offers a wealth of learning opportunities.

worthwhile physical exercise and science learning as well.

Few schools may be so fortunate to be located adjacent to an area managed for nature, like the forest preserve. Regardless, there are many other valuable activities and investigations that can be done outdoors. Gardening is one of them. The school garden can offer lots of opportunities for science lessons, connecting with topics such as reproduction; growth; plants; the structure of flowers, seeds, leaves, stems, and roots; photosynthesis, capillarity, nitrogen fixation, water and biogeochemical cycles, food chain and food pyramid (trophic levels), and parasitism, among others.

Butterfly, rock, herb, vegetable, and flower gardens are only a few of the many kinds of gardening projects. In a sense, your class could do a native plant restoration project in a corner of the schoolyard. Both native and heirloom seeds are available from a number of commercial sources (see Chapter 14). Many seed catalogs have interesting historical and scientific information. Advice and assistance is available in every area of the United States from the county land grant university extension agent. Local garden clubs in many places are often willing to contribute classroom speakers or conduct miniworkshops. You can easily find out methods and schedules for planting outdoors in your particular region.

After the class garden is planted, maintenance must begin. You can work with children to create a calendar of reminders about watering, weeding, and otherwise tending the garden. One way to manage maintenance is to schedule pairs of children to handle tasks on a rotating basis. The calendar could also mark the children's predictions for germination (the seed packet will usually include information on germination time). The class garden could be cared for during the summer holidays by volunteer parent-child pairs.

Another variation on the garden theme is the nature trail. In this case, what grows around your school is left undisturbed except for establishing a path through the area. Once a pathway is cleared, the plants that are indigenous to the area can be identified and labeled. In addition to seeing what is there, students can observe changes over time. Over the course of several years, these changes could be dramatic in plants such as small trees. A marker indicating the height of a sapling when your class measured it one year would be an interesting point of comparison for another class five years later.

Connecting the Classroom and the Home In the past, science homework has often been dry and boring stuff: "Read the chapter, answer questions 1 through 6 at the end of the chapter," or "Look up the vocabulary words in the glossary and write the definitions." This kind of homework doesn't draw upon the resources of a child's home and doesn't usually result in meaningful learning. As never before, however, educators are realizing the importance of linking classroom instruction with the home. Home-link science activities can be simple investigations that children and their parents or guardians can conduct at home. You can provide instructions on a take-home handout, or let the investigative teams come up with their own procedures. It is these kinds of activities that strengthen the connections between child, school, and home, and give children's caregivers opportunities to help and express interest in their children's work.

One elementary teacher sends the children in her third-grade class home on Friday with a science activity packed in a Ziploc resealable bag. Included in the bag are the science materials, the instructions for carrying out one or more investigations, a data sheet or worksheet, and a "Science Wizard Form" for the parent to verify the child has completed the activity at home. On Monday, the teacher recreates the activity that the child and parent have done at home. The experience of this teacher is that she receives immediate responses from most children because they have done the activity. Children are encouraged to discuss questions that came up at home. Examples of some take-home activities include exploring magnets;

learning the properties of Alka-seltzer; building a barge from aluminum foil, then estimating the number of pennies that will float on the barge; seed sorting and graphing; estimation, graphing, and sorting Gummi Bears candies; and finding the center of gravity of a ball of clay.

ACTIVITY 12.5

Science in a Bag

Choose any one of these science topics:

simple circuits	weather
magnets	plants

Design a take-home science activity, considering the following:

- All necessary materials must fit into a Ziploc bag.

- Assuming twenty students in the class, total materials cost cannot exceed $10.

- The assignment should include, or require the student to construct, some sort of data table or schematic (such as a classification scheme—refer to chapters 6 and 7).

- If you and your classmates each choose a different activity and prepare a bag for everyone in the class, you will have an excellent foundation collection of "science in a bag" activities.

Connecting the Classroom and the Community The outdoors and the school's community are invaluable instructional resources for science. The community has human resources as well. Children in your classroom are likely to have family members who have curriculum-related knowledge and skills. Some connections might even surprise you. For example, as part of a unit on forces, a carpenter or plumber who brought his tools to class probably could provide a wealth of examples of simple machines. There are many opportunities for investigations in every community, and there are always community members who are willing and interested in helping children learn.

Your local science or children's museum, zoo, aquarium, arboretum, botanical garden, nature/ecology center, and planetarium can be among your greatest allies in teaching science. These places are not just places where exhibits are stored; they are a treasure trove of ideas for investigations, people with special expertise, and resources for investigations.

Animals in the Classroom Living things are what the biological, or life, sciences are all about. The direct study of living things is an appropriate and necessary part of science teaching. Children can learn much from observing the living patterns and behaviors of organisms in the outdoors and in the classroom. Animals, however, must be properly cared for in the classroom, which means having appropriate, clean living space where the animals are free from undue stress and have the ability to exercise. Also important is providing proper food and clean water in suitable containers along with proper ventilation, light, and heating.

Many different organisms can be kept in the classroom. Mammals that are usually selected include rabbits and varieties of rodents (guinea pigs, mice, rats, hamsters, and gerbils), because they are clean and easy to care for. Be sure to keep in mind, however, that some children may have allergic reactions to these animals. Find out what you can about this situation before bringing animals into the classroom. Children are usually highly motivated to care for classroom organisms and often are willing to take them home over school holidays.

Chapter 14 contains information on the feeding requirements of several kinds of animals. Your public library has books on the animals you are likely to have available. Carolina Biological Supply Company has a number of booklets on the care of various organisms in the classroom (see chapter 14).

There is another side to this, of course. Some people take the view that animals do not belong in the school. Peter Singer, a professor at Australia's Monash University, wrote *Animal Liberation* in 1975. He used the term "speciesism," which he compared to racism and which he defined as "a prejudice or attitude of bias toward the interest of members of one's own species and against those of members of other species" (p. 7). Some animal rights advocates say that the educational benefits of using animals in the classroom are overstated, and that the suffering of the animals involved is underestimated. What do you think about this issue?

Planning for a Safe Environment

Both inside and outside the classroom, safety has got to be a prime consideration for the teacher in planning for science, if only for issues of liability. In fact, you and the children in your class should talk about classroom safety right at the start of the school year. Safety has been described as simply using plain common sense in planning ahead. You cannot guarantee that an accident will never happen in your classroom. We, the authors, consider ourselves considerate and aware of safety issues, but have had to manage emergencies in both classroom and field situations.

The first thing to do is to look ahead and be prepared. Within the school, keep classroom doors free from obstructions and never store flammable material near doors. Know the location of the nearest fire extinguisher and how to use it. Know school procedures for handling injuries. Unless circumstances offer no alternative, never treat injuries yourself. Excluding lifesaving measures, teachers may only stop bleeding and apply water (as to burns or acid spills).

FIGURE 12.4 A sample student safety contract, appropriate for intermediate or upper elementary grades.

STUDENT SAFETY CONTRACT

I will:

- Follow all instructions given by the teacher.
- Protect my eyes, face, hands, and body while conducting class activities.
- Carry out good housekeeping practices.
- Know where to get help fast.
- Know the location of first-aid and fire-fighting equipment.
- Conduct myself in a responsible manner at all times in a laboratory situation.

I, _____, have read and agree to abide by the safety regulations as set forth above and also any additional printed instructions provided by the teacher and/or district. I further agree to follow all other written and verbal instructions given in class.

Date: _____   _____

                                                                                          Signature

(National Science Teachers Association, 1977)

Determine appropriate safety rules for your class. In order to foster your students' investment in maintaining a safe environment, they should be able to contribute suggestions. Be sure to engage children in discussing safety rules at the start of the year. Post the resulting standards for safe behavior prominently in the classroom. A list of safety guidelines for the elementary classroom can be found in chapter 14.

Remind children of any special safety concerns before investigations or activities involving potential risks. These would include, for example, activities involving a lighted flame (e.g., burning candles or alcohol lamps), the use of chemicals, or the use of sharp instruments. Safety glasses should be available in the school for investigations in which a splash or projectile might harm the eyes. Contact lenses can be dangerous if a chemical splashes into the eyes because capillary action carries the irritant to the eye's surface. If the chemical is an alkali, eye damage can be done within ten to thirty seconds. Plan for safety, but don't let it inhibit activities. After all, many other things that children use in school could be misused, such as

scissors and pencils. You will never be able to establish an absolutely injuryproof environment. You can, however, establish an environment of conscientious attention to safety.

Your liability as a teacher falls under *tort law,* where negligence or breach of contract or trust results in injury to another person or damage to property. A student generally acquires the status of an *invitee,* which means that no contractual basis exists for assumed risk on his or her part. The student is also assumed not to possess the knowledge of potential danger or to appreciate a potential risk. The teacher's responsibility is related to the legal concept of negligence, which means neglecting particular instruction, supervision, or upkeep of equipment and supplies. If there is no precedent or statute involved, then the actions or inactions of the teacher are to be measured against what a hypothetical reasonably prudent individual would have done under the same circumstances. Of course, the reasonable person is one who anticipates that things can happen.

For older children, a good strategy is to work with the class to develop safety contracts that everyone in class will sign. The signed contracts should be kept on file. A sample student safety contract, appropriate for upper elementary grades, is shown in Figure 12.4. Keep in mind, however, that a document signed between you and a student serves only to communicate the importance of safety as part of the total learning experience. *Such a document does not absolve you of responsibility.*

Quick Review

You are literally surrounded at all times by resources for science. Try to break free of the idea that all science must occur on the top of a student's desk. When you consider that science is a study of the world around us, do not hesitate to make that world your resource. Though field trips are increasingly difficult to get approved, do not let that stop you. A well-planned trip has the chance of getting someone to finally say yes. Be specific in where and when you will go, why you are going, why it is just absolutely crucial to these children and the future well-being of the world that they go, and what they will do when they get there. Try. The worst scenario is that the answer is no.

But even "no" is not the end of the world. Look out of your classroom window and ask how you can make what you see a part of your science lessons. And ask who out there can help with those lessons.

Make safety a part of your plan rather than a reason not to plan. Be conscientious in your approach. While it simply is not possible to plan for every contingency that might arise when children are involved, take the time to consider the likely contingencies and what you will do to accommodate them.

CONCLUSION

Planning and managing inquiry-oriented science in the classroom has been the topic in this chapter. We have addressed some very practical matters, including organizing the classroom space and deciding what tools and resources to have in the classroom to support science learning, conducting field studies, scheduling, and safety. The physical setup of the room reflects what the teacher believes is important about the learning that is to go on there. Time for science is important, too—children's knowledge construction requires time for investigating and time for discussing, drawing, writing, and other process activities.

In between, we have also addressed some of the deeper aspects of planning and management. We acknowledged the importance of working with children to establish reliable routines in the classroom process. Excitement about learning grows when daily routines give way to exploration and adventure, as in doing studies in the field and community. Being sensitive to the interactions in the classroom, the teacher must allow some detours on the journey if the interests of the children point that way. Lesson plans are meant to guide, not bind.

Other matters introduced in this chapter were how to plan for the use of the outdoors and community resources in science instruction. The outdoors is especially relevant to studying nature and the built environment. Science investigations inside and out-of-doors should be carefully planned to take into account risks and hazards. The teacher of science needs to be pro-active in maintaining safe conditions for learning.

Neil Postman has written, "Children enter school as question marks and leave as periods." Unfortunately, this situation is true more often than not, and it can be the result of inept classroom planning and management. But in many classrooms, teachers work with children to plan and manage a place of inquiry, where children's interests and ideas are respected and are, in fact, the foundation of the curriculum.

13   ⚜   Assessment of Student Learning

The Nature of Assessment

Alternative Forms of Assessment

Authentic Assessment Using Portfolios

Scoring Rubrics

Conclusion

Your Academic Roadmap

Study of this chapter should help you to understand the following concepts:

- Assessment serves many purposes, from diagnostic to lesson design to evaluation.

- The application of acquired skills is performance-based assessment.

- There are alternative forms of assessment that are dynamic and encourage thinking on higher levels of Bloom's taxonomy of educational objectives.

- The outstanding advantage of portfolios as authentic assessment is that they provide evidence of individual gains in cognitive growth.

- Effective alternative assessment techniques appropriately reflect the content required by the curriculum, though in a manner most suitable for a child in the process of constructing new knowledge.

What happens to the stars during the day? *They go to the sun. After the stars go into the sun, the sun gets brighter and brighter. The stars make the sun light up.*

—Sha'Lee, six years old

THE NATURE OF ASSESSMENT

If we accept the notion that science is what scientists do, that through investigations they produce knowledge, then science is a systematic search for new information. Therefore, if we want to know how well children are doing in science, as teachers we must examine not only their skills of investigation but also the information they have discovered. Unfortunately, traditional means of testing have focused only on the information. The processes involved in the search for information have been typically overlooked or excluded. As the emphasis in the teaching of science has shifted to the active process of investigations, the science process skills and various forms of investigation as presented in chapters 6 and 7 must become an integral part of assessment as well as instruction.

This chapter examines performance-based assessment. Alternative forms of assessment are surveyed and various means of documenting student learning are discussed. Sample forms for assessing students' knowledge, skills, and attitudes are also included. In conclusion, attention is given to the importance of aligning curriculum, instruction, and assessment.

In its strictest interpretation in an educational setting, assessment refers to examining information in order to answer questions and make instructional decisions. What changes in the children have occurred as a result of instruction? What do the children know at this point? What skills have they acquired or further developed? What are their attitudes toward science and learning? When the information collected through assessment is used to assign a grade, it becomes evaluation. And this is what people typically think of when they hear the term assessment.

It is obvious, however, that assessment serves many purposes other than assigning grades. The information obtained with assessment instruments may be used from one end of the educational spectrum to the other, from designing tomorrow's lesson to making funding decisions for entire districts. At state and district levels, the most common purposes of assessment (usually in the form of testing) are for accountability, instructional improvement, and program evaluation. Often, but in fewer numbers, district testing is done for the purpose of making an individual diagnosis of instructional needs or for student placement. As classroom teachers our concern with assessment is primarily in two areas: designing effective instruction and measuring student performance.

Traditional Assessment versus Performance-Based Assessment

There are three general approaches, or categories, to assessment in terms of the tasks required of students: The first two characterize the assessment techniques with which we are all so familiar; the third takes a different approach.

In the first of the three categories, students demonstrate *familiarity* with a science concept through identification of information. They typically select correct answers from among a list of possibilities. For example, tests that make use of matching or multiple-choice questions measure familiarity. In such a situation, it is impossible to say whether the student would have been able to provide the appropriate information had it not been supplied as a potential response.

The second general approach is when students demonstrate *awareness* of information related to a particular concept by supplying discrete or specific pieces of informa-

tion. Most often, this occurs in tests that use a fill-in-the-blank format. Though this approach requires that the student supply the requested information, the format is necessarily so context-specific that there is little evidence that the student understands the concept well enough to apply it in a different setting.

The third general approach, performance-based assessment, calls for students to *demonstrate understanding* through the application of information and newly acquired skills. This approach involves placing students in problem-solving situations that reflect, though not necessarily duplicate, the context in which instruction took place. Some subjects in the elementary school rely on performance-based assessment. Of the "academic" subjects, mathematics comes closest to using performance-based assessment, though even in that situation the skills to be used and the procedures to follow are often very narrowly defined.

ACTIVITY 13.1

Assessing the Assessing

Note that this activity is assessing the assessing, not the assessors. The concern is with the assessment instrument.

- Ask teachers of science from various grade levels for copies of the assessments they use in class. The more samples you can obtain, the better.

- When you have acquired a number of tests, separate them by grade level.

- Consider each test and determine whether it falls into the category of familiarity, awareness, or demonstration of understanding.

- Construct a data table with the three categories across the top, and a row for each grade level represented in the tests you have collected.

- What trends or patterns can you identify?
- Is there a preference of one type of test over the others?
- What conclusions can you draw about the science programs and assessment programs represented by this data?

Indirect Assessment versus Direct Assessment

Traditional tests measure learning indirectly; that is, the questions ask for responses that suggest that something has been mastered or learned. This type of assessment is characterized by the first two approaches just discussed. The focus is clearly on the knowledge level of Bloom's taxonomy of cognitive development. There was a time when this may have been appropriate, for instance, when information was not so readily available. However, given the phenomenal access to information resources available to students of all ages, an emphasis on memorization is neither prudent nor warranted.

Instead, teachers have the opportunity to make information meaningful by allowing students to have an active role in its application. Direct measures of assessment are more consistent with current best practices for instruction and the emphasis on teaching science through inquiry and use of science process skills. The advantage to direct assessment is that students are challenged to generate solutions to problems by utilizing their newly acquired skills and knowledge.

Performance-based assessment and, in particular, performance tests that are conducted as hands-on science activities, use direct measures of learning rather than elicit responses that suggest that cognitive changes have occurred (Borich, 1995). This type of assessment is illustrative of the third general approach. Notice that the demonstration of understanding includes both factual knowledge and the ability to apply it. Thus, performance-based assessment may be seen as an improvement of traditional methods as it exemplifies the ancient Chinese proverb first mentioned back in chapter 8:

> I hear . . . and I forget.
> I see . . . and I remember.
> I do . . . and I understand.

Art, music, and physical education are components of the elementary curriculum that are typically studied outside the regular classroom. The responsibilities for instructional planning and student assessment belong to other teachers. Teachers in these curricular areas have been using performance-based assessment for a long time, specifically performance testing. It seems quite obvious that the best way to determine how well a student is doing in physical education is to observe the student's performance. For example, if you want to know how well a child can swim, watch him swim. A written test would not provide the necessary information to determine that child's mastery of particular swimming skills; performance testing is more appropriate.

Performance testing is appropriate for assessing skill development and is also useful in many other ways. For instance, not only can individual swimming skills such as arm stroke, leg kick, and breathing be assessed, but the ability to combine those skills in a coordinated fashion can also be determined. In addition, the instructor can observe the student's knowledge for application—that is, the student's ability to decide when to use what information or skill. If the focus is on aesthetic qualities or if competitive applications are important, the instructor can also make that type of assessment by observing student performance. Even attitudes that affect the learning process or the intended outcome (e.g., overcoming fear; enjoyment; physical fitness) can be assessed.

FIGURE 13.1 Characteristics of performance-based assessment (from Baron, 1991).

1. Problem-solving tasks require active student involvement.
2. Solutions to problems are produced by students rather than identified from a list of choices.
3. Responses are constructed by students rather than recalled from a text.

The same is true in science. While written tests are limited to indirect assessment of knowledge, performance-based assessments can measure students' understanding of science knowledge as well as their skills and attitudes toward science. Thus, it is the teacher's responsibility to put students in situations where they supply and apply information. These tasks need to be observable by the teacher in order to allow evaluation.

Performance-based assessment requires that students be actively involved in solving problems rather than merely recalling information or guessing at correct choices. There are numerous techniques, or alternative forms of assessment, that can be employed. Common to all forms, however, are the characteristics listed in Figure 13.1.

ALTERNATIVE FORMS OF ASSESSMENT

Alternative assessment is a phrase used to describe new assessment techniques in contrast to traditional approaches. The newer techniques ask students to construct responses to open-ended tasks rather than select responses from sets of options, as in the more traditional approaches. Some of these assessment forms, such as interviews and checklists, have teachers observing or interacting with children as the data is collected. Teachers do supply guidelines or initiate activities when using the other assessment forms, but the children generate the information in the form of products to be used for assessment.

Interviews

Chapter 5 closely examined interviewing as a means of eliciting what children know about a topic prior to instruction. Because interviewing allows for individual conversations with follow-up questions, personal explanations for natural phenomena can be probed and misconceptions can be identified. By sampling several students, group patterns can also be identified.

Interviews can also be used as a means of assessment following instruction. By interviewing each child at the end of an instructional unit, the teacher can determine what knowledge has been acquired. If the teacher has a progressive development model for the topic of instruction, the individual's responses can be compared to the model and decisions related to the level of understanding can be made. The enabling and facilitating concepts that the student correctly incorporates into his or her explanation can be recorded. Areas of persistent misunderstanding can also be noted. Although interviewing each child can be time-consuming, there is a tremendous advantage to using interviewing as a means of assessment. Teachers have the opportunities to use probing questions that are individually appropriate in order to elicit subtleties in the explanations that would otherwise go unnoticed.

Checklists

Teachers recognize the need to observe students as they conduct individual and group investigations. The purpose might be to assure that students follow the directions correctly. More often, teachers want to observe students in action to see them making measurements, testing predictions, classifying objects, and so on. Checklists allow for record-

CHECKLIST FOR BASIC PROCESS SKILLS

Name: _____ Date: _____

                    <u>Yes</u>   <u>No</u>   <u>Comments</u>

Made prediction:

Shared prediction:

Tested prediction:

Listed observations:

Constructed inference:

FIGURE 13.2 Sample checklist assessment.

ing observable behaviors or demonstration of skills that are important to learning in science. If checklists, such as the one in Figure 13.2, are designed in advance, the teacher can simply indicate the behavior as (1) "present" or "absent," (2) "demonstrated" or "not demonstrated," or (3) simply as observed "yes" or "no." The need for writing lengthy descriptions of individual student behavior is minimized.

Using checklists is an efficient way for teachers to document student performance during classroom activities; however, checklists do not allow for an assessment regarding the quality of skills demonstrated, unless the teacher adds comments. Comments are worthwhile because they add more depth to the recorded evidence. The opportunity to make them should be maintained, as the space on the checklist in Figure 13.2 indicates, but teachers should not feel compelled to complete that portion during class time or necessarily to utilize it each time. The primary function of a checklist is to provide a well-organized system for documenting student achievement in a minimum amount of time.

Open-ended Questioning

Open-ended questions do not have a single correct answer but are specifically designed to allow for a variety of acceptable responses. They encourage thinking on multiple levels simultaneously and allow teachers to value

Christine Ebert

PHOTO 13.1 Checklists allow for recording observable behaviors easily and efficiently.

all ideas expressed by children. Used formally or informally, open-ended questions challenge students to supply and apply information. The divergent nature of the questions allows for a diversity of responses that may or may not be in agreement or support of one another. When formulating answers, the children are encouraged to draw on personal experiences as well as newly acquired information gained through classroom experiences.

Sometimes the differences in the wording of the open-ended questions is subtly different from other questions. A few examples may help clarify that point. For instance, if you were to ask your students the question, "What color was the object?" the answers would essentially be the same regardless of who responded. However, by changing the question to "How would you describe the object?" the answers could be quite diverse. Some children might provide information about the color of the object. Others might describe shape and size. It is very likely that senses, other than visual, would be utilized. The descriptions might include texture, smell, or sounds produced by the object. As the first question limits the potential responses, the second question encourages diversity and elaboration.

A different type of limitation occurs in this next example. Consider the differences evoked by these two questions about an investigation involving mealworms.

- How many different responses did you notice?
- What different responses did you notice?

Do you think that the teacher really wanted a "number" response, or do you think that the intent was to generate a list of the many ways that mealworms responded to various stimuli?

When questions are used to stimulate oral discussion, responses that include expressions of personal perspective are often quite enlightening to the teacher as well as the other students. Besides indicating the understanding of newly acquired information, students' responses sometimes reflect connections that were not anticipated by the teacher. For example, second-grader Saya shared this observation: "I noticed that the mealworm moved into the dark area each time. Maybe he is afraid of his shadow, too." The teacher had expected the observation but not the inference that was added. At this point, the teacher may not wish to draw attention away from the mealworm investigation but may make a mental note to design opportunities for Saya to study and better understand shadows. Had it not been for the use of open-ended questioning, the teacher would probably not have learned as much from the student.

When this form of questioning is used only in the oral format, it is difficult to capture the answers as evidence of student progress. On the other hand, if the same type of questioning is used for written responses, the answers themselves serve as evidence of student performance.

Science Journals

Written journal entries provide physical evidence of student progress and cognitive growth. Journals can serve many purposes which may vary according to subject matter. Science journals are often used to collect data during investigations. So, if assessing students' abilities to collect and organize data is important in your classroom, journal entries can be very effective. If you consider it important for children to make connections between what they do in class and their lives outside of school, you can request that they make entries that do that. For example, students may complete the following: "What we did in class today is similar to . . ." You can also gain significant information about their learning by asking students to make entries such as "Today, I learned . . ." and "My question now is . . ."

Assessment of students' journals depends on the purpose for the assignment. If the intent is to chronicle activities such as observing bird behavior at a bird feeder, then regularity of journal entries becomes important. If the purpose of the journal is to collect and record data, then the accuracy and organization of information becomes important. If the purpose is to encourage children to reflect on their own learning, then feedback in terms of words encouraging the children to think deeply is most appropriate. In any case, it is important for the teacher to decide in advance what the purpose will be and to communicate that purpose to the children.

ACTIVITY 13.2

"Before and After" Journals

When working in a field service or practicum placement, you can easily demonstrate the effectiveness of journals for evidence of cognitive gain. As a simple exercise, prepare a set of booklets for use by the students. These booklets need be only one sheet of paper folded in half. If you want to be fancy about it, use a computer and printer to label and decorate the "cover" of the booklet. If you set the page orientation of your word processor to "landscape," you might want to type the heading "What I know before we start . . ." in the upper-left corner of the page. Type "What I know now . . ." in the upper-right corner. When folded in half, these two headings will be on opposing pages inside the booklet.

- Arrange with your cooperating teacher to visit the class on the day a new topic is to be started.

- Before instructions begin, provide each student with a booklet, and ask that they write what they know about the topic already. Collect the booklets.

- It would be worthwhile for you to review the booklets before visiting the class again.

PHOTO 13.2 Encourage reflective thinking by asking for journal entries such as "Today I learned . . ." and "My question now is . . ."

- Visit the class again when the teacher has completed the lesson or unit. Redistribute the booklets, and ask the students to write what they know now about the topic.

- Review the booklets and look for evidence of cognitive gain.

Inquiry Reports

Inquiry reports are written communications created by children to document investigations that are essentially designed and conducted by the children. Each inquiry project begins with a question formulated by the child. The child identifies a topic of personal interest, usually related to one of the topics

FIGURE 13.3 Reflection form for inquiry reports.

WHAT I LEARNED DURING MY INQUIRY PROJECT

Name: _____

Circle the number that best reflects how you feel about each statement.

	A little bit				A lot
1. I know more about this topic now than I did before I started my project.	1	2	3	4	5
2. I used a variety of sources to collect information.	1	2	3	4	5
3. I could explain what I have learned to somebody else.	1	2	3	4	5
4. Answering my inquiry question has increased my interest in the topic.	1	2	3	4	5

Complete each of the following statements:

5. The most important or interesting piece of information I found during the inquiry was . . .

6. If somebody else were to study this topic, my advice would be . . .

being studied in the classroom. For example, the class may be studying oceans and ocean life. The class experiences may satisfy the interest of some of the children while it stimulates in some children the desire to know more. One child may want to inquire about the habits of sharks. Another may be interested in knowing more about hurricanes, and still another wants to investigate beach erosion. Each child would formulate a question to serve as a focus of inquiry. Then a variety of ways to collect information would be pursued. Collection of information may involve personal investigations, on-site visits (local beaches, aquarium, museum, university, etc.), communication with experts in the field, as well as finding information in books and using computers to locate other data.

Once the information has been collected, each student shares his or her information with others in the class. The actual report may take many forms. It may be a combination of oral and written material and include artifacts such as photographs, drawings, charts, maps, and the like. The inquiry report, in whatever format, would certainly constitute evidence of student progress.

While inquiry reports are good evidence for student performance, they present special challenges for evaluation. One student's inquiry project may arise from an intense desire to learn more about a topic or the need to resolve personal uncertainty. Another inquiry project may result from a more superficial desire. The time and effort put into each of those projects is not likely to be equal. Experience with such assignments is also going to have an impact on the quality of the product. The goal for this type of experience is that children learn to value the vast number and types of information sources that are helpful in the pursuit of answers to questions. Criteria for evaluation may then reflect the use of an increasing number of sources each time a child conducts another inquiry project.

When it comes to assessing the amount of information learned, perhaps the child is the best one to make that decision. General guidelines such as those in Figure 13.3 may be used with children to help them self-evaluate their own progress. Notice that the intent of the guidelines focuses on reflection rather than on self-evaluation. Under these circumstances, the child is more apt to respond in ways that provide the teacher with insights that otherwise would not have been forthcoming.

Inquiry projects are found in many elementary curricula that have an integrated or interdisciplinary focus. And while they are not confined to science, they are truly exemplary of the type of science that is most appropriate for children.

Investigation Reports

Investigation reports are similar to inquiry reports in that they are open-ended tasks allowing for individuality to occur. As with inquiry reports, the student conducts an investigation and concludes by making a report, but these investigations are the same as the ones discussed in chapter 7—they are not inquiry reports. These forms of investigation include trial and error, documenting, prediction testing, product testing, generating models, experimenting, reflecting, and inventing. Though the investigation is largely self-directed, the investigative technique has a particular format to follow. A trial-and-error investigation is quite distinct from an experimental design. As such, adhering to the appropriate format for the particular investigative technique would have an impact on evaluation.

Another distinction between inquiry reports and investigation reports is that the investigations are often, although not always, conducted by students working in small groups rather than individually. An inquiry-based project stems from some personal question that the child wishes to answer. This was referred to in chapter 6 as "wonderings" and lends itself well to a project to be worked on alone. A child may select one of the investigative approaches, but the decision of which one to use should not be a "committee" decision. On the other hand, when investigating a topic suggested or assigned by the teacher, a small group of students may easily identify which of the techniques would be best to use.

Ultimately, the purpose of investigation reports is to allow children to share what they learned. If you were to compare the reports of children conducting the investigations, similarities should be apparent. However, as children construct their own understanding, subtle differences in observations and conclusions are likely to occur. Open-ended reports allow for these differences to be expressed. If the children were expected to complete laboratory worksheets by only supplying pieces of information collected, the diversity in learning may go unnoticed.

That is not to say that there are no guidelines. The teacher and students discuss expectations and criteria to be used to evaluate the product. These guidelines will vary according to the form of investigation being conducted. Common to all of the investigation reports would be the following elements:

1. A statement of the problem or question that served to focus the investigation.

2. A description of all the steps involved in the investigation.

3. A report of the data or information collected, if appropriate.

4. A presentation of the solution to the problem or answer to the question.

The last element in the report varies the most. When the children are investigating using generating models or inventing, the fourth element will take the form of a product separate from the report. The final element of an investigation report using reflecting would take the form of guidelines or questions leading to additional investigation.

Based on these four guidelines, criteria for assessment can be created. Completion of each of the four elements would be the primary concern. The quality of presentation and expectations related to detail depends greatly on the age, ability, and experience of the children. Teachers need to generate standards by which to evaluate student performance. At the same time, there is a need for flexibility. Each child is going to personalize the investigation with slight differences in questions, observations, inferences, and insights. For children, the importance of the activity is to develop the skills and confidence to solve real problems in the real world. Therefore, evaluation of the investigation report should place greater emphasis on the process involved than on the precision of the resulting information or product.

Inventions and Models

Investigations focusing on the development of inventions and models are also excellent examples of student performance. However, reports are not necessary for assessment to occur because the model or invention provides the teacher with a concrete example of the student's explanation for how things work. When children generate their own models they include previously existing components and indicate how those parts are related. Inventions are unique in that the product is something that did not previously exist. The children combine the parts or ideas into newly created systems. Either type of investigation leads to the generation of a novel and personally satisfying product. So how do you assess something that has never existed before?

Whether assessing inventions or models, it is important to focus on the process rather than the product. These forms of investigation are opportunities for children to apply information in creative, nonverbally dependent ways. Children who have weak verbal skills and typically do not perform well on written tests, often excel when provided the opportunity to demonstrate their understanding in this very concrete manner.

The purpose for the activity is again the most important perspective to consider when generating criteria. If the invention is a Rube Goldberg contraption, then by definition it must be humorous and complex. If the purpose is to identify a personal problem and subsequently invent a practical solution to the problem, then the criteria needs to reflect the effectiveness and practicality of the solution.

Model generation typically is done as a means of considering possibilities prior to the exploration of the existing model or the one espoused by the scientific community. If done the other way around, the child is faced with coming up with a model that is "better" than what scientists already believe to be true. Talk about intimidating! And certainly, when it is time to assess the student's work, it would be most inappropriate to assess the children's models for accuracy in a comparison with the scientifically accepted model. Instead, ideas that express possible solutions must be valued. The inclusion of components and some indication of how those parts work together are the principle ingredients. Perhaps a modification of the reflection form for inquiry reports in Figure 13.3 would also be appropriate.

Performance Tests

Each of the techniques discussed thus far tends to fall into the category of projects rather than testing techniques. There is a place in your science classroom for testing, though we are not about to say that multiple choice is the option we prefer. In science, performance tests are used to assess students' abilities to supply and apply newly acquired knowledge and skills under the same time and access constraints normally associated with tests. The difference is that the tests are not limited to pencil-and-paper activities. The activities require that children interact with manipulatives just as they do during instructional times. This type of testing allows children to actually demonstrate the skills rather than write about them.

For example, if the class has been learning how to classify leaves, the test would challenge them to actually classify leaves. The leaves may or may not be exactly the same as those used during instruction. The challenge is to be able to classify similar objects in a slightly different setting. So, in this performance test situation, children would be provided with the leaves and would have been asked to classify the leaves in a multistage classification scheme. In addition, they may be required to translate the scheme that they developed into a taxonomic key.

Similarly, activities such as the "dancing raisins" provide opportunities, in a testing situation, for students to demonstrate their skills of observation, prediction, and inference. Here's how it works: Children are given several raisins and a container of 7UP or some other clear, carbonated beverage, but none of the objects are referred to by any name. They are asked to list five observations of the solid and liquid objects and three related inferences. Next, they are to write a prediction as to what will happen if the solid objects are dropped into the container of liquid. Finally, they are directed to test their predictions, record at least five more observations and three additional inferences. The information collected through these performance tests demonstrates to the teacher the students' understanding and ability to apply these basic science process skills. Have you ever seen the dancing raisins? If not, give it a try and observe what happens.

Quick Review

The alternative forms of assessment that we have discussed are all dynamic in that they seek particular behaviors and encourage thinking on the higher levels of Bloom's *Taxonomy of Educational Objectives* (1956). In fact, the approaches described here give assessment a much different character than the paper-and-pencil, selected-response approach that has become so pervasive. We have emphasized throughout this book that science education in your classroom should exemplify what scientists do rather than what scientists did. These alternative forms of assessment continue that theme by allowing your assessment techniques to focus on the doing of science as well.

AUTHENTIC ASSESSMENT USING PORTFOLIOS

Authentic assessment, a phrase used to mean a collection of alternative assessment strategies, is an important principle in the belief of newer approaches to assessment. The idea is that multiple sources of information about each student lends more validity to the process of student assessment. Portfolios are the most familiar form of authentic assessment in that they combine various forms of alternative assessments and so contain multiple and diverse examples of student-generated products.

The Nature of Portfolios

Portfolios are representative collections of work samples over a given period of time that allow for reflection. While tests provide a brief look at student achievement at a particular moment, portfolios allow for a lingering view of student achievement by showing diversity of tasks and personal growth. Portfolios can be used to determine students' achievement and progress over a given period of time, whether that is a six- or nine-week grading period, a semester, or several years of schooling. In addition, they can include samples across various subject areas. Not only do the portfolios indicate students' skills and knowledge, they also tell teachers something about how those students organize and communicate information.

FIGURE 13.4 Assumptions about portfolios (from De Fina, 1992).

- Portfolios are systematic, purposeful, and meaningful collections of students' works in one or more subjects.

- Students of any age can learn not only to select pieces to be placed into their portfolios but also to establish criteria for selection.

- Portfolios should be ongoing so that they show student effort, progress, and achievement over a period of time.

- In all cases, portfolios should reflect the actual day-to-day learning activities of students.

- Portfolio collections may include input by teachers, parents, administrators, and peers.

- Portfolios may contain several compartments or subfolders.

- Selected works in portfolios may be in a variety of media and may be multidimensional.

Portfolios, by definition and intent, vary greatly as they reflect individual application of the process. However, the assumptions about portfolios made by De Fina (1992) in Figure 13.4 are helpful in understanding portfolio assessment in a general sense.

In some cases, teachers select entries that go into the portfolios. More often, teachers give students guidance related to the selection of materials that go into the portfolios and the students select the entries. The purpose of the portfolio will greatly influence the actual entries.

The Purpose of Portfolios

Without an identified purpose, a portfolio is a meaningless collection of work samples. And they are much too time–consuming to be done without a purpose. Since the purpose varies greatly from one setting to another, the nature of the portfolios varies as well. For example, when portfolios are used to celebrate students' accomplishments, they include a variety of elements but typically are composed of the individual's favorite work samples. The portfolio then takes on the appearance of a keepsake. If the portfolios are used to see how students accomplish a project, then evidence of the entire process from predictions and drafts to revisions, final versions, and complete displays will be included. If large-scale assessment is the focus, then standardized work samples will be required. The intent is not to create a system for storing papers, but to provide the opportunity to assemble a meaningful compendium of one's work.

The Value of Portfolios

You may wish to utilize portfolios for any one of the purposes described above. In such situations, the portfolio serves, to one degree or another, as a display of work accomplished. Documenting individual student growth is an important consideration for using portfolios, because they are very useful when communicating student progress with parents. We suggest the use of portfolios in another way, one that makes the portfolio itself a part of your assessment process by letting the student do something with the materials placed in the portfolio. Providing your students with opportunities to reflect on their own work and self-evaluate progress is a tremendously valuable lifelong skill. Portfolios are particularly well suited to providing this experience because they allow the student to see an organized representation of their work over time. Nowhere else in the traditional assessment approaches do children learn to evaluate their own progress. Not only does self-evaluation give each child the opportunity to recognize personal strengths and weaknesses, but the child also learns to appreciate the relationship between the amount of time and effort put forth and the quality of the results. The whole sense of ownership of the learning process becomes real for learners when they have opportunities to evaluate their own efforts. Though we do not diminish the value of a portfolio as documentation, we believe that its greatest value is found when used as a vehicle for reflecting on what has been done.

Components for Science Portfolios

Though portfolios are often used to examine student achievement in an interdisciplinary fashion, they can indeed be subject specific. Figure 13.5 lists various types of documentation related to science that could serve as evidence appropriate for portfolios that are specific either to student achievement in science or to science as one portion of the whole curriculum.

An effective portfolio design in science should reflect the conceptualization of science as a combination of scientific process, content, and attitude. The process of science has been described in terms of the science process skills (e.g., observing, predicting, classifying) and various forms of scientific investigation (e.g., documenting, inventing, experimenting). The content of science is described as the information gained through investigation and research. It can take the form of answers to questions or of new questions that continue the search. A scientific attitude is the driving force, the inquisitive nature, which generates investigation and subsequently the acquisition of new information. Elements of this category could come through most strongly in the reflection/evaluation component of the portfolio. The portfolio should include an appropriate balance of process, content, and attitude elements, and that balance should be reflective of the instructional setting. How to determine that balance is the next question to answer.

If, for instance, you are teaching first or second grade where great emphasis and instructional time (perhaps 50 percent) is

FIGURE 13.5 Types of evidence appropriate for science portfolios.

POSSIBLE COMPONENTS FOR SCIENCE PORTFOLIOS

- Investigation reports
- Inventions and models
- Observational checklists completed by students and teachers
- Inquiry records
- Reports of group work
- Logs or journals
- Tests
- Individual questions and wonderings
- Reflection and self-evaluation (on the portfolio as a whole, on each section, or on both)

placed on activities that foster the science process skills and investigations, then the largest portion of portfolio entries ought to also focus on these skills. Perhaps 50 percent of the work samples will relate to skills, while 20 percent focus on newly acquired information and another 30 percent on demonstrating a positive scientific attitude. If you are teaching fifth- or sixth-graders and the instructional time is distributed as 40 percent for process, 40 percent for new information, and 20 percent for attitude, then the balance of the portfolio should have similar representation.

In this instance, the portfolio criteria would likely include evidence of (1) each form of investigation conducted in this given time period, (e.g., prediction testing, documenting, and experiment); (2) construction of two different types of graphs; (3) a minimum of one drawing showing multistage classification; (4) one inquiry project report; (5) a minimum of one personal wondering or question that you want to pursue next grading period; and (6) the student's own evaluation of the materials in the portfolio

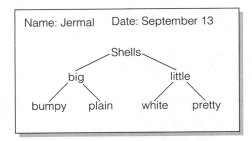

FIGURE 13.6 Jermal's first classification scheme.

and some conclusion as to what it all represents in terms of change, growth, or achievement. The first three criteria concentrate on process, one examines newly acquired information, and two reflect a kind of scientific attitude the teacher wants to foster. A portfolio is a vehicle for collecting materials and products that reflect student performance, skills, and attitudes. If the portfolio itself is considered a product, specific criteria will need to be generated for it.

Some student work will occur in written form, such as students' reports, journal entries, personal wonderings, and tests. The collection may also include photographs and/or drawings of the students' projects, as in the case of inventions and models. The collection might include objects such as videotapes, in which case the portfolio takes on various dimensions. It will be important to decide how projects can best be represented: by photographs and drawings or by pieces of paper indicating where the project is stored. In any case, the notion of portfolio should not be limited to "a folder."

The criteria used to assess the portfolio must match the purpose of the task. The criteria for a science portfolio, as discussed earlier, would reflect the definition of science. If the intent within science is to illustrate an individual student's ability to accomplish certain types of investigations, such as product testing, inventing, or prediction testing, then the child should be encouraged to include best evidence of those tasks.

Portfolio as Evidence of Cognitive Gain

A truly outstanding advantage of portfolios is not for assessment in its own right, or even as a means of sampling student work, but to evidence the most significant student accomplishment—individual gains in cognitive growth. Portfolios are an excellent way to show how much improvement a child has made over a given period of time. Samples of student work from September can be compared with similar work in January and May. Relevant progress will be apparent and available for reflection on the part of the child, the teacher, and the parents or other interested parties. For example, the two drawings in Figures 13.6 and 13.7, which represent classification systems constructed by Jermal, a second-grader, show considerable differences in complexity and attention to detail.

In September, when just learning to diagram his own classification scheme, he was satisfied with four separate groups of shells. After seven months, he classified the same set of shells. This time Jermal created eleven separate groups. He used quantitative as well as qualitative categories and the criteria included size, color, texture. When asked what he thought about his two classification papers, he responded, "Well, I know more differences. This time I studied the shells real close. I even smelled them, but I didn't know how to say that part."

ACTIVITY 13.3

Designing a Portfolio

Using the activities, projects, and tests that you have completed, design a portfolio representing your work in this course. Write out your plan as if it were to be distributed to students just beginning the course. Be sure that your design indicates the following:

- The balance of process, content, and attitude that is expected.

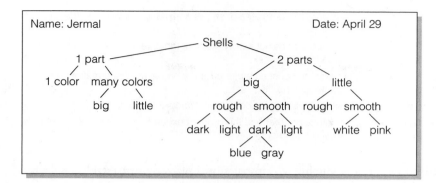

FIGURE 13.7 Jermal's advanced classification scheme.

- The specific elements that will be required.
- How reflection/self-evaluation will be a part of the portfolio.
- If the portfolio were to account for a portion of your grade in the course, how much emphasis should it receive?

Construct your portfolio and share it with your classmates.

Quick Review

The nature of portfolios as an ongoing record of progress becomes evident. In order to demonstrate individual student gains, samples of work must be placed in the portfolios at regular intervals throughout the instructional period, for instance, on a monthly basis. Perhaps the most valuable guidelines are these: Communicate the purpose of the portfolios and the evaluation criteria to your students, and allow your students an active role in deciding what examples of their work should be placed in the portfolio.

SCORING RUBRICS

It now seems obvious that alternative assessment and portfolios become more meaningful when criteria for evaluation are established and communicated to students. In Kuhs's (1997) discussion of portfolio evalu-

ation and grading, she stresses the importance of rubrics by explaining it in this way: "The point is, that evaluation that involves more than a 'right answer' approach requires guidelines to govern scoring. If the criteria, or focus, of the evaluation are not specifically defined and made known to students, the teachers' subjectivity may be questioned" (p. 58). Scoring rubrics provide a means for teachers to know what they expect and for children to know what is expected of them. For each learner outcome, the rubric describes anticipated levels or standards of accomplishment. Once the rubric is generated, the teacher can compare each student's work sample to the rubric and determine a numerical score. The scoring rubric in Figure 13.8 is a modification of Price and Hein's (1994) General Scoring Rubric. It provides descriptions in terms so general that they would apply to most any project. From that example, you could develop more specific rubrics for your classroom situation. Though this example has five categories, you may want to give more weight to one category than to another. Based on your own instructional goals, you can establish point values that are appropriate. Again, be sure to communicate this to your students before the assignment is completed.

A more specific example may help to demonstrate the versatility of scoring rubrics. The children in Ms. Davis's class are conducting product tests, examining the effectiveness

FIGURE 13.8 General scoring rubric. (Adapted from Price & Hein, 1994)

Poor: The product was not completed or shows no evidence that the student comprehends the activity.

Inadequate: The product does not satisfy many of the criteria, contains errors, or does not accomplish the given task.

Fair: The product does not contain major errors or omit crucial information, and does meet some of the criteria.

Good: The product substantially or completely meets the criteria.

Outstanding: All criteria are met and the product exceeds expectations or includes additional, outstanding features.

of dish-washing liquids to determine which is best. When each child has completed the specific tests and determines his or her own dish-washing liquid preference, the class results can be tabulated on the board. A logical extension of the activity is to graph the data. In the past, Ms. Davis's students have worked on graphing skills. Since graphing is an appropriate way to analyze the data collected in product testing, she decided to ask each child to construct a graph that represents the results of the activity. So far, so good.

As the teacher, her responsibility is to then evaluate the student work. She needs to provide feedback to students on the quality of the work and whether or not it was done correctly. She also knows that there is not just one way of graphing the information. The assessment must allow for some flexibility but meet certain standards. So the question is, how will the teacher decide how well each child has done on the graphing?

"Standards" is the key word. First, the criteria appropriate for measuring the quality and accuracy of the work must be identified. (Sounds very similar to product testing, doesn't it?) Once the criteria are listed, statements that reflect degrees of quality and describe accuracy can be written. The scoring rubric that Ms. Davis felt would be appropriate for evaluating the graphing activity is given in Figure 13.9.

A scoring rubric assumes its greatest value when it is understood by the teacher and the students before the activity begins. The teacher can better define his or her own instructional plans by first establishing what will be considered important in terms of assessment. The students will be able to perform with much more focus if they know what is expected of them. It is often beneficial in this regard to involve the students in the design of the scoring rubric. Certainly this is not appropriate under all circumstances, but even young children can indicate what they feel to be important when given particular tasks. You can then indicate what you consider to be of greatest importance. Notice that this does not lead to a lowering of standards, but can in fact lead to raising standards. Consider the last time you were given input into establishing expectations on a college assignment. Did you or any of your classmates first look to find the "easiest" way out? What do you suppose would have happened with students who were raised to set realistic and challenging standards?

CONCLUSION

Being able to align the *curriculum* (expectations for student learning), *instruction* (experiences to facilitate acquisition of new skills and information), and *assessment* (the means for describing student progress) is what makes teaching science both an art and a science. The theory, instructional techniques, and assessment techniques described in this book specifically seek to accomplish such an alignment. They provide the means for making the learning of science an interactive and positive educational experience that capitalizes on the child's natural curiosity and the cognitive process of constructing knowledge.

While examining how children learn (chapter 4) and eliciting children's concepts (chapter 5), it becomes apparent that children do not always construct their understanding of events and phenomena as teachers intend. This idea is important to keep in mind while focusing on assessment. As teachers, we need to be aware that it is reasonable to expect differences to occur among a group of children as each one goes through the process of constructing and reconstructing personal knowledge. Remember, some children will not change personal explanations until the new information is considered plausible or personally meaningful. At the elementary level, teachers need to accept this as realistic and appropriate for young children. Some change has probably occurred even if it doesn't meet the teacher's desired level of understanding of the concept. And that is the purpose of assessment techniques, to find out how much change has occurred.

Assessment is something that many educators are reluctant to address because they find it difficult to make value judgments about someone's work and assign a grade to it. And it *is* often difficult to declare one set of values to be the correct one. Without assessment, however, there would be no way of describing all of the exciting cognitive changes that have occurred. With assessment, teachers can describe children's levels of understanding at the beginning of the school year and again at the end of the year. Assessment allows the teacher to collect evidence and describe the individual growth and progress of each child.

Another reason for reluctance of some educators to face the challenges of assessment is the conceptual block associated with traditional assessment. The typical concep-

FIGURE 13.9 Scoring rubric for graphing.

SCORING KEY FOR GRAPHING ACTIVITY

Criteria	Yes	No
Accurate display of data using bar graph:		
Correct label for both axes:		
Key is accurate:		
Title is relevant:		
Data is displayed at equal intervals on both axes:		

Points

Score equals the total number of checks under "Yes"

tualization has been that all tests were done with paper and pencil, and that these indirect measures of knowledge were most appropriate for students of all ages. Yet there often seemed to be an underlying dissatisfaction with the limited information obtained from such tests.

With the use of performance-based assessment, the conceptual block can be broken. The many alternative forms of assessment are consistent with the types of activities known to be most effective in instructional settings. No longer do we have to think of instruction as a time of activity and purposeful problem solving, and consider testing as being a totally different type of experience. Now the settings are very similar. While instruction allows for discovery, exploration, and clarification, assessment allows for application of newly acquired skills and information.

Effective alternative assessment techniques appropriately reflect the content required by the curriculum, though in a manner most suitable for a child in the process of constructing new knowledge. Under these conditions, the items that find their way into the child's portfolio provide a meaningful representation of that child's cognitive progress.

ACTIVITY 13.4

INFOTRAC COLLEGE EDITION INVESTIGATION:

Tracking the Current Trend

Accountability and assessment are two of the hottest topics in education. Traditional assessment techniques are in place and readily available, though many educators believe that they are not reflective of cognitive gain and are not good measures for school accountability initiatives. Alternative assessments such as portfolios provide a much clearer picture of cognitive gain but are difficult and time-consuming to evaluate. So what's a school district to do?

InfoTrac College Edition will not be able to resolve this issue for you, but it can provide the most up-to-date information on the status of the assessment debate. Put InfoTrac College Edition to work to find the current thinking on the use of techniques such as portfolios and performance-based assessments versus traditional assessment techniques.

Based on the information you find, what is your opinion? Share this information with your classmates, and see whether the consensus within your class is aligned with the current trend in education.

Section V   Resources

CHAPTER 14   A Compendium of Resources for Teaching Science

Chapter 14, "A Compendium of Resources for Teaching Science," is such a varied collection that we felt it deserved chapter status. The materials have been annotated to provide the reader with more than just a series of lists. Included are information about science goals, sample interview questions, and Internet Web sites of interest that were available at the time of publication. No doubt, more Web sites will be available by the time the reader puts this book to use; however, those listed here should provide some guidance.

Following Chapter 14 are the references and the index. The references are considered to be a valuable part of scholarly writing because they point the way for a reader to find more information. The works of many thinkers, authors, educators, and instructional designers are represented in a book such as this one. You may find numerous books and materials listed in the references that, as primary sources, would contribute greatly to the design and presentation of science lessons.

And finally, in addition to the resources listed here, you have InfoTrac College Edition. We have included InfoTrac College Edition investigations throughout the chapters of this book in order for you to practice searching databases and finding the most current information about the topics we have discussed. However, you need not confine your use of InfoTrac College Edition to the activities provided. Utilize this source of research and publication to answer as many questions as it possibly can as you consider the world of science, and more.

14 A Compendium of Resources for Teaching Science

The roads that lead to knowledge are as wondrous as that knowledge itself.

—Johannes Kepler

GOALS AND OBJECTIVES FOR SCIENCE AND ENVIRONMENTAL EDUCATION: A SAMPLER

Curriculum standards or frameworks for science for all fifty states can be found at this Web site:

http://putwest.boces.org:80/standards.html

The complete text of the National Research Council's 1996 National Science Education Standards can be found at

http://www.nap.edu/readingroom/books/nses/html/3.html

The complete text of the American Association for the Advancement of Science's 1993 Benchmarks for Science Literacy (Project 2061) can be found at

http://project2061.aaas.org/tools/benchol/bolframe.html

According to the North American Association for Environmental Education (NAAEE), 1997 Framework for Environmental Literacy (Legro, Bybee, & Simmons, 1997), students should acquire:

1. Knowledge of environmental processes and systems.
   - Earth as physical system
   - The living environment (e.g., diversity, interdependence, matter/energy flow)
   - Humans and their societies
2. Inquiry skills.
   - Willingness and ability to ask questions, speculate and hypothesize, seek information, and develop answers
   - Familiarity with basic modes of inquiry
   - Skills for gathering and organizing information
   - Ability to interpret and synthesize information and develop explanations

3. Skills for decision and action.
   - Ability to draw conclusions, develop solutions, make decisions, and participate in resolving environmental issues
   - Ability to consider implication of alternative course of action and arrive at own conclusions
   - Understand ideals, principles, and practices of citizenship in democracy

4. Personal responsibility.
   - Possess the motivation and empowerment to act on conclusions about what should be done to ensure environmental quality

MAJOR SCIENCE CURRICULUM REFORM PROJECTS

The major reform projects of the late 1980s and the 1990s include Project 2061 (AAAS, 1989, 1993), the Scope, Sequence, and Coordination of Secondary School Science Project of the National Science Teachers Association (1992), and the National Research Council's National Science Education Standards (1996). The main Project 2061 documents are Science for all Americans (1989) and Benchmarks for Science Literacy (1993). The NSTA project primarily concerned secondary science. The principal goal was to reform the traditional biology, chemistry, physics sequence in high school so that each science would be taught each year in high school. In the following sections are some of the major aspects of the National Science Education Standards, focusing particularly on the content standards for the K–8 years. The National Science Education Standards can be accessed on the Internet at http://www.nap.edu/readingroom/books/nses/html/3.html.

Guidelines for the National Science Education Standards

- All students must have the opportunity to learn the science as defined.
- With appropriate opportunities and experiences, all students can learn this science.
- The learning process should reflect the inquiry processes used by scientists.
- Learning is an active process and occurs best within a learning community.
- Focus should be on essential/fundamental knowledge and skills to allow for deep understanding and powerful thinking.
- Content, teaching, and assessment standards guide the central features of an education program.

Areas Addressed by the National Science Education Standards

- Content
- What all students should know or be able to do (the content standards are narrative criteria covering K–12 in spans of K–4, 5–8, 9–12)
- Teaching
- What teachers need to understand and do
- Assessment
- Characteristics of fair and accurate evaluations
- Science program
- The coordination of content, teaching, and assessment K–12
- Educational system
- Supporting a quality science program through policies and practices outside the classroom

The Eight Categories of the Content Standards

Science Content Standards are divided by grades K–4, 5–8, and 9–12.

1. Unifying Concepts and Processes in Science
2. Science as Inquiry
3. Physical Science
4. Life Science
5. Earth and Space Science
6. Science and Technology
7. Science in Personal and Social Perspectives
8. History and Nature of Science

Content Standards by Category

Unifying Concepts and Processes in Science

- Systems, order, and organization
- Evidence, models, and explanation
- Change, constancy, and measurement
- Evolution and equilibrium
- Form and function

Science as Inquiry
Levels K–4, 5–8, 9–12:

- Abilities necessary to do scientific inquiry
- Understanding about scientific inquiry

Physical Sciences
K–4:

- Properties of objects and materials
- Position and motion of objects
- Light, heat, electricity, and magnetism

5–8:

- Properties and changes of properties in matter

- Motions and forces
- Transfer of energy

Earth and Space Science
K–4:

- Properties of earth materials
- Objects in the sky
- Changes in earth and sky

5–8:

- Structure of the earth system
- Earth's history
- Earth in the solar system

Life Science
K–4:

- Characteristics of organisms
- Life cycles of organisms
- Organisms and environments

5–8:

- Structure and function in living systems
- Reproduction and heredity
- Regulation and behavior
- Populations and ecosystems
- Diversity and adaptations of organisms

Science and Technology
K–4:

- Abilities to distinguish between natural objects and objects made by humans
- Abilities of technological design
- Understanding about science and technology

5–8 and 9–12:

- Abilities of technological design
- Understanding about science and technology

Science in Personal and Social Perspectives
K–4:

- Personal health
- Characteristics and changes in populations
- Types of resources
- Changes in environments
- Science and technology in local challenges

5–8:

- Personal health
- Populations, resources, environments
- Dynamics of populations
- Natural hazards
- Risks and benefits
- Science and technology in society

History and Nature of Science
K–4:

- Science as a human endeavor

5–8:

- Science as a human endeavor
- Nature of science
- History of science

SCIENCE TOPICS COMMON TO K–8 SCIENCE

Earth-Space Science

The Earth and Its Structure
Plate tectonics (earthquakes, volcanoes, mountains)

Kinds of rock   Minerals in rock

Age of rocks   Oceans

Forces that change
the earth

The Solar System
Origin and structure of the solar system

The sun (structure, energy)

The moon (origin and structure, phases, tides, eclipses)

The planets, comets, meteoroids

The Stars and the Universe
The stars (origin and evolution, types, distance, size, color, magnitude)

The constellations   The Milky Way

The universe   How stars and galaxies
are studied

The Air and Weather
The atmosphere (structure, composition)

Sun/air/water   Wind

Measuring   Water in the
weather   atmosphere

Forecasting   Air masses, systems,
weather   and fronts

Climate and   Severe weather
climate history   (thunderstorms,
hurricanes, tornadoes)

Energy in the Biosphere
Solar energy   The disposal of wastes

Nuclear fission   Biomass and other
and fusion   energy sources

Conservation of Soil
Erosion   Maintaining soil
fertility

Conservation of Water
Watersheds   Water table

Water quality

Conservation of Air
Pollution   Acid rain

The ozone hole   The greenhouse effect

Living Things

The Nature and Variety of Life
Where life is found

Cells and their structure

Meaning of "living" (adaptation, sensitivity, securing energy, growth, reproduction)

Organization and Method of Classification

Viruses	Kingdom Monera
Kingdom Protista	Kingdom Fungi
Kingdom Plantae	Kingdom Animalia

Mosses, Ferns, Seed Plants

Leaves	Stems
Roots	Flowers
Seeds	Seed dispersal

Kingdom Animalia

Sponges	Corals
Worms	Mollusks
Joint-legged invertebrates	Spiny-skinned animals
Vertebrates	Fish
Birds	Reptiles
Amphibians (frogs, newts, salamanders)	Mammals

The Human Body
The study of the body

Nutrition

Cells/tissues/organs/systems

Food and diet

Digestion and digestive structures

Respiration (mechanics of breathing, lung structures/air pathways/air sacs, smoking and health)

Circulation and material transport (heart, blood, excretion of body wastes)

The body framework and movement (bones, muscles, joints)

Body control (the nervous system, chemical control)

Heredity (sex determination, genes, DNA)

Reproduction (male and female anatomy, egg and sperm, fertilization, embryo development, the menstrual cycle)

Health and disease (germ theory of disease, vaccines/serums/antibiotics/other drugs, cancer, AIDS)

The History of Life
The changing earth   Records of past life

How life changes

The Eras of Earth
Precambrian (Cryptozoic) era (Life begins, life develops)

Paleozoic (Ancient Life) era (Age of fish, plants invade the land, coal forests, the first terrestrial animals, land vertebrates)

Mesozoic (Middle Life) era (Reptiles to dinosaurs to birds and mammals, mass extinctions)

Cenozoic (Recent Life) era (Age of mammals, human evolution)

Ecology, Energy, and the Environment
Spaceship Earth

The earth's environment over time

Ecology (food webs, pyramid of numbers, carrying capacity)

Biogeochemical Cycles in Nature

Cycles operating in the environment	Carbon, oxygen, nitrogen cycles
Water cycle	

Resources

Renewable resources	Nonrenewable resources
Population and the limits to growth	Conservation of forests
Conservation of wildlife	Conservation of wilderness

Causes and effects
of extinction

Conservation
of the urban
environment

Wetlands, prairies,
desert, forest

The environmental
movement and society

Matter and Energy

Molecules and Atoms

Dalton and the
Atomic Theory

The elements

Nuclear energy

Chemical changes (fire,
extinguishing fire)

The structure of the
atom

Heat

Sources of heat

Temperature

Changes of state

Heating buildings

Solar energy

The nature of heat

Measurement of heat

Insulation

Evaporation cools/
refrigeration

Heat movement
(conduction, convection, radiation)

Machines

Early machines

Friction

Simple machines (lever, pulley, wheel and
axle, gears, inclined plane, wedge, screw)

Magnetism and Electricity

Magnetism (natural and artificial magnets,
compass, magnetic fields, the earth as a
magnet)

Static electricity

Measuring electricity

Current electricity
(electric circuits, resistance)

Generating current electricity (Volta's discovery, generators, AC and DC)

Electromagnets

The electric motor

Electricity for heat and light

The telegraph and the telephone

Superconductors

Sound

What causes sound

Hearing

Speaking

Focusing sound

How sound travels (sound waves, the speed
of sound, bouncing sound—echos)

Characteristics of sound (loudness, pitch,
quality)

Sympathetic vibrations (entrainment)

Light

How light travels

Shadows

Mirrors

Lenses

What is light?

Sight

Light bends

The eye

The electromagnetic (EM) spectrum

Why the sky is blue, and What causes
rainbows

Flight and Space Travel

History of the space era

Aircraft control

How an airplane flies (resistance of the air,
Bernoulli's principle)

Jets

Rockets

Supersonic flight

Orbit

An Earth-moon or Earth-Mars trip

Life support in space (pressure, oxygen,
wastes, temperature, food, radiation,
acceleration, weightlessness)

Space stations and space colonization

(Adapted from Blough, 1990)

SAFETY IN THE CLASSROOM

Teacher's Liability

The teacher's liability falls under tort law, where negligence or breach of contract or trust results in another person or property being injured. A student generally acquires the status of an invitee, that is, no contractual basis exists for assumed risk on his or her part. The student also is assumed not to possess the knowledge of potential danger or appreciate potential risk.

Teacher responsibility is related to the legal concept of negligence, for example, in being negligent regarding instruction, supervision, or the upkeep of equipment and supplies. If there is no precedent or statute in a particular case, then actions or inactions of an individual are to be measured against what a hypothetical reasonably prudent individual would have done under the same circumstances. *A reasonable person is one who anticipates.*

First Aid

Excluding lifesaving measures, teachers may only stop bleeding and apply water (as to burns, acid spills).

Safety Glasses

Be aware that some children wear contact lenses. These can be dangerous if a chemical gets splashed into the eyes, because capillarity carries the irritant to the eye surface. If the chemical is an alkali, damage can be done within ten to thirty seconds. In general, whenever any chemicals are in use in any science activities, or where objects or liquids might fly into the air, children should wear safety glasses.

Science-Related General Safety Practices for Teachers

1. Check the federal, state, and local regulations related to school safety, as well as your school district's policies and procedures.
2. Check your classroom regularly to be sure that safety is being maintained. Equipment and materials should be properly stored. Hazardous materials should never be left in the classroom.
3. Before handling equipment and materials, become familiar with any possible hazards.
4. Be particularly cautious when using fire.
5. Be familiar with school fire regulations, evacuation procedures, and the location and use of the classroom fire extinguisher.
6. Know the school procedures for dealing with accidents.
7. At the start of the science activity, point out potential hazards and the precautions to be taken.
8. Limit the number of students working in a group to a number that can safely carry out the activity without creating confusion or an accident.
9. Plan sufficient time for children to perform activities. Cleanup and store equipment and materials properly after use.
10. Remind children never to taste or touch substances in the science classroom without first obtaining the teacher's specific permission.
11. Tell children to report accidents or injuries to you immediately, no matter how minor.
12. Tell children not to touch the face, mouth, eyes, or other parts of the body while working with plants, animals, or chemical substances, until they have washed their hands.

13. Whenever possible, substitute plastic for glassware in activities.

14. Hard glass test tubes should not be heated from the bottom: tip them slightly, but not toward a student.

15. Have a whisk broom and dustpan available for cleaning up.

16. Caution children not to drink from plasticware or glassware used in science activities.

17. Thermometers used in the elementary classroom should be filled with alcohol, not mercury.

18. Classroom doors must not be blocked, and flammable materials never should be stored near doors.

Suggestions for Working with Chemicals

1. Tell children not to mix chemicals "just to see what happens."

2. Tell children never to taste chemicals, and to wash their hands after use.

3. Children should not be allowed to mix acids and water.

4. Combustible materials should be kept in a locked metal cabinet.

5. Store chemicals under separate lock in a cool, dry place, but not in a refrigerator.

6. Store only small amounts of chemicals in the classroom. Any unused chemicals that could become unstable should be properly discarded.

Suggestions for Working with Electricity

1. Teach about safety related to the use of electricity in all everyday circumstances.

2. Caution children not to experiment with the electric current of their home circuits.

3. All extension cords should be in good condition. Connecting cords should be short, and plugged in at the closest outlet.

4. Tapwater conducts electricity. Children should dry their hands before touching electrical cords, switches, or appliances.

(Adapted from NSTA, nd, and NSTA, 1977)

SAMPLE INTERVIEW QUESTIONS

Day and Night

1. What is day?

2. What is night?

3. Where does the light of day come from?

4. Where does the darkness of night come from?

5. Why does a day end?

6. What makes day change to night?

7. What happens to the sun during the day?

8. What happens to the stars during the day?

9. What happens to the moon during the day?

10. Have you ever seen the moon at night? If yes, what did it look like? If no, why not?

11. Have you ever seen the moon during the day? If no, why not? If yes, what did it look like?

12. Is the moon always the same shape? If yes, why? If no, why does the moon's shape change?

13. If you were on the moon and looked up at the sky during the day, what would the sky look like?

14. If you were on the moon and looked up at the sky during the night, what would the sky look like?

Sound

For this interview you will need two glass bottles (soft drink bottles) partially filled with water. One bottle needs to have noticeably more water than the other bottle.

1. What is sound?

2. Where does sound come from?

3. How does sound travel?

4. Does sound travel through air? How or why not?

5. Does sound travel through water? How or why not?

6. Does sound travel through wood? How or why not?

7. How is it that you can hear noise from one room while you are in another room?

8. (Point to the bottle with the small amount of water.) If you were to blow air across the top of the bottle, would it make a higher or lower sound than the other bottle? Why?

9. (Point to the bottle with the larger amount of water.) If you were to tap the bottle with an object, would it make a sound? Why? or why not?

10. (Point to the bottle with the larger amount of water.) If you were to tap the bottle with an object, would it make a higher or lower sound than the other bottle? Why?

11. Why can you not hear the sounds being broadcast from a radio station unless you have a radio turned on?

Shadows

For this interview you will need a rod-shaped object. A wooden dowel works very well. An unused piece of chalk will also work.

1. What can you tell me about shadows?

2. Where does a shadow come from?

3. Can you make a shadow disappear? How or why not?

4. Can you make a shadow appear where you want it? How or why not?

5. Can you make your own shadow smaller? How or why not?

6. Can you make your own shadow larger? How or why not?

7. What would the shadow of this object look like? (Show the child a rod.) Might the shadow be another shape? What would that shape be?

8. Can you make the shadow of this object smaller? How or why not?

9. Can you make the shadow of this object larger? How or why not?

10. What is the largest shadow you have ever seen?

Light

1. Does a candle make light? How or why not?

2. How far from the candle does the light go?

3. How is it that you can see the candlelight?

4. How is it that you can see the candle?

Repeat all five questions in the same sequence three times substituting "sun," "moon," and "flashlight" for the word "candle."

Seasons

1. What can you tell me about the seasons? Name them please.

2. Why are there different seasons? Is there a particular order for the seasons? What is the order? or, Why not?

3. How can you tell when it is winter?

4. Are there any other signs that suggest it is winter?

5. How can you tell when it is spring?

6. Are there any other signs that suggest it is spring?

7. How can you tell when it is summer?

8. Are there any other signs that suggest it is summer?

9. How can you tell when it is fall?

10. Are there any other signs that suggest it is fall?

11. What causes the seasons to change?

Note: This set of questions may need to be changed based on your local conditions. If you have rainy seasons and dry seasons, then the questions should reflect that situation.

Electricity

1. What is electricity?

2. Where does electricity come from?

3. How does electricity make a lightbulb light?

4. What happens inside the bulb?

5. What happens inside the wires?

6. How does a battery make electricity?

7. What is the difference between static electricity and current electricity?

8. What is the difference between parallel and series circuits?

9. Can you make electricity? How? or, Why not?

Magnetism

1. What is a magnet?

2. Where do magnets come from?

3. Can you make a magnet?

4. Is a penny attracted to a magnet? Why or why not?

   a dime?

   a nickel?

   aluminum foil?

   a juice can?

   a pencil?

   a paper clip?

5. Will a magnet attract an object if the object is in water?

6. Will a magnet attract an object if the object is in a cardboard box?

7. What is the difference between a temporary magnet and a permanent magnet?

8. Can you make a magnet with electricity? How? or, Why not?

9. Can you make electricity with a magnet? How? or, Why not?

10. Why is a magnet marked N and S?

11. If like poles repel each other, why does the "north" magnetic pole of a compass point to the North Pole of the earth?

PLANNING SCIENCE FIELD TRIPS

Field Trip Safety

Field trips are valuable in the science program. Successful field trips are well planned ahead of time. Educational objectives should be identified and matched to trip activities. When the study in the field is well organized, a few precautions can foster safety for all participants.

1. Teachers should never be complacent when children are in their care and should always be alert for the unexpected.

2. One or more additional responsible adults, known and approved by the school administration, should accompany the teacher on the trip.

3. Parent permission should be solicited and received before a student is allowed to go on a field trip.

4. A list of appropriate clothing to be worn and the necessary equipment or

supplies to be taken on the trip should be sent home with each participant.

5. To prevent mites and ticks, plant poisoning, or scratches, participants should wear clothing that covers legs and arms.

6. First-aid kits should be carried on the trip. Periodically check the kit to see that it contains the essential first-aid items.

7. No trip should be taken to any body of water unless an adult in the group is familiar with rules of water safety as described in first-aid handbooks or the American Red Cross Senior Lifesaving manual.

8. If the trip is near or in the water of a stream, river, lake, or ocean, participants should be taught to recognize any dangerous aquatic or marine plants and animals common to the area.

9. If wading in the water is part of the field experience, the buddy system should be used and life jackets should be available.

10. Trips to industrial or construction sites and laboratories must be well supervised. An official plant representative should be present.

11. When in the field, children should be taught never to pick any unknown wildflowers, seeds, berries, or cultivated plants.

Toxic Plants

The following are some specific examples of toxic (poisonous) plants. *This list is only partial;* teachers should become aware of toxic plants of the field trip locality.

Plants Poisonous to the Touch

Poison ivy (often found on school grounds)

Poison oak

Poison sumac

Plants Poisonous When Eaten

Belladonna	Wake robin
Henbane	Water hemlock
Pokeweed	Tansy
Foxglove	Indian tobacco
Jimson weed	Aconite
Many fungi (mushrooms)	

Plants with Toxic Saps

Oleander	Poinsettia and other
Trumpet vine	*Euphorbia*

Note: Many common house plants also are toxic.

(Hardin and Arena, 1977)

Materials and Supplies for an Overnight Camping Experience

Necessary Items

Daily change of underwear	Daily change of socks
Pajamas	Walking shoes
Sneakers	Raincoat
Hat or hood	Waterproof boots
2 warm trousers or jeans	Shorts (seasonal)
Jacket (seasonal)	Heavy sweater/ sweatshirt
Warm shirts	Lights
1 laundry bag	1 washcloth
Tissues	Soap
Comb or brush	Toothbrush & toothpaste
Writing materials	Clipboard or notebook
2 pencils	

Suggested Options

Gloves (needed in cold weather)	Stamps, stationery, envelopes
Canteen	Lip gloss

Slippers

Reading materials

Camera & film (should be labeled with child's name)

Suggested Winter Weather Additions

Winter boots (insulated, waterproof)	2 pair warm mittens
Scarf for face	Lip gloss
Winter jacket or parka	2 extra pairs wool or warm socks
Warm ski hat (must cover ears)	

Suggested Prohibitions

Radio or tape player	Hair dryer/ curling irons
Portable TV	Knives
Candy or gum	Snack food
Fireworks	Electronic games
Matches	

The weather may vary, extremes are always possible. Children should be prepared for inclement weather. Many of the activities are out-of-doors even in rainy or chilly weather. Rain gear and rubber boots are required for spring and fall, and a warm coat, hat and mittens are recommended. During the winter, essential items include warm boots, extra socks, two pairs of mittens or gloves, and a hat.

USEFUL RECIPES AND FORMULAS

Sterilizer for Goggles

Pour one-half cup chlorine bleach in a pail (5 gallons) of water. Dip the goggles and dry.

Regular Cleaning Solution

Mix 2 oz. trisodium phosphate and 1 oz. sodium oleate in one pint distilled water. Soak apparatus in a warm solution ten to fifteen minutes, then brush with stiff brush. The chemicals are available from a paint supply store.

Goop

Keep goop in a well-sealed jar or can. Goop can be refreshed by adding water. (*Caution:* will stain wood and fabrics.) This recipe makes about 1½ cups.

½ tsp. Borax detergent (soaps and detergents section in supermarkets)

¼ cup water	4 oz. white craft glue
¼ cup cornstarch	2 tsp. food coloring (optional)

Dissolve the Borax in the water. Put the cornstarch in another bowl, and add the glue and stir until mixed. Add the Borax liquid, stirring constantly for about two minutes, even after the goop forms. Knead until no longer sticky.

Play Dough

Store play dough for up to six months in sealed plastic bags or lidded plastic containers in the refrigerator (return to room temperature before use). Food coloring can be mixed in as play dough is made. The work surface can be protected with wax paper. This recipe makes 2 cups:

1½ cups water	2 cups flour
2 tsp. food coloring	2 Tbsp. cooking oil
½ cup salt	4 Tbsp. cream of tartar

Combine water, coloring, and oil in a bowl. Put flour, salt, and cream of tartar in a saucepan. Pour the liquid mix into the saucepan, stirring and heating (medium heat) until a ball of dough forms (about five minutes). Cool for several minutes and knead until uniform.

Bubbles

Store in half-liter plastic soda bottles. Children can create bubble makers from a variety of materials, including a pair of glasses without lens, a length of wire or clothes hanger curved into a wand, or the tops cut off of any size plastic soda bottle. This recipe makes 2 cups:

1 cup dishwashing detergent

½ cup or less glycerine (available at pharmacies)

½ cup water

Combine all ingredients and mix. Pour into containers that have a large opening for dipping wands. Mix can also be poured on flat formica tabletops in thin puddles, then bubbles can be blown from soda straws. When these bubbles pop they leave a "footprint" that can be measured with a ruler or measuring tape. An investigation might be to compare various recipes or different detergents for the largest bubble. A math link would be to measure radius, diameter, and circumference.

If you can't get glycerine, clear corn syrup can be added to a water-detergent mix to give better bubbles. For a small quantity, mix ½ cup water to 3 tablespoons of liquid detergent and 1½ tablespoons of corn syrup, or try experimenting with proportions for the best mix.

Finger Paints

This recipe makes ¾ cup of each color:

2½ cups cold water

1 envelope unflavored gelatin

1 cup cornstarch

½ cup soap flakes

2 drops each of four colors of icing color paste (available at craft or baking supply stores)

Put ½ cup of the water into a bowl and sprinkle in the gelatin until dissolved. In a saucepan over medium heat, mix the cornstarch, soap flakes, and the rest of the water. Stir in the gelatin mixture and continue to stir until the mixture thickens. Prepare four containers for the different colors. Strain the warm mix equally into the containers. Let cool for about an hour, then fold in icing color paste for each container. Store in the refrigerator. *Note:* The materials are safe for children to use but should not be eaten.

NOTES ON ANIMALS IN THE CLASSROOM

Before bringing animals into the classroom, check your school district's policy to determine if there are any local regulations to be observed. Personnel at the local humane society or zoo are often very cooperative in helping teachers to provide a healthy environment for animals in the classroom. When animals are in the classroom, be sure children do not harm them. Mammals bite, scratch, and kick to protect themselves and their young. Dogs, cats, rabbits, guinea pigs, and similar pets should be handled with care and should not be disturbed when eating.

The following are some points to consider when planning rules to adopt for your classroom.

1. Do not allow students to bring wild animals, either alive or deceased, into the classroom. Snapping turtles, snakes, insects, or arachnids (spiders, ticks, mites) should be restricted or handled only by competent adults.

2. Provide proper living quarters for classroom animals. Keep the animal quarters clean and free from contamination. Be sure the cage can be securely closed. Plan ahead for animal care on weekends and holidays.

3. Obtain the classroom animals from a reputable supplier. Choose fish from tanks in which all the fish appear healthy.

4. When observing unfamiliar animals, don't permit children to touch or pick them up.

5. Children should be taught never to tease animals, or to put their fingers or objects through wire mesh cages. Children with animal bites or scratches should be taken to the school nurse.

6. Pick up rats, rabbits, hamsters, and mice by the scruff of the neck, placing a hand under the body to give support. Because the mother will be protective, if young animals are being handled, move the mother to another cage.

7. Use heavy gloves for handling animals, and have children wash their hands before and after they handle animals.

For additional information, see:

Humane Society of the United States. (nd). *HSUS guiding principles for use of animals in elementary and secondary education.* Washington, DC: Author.

Pratt-Butler, G.K. (nd). *How to care for living things in the classroom.* Revised edition. Arlington, VA: National Science Teachers Association.

RESOURCES FOR TEACHING SCIENCE

Books about Science Teaching Resources

National Science Resources Center. (1996). *Resources for teaching elementary school science.* Washington, DC: National Academy Press. (available from NSRC, 2101 Constitution Ave., N.W., Washington, DC 20418, ph. 1-800-624-6242)

National Science Resources Center. (1989). *Science for children.* Washington, DC: National Academy Press. (as above)

Periodicals

Journals and Magazines for Developing Content

Science	*New Scientist*
Scientific American	*Technology Review*
American Scientist	*High Technology*
Discover	*Popular Science*
Science News	*National Geographic*
Radical Science	*Smithsonian*
Natural History	*Science for the People*
Science Digest	*Nature*
Analog (science fiction)	*New England Journal of Medicine*
Issues in Science and Technology	*The Sciences* (New York Academy of Science)

Magazines That Address Issues in Science, Technology, and Society

The Conservationist	*E: The Environmental Magazine*
Environment	
The Earthwise Consumer	*The Practical Journal for the Environment*
Greenpeace	*National Wildlife*
Sierra	*Wilderness*
World Watch	*The Amicus Journal*
Backyard Composting	*Buzzworm: The Environmental Journal*
Audobon	*Environment*

Professional Journals for Theory and Research in Science Education

Australian Science Teachers Journal
Edith Cowan University
2 Bradford St.
Mount Lawley, W.A. 6050

Journal of Research in Science Teaching
John Wiley and Sons, Inc.
605 Third Ave.
New York, NY 10158

Journal of Science Teacher Education
219 Bluemont Hall
Kansas State University
Manhattan, Kansas 66506

Journal of Science Education and Technology
Karen C. Cohen, Editor
9 Cliff Road
Weston, MA 02193

Journal of Elementary Science Education
University of West Florida
11000 University Parkway
Bldg. 85, Rm 186
Pensacola, FL 32514-5753

Phi Delta Kappan
8th & Union, Box 789
Bloomington, IN 47401

Research in Middle Level Education
Judith Irvin, Center for the Study
of Middle Level Education
Florida State University NO
Dept. of Educational Leadership
113 Stone Bldg B-190
Tallahassee, FL 32306

School Science and Mathematics
P.O. Box 1614
Indiana University of Pennsylvania
Indiana, PA 15701

Science Education
John Wiley and Sons, Inc.
605 Third Ave.
New York, NY 10158

*Science Education International—Journal of the
International Council of Associations for Science
Education (ICASE)*
211 Henzlik Hall
University of Nebraska
Lincoln, NE 68588-0355

Periodicals for Teaching Ideas

Art to Zoo
Office of Elementary
and Secondary Education
Smithsonian Institution
Washington, DC 20560

Science Activities
Heldref Publications
1319 Eighteenth St., N.W.
Washington, DC 20036-1802

Science and Children (elementary—
a journal of the National Science
Teachers Association)
3140 N. Washington Blvd.
Arlington, VA 22201

Science Scope (middle grades—a journal of
the National Science Teachers Association)
3140 N. Washington Blvd.
Arlington, VA 22201

Astronomy Educator
Kalmbach Publishing Co.
1027 N. 7th St.
Milwaukee, WI 53233

Periodicals with Science Content for Children

Chickadee (ages 3–9)
Box 304
255 Great Arrow Ave.
Buffalo, NY 14207

Dinosaurs!
Atlas Editions Partworks
800-243-3484

Dolphin Log (ages 7–15)
Cousteau Society
930 W. 21 St.
Norfolk, VA 23517

Dragonfly
National Science Teachers Association
3140 No. Washington Blvd.
Arlington, VA 22201

National Geographic World (ages 8–14)
P.O. Box 2330
Washington, DC 20077

Odyssey
Cobblestone Publishing
30 Grove St.
Peterborough, NH 03458

Ranger Rick and Our Big Backyard
National Wildlife Federation
8925 Leesburg Pike
Vienna, VA 22184
703-790-4000
http://www.nwf.org/nwf/

Science Matters (ages 10–17)
National Science Gang
Cathedral Station
P. O. Box 1034
New York, NY 10025

Science Weekly (K–8)
Science Weekly, Inc.
Levels Pre-A, A, B, C, D, E, F
2141 Industrial Parkway, Suite 202
Silver Spring, MD 20904
Subscription Dept.: P.O. Box 70154
Washington, DC 20088-0154

WonderScience (grades 4–6)
American Chemical Society
P.O. Box 57136
Washington, DC 20037

Zoobooks
Wildlife Ed Ltd
9820 Willow Creek Rd., Suite 300
San Diego, CA 92131

Science Trade Books

Life Science

Aliki. (1989). *Digging up dinosaurs*. New York: HarperCollins.

Bittinger, G. (1990). *Learning and caring about our world*. Everett, WA: Warren Publishing House.

Branley, F.M. (1989). *What happened to the dinosaurs*. New York: Thomas Y. Crowell. (Primary level)

Carter, F. (1976). *The education of Little Tree*. Albuquerque: University of New Mexico Press.

Cherry, L. (1990). *The great kapok tree*. Gulliver Books.

Coulombs, D. (1984). *The seaside naturalist: A guide to study at the seashore*. New York: A Fireside Book.

Crichton, M. (1993). *Jurassic park: The junior novelization*. New York: Grosset & Dunlap.

Darling, L., and Darling, L. (1972). *Worms*. New York: William Morrow.

DeStefano, S. (1993). *Chico Mendes: Fight for the forest*. New York: Twenty-First Century Books. (Intermediate level)

Dunlap, J. (1993). *Aldo Leopold: Living with the land*. New York: Twenty-First Century Books. (Intermediate level)

Hogner, D.C. (1953). *Earthworms*. New York: Thomas Y. Crowell.

Mackie, D. (1987). *Undersea*. Burlington, Ontario: Hayes Publishing Ltd.

Morgan, N. (1992). *Pioneers of science: Louis Pasteur*. New York: The Bookwright Press. (Other titles in Pioneers of Science series: Archimedes, Alexander G. Bell, Karl Benz, Marie Curie, Thomas Edison, Albert Einstein, Michael Faraday, Galileo, G. Marconi, I. Newton, Leonardo da Vinci)

Nolan, D. (1990). *Dinosaur dreams*. New York: Macmillan.

Penner, L.R. (1991). *Dinosaur babies*. New York: Random House.

Pohrt, T. (1995). *Coyote goes walking*. Farrar, Straus & Giroux.

Teitelbaum, M. (1993). *Jurassic Park dinosaur hunter's guide: How to dig up fossils*. Racine, WI: Golden Book.

Physical Science

Amery, H. & Little, A. (1989). *The know how book of batteries and magnets*. London: Usborne Publishing, Ltd.

Ardley, N. (1983). *Exploring magnetism*. New York: Franklin Watts.

Ardley, N. (1991). *Light: The way it works*. New York: New Discovery Books.

Bender, L. (1991). *Eyewitness books: Invention.* London: Dorling Kindersley.

Berger, M. (1989). *Our atomic world.* New York: Franklin Watts.

Berger, M. (1989). *Switch on, switch off.* New York: Thomas Y. Crowell. (Primary level)

Catherall, E. (1990). *Exploring electricity.* Austin, TX: Stieck Vaugh Library.

Cash, T. & Taylor, B. (1989). *Fun with science: Sound.* New York: Warwick Press.

Challand, H.J. (1986). *Experiments with magnets.* Chicago, IL: Children's Press.

Chapman, P. (1991). *The Usborne young scientist: Electricity.* London: Usborne Publishing, Ltd.

Dempsey, M. (Ed.). (1985). *The children's first science encyclopedia.* New York: Exeter Books.

Epstein, S. & Epstein, B. (1977). *The first book of electricity.* New York: Franklin Watts.

Gibbons, G. (1989). *Catch the wind: All about kites.* New York: Little, Brown & Co.

Jonas, A. (1987). *Reflections.* New York: Greenwillow Books.

Kaufman, J. (1971). *What makes it go? What makes it work? What makes it fly? What makes it float?* New York: Golden Press.

Kent, A. & Ward, A. (1990). *Introduction to physics.* London: Usborne Publishing, Ltd.

Leon, G.L. (1983). *The electricity story: 2500 years of experiments and discoveries.* New York: Arco Publishing.

Levi, B.T. (1990). *Atoms: Building blocks of matter.* San Diego, CA: Locent Books.

Macaulay, D. (1988). *The way things work.* New York: Houghton Mifflin Company.

McPherson, J.G. (1981). *Pocket scientist: Fun with electronics.* London: Usborne Publishing, Ltd.

Michael, D. (1993). *Step by step, Making kites.* New York: Kingfisher.

Neugebauer, B. (1989). *The wonder of it: Exploring how the world works.* Redmond, WA: Exchange Press.

Pape, D.L. (1988). *The book of foolish machinery.* New York: Scholastic.

Taylor, B. (1991). *Sink or swim: The science of water.* New York: Random House.

Thomas Edison Foundation. (1988). *The Thomas Edison book of easy and incredible experiments.* New York: John Wiley & Sons.

VanCleave, J. (1991). *Astronomy for every kid: 101 easy experiments that really work.* New York: John Wiley & Sons.

Whyman, K. (1986). *Electricity and magnetism.* New York: Gloucester Press.

Williams, B. & Williams, B. (1990). *The Random House book of 1001 wonders of science.* New York: Random House.

Woodward, K. (1991). *Science with light and mirrors.* London: Usborne Publishing, Ltd.

Earth Science

Apfel, N. (1984). *Astronomy projects for young scientists.* New York: Arco Publishing.

Barrett, N. (1989). *Hurricanes and tornadoes.* New York: Franklin Watts.

Branley, F.M. (1962, 1986). *Air is all around you.* New York: Thomas Y. Crowell. (Primary level)

Buller, L. & Taylor, R. (1990). *More science in action: Earth and space.* Freeport, Long Island, NY: Marshall Cavendish Corporation.

Cochrain, J. (1987). *Air ecology.* New York: The Bookwright Press.

Cole, J. (1987). *The magic school bus inside the earth.* New York: Scholastic (see others in series).

Darling, D.J. (1984). *Comets, meteors, and asteroids: Rocks in space.* Minneapolis, MN: Dillon Press.

Eldredge, N.G. & Eldredge, D. (1989). *The fossil factory.* Reading, MA: Addison-Wesley.

Flint, D. (1991). *Weather and climate.* New York: Gloucester Press.

Gardner, R. (1988). *Projects in space science.* New York: Simon & Schuster.

Johnston, T. (1985). *Air, air everywhere.* Milwaukee, WI: Gareth Stevens Publishing.

Knapp, B. (1991). *Science in our world: Weather.* Danbury, CT: Grolier Educational Corp.

Knight, D.C. (1980). *The moons of our solar system.* New York: William Morrow.

Michael, G. (1991). *The sun.* Mankato, MN: Creative Education.

Moeschl, R. (1993). *Exploring the sky: Projects for beginning astronomers.* 2nd ed. Chicago: Chicago Review Press.

Nourse, A.E. (1982). *The giant planets.* New York: Franklin Watts.

Parker, S. (1992). *Galileo and the universe.* New York: HarperCollins.

Poth, C. (1988). *The air.* Englewood Cliffs, NJ: Silver Burdett Press.

Raymo, C. (1982). *365 starry nights: An introduction to astronomy for every night of the year.* New York: Simon & Schuster.

Roettger, D. (1992). *Weather watch.* New York: Fearon Teacher Aids (Simon & Schuster).

Rogers, D. (1989). *Weather.* New York: Marshall Cavendish Corporation.

Schaaf, F. (1990). *Seeing the sky: 100 projects, activities, and explorations in astronomy.* New York: John Wiley & Sons.

Simon, S. (1984). *Earth: Our planet in space.* New York: Four Winds Press.

Soutter-Perrot, A. (1993). *Water.* New York: American Education Publishing. (Primary level: Other books in the Brighter Child Series are *The earth* and *Air*)

Srogi, L. (1989). *Start collecting rocks and minerals.* Philadelphia, PA: Running Press.

Taylor, B. (1993). *Young discoverers: Rivers and oceans.* New York: Kingfisher Books. (Also in series: *Maps and mapping, Mountains and volcanoes, Weather and climate*)

Vita-Finzi, C. (1989). *Planet earth: A pop-up guide.* New York: Simon & Schuster.

Resources for Planning Outdoor Activities

Baker, A. & Baker, J. (1991). *Counting on a small planet: Activities for environmental mathematics.* Portsmouth, NH: Heinemann.

Comstock, A. (1967). *Handbook of nature study.* New York: Cornell University Press.

Perdue, P.K. & Vaszily, D.A. (1991). *City science.* Glenview, IL: Goodyear Books.

Roth, C.E., Cervoni, C., Wellnitz, T., & Arms, E. (1991). *Beyond the classroom: Explorations of schoolground and backyard.* Lincoln, MA: The Massachusetts Audubon Society.

Russell, H.R. (1973). *Ten-minute field trips.* Chicago: J. G. Ferguson Publishing Company.

Schmidt, V.E. and Rockcastle, V.N. (1982). *Teaching science with everyday things.* 2nd ed. New York: McGraw-Hill.

Shaffer, C. and Fielder, E. (1987). *City safaris.* San Francisco: Sierra Club Books.

Sisson, E.A. (1982). *Nature with children of all ages.* Englewood Cliffs, NJ: Prentice-Hall.

Western Regional Environmental Education Council. (1977, 1983). *Project learning tree and Project wild.* Boulder, CO: Author.

Suppliers of Equipment, Materials, and Media for Teaching Science

Addison-Wesley Publishing Co.
2725 Sand Hill Rd.
Menlo Park, CA 94025

Advanced Ideas
2902 San Pablo Ave.
Berkeley, CA 94702

Beacon Films
1560 Sherman Ave., Suite 100
Evanston, IL 60201

Biological Sciences Curriculum Study
(BSCS)
830 N. Teton St., Suite 405
Colorado Springs, CO 80903-4720

Broderbund Software
P.O. Box 12947
San Rafael, CA 94913-2947

Cambridge Development Laboratory, Inc.
214 Third Ave.
Waltham, MA 02154

Celestial Products
P.O. Box 801
Middleburg, VA 22117

Chancery Software
450-1122 Mainland St.
Vancouver, BC CANADA V6B 5l1

Charles E. Merrill Books
1300 Alum Creek Dr.
Columbus, OH 43216

Churchill Media
12210 Nebraska Ave.
Los Angeles, CA 90025-3600

Communication Skill Builders
3830 E. Bellevue
Box 42050
Tucson, AZ 85733

CONDUIT—University of Iowa
Oakdale Campus
Iowa City, IA 52242

Crowell Junior Books
Education Dept.
10 E. 53rd St.
New York, NY 10022

Davidson & Assoc.
3135 Kashiwa St.
Torrance, CA 90505

D. C. Heath and Co.
125 Spring St.
Lexington, MA 02173

Electronic Arts
1820 Gateway Dr.
San Mateo, CA 94404

Elementary Specialties
917 Hickory Lane
Mansfield, OH 44901-8105

Emerging Technology Consultants, Inc.
P.O. Box 120444
St. Paul, MN 55112

First Byte
3100 So. Harbor Blvd., Suite 150
Santa Ana, CA 92704

Encyclopedia Britannica Educational
Corporation
30 S. Michigan Ave.
Chicago, IL 60604

Great Wave Software
5353 Scotts Valley Dr.
Scotts Valley, CA 95066

Harcourt Brace Jovanovich
School Dept.
Orlando, FL 32887

HarperCollins Publishers
10 East 53rd St.
New York, NY 10022

Holt, Rinehart and Winston
1120 South Capital of Texas Hwy.
Austin, TX 78746-6487

IBM PC Software Dept.
One Culver Rd.
Dayton, NJ 08810

Insights Visual Productions, Inc.
P.O. Box 230644
Encinitas, CA 92023

Instructional Video
P.O. Box 21
Maumee, OH 43537

Kendall-Hunt Publishing Co.
4050 Westmark Dr.
P.O. Box 1840
Dubuque, IA 52004-1840

Kons Scientific Co., Inc.
P.O. Box 3
Germantown, WI 53022-0003

Learning Spectrum
1390 Westridge
Portola Valley, CA 94025

Macmillan/McGraw-Hill
4635 Hilton Corporate Dr.
Columbus, OH 43232-4163

MECC
3490 Lexington Ave. North
St. Paul, MN 55126

Microsoft Corporation
16011 NE 136th Way
Redmond, WA 98073-9717

Mimosa Publications
90 New Montgomery St., Suite 1414
San Francisco, CA 94105

Miramar Productions
200 Second Ave., W.
Seattle, WA 98119-4204

MMI Corp.
2950 Wyman Parkway
P.O. Box 19970
Baltimore, MD 21211

Modern Talking Picture Service, Inc.
5000 Park St. N.
St. Petersburg, FL 33709

National Geographic Society
Educational Services
11451 7th St., N.W.
Washington, DC 20036-4688

Optical Data Corporation
30 Technology Drive
Warren, NJ 07059

PC Globe, Inc.
2100 So. Rural Rd.
Tempe, AZ 85282

Peterson's Guides, Inc. (field guides for
wildflowers, rocks and minerals, fossils,
butterflies, insects, stars and constellations,
mammals, reptiles and amphibians, seashells, trees, mushrooms, etc.)
P.O. Box 2123
Princeton, NJ 08543-2123

Phoenix/BFA Films and Video, Inc.
2349 Chaffee Dr.
St. Louis, MO 63146

Raintree Publishers, Inc.
310 W. Wisconsin Ave.
Milwaukee, WI 53203

Rigby Education, Inc.
500 Coventry Lane
Crystal Lake, IL 60014

RightSoft, Inc.
4545 Samuel St.
Sarasota, FL 34233-9912

Scholastic, Inc.
730 Broadway
New York, NY 10003

Scholastic Software
2931 E. McCarthy St.
Jefferson City, MO 65102-9968

Scott, Foresman and Co.
1900 E. Lake Ave.
Glenview, IL 60025

Scott Resources
P.O. Box 2121 F
Ft. Collins, CO 80522

Charles Scribner's
866 Third Ave.
New York, NY 10022

Silver Burdett and Ginn
250 James St.
Morristown, NJ 07960-1918

Society for Visual Education
1345 Diversey Parkway
Chicago, IL 60614-1299

South-Western Publishing Co.
5101 Madison Rd.
Cincinnati, OH 45227

Springboard Software
7808 Creekridge Circle
Minneapolis, MN 55435

Sunburst Communications, Inc.
39 Washington Ave.
Pleasantville, NY 10570

Teacher Support Software
1035 NW 57th St.
Gainesville, FL 32605

Terrapin, Inc.
400 Riverside St.
Portland, ME 04103

The Learning Team
Armonk, New York
(914-273-2226)
Publishers of Mary Budd Rowe's 1987,
Science helper K−8.

The Planetary Society, Education Division
65 N. Catalina
Pasadena, CA 91106

Tom Snyder Productions
80 Coolidge Hill Rd.
Watertown, MA 02172

Troll Associates
100 Corporate Dr.
Mahwah, NJ 07430

The Wild Goose Co.
5181 S. 300 W.
Murray, UT 84107

Wings for Learning/Sunburst
1600 Green Hills Rd.
P.O. Box 660002
Scotts Valley, CA 95067-9908

Vernier Software (for probeware—
electronic measuring instruments that
transfer data directly into computer data
processing software)
2920 SW 89th St.
Portland, OR 97225

Videodiscovery, Inc.
1700 Westlake Ave. N., Suite 600
Seattle, WA 98109-3012

Science Activity Booksellers
Lawrence Hall of Science
Discovery Corner
University of California, Berkeley
Berkeley, CA 94720

National Science Teachers Association
3140 N. Washington Blvd.
Arlington, VA 22201

Science News Books
448 East 6400 South, Suite 125
Salt Lake City, UT 84017
1-800-552-4412
http://www.sciencenewsbooks.org/

Young Entomologists' Society, Inc.
1915 Peggy Place
Lansing, MI 48910

Equipment and Supply Catalog Companies

Carolina Biological
2700 York Rd.
Burlington, NC 27215
800-334-5551
http://www.carosci.com/

Central Scientific Co.
11222 Melrose Ave.
Franklin Park, IL 60648

Delta Education (materials kits and
general elementary/middle school
science equipment)
P.O. Box 915
Hudson, NH 03051-0915

Edmund Scientific
101 E. Gloucester Pike
Barrington, NJ 08007

Fisher Scientific
4901 W. LeMoyne St.
Chicago, IL 60651

Frey Scientific
905 Hickory Lane
Mansfield, OH 44905

Hubbard Scientific
P.O. Box 104
1946 Raymond Dr.
Northbrook, IL 60062
847-272-7810

Nasco
901 Janesville
Ft. Atkinson, WI 53538
800-558-9595

Sargent-Welch
7400 N. Linder Ave./Box 1026
Skokie, IL 60076
847-677-0560

Science Kit & Boreal Laboratories
777 East Park Dr.
Tonawanda, NY 14150
716-874-6020

Wards
800-962-2660

Native and Heirloom Seeds

Fox Hollow Herb and Heirloom Seed Co.
P.O. Box 148
McGrann, PA 16236

Harris Seeds at Moreton Farm
3670 Buffalo Rd.
Rochester, NY 14624

Pinetree Garden Seeds
Box 300
New Gloucester, ME 04260

Seeds of Change
P.O. Box 15700
Santa Fe, NM 87506

R.H. Shumway's
P.O. Box 1
Graniteville, SC 29829

Sites Related to Science Education on the World Wide Web

On-line Encyclopedias
Microsoft Encarta: http://encarta.msn.com

IBM World Book:
http://www.worldbook.com

Grolier Multimedia Encyclopedia:
http://www.grolier.com

Britannica Online: http://www.eb.com

Compton's Interactive Encyclopedia:
http://www.comptons.com

A Useful Search Tool—The Argus
Clearinghouse
An excellent meta-directory, it lists only
guides and directories, not content sites
themselves. This directory includes notes
about scope of each topic area and is supplemented by a general search utility:
http://www.clearinghouse.net/

Another search engine is SavvySearch—
conduct keyword Net searches using
nineteen search engines simultaneously
(via Colorado State U):
http://guaraldi.cs.colostate.edu:2000/

Science Education Associations Homepages
The National Science Teachers Association
(NSTA)—the major national organization
of science teachers at all levels: http://
www.nsta.org

For NSTA's position on teaching evolution,
access: http://www.nsta.org/handbook/
evolve.htm

The NEA homepage—many education
links: http://www.nea.org/

Research and Resource Sites
Education Resource Information Center
(ERIC)—Huge clearinghouse of a variety
of educational support services, information
networks, and publishers of materials; one
component, "AskERIC," is a service that
contains a question and answer link plus
lesson plans in a virtual library:
   http://www.aspensys.com/eric

The Library of Congress—Web site includes an excellent educator guide and index for using primary sources; has suggestions for class activities using primary
sources.
   http://rs6.loc.gov/ammem/ndlpedu/
primary.html

On-line Educator—links to teachers, resources, informative on-line magazine.
http://www.ole.net/ole/

Middle School Resource Guide—Complete text of the National Academy Press publication, Resources for teaching middle school science:
http://www.nap.edu/readingroom/

The National Archives and Records—Useful for primary source material:
http://www.nara.gov

Ideas for student research—A resource with links for topics, ideas, and how-to for developing a research project:
http://www.researchpaper.com

NOVA Online—Teachers—A starting point for lesson plans and scientific activities. Topics include animals, the human body, ancient cultures, space, earth, physics, and an odds and ends compendium. The Hot Science section provides many activities. Lesson Ideas and Teacher's Exchange allow teachers to share concepts and lesson plans:
http://www.pbs.org/wgbh/nova/teachers

FDA Kids Homepage—The U.S. Food and Drug Administration's Kids Homepage includes Yorick, a skeleton model that allows users to see the various medical devices and implants that can replace real body parts. Included are a glass eye, a silicon cochlear implant, a hip and a knee, etc.:
http://www.fda.gov/oc/opacom/kids/

Environmental education resources: EE-Link—Maintained by the National Consortium for Environmental Education and Training; hot links include classroom resources, organizations to contact, regional information, and an education directory:
http://www.nceet.snre.umich.edu/

Chem4Kids—An expansive Web site with resources on matter, atoms, elements, reactions, the math in chemistry, as well as a glossary and a quiz section. Written for students, includes clear definitions and fun graphics:
http://www.chem4kids.com

The Animal Diversity Web—A listing of Kingdom Animalia to the level of orders, with details of North American species. Many images and some photos of skulls:
http://www.oit.itd.umich.edu/bio108/

Physical Science—Chem 101 Home—Good for background on content, has some experiments and videos. Recommend the low graphic version:
http://tqd.advanced.org/3310/

News about science—The AAAS calls this site "your global gateway to science, medicine and technology news." Weekly updates and media and journal links:
http://www.eurekalert.org/

Athena Earth and Space Science—Focuses on the use of real-time data, activities include real-time changes for earthquakes, storms, and volcanoes. Activities have teacher's guide, activity sheets, and Internet links to remote-sensed data:
http://athena.wednet.edu

The Charlotte Science Resource Pages—Designed to assist teachers "engaged in teaching curriculum-based science topics to K–7 students." Modules include Energy Sciences, Forest Ecology, and Human Environments:
http://tqd.advanced.org/3310/

Middle School Science Teachers—Teacher Charlene Hoover has gathered a wide assortment of resources. The "Ready to Use Lesson Plans" may be very helpful:
http://www.geocities.com/CapeCanaveral/Launchpad/6576/

Earth First! On-line environmental education magazine—Environmental information, articles, and opinions:
http://www.envirolink.org/orgs/ef/

CARE—Information about food and international programs to relieve hunger. Click on "Programs and Regions" to get facts about countries:
    http://www.care.org

United Nations Food and Agriculture Organization (FAO)—This site has great pictures in the "PhotoFile":
    http://www.fao.org/

Zero Population Growth—Information on workshops, population-related classroom activities:
    http://www.zpg.org

Astronomical Society of the Pacific—Educators are eligible for a free subscription to *The Universe in the Classroom* quarterly newsletter. Fill out the subscription form on the Web site:
    http://www.aspsky.org

College chemistry on-line, from Brown University—Labs, problem sets, and twenty lectures all for the taking; there is even a question-and-answer line:
    http://www.chem.brown.edu/chem31/

HyperDoc—U.S. Library of Medicine—Health and medical education resource; access to The Visible Man (a sampler of fresh cryosections and CAT scans):
    http://www.nlm.nih.gov/

Hubble Space Telescope Project—Has a teachers' lounge, images to browse, and a project for children to do research on the telescope:
    http://quest.arc.nasa.gov/livefrom/hst.html

Institute for Academic Technology at UNC-Chapel Hill—Interactive education web, resources for using technology in education:
    http://www.iat.unc.edu/

Current sites from University of California, Berkeley—Stock Market game simulation, also on-line journal about technology; can access articles and search back issues by topic:

    http://www.ncsa.uiuc.edu/edu/RSE/RSEyellow/gnb.html

American Chemical Society—Plenty of links for resources for teaching physical science:
    http://www.acs.org/

U.S. Census Bureau—Up-to-the-minute population data and more; check out the "popclock":
    http://www.census.gov/

Ishmael Homepage—Eco-philosophy:
    http://www.ishmael.com/

Massachusetts Institute of Technology Web site includes a database of information on American inventions and discoveries:
    http://web.mit.edu/invent/

More MIT—Linked to this site is a hot list of science sites for children:
    http://web.mit.edu/afs/athena.mit.edu/org/i/invent/www/kids_list.html

Healthweb—Health and medicine, lists health science resources:
    http://www.ghsl.nwu.edu/healthweb/

Northwestern University—References and directories of all kinds, e.g., ZIP codes, AREA codes, the Periodic Table, etc.:
    http://www.nwu.edu/world/desk-reference.html

Monterey Bay Aquarium Research Institute—Oceanography; research and engineering; images of the ocean; sounds of dolphins, fish, or whales; also lots of marine science data:
    http://www.mbari.org/

Rainforest Action Network—Environmental education projects and rain forest information:
    http://www.igc.apc.org/ran/./

Kidscom—For kids ages 4–15, "a communication playground for kids"; links to sites for children, site of the month, etc.:
    http://www.kidscom.com/index1.html?

PBS Online—Links to the Web of Life, NOVA, Scientific American Frontiers, Nature, Bill Nye, Newton's Apple, National Geographic, the Magic School Bus, etc.:
http://www.pbs.org/

Geological Sciences Department, University of Manitoba, Canada—Links to geosciences information:
http://www.umanitoba.ca/geosci/gslf.html

National Aeronautics and Space Administration (NASA)—NASA Education Homepage:
http://www.hq.nasa.gov/education

NASA's K–12 Internet Initiative—Programs, materials, and opportunities for teachers and students to use NASA resources as learning tools to explore the Net, and lots of links to space science information, using the Net in school, NASA on-line resources, schools on-line, etc.:
http://quest.arc.nasa.gov/

NASA Spacelink—Current and historical information related to aeronautics and space research:
http://spacelink.nasa.gov

Another NASA site—The Observatorium, NASA's public site for space data:
http://www.rspac.ivv.nasa.gov/

National Teachers Enhancement Network—Courses on-line, resources, connections:
http://www.montana.edu.nten

National Wildlife Foundation—Links to kids' sites, links to issues and actions:
http://www.nwf.org/

U.S. Fish and Wildlife Service:
http://www.fws.gov/

National Oceanic and Atmospheric Administration (NOAA) Office of Oceanic and Atmospheric Research (OAR)—Series of on-line activities for middle school, using current and archived global data:
http://www.oar.noaa.gov/education/

Project WILD:
http://eelink.umich.edu/wild/wildhome.html

KIE Network (via University of California, Berkeley)—Science in the curriculum; classroom projects and activities; collections of scientific evidence; download software; contact other teachers, students, scientists; links to other education sites:
http://www.kie.berkeley.edu/KIE.html

National Geographic—Lots of pictures and articles:
http://www.nationalgeographic.com

Access Excellence—Has lesson plans for biology teachers; useful background:
http://www.gene.com/ae/

USA Today—Lesson plans for using news in the classroom and a reporter ready for student interaction:
http://www.usatoday.com/classlin/clfront.htm

Cockroach World—Interesting site many kids will love:
http://www.nj.com/yucky/roaches/index.html

Al Bodzin's Homepage—Lots of good links and pointers for science teachers K–12:
http://www4.ncsu.edu/unity/users/a/ambodzin/public/home.htm

The Why Files—This NSF site attempts to explain the science behind current events in the news:
http://whyfiles.news.wisc.edu/index.html

Kids World 2000—Has references for zoos and aquariums across the United States, and more:
http://www.now2000.com/bigkidnetwork/zoos.html#zoos

B.J. Pinchbeck's Homework Helper—Lots of links and resources for all curriculum areas:
http://tristate.pgh.net/~pinch13/index.html#i

Science activities on-line—Also a joke of the day:
> http://north.pacificnet.net/~mandel/Science.html

Discover Magazine Homepage:
> http://www.discover.com

Science and the Environment—Electronic news summary magazine:
> http://www.voyagepub.com/publish/

Earth Viewer—Map of Earth, views of sun, moon, planets, interactive orrery, lots of astronomy links:
> http://www.fourmilab.ch/earthview/vplanet.html

Annenberg Guide to Math and Science Reform—Links to model programs, grants:
> http://www.learner.org/k12/The_Guide/

Electronic Elementary Magazine—Highlights activities of elementary kids around the world; ideas for projects, activities; lots of links:
> http://www.inform.umd.edu/MDK-12/homepers/emag

Reinventing Schools—The Technology Is Now (via National Academy of Sciences):
> http://www.nas.edu/nap/online/techgap/welcome.html

"Thomas"—Legislative information (good for STS projects):
> http://thomas.loc.gov/

Science and Math (Minnesota schools)—Good links to resources for teaching:
> http://www.scimathmn.org/

Concord Consortium—Educational technology:
> http://www.concord.org/

Uppsala Astronomical Observatory—Good astronomy resource:
> http://www.astro.uu.se/

Louisiana Energy and Environment Center—Resources, environmental education activities:
> http://www.leeric.lsu.edu/

Earth Island Institute—Information on the environment, good source of STS issues for discussion for the middle grades:
> http://www.earthisland.org

Materials and Supplies Commonly Used in Teaching Science

aluminum foil	funnels (small and large)
aquarium	
baby food jars	glue
bags (paper, plastic)	hotplate
baking soda	iron filings
balances	lenses
balloons	magnets
balls	magnifiers/hand lenses
barometer and wind vane	
	masking tape
batteries	matches or lighter (keep secure)
buttons	
candles (birthday candles and table size)	measuring cups (metric and customary)
cellophane tape	mechanical toys (e.g., tops, toy cars, etc.)
clothespins	
coat hangers	medicine droppers
compasses	meter sticks
construction paper	metric weights
containers	microscopes
copper wire	mirrors
cotton balls	modeling clay
craft sticks	multipurpose small animal cage
dowel rods	
egg cartons	paper cups
extension cords	paper towels
film canisters	paraffin wax
flashlight	pill bottles
food coloring	pipe cleaners

plastic spoons and knives

plastic wrap

pulleys

rock mineral specimens

rubber bands

rulers (metric)

salt

sand

sandpaper

saw, hammer, screwdriver, and pliers

scissors

seeds (such as radish)

shoe boxes

small bulbs, flashlight size

sponges

steel wool

straws and plastic tubing

string, twine, and rope

Styrofoam cups

sugar

thermometers (metric)

tongs

toothpicks

tweezers

vinegar

wax paper

Miscellaneous Resources

Professional Associations

National Science Teachers Association
3140 N. Washington Blvd.
Arlington, VA 22201

National Association of Geology Teachers
P.O. Box 368
Lawrence, KS 66044

American Society for Aerospace Education
821 15th St., N.W., Suite 432
Washington, DC 20005

School Science and Mathematics
Association
126 Life Science Bldg.
Bowling Green State University
Bowling Green, OH 43403

National Resource Center for Middle
Grades Education
EDU–118/Univ. of So. Florida
Tampa, FL 33620

National Science Resources Center
of the Smithsonian Institution
Arts & Industry Bldg. 1201
Washington, DC 20560

Governmental Agencies

Fermi National Accelerator Lab
Education Office, MS 777
P.O. Box 500
Batavia, IL 60510

National Aeronautics and Space Administration (check the NASA homepage for other regional centers)
Lewis Research Center
Teacher Resource Center
Mail Stop 8–1, Cleveland, OH 44135

U.S. Department of Energy
1000 Independence Ave., S.W.
Washington, DC 20585

National Energy Information Center
Rm 1F-048, Forrestal Bldg.
1000 Independence Ave., S.W.
Washington, DC 20585

U.S. Dept. of Agriculture—Forest Service
Eastern Region
633 W. Wisconsin Ave.
Milwaukee, WI 53203

U.S. Department of the Interior/
U.S. Geological Survey
507 National Center
Reston, VA 22092

National Geophysical Data Center
E/GCZ, 325 Broadway
Boulder, CO 80303

Environmental Protection Agency
401 M St., S.W.
Washington, DC

National Oceanic and Atmospheric
Administration
Office of Public Affairs, U.S. Dept.
of Commerce
Washington, DC 20230

National Climatic Center
Federal Bldg.
Asheville, NC 28801

National Center for Atmospheric Research
Information Office, NCAR, Box 3000
Boulder, CO 80307

Superintendent of Documents
U.S. Government Printing Office
Washington, DC 20402

Smithsonian National Air and Space
Museum
Educational Services Division
Washington, DC 20560

Smithsonian Astrophysical Observatory
60 Garden St.
Cambridge, MA 02138

The President's Council for Sustainable
Development
730 Jackson Pl, N.W.
Washington, DC 20503

Other agencies include the U.S. Fish &
Wildlife Service, U.S. Soil Conservation
Service, National Science Foundation, and
the Census Bureau.

Quasipublic, Not-for-Profit, and Private Organizations

American Geological Institute
National Center for
Earth Science Education
4220 King St.
Alexandria, VA 22302

American Geophysical Union
2000 Florida Ave., N.W.
Washington, DC 20009

Acid Rain Information Clearinghouse
33 S. Washington St.
Rochester, NY 14608

American Association for the
Advancement of Science
1333 H St., N.W.
Washington, DC 20005

American Chemical Society
1155 16th St., N.W.
Washington, DC 20036

American Wind Energy Association
777 No. Capitol St., N.W., Suite 805
Washington, DC 20002

American Astronomical
Society Education Office
1816 Jefferson Pl., N.W.
Washington, DC 20036

American Institute of Biological Sciences
730 11th St., N.W.
Washington, DC 20001

American Institute of Physics
and American Physical Society
335 East 45th St.
New York, NY 10017

American Astronomical Society
211 Fitz Randolph Rd.
Princeton, NJ 08540

American Society for Horticultural Science
600 Cameron St.
Alexandria, VA 22314–2562
703–836–4606
http://www.ashs.org

American Society for
Engineering Education
One Dupont Circle, Suite 200
Washington, DC 20036

American Society of Microbiology
1913 I St., N.W.
Washington, DC 20005

American Forestry Institute
1619 Massachusetts Ave., N.W.
Washington, DC 20036

Animal Welfare Information Center
National Agricultural Library
Beltsville, MD 20705

Astronomical Society of the Pacific
1290 24th Ave.
San Francisco, CA 94122

Biodiversity Resource Center at
the California Academy of Science
Golden Gate Park
San Francisco, CA 94118

Carrying Capacity Network
2000 P St., N.W., Suite 240
Washington, DC 20036

Earth Force (a national nonprofit
environmental organization for children)
1501 Wilson Blvd., 12th fl.
Arlington, VA 22209

Educators for Social Responsibility
23 Garden St.
Cambridge, MA 02138

Electrical Power Research Institute
3412 Hillview Ave.
Box 50490
Palo Alto, CA 94304

Geological Society of America
3300 Penrose Pl
P.O. Box 9140
Boulder, CO 80301

Girls Clubs of America
205 Lexington Ave.
New York, NY 10016

Human Ecology Action League, Inc.
Box 49126
Atlanta, GA 30359

Marine Science Society
P.O. Box 2079
Poulsbo, WA 98370

National Academy of Sciences
2101 Constitution Ave.
Washington, DC 20418

National Center for Environmental
Health Strategies
1100 Rural Ave.
Voorhees, NJ 08043

National Energy Foundation
(publishers of *The Energist*)
5160 Wiley Post Way
Salt Lake City, UT 84116

Population Reference Bureau, Inc.
1875 Connecticut Ave., N.W. Suite 520
Washington, DC 20009

Royal Astronomical Society of Canada
124 Martin St.
Toronto, Ontario M4S 222

Science Olympiad
5955 Little Pine Lane
Rochester, MI 48064

Scripps Institute of Oceanography
950 Gilman Dr., UCSD-0207
La Jolla, CA 92093-0205

Society of Women Engineers
345 E. 47th St.
New York, NY 10017

The Planetary Society
65 No. Catalina Ave.
Pasadena, CA 91106

Union of Concerned Scientists
26 Church St.
Cambridge, MA 02238

World Future Society
4916 St Elmo Ave.
Bethesda, MD 20814

World Resources Institute
1709 New York Ave., N.W.
Washington, DC 20006

World Watch Institute
1776 Massachusetts Ave., N.W.
Washington, DC 20036

World Wildlife Fund Environmental
Education Department
1250 24th St., N.W.
Washington, DC 20037

Young Astronaut Council
P.O. Box 65432
Washington, DC 20036

Zero Population Growth, Inc.
1400 16th St., N.W.
Washington, DC 20036

Note that many government agencies and
nongovernmental science and education

organizations have Web sites on the Internet. Use a search function in your browsing software.

Subject Headings in a Typical City Telephone Book

Animals—Laboratory Use

Biological Products

Biological Supplies

Chemicals

Pet Shops

Scientific Apparatus

Laboratory Equipment

Sources for General Materials for Science Activities

The Nature Company (rock and mineral specimens, maps and globes)

Kmart, Wal-Mart, Target, and other discount stores

Hardware stores and lumber yards

Pharmacies

Grocery stores

Gardening stores (seeds, potting soil, sand, etc.)

Toy stores (e.g., Toys "R" Us)

References

Aikenhead, G.S. (nd). *Research matters . . . to the science teacher: Authentic science: What do students believe?* Washington, DC: National Association for Research in Science Teaching (monograph).

Albert, T. (1993). *Endangered rain forests.* Greensboro, NC: Carson-Dellosa Publishing Company.

American Association for the Advancement of Science. (1993). *Benchmarks for science literacy: Project 2061.* New York: Oxford University Press.

American Association for the Advancement of Science. (1990). *The liberal art of science: Agenda for action.* Washington, DC: Author.

American Association for the Advancement of Science. (1989). *Science for all Americans* (Project 2061). Washington, DC: Author.

American Association for the Advancement of Science. (1975). *Science: A process approach.* Lexington, MA: Ginn.

Arnheim, R. (1969). *Visual thinking.* Berkeley, CA: University of California Press.

Arter, J., & Spandel, V. (1992). Using portfolios of student work in instruction and assessment. *Instructional Topics in Educational Measurement,* Portland, OR: National Council on Measurement in Education.

Atkins, J.M., & Karplus, R. (1962, September). Discovery or invention? *Science Teacher, 29,* 5, 45–51.

Atwater, M., & Riley, J. (1993). Multicultural science education: Perspectives, definitions, and research agenda. *Science Education, 77*(6), 661–668.

Ausubel, D. (1968). *Educational psychology.* New York: Holt, Rinehart & Winston.

Baker, A., & Baker, J. (1991). *Counting on a small planet: Activities for environmental mathematics.* Portsmouth, NH: Heinemann.

Banks, J.A. (1994). *An introduction to multicultural education.* Boston, MA: Allyn & Bacon.

Barney, G.O. (1980). *The global 2000 report to the President: Entering the twenty-first century.* Washington, DC: U.S. Government Printing Office.

Baron, J. (1991). Performance assessment: Blurring the edges of assessment, curriculum, and instruction. In G. Kulm & S. Malcom (Eds.), *Science assessment in the service of reform.* Waldorf, MD: AAAS.

Benniga, J.S. (1988, Feb.). An emerging synthesis in moral education. *Phi Delta Kappan, 69*(6), 415–418.

Bloom, B.S. (Ed.). (1956). *Taxonomy of educational objectives: Cognitive domain.* New York: Longmans, Green & Company.

Blough, G.O. (1990). *Elementary school science and how to teach it* (8th ed., pp. xi–xii). Fort Worth: Holt, Rinehart and Winston.

Bohm, D., & Peat, F.D. (1987). *Science, order, and creativity.* New York: Bantam Books.

Borich, G. (1995). *Effective teaching methods* (3rd ed.). Englewood Cliffs, NJ: Merrill.

Bowers, C.A., & Flinders, D.J. (1990). *Responsive teaching.* New York: Teachers College Press.

Braus, J. (Ed.). (1994). *Windows on the wild* (pp. 38–39). Washington, DC: World Wildlife Fund.

Bredderman, T. (1983). Effects of activity-based elementary science on student outcomes: A quantitative synthesis. *Review of Educational Research, 53,* 499–518.

Brooks, J.G. (1990). Teachers and students: Constructivists forging new connections. *Educational Leadership* (February), 68–71.

Brophy, J. (1987, October). Synthesis of research on strategies for motivating students to learn. *Educational Leadership, 45*(2), 40–48.

Brown, L., et al. (Eds.). (1998, 1997, 1996, 1995, 1994, 1993, 1992, 1991, 1990, 1989, 1988, 1987, 1986, 1985, 1984). *State of the world.* Washington, DC: Worldwatch Institute.

Brown, L.R., Flavin, C., & Kane, H. (1992). *Vital signs: The trends that are shaping our future.* New York: W.W. Norton.

Brown, L.R. (1990, April). Earth day—20 years later. *World Watch, 3*(2).

Brown, L.R., Flavin, C., & Postel, S. (1990, March–April). Earth Day 2030. *World Watch, 3*(1), 12, 12–21.

Bruner, J. (1982, Jan.). Schooling children in a best climate. *Psychology Today, 16*(1), 57–68.

Bullock, L.D. (1996). *The efficacy of a gender and ethnic equity in science education curriculum for preservice teachers.* Paper presented at the International Meeting of the Association for the Education of Teachers in Science, Seattle, Washington.

Bybee, R. (1985). The Sisyphean question in science education: What should the scientifically and technologically literate person know, value, and do—as a citizen? In R.W. Bybee (Ed.), *Science technology society.* Washington, DC: National Science Teachers Association.

Bybee, R. (1977). The new transformation of science education. *Science Education, 61*(1), 85–97.

Byrne, E.M. (1993). *Women and science: The Snark syndrome.* Washington, DC: The Falmer Press.

Byrnes, P. (1995, Fall). Wild medicine. *Wilderness, 28–33.*

Caduto, M.J., & Bruchac, J. (1991). *Keepers of the animals: Native American stories and environmental activities for children.* Golden, CO: Fulcrum.

Caduto, M.J., & Bruhac, J. (1988). *Keepers of the earth: Native American stories and environmental activities for children.* Golden, CO: Fulcrum.

Carin, A.A. (1993). *Teaching modern science* (6th ed.). Columbus, OH: Merrill Publishing Company.

Carin, A.A., & Sund, R. (1981). *Teaching modern science* (5th ed.). Columbus, OH: Merrill Publishing Company.

Carlsen, W.S. (1991, Spring). Saying what you know in the biology laboratory. *Teaching Education, 3*(2), 17–29.

Carson, R. (1972). *Silent spring*. Boston: Houghton Mifflin.

Cash, T., & Taylor, B. (1989). *Fun with science: Electricity and magnets*. New York: Warwick Press.

Cash, T., & Taylor, B. (1989). *Fun with science: Sound*. New York: Warwick Press.

Catton, W.R. Jr., & Dunlap, R.E. (1980). A new ecological paradigm for post-exuberant sociology. *American Behavioral Scientist, 24*(1), 27.

CCN/Clearinghouse Bulletin, 1995, 3(1), 5.

Chadwick, D.C. (1994, Summer). Nurturing nature. *Defenders*, 8–16.

Chaillé, C., & Britain, L. (1991). *The young child as scientist: A constructivist approach to early childhood science education*. New York: HarperCollins.

Chambers, D.W. (1983). Stereotypic images of the scientist: The Draw-a-Scientist Test. *Science Education, 67*, 255–265.

Champagne, A.B. (Ed.). (1988). *Science teaching: Making the system work*. Washington, DC: American Association for the Advancement of Science.

Cheek, D. (1992). Introduction. In M. O. Thirunarayanan (Ed.), *Think and act— make an impact: Handbook of science, technology and society: Vol. 1*. Tempe: Arizona State University.

CIDIAC Communications. (1995, Fall). Carbon dioxide information analysis, 5.

Clark, B. (1986). *Optimizing learning: The integrative education model in the classroom*. Columbus, OH: Merrill Publishing Company.

Cole, K.C. (1982, March). Ask a stupid question . . . *Washington Post Magazine*, 18.

Cole, M., & Griffin, P. (1987). *Contextual factors in education*. Madison: Wisconsin Center for Education Research, University of Wisconsin.

Crews, K.A. (1992). Making connections: Linking population and the environment. *Elementary Teacher's Guide*. Washington, DC: Population Reference Bureau.

Cronbach, L.J. (1963). *Educational psychology*. New York: Harcourt Brace & World.

Csikszentmihalyi, M. (1994, February). *The importance of meaning: Current understanding of the processes by which we acquire a sense that our lives are "meaningful" (or "meaningless") and the implications of this understanding for our mental and spiritual health*. Paper presented at the Chicago Center for Religion and Science, Chicago, IL.

Csikszentmihalyi, M. (1991). *The psychology of optimal experience*. New York: HarperCollins.

Culliton, B.J. (1989). The dismal state of scientific literacy. *Science, 243*, 600.

Daintith, J.D., & Martin, E. (Eds.). (1991). *Concise science dictionary* (2nd ed.). London: Oxford University Press.

Dale, T., & Carter, V.G. (1955). *Topsoil and civilization*. Norman: University of Oklahoma Press.

De Fina, A. (1992). *Portfolio assessment: Getting started*. New York: Scholastic Professional Publications.

Dean, S.W., & Shayon, R.L. (1989, Oct. 9). Grabbing an electronic bonanza. *The Nation, 249*(11), 369, 387–388.

DeBoer, G.E. (1991). *A history of ideas in science education: Implications for practice*. New York: Teachers College Press.

di Sessa, A.A. (1982). Unlearning Aristotelian physics: A study of knowledge–based learning. *Cognitive Science, 6*, 37–75.

Driver, R., Guesne, E., & Tiberghien, A. (1985). *Children's ideas in science*. Milton Keynes: Open University Press.

Dubos, R. (1974). *Beast or angel? Choices that*

make us human. New York: Charles Scribner's Sons.

Duschl, R. (1989). *Restructuring science education: The importance of theories and their development*. Wolfeboro, NH: Teachers College Press.

Duschl, R. (1988). Abandoning the scientistic legacy of science education. *Science Education, 72*(1), 51–62.

Duschl, R., & Hamilton, R.J. (Eds.). (1992). *Philosophy of science, cognitive psychology, and educational theory and practice*. Albany: State University of New York Press.

Earth Island Journal. (1993). Consumption patterns, 21.

Ebert, C., & Ebert, E. (1998). *The inventive mind in science*. Englewood, CO: Teacher Ideas Press.

Ebert, C., & Ebert, E. (1993). An instructionally oriented model for enabling conceptual development. In J. Novak (Ed.), *Third international seminar on misconceptions and educational strategies in science and mathematics*. Ithaca, NY: Cornell University.

Ebert, E. (1994). The cognitive spiral: Creative thinking and cognitive processing. *The Journal of Creative Behavior, 28*(4), 275–290.

Eby, D., & Tatum, R. (1977). *The chemistry of food: A consumer chemistry learning activity package*. Seattle, WA: Unigraph.

Edwards v. Aguillard, 482 U.S. 578 (1987).

Ehrlich, P., & Ehrlich, A. (1992). The most overpopulated nation. *Carrying Capacity Network, 2*(8), 1–3.

Eisner, E. (Ed.). (1985). *Learning and teaching the ways of knowing* (84th Yearbook of the National Society for the Study of Education). Chicago, IL: National Society for the Study of Education.

Enright, J.B. (1993). Asking the right questions. *New Dimensions, 20*(3), 4.

Erikson, E.H.(1950). *Childhood and society*. New York: W.W. Norton.

Facing facts. (1994). *Human Survival, 20*(1), 1.

Farndon, J. (1992). *How the earth works*. Pleasantville, NY: The Reader's Digest Association.

Feather, N. (Ed.). (1982). *Expectations and actions*. Hillsdale, NJ: Erlbaum.

Ferguson, M. (1982). New theory: Feelings code, organize thinking. *Brain/Mind Bulletin, 7*(6), 1, 2.

Fetzer, J.H., & Almeder, R.F. (1993). *Glossary of epistemology/philosophy of science*. New York: Paragon House.

Fisher, B. (1992, August–September). Starting the year in a first grade classroom. *Teaching K–8*, 57–58.

Gallant, R.A. (1986). *Picture atlas of our universe*. Washington, DC: National Geographic Society.

Gallas, K. (1995). *Talking their way into science: Hearing children's questions and theories, responding with curricula*. New York: Teachers College Press.

Gallas, K. (1994). *The languages of learning: How children talk, write, dance, draw, and sing their understanding of the world*. New York: Teachers College Press.

Garrison, J.W., & Bentley, M.L. (1990). Teaching scientific method: The logic of confirmation and falsification. *School Science and Mathematics, 90*(3), 188–197.

Geography Education Standards Project. (1994). *Geography for life: National geography standards*. Washington, DC: National Geographic Research and Exploration.

Gerbner, G., Gross, L., Morgan, M., & Signorielli, N. (1985). *Television entertainment and viewers' conceptions of science*. Philadelphia: University of Pennsylvania, Annenberg School of Communications.

Gilbert, J.K., Watts, D.M., & Osborne, R.J. (1985). Eliciting student views using an interview-about-instances technique. In L.H.T. West & A.L. Pines (Eds.), *Cognitive structure and conceptual change* (pp. 11–27). New York: Academic.

Gilbert, J.K., & Watts, D.M. (1983). Concepts, misconceptions and alternative conceptions: Changing perspectives in science education. *Studies in Science Education, 10,* 61–98.

Glasser, W. (1990). *The quality school.* New York: Harper & Row.

Glasser, W. (1969). *Schools without failure.* New York: Harper & Row.

Gleick, J. (1987). *Chaos: Making a new science.* New York: Penguin Books.

Goldsmith, E. (1992). Development, biospheric ethics and a new way forward. In E. Goldsmith, M. Khor, H. Norberg-Hodge, & V. Shiva (Eds.), *The future of progress: Reflections on environment & development* (pp. 189–209). Berkeley, CA: International Society for Ecology and Culture.

Good, R. (1977). *How children learn science: Conceptual development and implications for teaching.* New York: Macmillan.

Gowin, B. (1987). *Educating.* Ithaca, NY: Cornell University Press.

Greenhouse Gas-ette (1993, Oct.). The story of "Goat Island," 4.

Hampton, S. (1992). *Security systems simplified: Protecting your home, business, and car with state-of-the-art burglar alarms.* Boulder, CO: Paladin Press.

Hann, J. (1991). *How nature works.* Pleasantville, NY: Reader's Digest Association, Inc.

Hann, J. (1991). *How science works.* Pleasantville, NY: Reader's Digest Association, Inc.

Hanson, B. (1989, Summer). Spoiled soil. *The Amicus Journal, 11*(3), 3–7.

Hardin, G. (1985). Human ecology: The subversive, conservative science. *American Zoology, 25,* 469–476. (Science as a Way of Knowing Project, American Society of Zoologists.)

Hardin, G. (1982). Discriminating altruisms. *Zygon, 17*(2), 179.

Hardin, G. (Ed.). (1969). *Population, evolution, and birth control* (2nd ed.). New York: W. H. Freeman.

Hardin, J.W., & Arena, J.M. (1977). *Human poisoning from native and cultivated plants.* Durham, NC: Duke University Press.

Harms, N. (1981). Project Synthesis: Summary and implications for teachers. In N. Harms & R. Yager (Eds.), *What research says to the science teacher.* Washington, DC: National Science Teachers Association.

Haury, D.L. (1994, Nov.). From the Director . . . Cultivating human potential in science and mathematics. *CSMEE Horizon, 2*(2), 1–2.

Hawkins, D. (1990). Defining and bridging the gap. In Duckworth, E., Easley, J., Hawkins, D., Henriques, A. (Eds.), *Science education: A minds-on approach for the elementary years.* Hillsdale, NJ: Lawrence Erlbaum.

Hazen, R.M., & Trefil, J. (1991). *Science matters—Achieving scientific literacy.* New York: Doubleday.

Hestenes, D. (1992). Modeling games in the Newtonian world. *American Journal of Physics, 60*(8), 732–748.

Hively, W. (1988). How much science does the public understand. *American Scientist, 76*(5), 439–444.

Holden, C. (1989, June 30). Wanted: 675,000 future scientists and engineers. *Science, 244,* 1536–1537.

Holton, G. (1992). How to think about the "anti-science" phenomenon. *Public Understanding of Science, 1*(1), 103–128.

Holton, G., & Brush, S. (1985). *Introduction to concepts and theories in physical science* (2nd ed.). Princeton, NJ: Princeton University Press.

Hunter, M., & Barker, G. (1987, October). "If at first . . .": Attribution theory in the classroom. *Educational Leadership, 45*(2), 50–53.

Ingram, J. (1989). *The science of everyday life.* New York: Penguin.

International Association for the Evaluation of Educational Achievement. (1988). *Science achievement in 17 countries: A prelimi-*

nary report. New York: Teachers College, Columbia University.

Iozzi, L.A., & Bastardo, P.J. (1987). *Decisions for today and tomorrow: Teaching notes.* Salt Lake City: National Energy Foundation (ED 289 735).

Jones, R.S. (1992). *Physics for the rest of us: Ten basic ideas of twentieth century physics that everyone should know . . . and how they have shaped our culture and consciousness.* Chicago, IL: Contemporary Books.

Kimball, M. (1968). Understanding the nature of science: A comparison of scientists and science teachers. *Journal of Research in Science Teaching, 5,* 110–120.

Knapp, C.E. (1993, June). An interview with Eliot Wigginton: Reflecting on the Foxfire Approach. *Phi Delta Kappan, 74*(10), 779–782.

Kohn, A. (1991, March). Caring kids: The role of the schools. *Phi Delta Kappan, 72*(7), 496–506.

Krech, D. (1969). Psychoneurobiochemeducation. *Phi Delta Kappan, 1,* 370–375.

Kuehn, C. (1985). *The analysis of fifth and sixth grade students' acquisition of the process of inventing.* Unpublished doctoral dissertation, Purdue University, West Lafayette, IN.

Kuehn, C., & McKenzie, D. (1989). Using interviewing as a teacher education technique. *Journal of Science Teacher Education, 1*(2), 27–29.

Kuehn, C., & McKenzie, D. (1988). The art of the interview. *Science Scope, 11*(5), 22–23.

Kuhn, T. (1962). *The structure of scientific revolutions.* Chicago: The University of Chicago Press.

Kuhs, T.M. (1997). *Measure for measure: Using portfolios in K–8 mathematics.* Portsmouth, NH: Heinemann.

Kumar, D., & Voldrich, J.F. (1994). Situated cognition in second grade science: Literature books for authentic contexts.

Journal of Elementary Science Education, 6(2), 1–10.

Lamb, L. (1989, Sept./Oct.). Environmental illness: The new plague. *Utne Reader,* 14–15.

Lampton, C. (1983). *Space sciences: A reference first book.* New York: Franklin Watts.

Larochelle, M., & Desautels, J. (1991a). *The epistemological turn in science education: The return of the actor.* A paper presented at the International Workshop: "Research in Physics Learning: Theoretical Issues and Empirical Studies," Bremen, Germany.

Larochelle, M., & Desautels, J. (1991b). "Of course, it's just obvious": Adolescents' ideas of scientific knowledge. *International Journal of Science Education, 13*(4), 373–389.

Lauerman, C. (1988, August 7). Failing science: Too many Americans have a Fred Flintstone view of the world, and it's no laughing matter. *The Chicago Tribune Magazine,* 9–10, 12–13.

Lawrence Hall of Science. (1979). *Outdoor biology instructional strategies.* Berkeley, CA: University of California.

Lederman, N.G. (1992). Students' and teachers' conceptions of the nature of science: A review of the research. *Journal of Research in Science Teaching, 29*(4), 331–359.

Legro, P., Bybee, R., & Simmons, B. (1997, Mar.–Apr.). Finding synergy—connecting the National Science Education Standards and the Environmental Education Learner Guidelines. *Environmental Communicator, 27*(2), 10–12.

Lemke, J.L. (1990). *Talking science: Language, learning, and values.* Norwood, NJ: Ablex Publishing Corporation.

Levin, B. (1994, June). Improving educational productivity: Putting students at the center. *Phi Delta Kappan,* 758–760.

Levy, J. (1980). Cerebral asymmetry and the psychology of man. In M. Wittrock

(Ed.), *The Brain and psychology* (pp. 245–321). New York: Academic Press.

Lewenstein, B.V. (1988). How much science does the public understand? *American Scientist, 76*(5), 440.

Lightman, A., & Sadler, P. (1988, Feb.). The earth is round? Who are you kidding? *Science and Children, 25*(5), 24–26.

Lincoln, Y., & Guba, E. (1985). *Naturalistic inquiry.* Beverly Hills: Sage.

Little, C.E. (1995). *The dying of the trees: The pandemic in America's forests.* New York: Viking.

Lorenz, M. (1989, June). Ecology, community, and art. *Green Synthesis, 6,* 14.

Lotter, D. (1993). EnviroAccount. Davis, CA: EnviroAccount Software.

Macaulay, D. (1988). *The way things work.* New York: Houghton Mifflin.

Macaulay, D. (1976). *Underground.* Boston: Houghton Mifflin.

Mann, D.W. (1995, Dec.). Letter from NPG president. Teaneck, NJ: Negative Population Growth.

Marturano, A. (1995, Feb.). Horticulture and human culture: Connect natural sciences and cultural geography through gardening. *Science and Children, 32*(5), 26–29, 50.

Matthews, M.R. (1987). Galileo's pendulum and the objects of science. *Philosophy of Education,* 309–319.

McCloskey, D.N. (1995, Feb.). Once upon a time there was a theory. *Scientific American, 272*(2), 19.

McCormack, A. (1981). *Inventors workshop.* Belmont, CA: David S. Lake Publishers.

McCutcheon, G. (1995). *Developing the curriculum: Solo and group deliberation.* New York: Longman Publishers USA.

McKibben, W. (1989). *The end of nature.* New York: Random House.

Meadows, D., Ronders, J., & Behrens, W. (1972). *The limits to growth.* New York: Universe Books.

Miller, J.D. (1988). The roots of scientific literacy. In P.G. Heltne & L.A. Marquardt (Eds.), *Science learning in the informal setting.* Chicago: The Chicago Academy of Sciences.

Moravcsik, M.J. (1981). Creativity in science education. *Science Education, 65,* 221–227.

Moyer, R., & Bishop, J. (1986). *General science.* Columbus, OH: Charles E. Merrill Publishing Company.

Mullis, I., & Jenkins, L.B. (1988). *The science report card: Elements of risk and recovery.* Princeton, NJ: Educational Testing Service.

National Center for Improving Science Education. (1989). *Getting started in science: A blueprint for elementary school science education.* Andover, MA: The NETWORK, Inc.

National Council for the Social Studies. (1994). *Curriculum standards for social studies.* Washington, DC: Author.

National Council of Teachers of Mathematics. (1989). *Curriculum and evaluation standards for school mathematics.* Reston, VA: Author.

National Research Council. (1996). *National science education standards.* Washington DC: National Academy Press.

National Science Board Commission on Precollege Education in Mathematics, Science, and Technology. (1983). *Educating Americans for the 21st century: A plan of action for improving mathematics, science, and technology education for all American elementary and secondary students so that their achievement is the best in the world by 1995* (p. v). Washington, DC: National Science Foundation.

National Science Resources Center. (1989). *Science for children.* Washington, DC: National Academy Press.

National Science Teachers Association (1992). *The content core: A guide for cur-*

riculum designers (Scope, Sequence, and Coordination of Secondary School Science Project). Washington, DC: Author.

National Science Teachers Association. (1982). *Science, technology and society: Science education for the 1980s.* Washington, DC: Author.

National Science Teachers Association. (Prepublication copy, 1977). *Safety in the secondary science classroom,* 4–18.

National Science Teachers Association. (nd). *Safety in the elementary science classroom.* Washington, DC: Author.

Newman, D., Griffin, P., & Cole, M. (1989). *The construction zone: Working for cognitive change in school.* New York: Cambridge University Press.

Newmann, F.M. (1988, January). Can depth replace coverage in the high school curriculum? *Phi Delta Kappan, 69*(5), 345–348.

Nickerson, R.S. (1981, October). Thoughts on teaching thinking. *Educational Leadership, 39*(1), 21–24.

Nicholson, S. (1972). The theory of loose parts. *BEE,* 1–3 (originally appeared in *Landscape Architecture Quarterly*).

Nielson, H. (1992). Paper presented at the International Conference on the History and Philosophy of Science in Science Teaching, Queen's University, Kingston, Ontario.

Nobel Prize geneticist Barbara McClintock, 90. (1992, Sept. 4). *Chicago Tribune,* p. B10.

Noddings, N., & Shore, P.J. (1984). *Awakening the inner eye: Intuition in education.* New York: Teachers College Press.

Novak, J.D., & Gowin, D.B. (1986). *Learning how to learn.* New York: Cambridge University Press.

Novelli, J. (1995, Sept.). Learning centers that work. *Instructor,* 82–85.

Oakes, J. (1990). *Lost talent: The underparticipation of women, minorities, and disabled persons in science* (Report No. R-3774-

NSF/RC). Santa Monica, CA: The Rand Corporation.

Osborne, R., & Freyberg, P. (1985). *Learning in science.* Portsmouth, NH: Heinemann.

Paschall, D. (1992). *Earth time.* Ketchum, ID: The EarthTime Project.

Perkins, K.W., & Whitten, R.H. (1981). *Reptiles and amphibians: Care and culture.* Burlington, NC: Carolina Biological Supply Company.

Peterson, J. (Ed.). (1983). *The aftermath: The human and ecological consequences of nuclear war.* New York: Pantheon Press.

Piaget, J. (1977). Problems in equilibration. In M. Appel & L. Goldberg (Eds.), *Topics in cognitive development: Vol 1. Equilibration: Theory, research and application* (pp. 3–13). New York: Plenum.

Piaget, J. (1929). *The child's conception of the world.* London: Routledge & Kegan, Paul.

Piasecki, B. (1989, August). Beyond dumping. *Calypso log,* 7–10.

Pimentel, G.C., & Coonrod, J.A. (1987). *Opportunities in chemistry: Today and tomorrow.* Washington, DC: National Academy Press.

Pinch, T. (1996). Science as Golem. *Academe, 82*(1), 16–18.

Population Reference Bureau. (1995). World population data sheet. Washington, DC: Author.

Posner, G., Strike, K., Hewson, P., & Gertzog, W. (1982). Accommodation of a scientific conception: Toward a theory of conceptual change. *Science Education, 66*(2), 211–227.

Powell, D., Needham, R.A., & Bentley, M.L. (1994, April). *Using big books in science and social studies.* Paper presented at Annual Meeting of the International Reading Association. Toronto, Canada.

Pratt-Butler, G.K. (1978). *How to . . . care for living things in the classroom* (Rev. ed.). Washington, DC: Monograph of the National Science Teachers Association.

Price, S., & Hein, G. (1994, October). Scoring active assessments. *Science and Children,* 26–29.

Prigogine, I. (1980). *From being to becoming: Time and complexity in the physical sciences.* San Francisco: W.H. Freeman.

Puls, D., & O'Brien, P. (1994). What's a zoo to do? *Science Scope, 17*(4), 17–20.

Quammen, D. (1988). *The flight of the iguana: A sidelong view of science and nature.* New York: Delacorte.

Quammen, D. (1985). *Natural acts: A sidelong view of science and nature.* New York: Laurel.

Quinn, D. (1993). *Ishmael.* New York: Bantam.

Raizen, S.A., & Michelson, A.M. (1994). *The future of science in elementary schools: Educating prospective teachers.* San Francisco: Jossey-Bass.

Reiss, M.J. (1993). *Science education for a pluralist society.* Philadelphia, PA: Open University Press.

Rensberger, B. (1986). *How the world works.* Washington, DC: Science News Books.

Restak, R.M. (1995). *Brainscapes: An introduction to what neuroscience has learned about the structure, function, and abilities of the brain.* New York: Hyperion.

Richards, S. (1987). *Philosophy and sociology of science,* 2nd ed. NY: Basil Blackwell. 35.

Roach, L.E., & Wandersee, J.H. (1995, November). Putting people back into science: Using historical vignettes. *School Science and Mathematics, 95*(7), 365–370.

Ronan, C.A. (1991). *The natural history of the universe: From the Big Bang to the end of time.* New York: Macmillan.

Rowe, M.B. (1987). *Science helper K–8.* Armonk, NY: The Learning Team.

Ruelle, D. (1991). *Chance and chaos.* Princeton, NJ: Princeton University Press.

Rumbaitis-del Rio, C. (1994, Mar.). Not a drop to drink: The end of the easy water days: What can we do about it? *Balance Data,* no. 31, 1–4.

Rutherford, F.J., & Ahlgren, A. (1990). *Science for all Americans* (p. viii). New York: Oxford University Press.

Ryan, A.G., & Aikenhead, G.S. (1992). Students' preconceptions about the epistemology of science. *Science Education, 76*(6), 559–580.

Ryan, J.C. (1989, Sept.–Oct.). Eyes in the sky. *World Watch, 2*(5), 11, 41.

Sagan, C. (1991, June 2). Science—Who cares? *Parade Magazine,* 10–12.

Sagan, C., & Druyan, A. (1992). *Shadows of forgotten ancestors: A search for who we are.* New York: Random House.

Sanders, M. (1993). Science and technology: A new alliance. *Science Scope, 16*(6), 56–60.

Sauer, C.O. (1971). Theme of plant and animal destruction in economic history. In P. Shepard & D. McKinley (Eds.), *Environmental.* Boston: Houghton Mifflin.

Schell, J. (1982). *The fate of the Earth.* New York: Alfred A. Knopf.

Scholnick, E.K. (Ed.). (1983). *New trends in conceptual representation: Challenges to Piaget's theory.* Hillsdale, NJ: Erlbaum.

Segal, L. (1986). *The dream of reality: Heinz von Foerster's constructivism.* New York: W.W. Norton & Company.

Selye, H. (1956). *The stress of life.* New York: McGraw-Hill.

Shaffer, C., & Fielder, E. (1987). *City safaris.* San Francisco: Sierra Club Books.

Simpson, R.D. (1979, November). Breeding success in science. *The Science Teacher,* 24–26.

Singer, P. (1975). *Animal liberation.* New York: New York Review.

Sisson, E.A. (1982). *Nature with children of all ages.* Englewood Cliffs, NJ: Prentice-Hall.

Sivertsen, M.L. (1993). *Transforming ideas for teaching and learning science: A guide for elementary science education.* Washington, DC: U.S. Department of Education.

Sizer, T.R. (1984). *Horace's compromise: The*

dilemma of the American high school. Boston: Houghton Mifflin.

Smith, E.L. (1991). A conceptual change model. In S.M. Glynn, R.H. Yeany, & B.K. Britton (Eds.), *The psychology of learning* (pp. 43–63). Hillsdale, NJ: Lawrence Erlbaum Associates.

Smith, F. (1995, Apr.). Let's declare education a disaster and get on with our lives. *Phi Delta Kappan, 76*(8), 584–590.

Smith, L. (1989, July–August). Public understanding of environmental issues. *Environmental Communicator, 9.*

Smith, L., Ryan, J., & Kuhs, T. (1993). *Assessment of student learning in science.* South Carolina Center for Excellence in the Assessment of Student Learning, University of South Carolina.

Snively, G. (1995). Bridging traditional science and Western science in the multicultural classroom. In G. Snively & A. MacKinnon (Eds.), *Thinking globally about mathematics and science education.* Vancouver: University of British Columbia, Research and Development Group.

Sprung, B. et al. (1986). *What will happen if . . .: Young children and the scientific method.* New York: Educational Equity Concepts.

Stangl, J. (1987). *The tools of science.* New York: Dodd, Mead & Company.

Starke, L. (Ed.). (1996). *State of the world 1996.* New York: W.W. Norton.

Stepans, J. (1994). *Targeting students' science misconceptions: Physical science activities using the conceptual change model.* Riverview, FL: Idea Factory.

Stockley, C., Oxlade, C., & Wertheim, J. (1988). *The Usborne illustrated dictionary of science.* Tulsa, OK: EDC Publishing.

Suter, L.E. (Ed.). (1993). *Indicators of science and mathematics education 1992.* Washington, DC: National Science Foundation.

The old farmer's almanac 1998. Dublin, NH: Yankee Publishing Incorporated.

Thirunarayanan, M.O. (Ed.). (1992). *Think and act—make an impact: Handbook of science, technology and society,* Vol. 2. Tempe: Arizona State University.

Thomas, L. (1979). *The medusa and the snail.* New York: Bantam Books.

Thomas, L. (1978). Address to the Mount Sinai School of Medicine. Reprinted in *The New York Times,* July 2, p. 15.

Thomas, L. (1974). *The lives of a cell.* New York: Bantam Books.

Tobin, K., & Tippins, D. (1993). Constructivism as a referent for teaching and learning. In K. Tobin (Ed.), *Constructivism: The practice of constructivism in science education* (pp. 3–21). Washington, DC: American Association for the Advancement of Science.

Trefil, J.S. (1983). *The unexpected vista: A physicist's view of nature.* NY: Collier Books.

Tressel, G.W. (1987). The role of informal learning in science education. In P.G. Heltne & L.A. Marquardt (Eds.), *Science learning in the informal setting.* Chicago: Chicago Academy of Sciences.

Tudge, C. (1991). *Global ecology.* London: Oxford University Press.

Turner, F. (1982). Sumerian implications. *Living wilderness, 46*(157), 6–13.

Van, J. (1988, February 15). Air conditioners a puzzle to many, survey finds. *Chicago Tribune,* sect. 1, p. 6.

von Glasersfeld, E. (1989). Cognition, construction of knowledge, and teaching. *Synthese, 80,* 121–140.

Vygotsky, L. (1978). *Mind in society: The development of higher psychological processes.* Cambridge, MA: Harvard University Press.

Vygotsky, L. (1962). *Thought and language.* Cambridge, MA: MIT Press.

Waks, L. (1995, April). *Citizenship in transition: Globalization, postindustrial technology and education.* Royal Bank Lecture presented at symposium "Life after school:

Education, globalization and the person." Kingston, Ontario: Queen's University.

Weiner, B. (1984). Principles for a theory of student motivation and their application within an attributional framework. In *Research on motivation education, Vol. I: Student motivation*. Orlando, FL: Academic Press.

Weininger, S. (1990, January 8). Science and "the humanities" are wedded, not divorced. *The Scientist, 4*(1), 15, 17.

Weiss, I.R. (1994). *A profile of science and mathematics education in the United States: 1993*. Chapel Hill, NC: Horizon Research.

Weiss, I.R. (1987). *Report of the 1985–86 national survey of science, mathematics, and social studies education*. Research Triangle Park, NC: Research Triangle Institute.

Western Regional Environmental Education Council. (1977, 1983). *Project learning tree and project wild*. Boulder, CO: Author.

Whittaker, R.H. (1975). *Communities and ecosystems* (2nd ed., p. 366). New York: Macmillan.

Willrich, M. (1989, Spring). Murder in acre. *The Amicus Journal, 11*(2): 10–13.

Wilson, E.O. (1992). *The diversity of life*. Cambridge, MA: Harvard University Press.

Winner, L. (1989). *Science, technology and social progress*. New York: Associated University Presses.

Wittrock, M.C. (1974). Learning as a generative process. *Educational Psychology, 11*, 87–95.

Woods, D.R. (1995, Feb.). More resources of developing problem solving. *Journal of College Science Teaching*, 284–285.

World POPClock. (1998). In U.S. Census Bureau [On-line]. Available HTTP: http://www.census.gov/cgi-bin/ipc/popclockw [1996, Jan. 20].

Worldwatch Institute. (1996). Database diskette. Washington, DC: Author.

Wright, R.G. (1992, February). Event-based science. *The Science Teacher, 59* (2), 22–23.

Wurman, S.A. (Ed.). (1972). *Yellow pages of learning resources*. Cambridge, MA: The MIT Press.

Yager, R.E. (1994, Oct.). Assessment results in the S/T/S approach. *Science & Children*, 34–37.

Yager, R.E., & McCormack, A.J. (1989). Assessing teaching/learning successes in multiple domains of science and science education. *Science Education, 73*(1), 45–58.

Yager, R., & Brunkhorst, H.K. (1986). A new rationale for science education—1985. *School Science and Mathematics, 86*(5), 365–368.

Index

About the Authors

Dr. Michael Bentley is an associate professor in the Department of Teaching and Learning at Virginia Polytechnic Institute and State University (Virginia Tech), where he teaches courses in methods of teaching science and elementary and secondary curriculum. He is the author of three books in addition to many journal articles, chapters in books, and curriculum materials. Dr. Bentley's research interests include the public understanding of science, K–12 curriculum, science teacher education, studies of the teaching-learning process and child development, and, particularly, the history, philosophy, and sociology of science as applied to science education. He lives in Salem, Virginia, with his wife, the Rev. Susan E. Bentley, a daughter, Sarah, and sons Alexander and Matthew.

Dr. Christine Ebert is an associate professor of science education and Interim Associate Dean for Administration, Research, and Technology in the College of Education, the University of South Carolina. She is also Director of International Programs for the College of Education. Her work in science education focuses on conceptual change and development in students' understanding of science principles. In addition, she teaches courses in thinking and reasoning, and is extensively involved with collaboration between elementary schools and the university. She has co-authored three other books related to science education and conceptual development. Dr. Ebert has presented her work on science education and creative thinking at conferences across the country and around the world. She and her husband, Dr. Edward Ebert, live in Columbia, South Carolina.

Dr. Edward S. Ebert II is an associate professor of education at Coker College in Hartsville, South Carolina. With a degree in psychological foundations of education, Dr. Ebert teaches courses in educational psychology, elementary science methods, child development, test and measurement, and creative problem solving.